Guide to Advanced Empirical Software Engineering

Forrest Shull • Janice Singer • Dag I.K. Sjøberg

Editors

Guide to Advanced Empirical Software Engineering

 Springer

Forrest Shull
Fraunhofer Center for Empirical
 Software Engineering
College Park
Maryland
USA

Janice Singer
NRC Institute for Information Technology
National Research Council
Ottawa
Canada

Dag I.K. Sjøberg
Simula Research Laboratory
Lysaker
Norway

British Library Cataloguing in Publication Data
A catalogue record for this book is available from the British Library

ISBN-13: 978-1-84996-712-9   e-ISBN-13: 978-1-84800-044-5

Printed on acid-free paper

9 8 7 6 5 4 3 2 1

Springer Science+Business Media
springer.com

Contents

Contributors

Bente C. D. Anda
Simula Research Laboratory, Department of Software Engineering
Lysaker, Norway, NO-1325
and
Department of Informatics, University of Oslo
Oslo, Norway, NO-0316
bentea@simula.no

Johanna Bragge
Helsinki School of Economics and Business Administration
Helsinki, Finland FIN-00101
johanna.bragge@hse.fi

Andy Brooks
University of Akureyri
Akureyri, Iceland IS 600
andy@unak.is

Marcus Ciolkowski
Software Engineering: Processes and Measurement Research Group (AGSE)
University of Kaiserslautern PO Box 3049
67653 Kaiserslautern
Germany
and
Fraunhofer Institute for Experimental Software Engineering, Fraunhofer-Platz 1
67663 Kaiserslautern
Germany
Marcus.Ciolkowski@iese.fraunhofer.de

John Daly
Formerly of the Department of Computer Science, University of Strathclyde
26 Richmond Street,
Glasgow, Scotland G1 1XH

Daniela Damian
Dept. of Computer Science, University of Victoria
Victoria, British Columbia, Canada V8W 3P6
DanielaD@cs.uvic.ca

Tore Dybå
Simula Research Laboratory, Department of Software Engineering
Lysaker, Norway, NO-1325
and
SINTEF ICT
Trondheim, Norway, NO-7465
tore.dyba@sintef.no

Steve Easterbrook
Department of Computer Science, University of Toronto
Toronto, Ontario, Canada M5S 2E4
sme@cs.toronto.edu

Raimund L. Feldmann
Fraunhofer Center Maryland
College Park, MD 20742, USA
rfeldmann@fc-md.umd.edu

Jo E. Hannay
Simula Research Laboratory, Department of Software Engineering
Lysaker, Norway, NO-1325
and
Department of Informatics, University of Oslo
Oslo, Norway, NO-0316
johannay@simula.no

Andreas Jedlitschka
Fraunhofer Institute for Experimental Software Engineering, Fraunhofer-Platz 1
67663 Kaiserslautern
Germany
Andreas.Jedlitschka@iese.fraunhofer.de

Barbara A. Kitchenham
Keele University, School of Computing and Mathematics
Keele, Staffordshire, United Kingdom
b.a.kitchenham@cs.keele.ac.uk

Jyrki Kontio
Software Business Laboratory, Helsinki University of Technology
Helsinki, Finland FIN-02015 TKK
jyrki.kontio@tkk.fi

Laura Lehtola
Software Business and Engineering Institute, Helsinki University of Technology
Helsinki, Finland FIN-02015 HUT
laura.lehtola@tkk.fi

Timothy C. Lethbridge
School of Information Technology and Engineering, University of Ottawa
Ottawa, Ontario, Canada K1N 6N5
tcl@site.uottawa.ca

Steve Lyon
Mitel Networks
350 Legget Drive
P.O. Box 13089
Ottawa, Ontario, Canada K2K 2W7
Steve_Lyon@mitel.com

James Miller
Department of Electrical and Computer Engineering, University of Alberta
Edmonton, Alberta, Canada T6G 2E1
jm@ece.ualberta.ca

Audris Mockus
Software Technology Research Department, Avaya Labs Research
Basking Ridge, NJ 07920, USA
audris@research.avayalabs.com

Mark Müller
Robert BOSCH GmbH
Corporate Sector Research and Advance Engineering
Dept. CR/AEC - Corporate Systems Engineering Process Group
Postfach 300240, 70442 Stuttgart, Germany
mark.mueller2@de.bosch.com

Peter Perry
Mitel Networks
350 Legget Drive
P.O. Box 13089
Ottawa, Ontario, Canada K2K 2W7
Peter_Perry@mitel.com

Dietmar Pfahl
Schulich School of Engineering, University of Calgary, Electrical and
Computer Engineering Department
Calgary, Alberta, Canada T2N 1N4
dpfahl@ucalgary.ca

Shari Lawrence Pfleeger
Rand Corporation
Arlington, VA 22202, USA
shari_pfleeger@rand.org

Jarrett Rosenberg
Sun Microsystems
Palo Alto, CA 94303, USA
Jarrett.Rosenberg@ACM.ORG

Marc Roper
Department of Computer and Information Sciences, University of Strathclyde
Glasgow, Scotland G1 1XH
Marc.Roper@cis.strath.ac.uk

Carolyn Seaman
University of Maryland Baltimore County, Department of Information Systems
Baltimore, MD 21250, USA
cseaman@umbc.edu

Forrest Shull
Fraunhofer Center Maryland
College Park, MD 20742, USA
fshull@fc-md.umd.edu

Susan Elliott Sim
Department of Informatics, Donald Bren School of Information and Computer
Sciences, University of California, Irvine
Irvine, CA 92967-3440, USA
ses@ics.uci.edu

Janice Singer
National Research Council Canada, Institute for Information Technology
Ottawa, Ontario, Canada K1A 0R6
janice.singer@nrc-cnrc.gc.ca

Dag I. K. Sjøberg
Simula Research Laboratory, Department of Software Engineering
Lysaker, Norway, NO-1325
and
Department of Informatics, University of Oslo
Oslo, Norway, NO-0316
dagsj@simula.no

Margaret-Anne Storey
Dept. of Computer Science, University of Victoria
Victoria, British Columbia, Canada V8W 3P6
mstorey@csr.uvic.ca

Norman G. Vinson
National Research Council Canada, Institute for Information Technology
Ottawa, Ontario, Canada K1A 0R6
Norman.Vinson@nrc-cnrc.gc.ca

Murray Wood
Department of Computer and Information Sciences, University of Strathclyde
Glasgow, Scotland, G1 1XH
Murray.Wood@cis.strath.ac.uk

Introduction

Empirical studies have become an important part of software engineering research and practice. Ten years ago, it was rare to see a conference or journal article about a software development tool or process that had empirical data to back up the claims. Today, in contrast, it is becoming more and more common that software engineering conferences and journals are not only publishing, but eliciting, articles that describe a study or evaluation. Moreover, a very successful conference (International Symposium on Empirical Software Engineering and Measurement), journal (Empirical Software Engineering), and organization (International Software Engineering Research Network) have all evolved in the last 10 years that focus solely on this area. As a further illustration of the growth of empirical software engineering, a search in the articles of 10 software engineering journals showed that the proportion of articles that used the term "empirical software engineering" doubled from about 6% in 1997 to about 12% in 2006.

While empirical software engineering has seen such substantial growth, there is not yet a reference book that describes advanced techniques for running studies and their application. This book aims to fill that gap. The chapters are written by some of the top international empirical software engineering researchers and focus on the practical knowledge necessary for conducting, reporting, and using empirical methods in software engineering. The book is intended to serve as a standard reference.

The goals of this book are:

- To provide guidance on designing, conducting, analysing, interpreting, and reporting empirical studies, taking into account the common difficulties and challenges encountered in the field.
- To provide information across a range of techniques, methods, and quantitative and qualitative issues, and in so doing provide a toolkit that is applicable across the diversity of software development contexts.
- To present material that is adapted from work in other disciplines such as statistics, medicine, psychology, and education, into a software engineering context.

We did not include introductory topics on how to design and run studies in empirical software engineering, as this information has been covered adequately

1

F. Shull et al. (eds.), *Guide to Advanced Empirical Software Engineering*.
© Springer 2008

in several other books and papers. To address these goals, the chapters in this book are grouped according to three primary themes:

"Research Methods and Techniques" presents discussions on the proper use of various strategies for collecting and analyzing data, and the uses for which those strategies are most appropriate. Our aim in this section is to present ideas about strategies that are less often used in our field, which perhaps may provide some ideas about less conventional but still rigorous and useful ways of collecting data. We also aim to provide detailed information on topics such as surveys that in our experience often contain methodological errors.

"Practical Foundations" provides a discussion of several basic issues that a researcher has to get right before a study becomes meaningful. This section discusses important, global issues that need to be considered from the very beginning of research planning. Chapters here discuss topics that are almost always going to be important, regardless of the specific choices that are made about running the study. Our aim in this section is to arm researchers with the information necessary to avoid fundamental risks. For example, an entire study may be inappropriate if a researcher doesn't understand enough about metrics and statistics to collect the right measures; a researcher may not get the chance to run the study he/she wants if there is no good way to cooperate with industry; or the results may be jeopardized if incomplete data is collected by the study and the researcher don't respond appropriately.

Finally, "Knowledge Creation" looks beyond the challenge of running an appropriate study to provide insight on what is becoming one of the most important challenges in empirical software engineering today–using a set of disparate studies (all of which may employ different designs and metrics) to provide useful decision support on a question of interest. The conversion of discrete scientific results into a broadly useful "body of knowledge" on a topic is a difficult process, with many opportunities for introducing bias if done incorrectly. Refining and employing appropriate techniques in addressing this problem is one of the most important challenges for ensuring the relevance of empirical software engineering and showing its practical impact.

While we feel that all of these topics are of interest to many workers in this field, we do wish to direct the attention of certain readers to certain parts of the book. There are four target audiences for this book:

1. Practising software engineering researchers, whether they reside in academia or in industrial research labs.

   Of primary interest to such readers may be the section on "Knowledge Creation," since building knowledge from multiple sources of data, suitable for providing higher level answers to problems, continues to be of more importance to the empirical software engineering community as a whole. At the same time, our methods for abstracting such knowledge are not yet well codified, and the chapters in this section raise awareness as well as inform researchers about the methods currently being employed.

   Researchers may be primarily either quantitatively or qualitatively inclined. Both types will find issues of direct relevance to the typical problems that they encounter in the "Research Methods and Tools" section. That section is designed to provide a mix of relevant and interesting content of both types, as we feel strongly that the quantitative-qualitative distinction is an arbitrary one, and interesting and relevant conclusions will always need to combine a mix of both types of data. Overall, the methodological material will inform readers about advanced and defensible techniques that they can use in their research.

One last topic of special interest may be that of reporting guidelines in "Practical Foundations," which can provide readers with guidelines that they can use for reporting their results, either internally within their organisations or in the scientific literature.

2. Practising software engineers whose work involves data analysis. This category includes, for example, quality assurance personnel.

As budgets are squeezed, there is more pressure to provide stronger evidence and more convincing business cases to implement new technologies or make process changes, and even to justify decisions already made. Therefore, any knowledge that the engineers can use to help them achieve this goal is welcomed. The "Research Methods and Tools" section is of relevance to this target group. Insofar as readers may be expected to address real problems of practical interest, we have tried to make available a set of techniques that may be able to help them. As no two project environments and constraints are exactly alike, having as wide a variety of methods to apply will be beneficial. Moreover, the chapters in "Practical Foundations" that deal with the science of measurement and how to deal with common problems, such as missing data, may also be of help.

For example, one may consider using data collected about a new technology to estimate its effect on a larger process (simulation), understanding whether there are hidden costs of such changes by understanding more than just the dollar figure involved (qualitative methods), evaluating the impact of process changes within the organisation (through surveys of technical staff), customer surveys (survey design and focus groups), and performing appropriate analysis of factors affecting the incidence of operational defects when there are missing values in the defect databases (dealing with missing values). In particular, organisations following the improvement path stipulated by contemporary maturity/capability models are primary targets since these models emphasize measurement and quantitative control at higher levels of maturity/capability.

Other topics that may be of particular relevance for individuals in industry performing empirical studies can be found in "Practical Foundations." For example, given that quality assurance personnel usually rely on the co-operation of the development and maintenance engineers, ethical behaviour will ensure that none of the engineers are alienated. Furthermore, there may be legal ramifications for unethical behaviour, particularly in countries with strong labour laws (e.g., North European countries). The management of co-operation with universities will be relevant for those involved in joint industry-university research projects. Since a successful collaboration depends on both parties, the industrial side would also contribute to this success if they are aware of these guidelines.

3. Graduate students in software engineering. The book could serve as a text for a graduate level course on empirical methods, and/or as reference material for students embarking on a research project.

All of the material in the book will be of direct relevance to graduate students. Specifically, such readers may find valuable the coverage of the different types of studies that can be performed in order to make a decision on which approaches to follow during their research projects ("Research Methods and Tools"). Even more importantly, topics under "Practical Foundations" will help novice researchers recognize some of the background requirements in running successful studies, contribute towards ensuring that their research is well reported, and mitigate against the tendency of over-interpreting the results of individual studies.

The section on "Knowledge Creation" will help students understand the body of knowledge that may exist on their research topic and the importance of relating their work to existing theories that have been built up in the area.

4. Reviewers of empirical research.

The overview of empirical methods with their strengths and weaknesses ("Research Methods and Tools"), especially the discussion of appropriate issues that can be tackled with the various methods, should help reviewers make a better judgement of the quality of an empirical study.

The section on "Knowledge Creation" is especially important to reviewers. First, it aims to inform such readers about, and increase the acceptance of, replication. Replication is critical for any discipline to progress, and reviewers are essentially the gatekeepers. The chapter on reporting guidelines would assist reviewers in ensuring that sufficient detail is reported in published manuscripts.

Perhaps the most relevant chapter under "Practical Foundations" for reviewers is the one concerned with ethics. Reviewers have to judge whether appropriate ethical behaviour was followed in published manuscripts. Again, being the gatekeepers for a discipline, they can encourage or discourage certain behaviours.

When we first set out to put this book together, we were motivated by what we as researchers felt was missing, a handy reference guide on some of the techniques we are called upon to apply as part of our work or to review in others' work. Little did we understand at the time the kind of process we were embarking upon in trying to fill that gap. We wish to thank all of the chapter authors for their high-quality work and for helping to move this project along. We especially wish to thank all of the external reviewers (listed below) for contributing their effort to improve the quality of the materials found here. We certainly hope that readers will find this, as we intended, a useful and practical reference for their own work.

Forrest Shull

Janice Singer

Dag Sjøberg

External Reviewers

David Budgen

Reidar Conradi

Yvonne Dittrich

Tore Dybå

Tracy Hall

Natalia Juristo

James Miller

Helen Sharp

Susan Sim

Bhekisipho Twala

Paul Wernick

Bernard Wong

Murray Wood

Section I
Research Methods and Techniques

Chapter 1
Software Engineering Data Collection for Field Studies[1]

Janice Singer, Susan E. Sim, and Timothy C. Lethbridge

Abstract Software engineering is an intensely people-oriented activity, yet little is known about how software engineers perform their work. In order to improve software engineering tools and practice, it is therefore essential to conduct *field studies*, i.e., to study real practitioners as they solve real problems. To aid this goal, we describe a series of data collection techniques for such studies, organized around a taxonomy based on the degree to which interaction with software engineers is necessary. For each technique, we provide examples from the literature, an analysis of some of its advantages and disadvantages, and a discussion of special reporting requirements. We also talk briefly about recording options and data analysis.

1. Introduction

Software engineering involves real people working in real environments. People create software, people maintain software, people evolve software. Accordingly to understand software engineering, one should study software engineers as they work – typically by doing field studies. In this chapter, we introduce a set of data collection techniques suitable for performing such studies that can be used individually or in combination to understand different aspects of real world environments. These data collection techniques can be used with a wide variety of methods under a wide variety of theoretical and philosophical traditions (see Easterbrook et al., Chap. 11).

To better showcase the qualities of the various techniques, we have created a taxonomy based on the degree to which interaction with software engineers is required. The next section details the taxonomy. In Sect. 3, each technique is described in detail. We talk briefly in Sect. 4 about recording options for the data and present a brief overview of data analysis. We conclude the chapter with a discussion of how these techniques can be used in the most appropriate fashion.

---

[1] Based on Lethbridge, T., Sim, S., & Singer, J. (2005). Studying software engineers: data collection techniques for software field studies, *Empirical Software Engineering 10*(3), 311–341.

F. Shull et al. (eds.), *Guide to Advanced Empirical Software Engineering*.

2. Field Study Data Collection Taxonomy

Table 1. presents a summary of the data collection techniques; the second column shows the kinds of questions each can answer; the third column indicates the amount of data generated by the technique, and the fourth column shows other areas in software engineering where the technique is applied. Each technique is categorized according to how much contact is required between the researchers and the participants[2]. Direct techniques require the researcher to have direct involvement with the participant population. Indirect techniques require the researcher to have only indirect access to the participants' via direct access to their work environment. Finally, independent techniques require researchers to access only work artifacts, such as source code or documentation. Selecting an appropriate technique will be influenced by the questions asked and the amount of resources available to conduct the study. Generally, direct techniques require more resources, both to collect the data and to analyse it. Direct techniques are, however, the only techniques that allow researchers to explore the thoughts and feelings of the software engineers.

3. Survey of Data Collection Techniques

In this section, we describe the data collection techniques listed in Table 1. We use the taxonomy to organize the presentation of the techniques, beginning with direct techniques, moving on to indirect techniques, and concluding with independent techniques. Each of the techniques is described in the same way. First the technique is described. Then its advantages and disadvantages are identified. Next, one or more examples of its use in software engineering research are given. Finally, some guidance is given regarding special considerations when reporting the technique (for more information on reporting in general, see Jedlitschka et al., Chap. 8).

3.1. Direct Techniques

The first five techniques listed in Table 1 are what we call *inquisitive* techniques (brainstorming, focus groups, interviews, questionnaires, conceptual modeling), while the remaining ones are primarily *observational*. Each type is appropriate for gathering different types of information from software engineers.

---

[2] We recognize that there is some debate about whether to properly characterize people who participate in research as subjects or participants. In this chapter, we have chosen to use the word participant because in field studies, there is frequently a greater degree of collaboration between those being studied and those doing the research.

Table 1 Questions asked by software engineering researchers (column 2) that can be answered by field study techniques

Technique	Used by researchers when their goal is to understand:	Volume of data	Also used by software engineers for
Direct techniques			
Brainstorming and focus groups	Ideas and general background about the process and product, general opinions (also useful to enhance participant rapport)	Small	Requirements gathering, project planning
Interviews and questionnaires	General information (including opinions) about process, product, personal knowledge etc.	Small to large	Requirements and evaluation
Conceptual modeling	Mental models of product or process	Small	Requirements
Work diaries	Time spent or frequency of certain tasks (rough approximation, over days or weeks)	Medium	Time sheets
Think-aloud sessions	Mental models, goals, rationale and patterns of activities	Medium to large	UI evaluation
Shadowing and observation	Time spent or frequency of tasks (intermittent over relatively short periods), patterns of activities, some goals and rationale	Small	Advanced approaches to use case or task analysis
Participant observation (joining the team)	Deep understanding, goals and rationale for actions, time spent or frequency over a long period	Medium to large	
Indirect techniques			
Instrumenting systems	Software usage over a long period, for many participants	Large	Software usage analysis
Fly on the wall	Time spent intermittently in one location, patterns of activities (particularly collaboration)	Medium	
Independent techniques			
Analysis of work databases	Long-term patterns relating to software evolution, faults etc.	Large	Metrics gathering
Analysis of tool use logs	Details of tool usage	Large	
Documentation analysis	Design and documentation practices, general understanding	Medium	Reverse engineering
Static and dynamic analysis	Design and programming practices, general understanding	Large	Program comprehension, metrics, testing, etc.

Inquisitive techniques allow the experimenter to obtain a general understanding of the software engineering process. Such techniques are probably the only way to gauge how enjoyable or motivating certain tools are to use or certain activities to perform. However, they are often subjective, and additionally do not allow for accurate time measurements.

Observational techniques provide a real-time portrayal of the studied phenomena. However, it is more difficult to analyze the data, both because it is dense and because it requires considerable knowledge to interpret correctly. Observational techniques can be used at randomly chosen times or when a software engineer is engaged in a specific type of activity (such as whenever she is using a debugger). Observational techniques always run the risk of changing the process simply by observing it; the Hawthorne (Draper, 2004; Robbins, 1994) effect was first identified when a group of researchers found that output was not related to environmental conditions as expected, but rather to whether or not workers were being observed. Careful consideration of this effect is therefore warranted in implementing the research and explaining its purpose and protocol to the research participants.

3.1.1. Brainstorming and Focus Groups

In brainstorming, several people get together and focus on a particular issue. The idea is to ensure that discussion is not limited to "good" ideas or ideas that make immediate sense, but rather to uncover as many ideas as possible. Brainstorming works best with a moderator because the moderator can motivate the group and keep it focused. Additionally, brainstorming works best when there is a simple "trigger question" to be answered and everybody is given the chance to contribute their opinions. A good seminal reference for this process, called Nominal Group Technique, is the work of Delbecq et al. (1975). Trigger questions, such as, "What are the main tasks that you perform?" or "What features would you like to see in software engineering tools?" can result in extensive lists of valuable ideas that can then be analysed in more detail.

Focus Groups are similar to brainstorming. However, focus groups occur when groups of people are brought together to focus on a particular issue (not just generate ideas). They also involve moderators to focus the group discussion and make sure that everyone has an opportunity to participate. For more information on how to conduct focus groups, see Kontio et al., Chap. 4.

Advantages: Brainstorming and focus groups are excellent data collection techniques to use when one is new to a domain and seeking ideas for further exploration. They are also very useful for collecting information (for instance about the usefulness of a particular tool) from large groups of people at once. They are good at rapidly identifying what is important to the participant population. Two important side benefits of brainstorming and focus groups are that they can introduce the researchers and participants to each other and additionally give the participants more of a sense of being involved in the research process. Conducting research in field environments is often stressful to the research participants; they are more likely to be willing participants if they feel comfortable with the researchers and feel they are partners in research that focuses on issues that they consider to be important.

Disadvantages: Unless the moderator is very well trained, brainstorming and focus groups can become too unfocused. Although the nominal group technique helps people to express their ideas, people can still be shy in a group and not say what they really think. Just because a participant population raises particular issues, this does not mean the issues are really relevant to their daily work. It is often difficult to schedule a brainstorming session or focus group with the busy schedules of software engineers.

Examples: Bellotti and Bly (1996) used brainstorming during an initial meeting with a product design group. The brainstorming meeting was held to identify problems and possible solutions as seen by the team. This meeting gave the researchers an initial understanding of the team's work and additionally let the researchers know how existing technology was either supporting or inhibiting the work. A nice side effect of the meeting was that it gave the researchers an entry point for communication about the design process with their colleagues in the design department at Apple.

Hall and her colleagues have published a number of papers based on a large study involving focus groups to understand software process improvement (see for example, Baddoo and Hall, 2002; Rainer and Hall, 2003). In their studies, 39 focus groups were implemented in 13 companies. The groups were comprised of between four and six participants. The companies were chosen based on certain characteristics, but overall were representative of the industry. Each session lasted 90 min. There were three types of groups: senior managers, project managers, and developers. The focus groups were moderated and tackled very specific questions aimed at understanding several factors leading to success and failure for software process improvement.

Storey et al. (2007) conducted a focus group with a number of users of a tool they developed. The focus group enabled the users to communicate with each other, and additionally allowed for greater time efficiency when collecting the data than interviews would have allowed.

Reporting guidelines: The reporting of brainstorming and focus groups is similar. For both, the number of participants seen, and the context in which they were seen should be reported. Where appropriate the role and expertise of the moderator should be described. If specific questions were used, they should be detailed. Additionally, the time spent on brainstorming or the focus group should be reported. Finally, the type of data recording used should be described (e.g., video, audio, notes, etc.).

3.1.2. Interviews

Interviews involve at least one researcher talking to at least one respondent. Interviews can be conducted in two ways. In a structured interview, a fixed list of carefully worded questions forms the basis of the interview. Usually, the questions are asked exactly as written, and no deviations occur. The data from structured interviews is usually analysed using statistical analyses. In a semi-structured interview, the interview generally follows more of a conversational flow. New questions may be devised as new information is learned. Typically, some open-ended questions that allow for greater interaction are asked. Furthermore, in some semi-structured interviews, the interview will be structured around a framework of potential topics as opposed to any specific questions. The data from semi-structured interviews is usually analysed using qualitative analysis methods (see Seaman, Chap. 2).

Advantages: Structured interviews are an efficient means of collecting the same data from a large number of respondents. Semi-structured interviews tend to be much more highly interactive. Researchers can clarify questions for respondents and probe unexpected responses. Interviewers can also build rapport with a respondent to improve the quality of responses.

Disadvantages: Interviews are time and cost inefficient. Contact with the respondent needs to be scheduled and at least one person, usually the researcher, needs to attend the meeting (whether in person, by phone, videoconference, or over the web). If the data from interviews consists of audio- or videotapes, this needs to be transcribed and/or coded; careful note-taking may, however, often be an adequate substitute for audio or video recording. Finally, participants' reports of events may not mirror reality. For instance, in one of our interview studies, developers reported that they spent a substantial amount of time reading documentation, but we did not observe this to be true.

Examples: Interviews have been used in many studies because they fit well with many types of methods and philosophical traditions. We have used interviews in longitudinal studies as an aid in understanding how newcomers adapt to a development team and software system (Sim and Holt, 1998). We interviewed newcomers once every three weeks over a number of months to track their progress as maintenance team members. Since this was an exploratory study, the interviews were semi-structured with open-ended questions.

Curtis et al. (1988) used interviews to study the design process used on 19 different projects at various organizations. They interviewed personnel from three different levels of the participating projects, systems engineers, senior software designers and project managers. The researchers conducted 97 interviews, which resulted in over 3000 pages of transcripts of the audio recordings. They found three key problems common to the design processes: communication and coordination breakdowns, fluctuating and conflicting product requirements, and the tendency for application domain knowledge to be located in individuals across the company. They characterized the problems at each level of a model they subsequently defined.

Damian et al. (2004) used interviews of experienced personnel and senior management to examine how changes in the requirements engineering process affected software development practice. Because there was limited historical data on the previous requirements process, the interviews were key to provide information on how the changes were affecting the current practice. In addition to the initial interviews, follow-up interviews were conducted after a questionnaire to elucidate the responses. Overall, Damian et al. found the improved requirements process was useful to the product development team in that it resulted in better documentation of requirements, understanding of the market need, and understanding of requirements.

Reporting guidelines: When reporting data from interviews, it is necessary to detail the number and type of interviewees seen, approximately how long the interviews took, the type of interview (semi-structured or structured), the way the interview is recorded, and how the participants were selected. Additionally, if possible, provide a copy of the questions in the report or an appendix.

3.1.3. Questionnaires

Questionnaires are sets of questions administered in a written format. These are the most common field technique because they can be administered quickly and easily. However, very careful attention needs to be paid to the wording of the questions, the layout of the forms, and the ordering of the questions in order to ensure valid results. Pfleeger and Kitchenham have published a six part series on principles of survey research starting with Pfleeger and Kitchenham (2001) (see also Chap. 3). This series gives detailed information about how to design and implement questionnaires. Punter et al. (2003) further provide information on conducting web-based surveys in software engineering research.

Advantages: Questionnaires are time and cost effective. Researchers do not need to schedule sessions with the software engineers to administer them. They can be filled out when a software engineer has time between tasks, for example, waiting for information or during compilation. Paper form-based questionnaires can be transported to the respondent for little more than the cost of postage. Web-based questionnaires cost even less since the paper forms are eliminated and the data are received in electronic form. Questionnaires can also easily collect data from a large number of respondents in geographically diverse locations.

Disadvantages: Since there is no interviewer, ambiguous and poorly-worded questions are problematic. Even though it is relatively easy for software engineers to fill out questionnaires, they still must do so on their own and may not find the time. Thus, response rates can be relatively low which adversely affects the representativeness of the sample. We have found a consistent response rate of 5% to software engineering surveys. If the objective of the questionnaire is to gather data for rigorous statistical analysis in order to refute a null hypothesis, then response rates much higher than this will be needed. However, if the objective is to understand trends, then low response rates may be fine. The homogeneity of the population, and the sampling technique used also affect the extent to which one can generalize the results of surveys. In addition to the above, responses tend to be more terse than with interviews. Finally, as with questionnaires, developers' responses to questions may not mirror reality.

Examples: Lethbridge (2000) used questionnaires that were partly web-based and partly paper-based to learn what knowledge software engineers apply in their daily work, and how this relates to what they were taught in their formal education.

Respondents were asked four questions about each of a long list of topics. Several questionnaires were piloted, but nonetheless a couple of the topics[3] were interpreted in different ways by different respondents. Despite this, useful conclusions about how software engineers should be trained were drawn from the study.

Iivari (1996) used a paper-based questionnaire to test nine hypotheses about factors affecting CASE tool adoption in 52 organizations in Finland. The author contacted organizations that had purchased CASE tools and surveyed key information systems personnel about the use of the tool. Companies and individuals were more likely to use CASE tools when adoption was voluntary, the tool was perceived to be superior to its predecessor(s) and there was management support.

Reporting guidelines: When reporting data from questionnaires, it is necessary to detail how the population was sampled (i.e., who the questionnaires were sent to, or how respondents were chosen) and the response rate for the questionnaire, if appropriate. Any piloting and subsequent modification of the questionnaire should be explained. Additionally, if possible, provide a copy of the questions in the report or an appendix.

3.1.4. Conceptual Modeling

During conceptual modeling, participants create a model of some aspect of their work – the intent is to bring to light their mental models. In its simplest form, participants draw a diagram of some aspect of their work. For instance, software engineers may be asked to draw a data flow diagram, a control flow diagram or a package diagram showing the important architectural clusters of their system. As an orthogonal usage, software engineers may be asked to draw a physical map of their environment, pointing out who they talk to and how often.

Advantages: Conceptual models provide an accurate portrayal of the user's conception of his or her mental model of the system. Such models are easy to collect and require only low-tech aids (pen and paper).

Disadvantages: The results of conceptual modeling are frequently hard to interpret, especially if the researcher does not have domain knowledge about the system. Some software engineers are reluctant to draw, and the quality and level of details in diagrams can vary significantly.

Examples: In one of our studies, we collected system maps from all members of the researched group. Additionally, as we followed two newcomers to a system, we had them update their original system maps on a weekly basis. We gave them a photocopy of the previous week's map, and asked them to either update it or draw a new one. The newcomers almost exclusively updated the last week's map.

In our group study, our instructions to the study participants were to "draw their understanding of the system." These instructions turned out to be too vague. Some

---

[3] For example, we intended 'formal languages' to be the mathematical study of the principles of artificial languages in general, yet apparently some respondents thought we were referring to learning how to program.

participants drew data flow diagrams, some drew architectural clusters, others listed the important data structures and variables, etc. Not surprisingly, the manager of the group subsequently noted that the system illustrations reflected the current problems on which the various software engineers were working.

We learned from this exercise that for conceptual modeling to be useful, it is important to specify to the greatest extent possible the type of diagram required. It is next to impossible to compare diagrams from different members of a group if they are not drawing the same type of diagram. Of course, this limits researchers in the sense that they will not be getting unbiased representations of a system. Specifying that data-flow diagrams are required means that software engineers must then think of their system in terms of data-flow.

In another project (Sayyad-Shirabad et al., 1997), we wanted to discover the concepts and terminology that software engineers use to describe a software system. We extracted a set of candidate technical terms (anything that was not a common English word) from source code comments and documentation. Then we designed a simple program that allowed software engineers to manipulate the concepts, putting them into groups and organizing them into hierarchies. We presented the combined results to the software engineers and then iteratively worked with them to refine a conceptual hierarchy. Although there were hundreds of concepts in the complex system, we learned that the amount of work required to organize the concepts in this manner was not large.

Reporting guidelines: The most important thing to report for conceptual models is the exact instructions given to the participants and a precise description of the tools that they had available to them to model. The way the data is recorded should also be outlined.

3.1.5. Work Diaries

Work diaries require respondents to record various events that occur during the day. It may involve filling out a form at the end of the day, recording specific activities as they occur, or noting whatever the current task is at a pre-selected time. These diaries may be kept on paper or in a computer. Paper forms are adequate for recording information at the end of the day. A computer application can be used to prompt users for input at random times. A special form of the work diary is time sheets. Many software engineers (particularly consultants) are required to maintain and update quite detailed time sheets recording how many hours are spent per day per activity category. These time sheets can be a valuable source of data.

If you are considering utilizing prompted work diaries, Karahasanovic et al. (2007) provide a comprehensive comparison of this technique to think-aloud protocol analysis (detailed below), evaluating its costs, impacts on problem solving, and benefits.

Advantages: Work diaries can provide better self-reports of events because they record activities on an ongoing basis rather than in retrospect (as in interviews and questionnaires). Random sampling of events gives researchers a way of understanding how software engineers spend their day without undertaking a great deal of observation or shadowing.

Disadvantages: Work diaries still rely on self-reports; in particular, those that require participants to recall events may have significant problems with accuracy. Another problem with work diaries is that they may interfere with respondents as they work. For instance, if software engineers have to record each time they go and consult a colleague, they may consult less often. They may also forget or neglect to record some events and may not record at the expected level of detail.

Examples: Wu et al. (2003) were interested in collaboration at a large software company. In addition to observations and interviews, they asked software engineers to record their communication patterns for a period of 1 day. The researchers were interested in both the interaction between the team members, and the typical communication patterns of developers. They found that developers communicate frequently and extensively, and use many different types of communication modalities, switching between them as appropriate, and that communication patterns vary widely amongst developers. As a slight variation, at the end of each day, Izquierdo et al. (2007) asked developers to complete a communication diary that detailed who they talked to and the purpose for the communication. These were used as the basis to create social networks for the group.

As another example, Jørgensen (1995) randomly selected software maintainers and asked them to complete a form to describe their next task. These reports were used to profile the frequency distribution of maintenance tasks. Thirty-three hypotheses were tested and a number of them were supported. For example, programmer productivity (lines of code per unit time) is predicted by the size of the task, type of the change, but it is not predicted by maintainer experience, application age, nor application size.

As a slight modification of the work diary, Shull et al. (2000) asked students to submit weekly progress reports on their work. The progress reports included an estimate of the number of hours spent on the project, and a list of functional requirements begun and completed. Because the progress reports had no effect on the students' grades, however, Shull et al. found that many teams opted to submit them only sporadically or not at all.

In an interesting application the use of time sheets as data, Anda et al. (2005) describe a project where Simula Research Laboratory acted as both clients and researchers in an IT project, where the actual contract was given to four different companies, which allowed for a comparative case study. Although the applicability of this model in empirical software engineering is limited (because of the large amount of resources required), the paper nonetheless highlights how this data can potentially be used in a study (when collected from accessible sources).

Reporting guidelines: When reporting work diaries, the precise task given to the software engineers (e.g., to record their communication patterns) must be described, as well as how it was accomplished (e.g., reported to experimenter, recorded periodically throughout the day, etc). Additionally, the tools made available to do so should be detailed.

3.1.6. Think-Aloud Protocols

In think-aloud protocol analysis (Ericcson and Simon, 1984), researchers ask participants to think out loud while performing a task. The task can occur naturally at work or be predetermined by the researcher. As software engineers sometimes forget to verbalize, experimenters may occasionally remind them to continue thinking out loud. Other than these occasional reminders, researchers do not interfere in the problem solving process. Think-aloud sessions generally last no more than 2 hours.

Think-aloud protocol analysis is most often used for determining or validating a cognitive model as software engineers do some programming task. For a good review of this literature, see von Mayrhauser and Vans (1995). Additionally, if you are considering utilizing this technique, Karahasanovic et al. (2007) provide a comprehensive comparison of this technique to a form of work diaries, evaluating its costs, impacts on problem solving, and benefits.

Advantages: Asking people to think aloud is relatively easy to implement. Additionally, it is possible to implement think-aloud protocol analysis with manual record keeping eliminating the need for transcription. This technique gives a unique view of the problem solving process and additionally gives access to mental model. It is an established technique.

Disadvantages: Think-aloud protocol analysis was developed for use in situations where a researcher could map out the entire problem space. It's not clear how this technique translates to other domains where it is impossible to map out the problem space a priori. However, Chi (1997) has defined a technique called Verbal Analysis that does address this problem. In either case, even using manual record keeping, it is difficult and time-consuming to analyze think-aloud data.

Examples: von Mayrhauser and Vans (1993) asked software developers to think aloud as they performed a maintenance task which necessitated program comprehension. Both software engineers involved in the experiment chose debugging sessions. The think-aloud protocols were coded to determine if participants were adhering to the "Integrated meta-model" of program comprehension these researchers have defined. They found evidence for usage of this model, and were therefore able to use the model to suggest tool requirements for software maintenance environments.

As another example of think-aloud protocol analysis, Seaman et al. (2003) were interested in evaluating a user interface for a prototype management system. They asked several subjects to choose from a set of designated problems and then solve the problem using the system. The subjects were asked to verbalize their thoughts and motivations while working through the problems. The researchers were able to identify positive and negative aspects of the user interface and use this information in their evolution of the system.

Hungerford et al. (2004) adopted an information-processing framework in using protocol analysis to understand the use of software diagrams. The framework assumes that human cognitive processes are represented by the contents of short-term memory that are then available to be verbalized during a task. The verbal protocols were coded using a pre-established coding scheme. Intercoder reliability scores were used to ensure consistency of codings across raters and internal validity of the coding scheme. Hungerford et al. found individual differences in search strategies and defect detection rates across developers. They used their findings to suggest possible training and detection strategies for developers looking for defects.

Reporting guidelines: When reporting think-aloud protocol analysis, it is important to provide an extremely precise characterization of the task the participant was asked to undertake, including any tools at the participant's disposal. The time taken to complete the task and any materials provided to the participant are also important to describe. Finally, the precise way in which the analysis occurs needs to be closely detailed, especially if it is based on information processing theory or a specific cognitive model.

3.1.7. Shadowing/Observation

In shadowing, the experimenter follows the participant around and records their activities. Shadowing can occur for an unlimited time period, as long as there is a willing participant. Closely related to shadowing, observation occurs when the experimenter observes software engineers engaged in their work, or specific experiment-related tasks, such as meetings or programming. The difference between shadowing and observation is that the researcher shadows one software engineer at a time, but can observe many at one time.

Advantages: Shadowing and observation are easy to implement, give fast results, and require no special equipment.

Disadvantages: For shadowing, it is often difficult to see what a software engineer is doing, especially when they are using keyboard shortcuts to issue commands and working quickly. However, for the general picture, e.g., knowing they are now debugging, shadowing does work well. Observers need to have a fairly good understanding of the environment to interpret the software engineer's behavior. This can sometimes be offset by predefining a set of categories or looked-for behaviors. Of course, again, this limits the type of data that will be collected.

Examples: We have implemented shadowing in our work in two ways (1997). First, one experimenter took paper-and-pencil notes to indicate what the participant was doing and for approximately how long. This information gave us a good general picture of the work habits of the software engineers. We also used *synchronized shadowing* where two experimenters used two laptop computers to record the software engineer's actions. One was responsible for ascertaining the participants' high level goals, while the other was responsible for recording their low-level actions. We used pre-defined categories (Microsoft Word macros) to make recording easier. Wu et al. (2003) also used pre-defined categories to shadow software engineers.

Perry et al. (1994) also shadowed software engineers as they went about their work. They recorded continuous real-time non-verbal behavior in small spiral notebooks. Additionally, at timed intervals they asked the software engineers "What are you doing now?" At the end of each day, they converted the notebook observations to computer files. The direct observations contributed to Perry et al.'s understanding of the software process. In particular, shadowing was good for observing informal communication in the group setting. Similarly, Ko et al. (2007) also shadowed software engineers. They asked the participants to think of the researchers as a new hire to which they should explain what they were doing. From this data, they were able to categorize the met and unmet information needs of software engineers.

As an example of observation, Teasley et al. (2002), were interested in whether co-locating team members affects development of software. In addition to interviews and questionnaires, they observed teams, conference calls, problem solving, and photographed various artifacts. The researchers found that satisfaction and productivity increased for co-located teams.

Reporting guidelines: In reporting shadowing, the precise form of shadowing and/ or observation needs to be detailed, including whether any verbal instructions were given to the participant to think out loud. Additionally, the way the information is recorded must be detailed as well as the length of the session, and any other special instructions given to the participants. It is also helpful to provide context information, such as what activities the shadowed and/or observed participants were engaged in, and whether this was typical or not.

3.1.8. Participant-Observer (Joining the Team)

Usually done as part of an ethnography, in the Participant-Observer technique, the researcher essentially becomes part of the team and participates in key activities. Participating in the software development process provides the researcher with a high level of familiarity with the team members and the tasks they perform. As a result, software engineers are comfortable with the researcher's presence and tend not to notice being observed.

Advantages: Respondents are more likely to be comfortable with a team member and to act naturally during observation. Researchers also develop a deeper understanding of software engineering tasks after performing them in the context of a software engineering group.

Disadvantages: Joining a team is very time consuming. It takes a significant amount of time to establish true team membership. Also, a researcher who becomes too involved may lose perspective on the phenomenon being observed.

Examples: Participant-Observer was one of the techniques used by Seaman and Basili (1998) in their studies of how communication and organization factors affect the quality of software inspections. One of the authors (Seaman) was integrated into a newly formed development team. Over seventeen months, Seaman participated in twenty-three inspection meetings. From her participation, Seaman and Basili developed a series of hypotheses on how factors such as familiarity, organizational distance, and physical distance are related to how much time is spent on discussion and tasks.

Porter et al. (1997) also used the participant-observer technique. One of the researchers, a doctoral student, joined the development team under study as a means of tracking an experiment's progress, capturing and validating data, and observing inspections. Here, the field study technique was used in the service of more traditional experimental methods.

More recently, Izquierdo et al. (2007) joined a team over a period of 4 months to understand how they processed information and became aware of changes. Izquierdo did not participate in any development, but rather used the opportunity of closeness to support data collection and a greater comprehension of the team dynamics.

Reporting guidelines: Using the participant-observer technique, it is important to report the role of the participant-observer in the team – whether they are actually involved in any of the meaningful team activities or not. It is also important to characterize how they interact with the team, and what access they have to team material. Additionally, the length of time of the interaction needs to be reported. Finally, a characterization of how data was collected, coded, and analysed must be provided.

3.2. Indirect Techniques

Indirect techniques require the researcher to have access to the software engineer's environment as they are working. However, the techniques do not require *direct* contact between the participant and researcher. Instead data collection is initiated, then the software engineers go about their normal work as the data is automatically gathered. As a result, these techniques require very little or no time from the software engineers and are appropriate for longitudinal studies.

3.2.1. Instrumenting Systems

This technique requires "instrumentation" to be built into the software tools used by the software engineer. This instrumentation is used to record information automatically about the usage of the tools. Instrumentation can be used to monitor how frequently a tool or feature is used, patterns of access to files and directories, and even the timing underlying different activities. This technique is also called system monitoring.

In some cases, instrumentation merely records the commands issued by users. More advanced forms of instrumentation record both the input and output in great detail so that the researcher can effectively play back the session. Others have proposed building a new set of tools with embedded instruments to further constrain the work environment (Buckley and Cahill, 1997). Related to this, Johnson and his group have developed Hackystat, an open-source server-based system for monitoring actions. Developers install sensors on their machines that then relay information to a centralized server (see www.csdl.ics.hawaii.edu/Research/hackystat for more information).

Advantages: System monitoring requires no time commitment from software engineers. Since, people tend to be very poor judges of factors such as relative frequency and duration of the various activities they perform, this technique can be used to provide such information accurately.

Disadvantages: It is difficult to analyze data from instrumented systems meaningfully; that is, it is difficult to determine software engineers' thoughts and goals from a series of tool invocations. This problem is particularly relevant when the working environment is not well understood or constrained. For example, software engineers often customize their environments by adding scripts and macros (e.g., in emacs). One way of dealing with this disadvantage is to play back the events to a software engineer and ask them to comment. Although in many jurisdictions, employers have the right to monitor employees, there are ethical concerns if researchers become involved in monitoring software engineers without their knowledge.

Examples: Budgen and Thomson (2003) used a logging element when assessing how useful a particular CASE tool was. The logger element recorded data whenever an event occurred. Events were predetermined before. Textual data was not recorded. The researchers found that recording events only was a shortcoming of their design. It would have been more appropriate to collect information about the context of the particular event.

As another example, Walenstein (2003) used VNC (Virtual Network Computing) to collect verbatim screen protocols (continuous screen captures) of software developers engaged in software development activities. Walenstein also collected verbal protocols and used a theory-based approach to analyse the data.

More recently, Storey et al. (2007) logged developers' use of their TagSEA tool. The logs were stored on the client machine. The software engineers downloaded them to a server at specified intervals. The logs enabled Storey et al. (2007) to understand how the tool was being used, and nicely complemented other data sources such as interviews and a focus group. Similar to this study, Zou and Godfrey (2007) used a logger to determine which artifacts software maintainers were just viewing, and which were actually changed.

Reporting guidelines: The precise nature of the logging needs to be reported, including any special instrumentation installed on the software engineer's machines. This should include a description of what exactly is logged, with what frequency. Any special considerations with respect to data processing and analysis should also be detailed.

3.2.2. Fly on the Wall (Participants Recording their Own Work)

"Fly on the Wall" is a hybrid technique. It allows the researcher to be an observer of an activity without being present. Participants are asked to video- or audiotape themselves when they are engaged in some predefined activity.

Advantages: The fly-on-the-wall technique requires very little time from the participants and is very unobtrusive. Although there may be some discomfort in the beginning, it fades quickly.

Disadvantages: The participants may forget to turn on the recording equipment at the appropriate time and as a result the record may be incomplete or missing. The camera is fixed, so the context of what is recorded may be hard to understand. There is a high cost to analyzing the resulting data.

Examples: Berlin (1993) asked mentors and apprentices at a software organization to audiotape their meetings in order to study how expertise is passed on. She later analyzed these recordings for patterns in conversations. She found that discussions were highly interactive in nature, using techniques such as confirmation and re-statement to verify messages. Mentors not only explain features of the system; they also provide design rationale.

Walz et al. (1993) had software engineers videotape team meetings during the design phase of a development project. Researchers did not participate in the meetings and these tapes served as the primary data for the study. The goal of the study was to understand how teamwork, goals, and design evolved over a period of four months. Initially the team focused on gathering knowledge about the application domain, then on the requirements for the application, and finally on design approaches. The researchers also found that the team failed to keep track of much of the key information; as a result they re-visited issues that had been settled at earlier meetings.

Robillard et al. (1998) studied interaction patterns among software engineers in technical review meetings. The software engineers merely had to turn on a video-tape recorder whenever they were conducting a meeting. The researchers analyzed transcripts of the sessions and modeled the types of interactions that took place during the meetings. Their analysis led to recommendations for ways in which such meetings can be improved

Reporting guidelines: The precise nature of the recording needs to be reported, along with any special instructions given to the participants. Additionally, any problems with the recording need to be reported, such as developers forgetting to record a meeting. Context information will also help to clarify the application of the technique, such as where the recording occurred, what the typical tasks were, who was involved, who was responsible for the recording, etc. Additionally, any methods used to transform, transcribe, and analyse the data need to be specified.

3.3. Independent Techniques

Independent techniques attempt to uncover information about how software engineers work by looking at their output and by-products. Examples of their output are source code, documentation, and reports. By-products are created in the process of doing work, for example work requests, change logs and output from configuration management and build tools. These repositories, or archives, can serve as the primary information source. Sometimes researchers recruit software engineers to assist in the interpretation or validation of the data.

3.3.1. Analysis of Electronic Databases of Work Performed

In most large software engineering organizations, the work performed by developers is carefully managed using issue tracker, problem reporting, change request and configuration management systems. These systems require software engineers to input data, such as a description of a problem encountered, or a comment when checking in a source code module. The copious records generated for such systems are a rich source of information for software engineering researchers. Besides the examples provided below, see the proceedings from the International Workshops on Mining Software Repositories.

Advantages: A large amount of data is often readily available. The data is stable and is not influenced by the presence of researchers.

Disadvantages: There may be little control over the quantity and quality of information manually entered about the work performed. For example, we found that descriptive fields are often not filled in, or are filled in different ways by different developers. It is also difficult to gather additional information about a record, especially if it is very old or the software engineer who worked on it is no longer available.

Examples: Work records can be used in a number of ways. Pfleeger and Hatton (1997) analyzed reports of faults in an air traffic control system to evaluate the effect of adding formal methods to the development process. Each module in the software system was designed using one of three formal methods or an informal method. Although the code designed using formal methods tended to have fewer faults, the results were not compelling even when combined with other data from a code audit and unit testing.

Researchers at NASA (1998) studied data from various projects in their studies of how to effectively use COTS (commercial off-the-shelf software) in software engineering. They developed an extensive report recommending how to improve processes that use COTS.

Mockus et al. (2002) used data from email archives (amongst a number of different data sources) to understand processes in open source development. Because the developers rarely, if ever, meet face-to-face, the developer email list contains a rich record of the software development process. Mockus et al. wrote Perl scripts to extract information from the email archives. This information was very valuable in helping to clarify how development in open source differs from traditional methods.

Reporting guidelines: The exact nature of the collected data needs to be specified, along with any special considerations, such as whether any data is missing, or uninterpretable for some reason. Additionally, any special processing of the data needs to be reported, such as if only a certain proportion is chosen to be analysed.

3.3.2. Analysis of Tool Logs

Many software systems used by software engineers generate logs of some form or another. For example, automatic building tools often leave records, as source code control systems. Some organizations build sophisticated logging into a wide spectrum of tools so they can better understand the support needs of the software engineers.

Such tool logs can be analyzed in the same way tools that have been deliberately instrumented by the researchers – the distinction is merely that for this independent technique, the researchers don't have control over the kind of information collected. This technique is also similar to analysis of databases of work performed, except that the latter includes data manually entered by software engineers.

The analysis of tool logs has become a very popular area of research within software engineering. Besides the examples provided below, see the proceedings from the International Workshops on Mining Software Repositories.

Advantages: The data is already in electronic form, making it easier to code and analyze. The behaviour being logged is part of software engineers normal work routine.

Disadvantage: Companies tend to use different tools in different ways, so it is difficult to gather data consistently when using this technique with multiple organizations.

Examples: Wolf and Rosenblum (1993) analyzed the log files generated by build tools. They developed tools to automatically extract information from relevant events from these files. This data was input into a relational database along with the information gathered from other sources.

In one of our studies (Singer et al., 1997) we looked at logs of tool usage collected by a tools group to determine which tools software engineers throughout the company (as opposed to just the group we were studying) were using the most. We found that search and Unix tools were used particularly often.

Herbsleb and Mockus (2003) used data generated by a change management system to better understand how communication occurs in globally distributed software development. They used several modeling techniques to understand the relationship between the modification request interval and other variables including the number of people involved, the size of the change, and the distributed nature of the groups working on the change. Herbsleb and Mockus also used survey data to elucidate and confirm the findings from the analysis of the tool logs. In general they found that distributed work introduces delay. They propose some mechanisms that they believe influence this delay, primarily that distributed work involves more people, making the change requests longer to complete.

Reporting guidelines: As with instrumentation, the exact nature of what is being collected needs to specified, along with any special concerns, such as missing data. Additionally, if the data is processed in any way, it needs to be explained.

3.3.3. Documentation Analysis

This technique focuses on the documentation generated by software engineers, including comments in the program code, as well as separate documents describing a software system. Data collected from these sources can also be used in re-engineering efforts, such as subsystem identification. Other sources of documentation that can be analyzed include local newsgroups, group e-mail lists, memos, and documents that define the development process.

Advantages: Documents written about the system often contain conceptual information and present a glimpse of at least one person's understanding of the software system. They can also serve as an introduction to the software and the team. Comments in the program code tend to provide low-level information on algorithms and data. Using the source code as the source of data allows for an up-to-date portrayal of the software system.

Disadvantages: Studying the documentation can be time consuming and it requires some knowledge of the source. Written material and source comments may be inaccurate.

Examples: The ACM SIGDOC conferences contain many studies of documentation.

Reporting guidelines: The documentation needs to be described as well as any processing on it.

3.3.4. Static and Dynamic Analysis of a System

In this technique, one analyzes the code (static analysis) or traces generated by running the code (dynamic analysis) to learn about the design, and indirectly about how software engineers think and work. One might compare the programming or architectural styles of several software engineers by analyzing their use of various constructs, or the values of various complexity metrics.

Advantages: The source code is usually readily available and contains a very large amount of information ready to be mined.

Disadvantages: To extract useful information from source code requires parsers and other analysis tools; we have found such technology is not always mature – although parsers used in compilers are of high quality, the parsers needed for certain kinds of analysis can be quite different, for example they typically need to analyze the code *without* it being pre-processed. We have developed some techniques for dealing with this surprisingly difficult task (Somé and Lethbridge, 1998). Analyzing old legacy systems created by multiple programmers over many years can make it hard to tease apart the various independent variables (programmers, activities etc.) that give rise to different styles, metrics etc.

Examples: Keller et al. (1999) use static analysis techniques involving template-matching to uncover design patterns in source code – they point out, "… that it is these patterns of thought that are at the root of many of the key elements of large-scale software systems, and that, in order to comprehend these systems, we need to recover and understand the patterns on which they were built."

Williams et al. (2000) were interested in the value added by pair programming over individual programming. As one of the measures in their experiment, they looked at the number of test cases passed by pairs versus individual programmers. They found that the pairs generated higher quality code as evidence by a significantly higher number of test cases passed.

Reporting guidelines: The documents (e.g. source code) that provide the basis for the analysis should be carefully described. The nature of the processing on the data also needs to be detailed. Additionally, any special processing considerations should be described.

4. Applying the Techniques

In the previous section, we described a number of diverse techniques for gathering information in a field study. The utility of data collection techniques becomes apparent when they can help us to understand a particular phenomenon. In this section, we outline how to record and analyze the data.

4.1. Record-Keeping Options

Direct techniques generally involve one of the following three data capture methods: videotape, audiotape, or manual record keeping. These methods can be categorized as belonging to several related continua. First, they can be distinguished with respect to the completeness of the data record captured. Videotape captures the most complete record, while manual record keeping captures the least complete record. Second, they can be categorized according to the degree of interference they invoke in the work environment. Videotaping invokes the greatest amount of interference, while manual recording keeping invokes the least amount of interference. Finally, these methods can be distinguished with respect to the time involved in using the captured data. Again, videotape is the most time-intensive data to use and interpret, while manual record keeping is the least time-intensive data to use and interpret.

The advantage of videotape is that it captures details that would otherwise be lost, such as gestures, gaze direction, etc.[4] However, with respect to video recording, it is important to consider the video camera's frame of reference. Videotape can record only where a video camera is aimed. Moving the video camera a bit to the right or a bit to the left may cause a difference in the recorded output and subsequently in the interpretation of the data. Related to videotaping, there are a number of software programs that allow screen capture and playback of the recorded interactions. To be used with videotape, the video and the screen capture must be synchronized in some way.

Audiotape allows for a fairly complete record in the case of interviews, however details of the physical environment and interaction with it will be lost. Audiotape does allow, however, for the capture of tone. If a participant is excited while talking about a new tool, this will be captured on the audio record.

Manual record keeping is the most data sparse method and hence captures the least complete data record, however manual record keeping is also the quickest, easiest, and least expensive method to implement. Manual record keeping works best when a well-trained researcher identifies certain behaviors, thoughts, or concepts during the data collection process. Related to manual record keeping, Wu et al. (2003) developed a data collection technique utilizing a PDA. On the PDA, they

---

[4] It is often felt that videotaping will influence the participants actions. However, while videotaping appears to do so initially, the novelty wears off quickly (Jordan and Henderson, 1995).

had predetermined categories of responses that were coded each time a particular behaviour was observed. The data were easily transported to a database on a PC for further analysis.

All three data capture methods have advantages or disadvantages. The decision of which to use depends on many variables, including privacy at work, the participant's degree of comfort with any of the three measures, the amount of time available for data collection and interpretation, the type of question asked and how well it can be formalized, etc. It is important to note that data capture methods will affect the information gained and the information that it is possible to gain. But again, these methods are not mutually exclusive. They can be used in conjunction with each other.

4.2. Coding and Analyzing the Data

Field study techniques produce enormous amounts of data—a problem referred to as an "attractive nuisance" (Miles, 1979). The purpose of this data is to provide insight into the phenomenon being studied. To meet this goal, the body of data must be reduced to a comprehensible format. Traditionally, this is done through a process of coding. That is, using the goals of the research as a guide, a scheme is developed to categorize the data. These schemes can be quite high level. For instance, a researcher may be interested in noting all goals stated by a software engineer during debugging. On the other hand the schemes can be quite specific. A researcher may be interested in noting how many times grep was executed in a half-hour programming session. Once coded, the data is usually coded by another researcher to ensure the validity of the rating scheme. This is called inter-coder or inter-rater reliability. There are a number of statistics that can be reported that assess this, the most common is Kendall's tau.

Audio and videotape records are usually transcribed before categorization, although transcription is often not necessary. Transcription requires significant cost and effort, and may not be justified for small, informal studies. Having made the decision to transcribe, obtaining an accurate transcription is challenging. A trained transcriber can take up to 6 hours to transcribe a single hour of tape (even longer when gestures, etc. must be incorporated into the transcription). An untrained transcriber (especially in technical domains) can do such a poor job that it takes researchers just as long to correct the transcript. While transcribing has its problems, online coding of audio or videotape can also be quite time inefficient as it can take several passes to produce an accurate categorization. Additionally, if a question surfaces later, it will be necessary to listen to the tapes again, requiring more time.

Once the data has been categorized, it can be subjected to a quantitative or qualitative analysis. Quantitative analyzes can be used to provide summary information about the data, such as, on average, how often grep is used in debugging sessions. Quantitative analyzes can also determine whether particular hypotheses are supported by the data, such as whether high-level goals are stated more frequently in development than in maintenance.

When choosing a statistical analysis method, it is important to know whether your data is consistent with assumptions made by the method. Traditional, inferential statistical analyzes are only applicable in well-constrained situations. The type of data collected in field studies often requires *nonparametric* statistics. Nonparametric statistics are often called "distribution-free" in that they do not have the same requirements regarding the modeled distribution as parametric statistics. Additionally, there are many nonparametric tests based on simple rankings, as opposed to strict numerical values. Finally, many nonparametric tests can be used with small samples. For more information about nonparametric statistics, Seigel and Castellan (1988) provide a good overview. Briand et al. (1996) discuss the disadvantages of nonparametric statistics versus parametric statistics in software engineering; they point out that a certain amount of violation of the assumptions of parametric statistics is legitimate, but that nonparametric statistics should be used when there are extreme violations of those assumptions, as there may well be in field studies.

Qualitative analyzes do not rely on quantitative measures to describe the data. Rather, they provide a general characterization based on the researchers' coding schemes. Again, the different types of qualitative analysis are too complex to detail in this paper. See Miles and Huberman (1994) for a very good overview.

Both quantitative and qualitative analysis can be supported by software tools. The most popular tools for quantitative analysis are SAS and SPSS. A number of different tools exist for helping with qualitative analysis, including NVivo, Altas/ti, and Noldus observer. Some of these tools also help with analysis of video recordings.

In summary, the way the data is coded will affect its interpretation and the possible courses for its evaluation. Therefore it is important to ensure that coding schemes reflect the research goals. They should tie in to particular research questions. Additionally, coding schemes should be devised with the analysis techniques in mind. Again, different schemes will lend themselves to different evaluative mechanisms. However, one way to overcome the limitations of any one technique is to look at the data using several different techniques (such as combining a qualitative and quantitative analyzes). A *triangulation* approach (Jick, 1979) will allow for a more accurate picture of the studied phenomena. Bratthall and Jørgensen (2002) give a very nice example of using multiple methods for data triangulation. Their example is framed in a software engineering context examining software evolution and development. In fact, many of the examples cited earlier, use multiple methods to triangulate their results.

As a final note, with any type of analysis technique, it is generally useful to go back to the original participant population to discuss the findings. Participants can tell researchers whether they believe an accurate portrayal of their situation has been achieved. This, in turn, can let researchers know whether they used appropriate coding scheme and analysis techniques.

5. Conclusions

In this chapter we have discussed issues that software engineering researchers need to consider when studying practitioners in the field. Field studies are one of several complementary approaches to software engineering research and are based on a recognition that software engineering is fundamentally a human activity: Field studies are particularly useful when one is gathering basic information to develop theories or understand practices.

The material presented in this chapter will be useful to both producers and consumers of software engineering research. Our goal is to give researchers a perspective on how they might effectively collect data in the field – we believe that more studies like this are needed. As well, the reporting guidelines presented here will help others evaluate published field studies: for example, readers of a field study may ask whether appropriate data gathering or analysis techniques were used.

In this chapter, we divided the set of field study techniques into three main categories. Direct techniques such as interviewing, brainstorming, and shadowing place the researcher in direct contact with participants. Indirect techniques allow researchers to observe work without needing to communicate directly with participants. Independent techniques involve retrospective study of work artifacts such as source code, problem logs, or documentation. Each technique has advantages and disadvantages that we described in Sect. 2.

In addition to deciding which techniques to use, the researcher must also determine the level of detail of the data to be gathered. For most direct techniques one must typically choose among, in increasing order of information volume and hence difficulty of analysis: manual notes, audio-taping and videotaping. In all three cases, a key difficulty is encoding the data so that it can be analyzed.

Regardless of the approach to gathering and analyzing data, field studies also raise many logistical concerns that should be dealt with in the initial plan. For example: How does one approach and establish relationships with companies and employees in order to obtain a suitable sample of participants? Will the research be considered ethical, considering that it involves human participants? And finally, will it be possible to find research staff who are competent and interested, given that most of the techniques described in this paper are labor intensive but not yet part of mainstream software engineering research?

Finally, as technology and knowledge evolve, new data collection techniques emerge – e.g., using web cameras to collect work diaries. A good place to learn more about these new techniques is by following the human computer interaction and psychology methods literature. As well, reading papers in empirical software engineering will highlight current accepted techniques in the field, and how they may be used in practice.

In conclusion, field studies provide empirical studies researchers with a unique perspective on software engineering. As such, we hope that others will pursue this approach. The techniques described in this paper are well worth considering to better understand how software engineering occurs, thereby aiding in the development of methods and theories for improving software production.

References

Anda, B., Benestad, H., and Hove, S. 2005. A multiple-case study of effort estimation based on use case points. In *ISESE 2005* (Fourth International Symposium on Empirical Software Engineering). IEEE Computer Society, Noosa, Australia, November 17–18, pp. 407–416.

Baddoo, N. and Hall, T. 2002. Motivators of software process improvement: an analysis of practitioners' views. *Journal of Systems and Software*, 62, 85–96.

Bellotti, V. and Bly, S. 1996. *Walking Away from the Desktop Computer: Distributed Collaboration and Mobility in a Product Design Team*. Conference on Computer Supported Cooperative Work, Cambridge, MA, pp. 209–219.

Berlin, L.M. 1993. *Beyond Program Understanding: A Look at Programming Expertise in Industry*. Empirical Studies of Programmers, Fifth Workshop, Palo Alto, pp. 6–25.

Briand, L., El Emam, K. and Morasca, S. 1996. On the application of measurement theory in software engineering. *Empirical Software Engineering*, 1, 61–88.

Bratthall, L. and Jørgensen, M. 2002. Can you trust a single data source exploratory software engineering case study? *Empirical Software Engineering: An International Journal*, 7(1), 9–26.

Budgen, D. and Thomson, M. 2003. CASE tool evaluation: experiences from an empirical study. *Journal of Systems and Software*, 67, 55–75.

Buckley, J. and Cahill, T. 1997. *Measuring Comprehension Behaviour Through System Monitoring*. International Workshop on Empirical Studies of Software Maintenance, Bari, Italy, 109–113.

Chi, M. 1997. Quantifying qualitative analyzes of verbal data: a practical guide. *The Journal of the Learning Sciences*, 6(3), 271–315.

Curtis, B., Krasner, H., and Iscoe, N. 1988. A field study of the software design process for large systems. *Communications of the ACM*, 31(11), 1268–1287.

Damian, D., Zowghi, D., Vaidyanathasamy, L., and Pal, Y. 2004. An industrial case study of immediate benefits of requirements engineering process improvement at the Australian Center for Unisys Software. *Empirical Software Engineering: An International Journal*, 9(1–2), 45–75.

Delbecq, A.L., Van de Ven, A.H., and Gustafson, D.H. 1975. *Group Techniques for Program Planning*. Scott, Foresman & Co, Glenview, IL.

Draper, S. 2004. *The Hawthorne Effect*. http://www.psy.gla.ac.uk/ steve/hawth.html

Ericcson, K. and Simon, H. 1984. *Protocol Analysis: Verbal Reports as Data*. The MIT Press, Cambridge, MA.

Herbsleb, J. and Mockus, A. 2003. An empirical study of speed and communication in globally distributed software development. *IEEE Transactions of Software Engineering*, 29(6), 481–494.

Hungerford, B., Hevner, A., and Collins, R. 2004. Reviewing software diagrams: a cognitive study. *IEEE Transactions of Software Engineering*, 30(2), 82–96.

Iivari, J. 1996. Why are CASE tools not used? *Communications of the ACM*, 39(10), 94–103.

Izquierdo, L., Damian, D., Singer, J., and Kwan, I. (2007). *Awareness in the Wild: Why Communication Breakdowns Occur*. ICGSE 2007, Germany.

Jick, T. 1979. Mixing qualitative and quantitative methods: triangulation in action. *Administrative Science Quarterly*, 24(4), 602–611.

Jordan, B. and Henderson, A. 1995. Interaction analysis: foundations and practice. *The Journal of the Learning Sciences*, 4(1), 39–103.

Jørgensen, M. 1995. An empirical study of software maintenance tasks. *Software Maintenance: Research and Practice*, 7, 27–48.

Karahasanovic, A., Hinkel, U., Sjøberg D., and Thomas, R. (2007). *Comparing of Feedback Collection and Think-Aloud Methods in Program Comprehension Studies*. Accepted for publication in Journal of Behaviour & Information Technology, 2007.

Keller, R., Schauer, R. Robitaille, S., and Page, P. 1999. Pattern-based Reverse Engineering of Design Components. *Proceedings, International Conference on Software Engineering*, Los Angeles, CA, pp. 226–235.

Ko, A.J., DeLine, R., and Venolia, G. (2007). Information needs in collocated software development teams. *International Conference on Software Engineering (ICSE)*, May 20–26, 344–353.

Lethbridge, T.C. 2000. Priorities for the education and training of software engineers. *Journal of Systems and Software*, 53(1), 53–71.

Miles, M.B. 1979. Qualitative data as an attractive nuisance: the problem of analysis. *Administrative Science Quarterly*, 24(4), 590–601.

Miles, M.B. and Huberman, A.M. 1994. *Qualitative Data Analysis: An Expanded Sourcebook*, Second Edition. Sage Publications, Thousand Oaks, CA.

Mockus, A., Fielding, R.T., and Herbsleb, J.D. 2002. Two case studies of open source software development: Apache and Mozilla. *ACM Transactions on Software Engineering and Methodology*, 11(3), 209–246.

NASA, *SEL COTS Study Phase 1 Initial Characterization Study Report, SEL-98–001*, August 1998. http://sel.gsfc.nasa.gov/website/documents/online-doc.htm.

Perry, D.E., Staudenmayer, N., and Votta, L. 1994. People, organizations, and process improvement. *IEEE Software*, 11, 37–45.

Pfleeger, S.L. and Hatton, L. 1997. Investigating the influence of formal methods. *Computer*, 30, 33–43.

Pfleeger, S. and Kitchenham, B. 2001. Principles of survey research Part 1: turning lemons into lemonade. *Software Engineering Notes*, 26(6), 16–18.

Porter, A.A., Siy, H.P., Toman, C.A., and Votta, L.G. 1997. An experiment to assess the cost-benefits of code inspections in large scale software development. *IEEE Transactions on Software Engineering*, 23(6), 329–346.

Punter, T., Ciolkowski, M., Freimut, B., and John, I. 2003. Conducting On-Line Surveys in Software Engineering. *Proceedings on the International Symposium on Empirical Software Engineering'03*, pp. 80–88.

Rainer, A. and Hall, T. 2003. A quantitative and qualitative analysis of factors affecting software processes. *Journal of Systems and Software*, 66, 7–21.

Robbins, S.P. 1994. *Essentials of Organizational Behavior*, Fourth edition. Prentice Hall, Englewood Cliffs, NJ.

Robillard, P.N., d'Astous, P., Détienne, D., and Visser, W. 1998. Measuring Cognitive Activities in Software Engineering. *Proceedings on the 20th International Conference on Software Engineering*, Japan, pp. 292–300.

Sayyad-Shirabad, J., Lethbridge, T.C., and Lyon, S. 1997. A Little Knowledge Can Go a Long Way Towards Program Understanding. *Proceedings of 5th International Workshop on Program Comprehension*, IEEE, Dearborn, MI, pp. 111–117.

Seigel, S. and Castellan, N.J. 1988. *Nonparametric Statistics for the Behavioral Sciences*, Second Edition. McGraw-Hill, New York.

Seaman, C.B. and Basili, V.R. 1998. Communication and organization: an empirical study of discussion in inspection meetings. *IEEE Transactions on Software Engineering*, 24(7), 559–572.

Seaman, C., Mendonca, M., Basili, V., and Kim, Y. 2003. User interface evaluation and empirically-based evolution of a prototype experience management tool. *IEEE Transactions on Software Engineering*, 29, 838–850.

Shull, F., Lanubile, F., and Basili, V. 2000. Investigating reading techniques for object-oriented framework learning. *IEEE Transactions on Software Engineering*, 26, 1101–1118.

Sim S.E. and Holt, R.C. 1998. The Ramp-Up Problem in Software Projects: A Case Study of How Software Immigrants Naturalize. *Proceedings on the 20th International Conference on Software Engineering*, Kyoto, Japan, April, pp. 361–370.

Singer, J., Lethbridge, T., Vinson, N., and Anquetil, N. 1997. An Examination of Software Engineering Work Practices. *Proceedings of CASCON*, IBM Toronto, October, pp. 209–223.

Somé, S.S. and Lethbridge T.C. 1998. Parsing Minimizing when Extracting Information from Code in the Presence of Conditional Compilation. *Proceedings of the 6th IEEE International Workshop on Program Comprehension*, Italy, June, pp. 118–125.

Storey, M.-A., Cheng, L., Singer, J., Muller, M., Ryall, J., and Myers, D. (2007). *Turning Tags into Waypoints for Code Navigation*. ICSM, Paris, France.

Teasley, S., Covi, L., Krishnan, M., and Olson, J. 2002. Rapid software development through team collocation. *IEEE Transactions on Software Engineering*, 28, 671–683.

von Mayrhauser, A. and Vans, A.M. 1993. From Program Comprehension To Tool Requirements for an Industrial Environment. *Proceedings of the 2nd Workshop on Program Comprehension*, Capri, Italy, pp. 78–86.

von Mayrhauser, A. and Vans, A.M. 1995. Program understanding: models and experiments. In M.C. Yovita and M.V. Zelkowitz (eds.), *Advances in Computers*, Vol. 40, Academic Press, New York, pp. 1–38.

Walz, D.B., Elam, J.J., and Curtis, B. 1993. Inside a software design team: knowledge acquisition, sharing, and integration. *Communications of the ACM*, 36(10), 62–77.

Walenstein, A. 2003. Observing and Measuring Cognitive Support: Steps Toward Systematic Tool Evaluation and Engineering. *Proceedings of the 11th IEEE Workshop on Program Comprehension*.

Williams, L., Kessler, R.R., Cunningham, W., and Jeffries, R. 2000. Strengthening the case for pair-programming. *IEEE Software*, July/Aug, 19–25.

Wolf, A. and Rosenblum, D. 1993. A Study in Software Process Data Capture and Analysis. *Proceedings of the 2nd International Conference on Software Process*, February, pp. 115–124.

Wu, J., Graham, T., and Smith, P. 2003. A Study of Collaboration in Software Design. *Proceedings of the International Symposium on Empirical Software Engineering'03*.

Zou, L. and Godfrey, M. 2007. An Industrial Case Study of Program Artifacts Viewed During Maintenance Tasks. *Proceedings of the 2006 Working Conference on Reverse Engineering (WCRE-06)*, 23–28 October, Benevento, Italy.

Chapter 2
Qualitative Methods[1]

Carolyn B. Seaman

Abstract Software engineering involves a blend of non-technical as well as technical issues that often have to be taken into account in the design of empirical studies. In particular, the behavior of people is an integral part of software development and maintenance. This aspect of our subject presents complexities and challenges for the empirical researcher. In many other disciplines, qualitative research methods have been developed and are commonly used to handle the complexity of issues involving people performing tasks in their workplace. This chapter presents several qualitative methods for data collection and analysis and describes them in terms of how they might be incorporated into empirical studies of software engineering, in particular how they might be combined with quantitative methods. To illustrate this use of qualitative methods, examples from real software engineering studies are used throughout.

1. Introduction

The study of software engineering has always been complex and difficult. The complexity arises from technical issues, from the awkward intersection of machine and human capabilities, and from the central role of the people performing software engineering tasks. The first two aspects provide more than enough complex problems to keep empirical software engineering researchers busy. But the last factor, the people themselves, introduces aspects that are especially difficult to capture. However, studies attempting to capture human behavior as it relates to software engineering are increasing and, not surprisingly, are increasingly employing qualitative methods (e.g. Lethbridge et al., 2005; Lutters and Seaman, 2007; Orlikowski, 1993; Parra et al., 1997; Rainer et al., 2003; Seaman and Basili, 1998; Singer, 1998; Sharp and Robinson, 2004).

Historically, qualitative research methods grew out of the interpretivist tradition in social science research. Interpretivism, in turn, arose as a reaction to positivism,

---

[1] Based on "Qualitative Methods in Empirical Studies of Software Engineering" by Carolyn B. Seaman, which appeared in *IEEE Transactions on Software Engineering*, 25(4):557–572, July/August 1999. © 1999 IEEE.

F. Shull et al. (eds.), *Guide to Advanced Empirical Software Engineering*.
© Springer 2008

which was and continues to be the prevailing (if implicit) philosophical underpinning of research in the natural and physical sciences, including computer science and software engineering. The positivist researcher views objective truth as possible, i.e. that there exists some absolute truth about the issues of relevance, even if that truth is elusive, and that the role of research is to come ever closer to it. Interpretivism, on the other hand, posits that all truth is socially constructed, meaning that human beings create their own truth about the issues of relevance to them, and these socially constructed truths are valid and valuable. Qualitative methods, then, were required to capture and describe these socially constructed realities. See Creswell (1998) for a fuller explanation of positivism, interpretivism, other related philosophical frameworks, and the role of qualitative research methods in them. For many social science researchers, qualitative methods are reserved exclusively for use by interpretivist researchers, and are not to be mixed with quantitative methods or positivist points of view. However, in recent decades, researchers in information systems, human–computer interaction, and software engineering have begun using qualitative methods, even though the predominant, implicit philosophical stance of these research areas remains positivist (Orlikowski and Baroudi, 1991). Thus, the perspective of this chapter is that qualitative methods are appropriate for (even implicitly) positivist research in software engineering, and a researcher does not have to subscribe wholeheartedly to the interpretivist world view in order to apply them.

Qualitative data are data represented as text and pictures, not numbers (Gilgun, 1992). Qualitative research methods were designed, mostly by educational researchers and other social scientists (Taylor and Bogdan, 1984), to study the complexities of humans (e.g. motivation, communication, understanding). In software engineering, the blend of technical and human aspects lends itself to combining qualitative and quantitative methods, in order to take advantage of the strengths of both.

The principal advantage of using qualitative methods is that they force the researcher to delve into the complexity of the problem rather than abstract it away. Thus the results are richer and more informative. They help to answer questions that involve variables that are difficult to quantify (particularly human characteristics such as motivation, perception, and experience). They are also used to answer the "why" to questions already addressed by quantitative research. There are drawbacks, however. Qualitative analysis is generally more labor-intensive and exhausting than quantitative analysis. Qualitative results often are considered "softer," or "fuzzier" than quantitative results, especially in technical communities like ours. They are more difficult to summarize or simplify. But then, so are the problems we study in software engineering.

Methods are described here in terms of how they could be used in a study that mixes qualitative and quantitative methods, as they often are in studies of software engineering. The focus of this chapter is rather narrow, in that it concentrates on only a few techniques, and only a few of the possible research designs that are well suited to common software engineering research topics. See Judd et al. (1991), Lincoln and Guba (1985), Miles and Huberman (1994) and Taylor and Bogdan (1984) for descriptions of other qualitative methods.

The presentation of this chapter divides qualitative methods into those for collecting data and those for analysing data. Examples of several methods are given for each, and the methods can be combined with each other, as well as with quantitative methods. Throughout this chapter, examples will be drawn from several software engineering studies, including (von Mayrhauser and Vans 1996; Guindon et al., 1987; Lethbridge et al., 2005; Perry et al. 1994; Lutters and Seaman, 2007; Singer, 1998; Orlikowski 1993). More detailed examples will also be used from studies described in Parra et al. (1997) and Seaman and Basili (1998) because they represent the author's experience (both positive and negative).

2. Data Collection Methods

Two data collection methods, direct observation and interviewing, are presented in this section. These are useful ways of collecting firsthand information about software development efforts. Historical qualitative information can also be gained by examining documentation. Techniques for analysing archival documents are discussed in Taylor and Bogdan (1984). Another useful technique is focus groups, which are treated extensively in the chapter by Kontio et al. (2007, this volume).

2.1. Participant Observation

Participant observation, as defined in Taylor and Bogdan (1984), refers to "research that involves social interaction between the researcher and informants in the milieu of the latter, during which data are systematically and unobtrusively collected." The idea is to capture firsthand behaviors and interactions that might not be noticed otherwise.

Definitions of participant observation differ as to whether it implies that the observer is engaged in the activity being observed (e.g. Barley, 1990), or only that the observer is visibly present and is collecting data with the knowledge of those being observed. To avoid this confusion in terminology, the term direct observation is more usefully used when the researcher is not actively involved in the work being observed.

Although a great deal of information can be gathered through observation, the parts of the software development process that can actually be observed are limited. Much of software development work takes place inside a person's head. Such activity is difficult to observe, although there are some techniques for doing so. For example, it is sometimes possible to capture some of the thought processes of individual developers by logging their keystrokes and mouse movements as they work on a computer (Shneiderman, 1998). This technique is sometimes used in usability studies, where the subjects are software users, but it has not been widely employed in studies of software developers.

Think aloud observation (Hackos and Redish, 1998) requires the subject to verbalize his or her thought process so that the observer can understand the mental process going on. Such protocols are limited by the comfort level of the subject and their ability to articulate their thoughts. A good software engineering example of this technique is the work of von Mayrhauser and Vans (1996), in which software maintainers were asked to verbalize their thought processes while working on understanding source code. The data was collected by audio- and video-taping the sessions. Another example of a software engineering study based on thinking aloud observations is Guindon, Krasner, and Curtis's study of software designers (Guindon et al., 1987).

A variation on think aloud observation is synchronized shadowing, described in Lethbridge et al. (2005). With synchronized shadowing, two observers watch a subject perform some task while the subject is thinking aloud. Both observers record their notes on laptops whose clocks have been previously synchronized to the second. The two observers record different types of information. For example, one might concentrate on the subject's actions (keystrokes, commands, mouse clicks) while the other concentrates on the subject's goals and motivations (as evidenced by the subject thinking aloud). Both observers timestamp individual observations (using a macro in the word processor) so that the notes can later be synchronized. The end result is a detailed set of field notes that relates actions to goals.

Software developers reveal their thought processes most naturally when communicating with other software developers, so this communication offers the best opportunity for a researcher to observe the development process. One method is for the researcher to observe a software developer continuously, thus recording every communication that takes place with colleagues, either planned or unplanned. A good example of a study based on this type of observation is Perry et al. (1994). A less time-consuming approach is to observe meetings of various types. These could include inspection meetings, design meetings, status meetings, etc. By observing meetings, a researcher can gather data on the types of topics discussed, the terminology used, the technical information that was exchanged, and the dynamics of how different project members speak to each other.

There are a number of issues of which an observer must be aware. Many of these are presented here, based in part on the literature (in particular Taylor and Bogdan, 1984) and partly on the particular experience of this researcher with studies of software engineering.

The observer must take measures to ensure that those being observed are not constantly thinking about being observed. This is to help ensure that the observed behavior is "normal," i.e. that it is what usually happens in the environment being observed, and is not affected by the presence of the observer. For example, observers should strive for "fly on the wall" unobtrusiveness. Ideally, all those being observed should know beforehand that the observer will be observing and why. This advance notice avoids having to do a lot of explaining during the observation, which will only remind the subjects that they are being observed. The observer, although visible, should not be disruptive in any way, in particular avoiding making noise or movement that is distracting. The observer should always look for signs that their presence makes any of the participants nervous or self-conscious, which again may affect their behavior. Any such signs should be recorded in the notes that the observer takes, and will be considered in the analysis later.

The observer's notes should not be visible to any of those being observed. In fact, the notes should be kept confidential throughout the study. This gives the researcher complete freedom to write down any impressions, opinions, or thoughts without the fear that they may be read by someone who will misinterpret them.

The data gathered during an observation is ultimately recorded in the form of field notes. These notes are begun during the actual observation, during which the observer writes what is necessary to fill in the details later. Then, as soon after the observation as possible, the notes are augmented with as many details as the observer can remember. The information contained in the field notes should include the place, time, and participants in the observation, the discussions that took place, any events that took place during the observation, and the tone and mood of the interactions. The notes can also contain observer's comments, marked "OC" in the text of the notes, which record the observer's impressions of some aspect of the activity observed, which may not correspond directly to anything that was actually said or that occurred. For example, impressions about the setting of the observation (e.g. quality of the light, temperature, noise level), the demeanor of the people observed (e.g. if someone appeared to be agitated, ill, or tired), or the internal state of the observer (e.g. if the observer is agitated, ill, or tired, or has some strong emotional reaction to what is being observed) could all be recorded in observer's comments. The level of detail in the notes depends on the objectives of the researcher. The most detailed are verbatim transcripts of everything said and done, plus detailed descriptions of the setting and participants. Writing such detailed notes is extremely time-consuming. Often what are needed are summaries of the discussions and/or some details that are specific to the aims of the study. The more exploratory and open-ended the study, the more detailed the field notes should be, simply because in such a study anything could turn out to be relevant. In any study, the observer should begin with very detailed notes at least for the first few observations, until it is absolutely clear what the objectives of the study are and exactly what information is relevant.

In many studies, there are very specific pieces of information that are expected to be collected during an observation. This is often true in studies that combine qualitative and quantitative methods, in which qualitative information from an observation will later be coded into quantitative variables, e.g. the length of a meeting in minutes, the number of people present, etc. When this is the case, forms will be designed ahead of time that the observer will fill in during the course of the observation. This will ensure that specific details will be recorded. These forms are used in addition to, not instead of, field notes.

An example of a study based largely on observation data is Seaman and Basili (1998), a study of code inspection meetings (hereafter referred to as the Inspection Study). Most of the data for this study was collected during direct observation of 23 inspections of C++ classes. The objective of the study was to investigate the relationship between the amount of effort developers spend in technical communication (e.g. the amount of time spent discussing various issues in inspection meetings) and the organizational relationships between them (e.g. how much a group of inspection participants have worked together in the past). Information about organizational relationships was collected during interviews with inspection participants, described in Sect. 2.2. Information about communication effort was collected during the observations of code inspections.

Figure 1 shows a form that was filled out by the observer for each observed meeting in the Inspection Study. The administrative information (classes inspected, date, time, names of participants), the responsibilities of each inspector (which products each was responsible for inspecting), each preparation time, and who was present were all recorded on the data form either before or during the observed inspection. The amount and complexity of the code inspected was addressed during interviews later.

Another form filled out during observations was a time log, an example of which is shown in Fig. 2. For each discussion that took place during the meeting, the observer recorded the time (to the closest minute) it started, the initials of the participants in that discussion, a code corresponding to the type of discussion, and some notes indicating the topic of discussion, the tone of the discussion, and any other relevant information. The arrows in some of the lists of participants' initials indicate that a comment or question was made by one participant, specifically targeted to another participant. In the margins of the time log, the observer also recorded other relevant information about the participants, the setting of the meeting, and other activities taking place. The number of minutes spent in each discussion category was calculated from the time logs after the meeting.

Extensive field notes were also written immediately after each meeting observed in the Inspection Study. These notes contained broader descriptions of observations noted on the inspection data forms. Below is a sanitized excerpt from these field notes:

[Inspector1] raised a bunch of defects all together, all concerning checking for certain error conditions (unset dependencies, negative time, and null pointers).

[Inspector2] raised a defect which was a typo in a comment. She seemed slightly sheepish about raising it, but she did nevertheless.

OC: [Inspector2] seemed more harsh on [Author] than I had ever seen her on any of the [subcontractor] authors. My impression of her is that she would never raise a typo as a defect with anyone else. Does she have something against [government agency] folks?

[Inspector2] raised a defect concerning the wrong name of a constant.

[Inspector3] raised a defect having to do with the previous single dependency issue. In particular, dereferencing would have to be done differently, although there were several ways to fix it. [Inspector3] recommended using the dot instead of the arrow.

In order to evaluate the validity and consistency of data collected during observations, rater agreement exercises (Judd et al., 1991) are often conducted. The basic idea is to ensure not only that the data being recorded are accurate, but also that the observer is not recording data in a form that is understandable only to him or her. During three of the inspection meetings observed in the Inspection Study (about 15%), a second observer was present to record data. The same second observer was used all three times. All three were among the first half of meetings observed, i.e. they occurred fairly early in the study. This was intentional, in order

Inspection Data Form

Class(es) inspected: Inspection date: Time:
Author:
Moderator:
Reviewers:
    Name   Responsibility   Preparation time   Present

Amount of code inspected:
Complexity of Classes:

Discussion codes:

D   **Defects**
Reviewer raises a question or concern and it is determined that it is a defect which the author must fix; time recorded may include discussion of the solution

Q   **Questions**
Reviewer asks a question, but it is not determined to be a defect.

C   **Classgen defect**
Reviewer raises a defect caused by classgen; author must fix it, but it is recognized as a problem to eventually be solved by classgen

U   **Unresolved issues**
Discussion of an issue which cannot be resolved; someone else not at the meeting must be consulted (put name of person to be consulted in () beside the code); this includes unresolved classgen issues. It also includes issues which the author has to investigate more before resolving.

G/D   **Global defects**
Discussion of global issues, e.g. standard practices, checking for null pointers, which results in a defect being logged (does not include classgen defects)

G/Q   **Global questions**
Same as above, but not defect is logged

P   **Process issues**
General discussion and questions about the inspection process itself, including how to fill out forms, the order to consider material in, etc., but not the actual excecution of these tasks.

A   **Administrative issues**
Includes recording prep time, arranging rework, announcing which products are being inspected, silence while people look through their printouts, filling out forms.

M   **Miscellaneous discussion**

Time logged (in minutes)

D—— Q—— C—— U—— G/D—— G/D—— P—— A—— M————

Fig. 1 Form used to collect data during observation of inspection meetings

freshly painted room – smells + is hot
just had a task meeting – 39 classes needed in 6 weeks
SM: "This is a nightmare, and it's going to get worse."
- started 30 minutes late because of meeting

Class(es) inspected: ANI.3, EVS, EVS.1   Date: 3/15/96   Time: 2:00   Page 1 of 2

Time	Participants	Code	Notes
30	SM	A	get started; SM having problems finding right files
31	AP → RK	G/D	o change to null / - actually several small different small defects / don't change now, wait for TB3
33	AP, SM, MI	Q	
34	AP	D	couts
35	MI	G/D	"good thorough test plan" – some FYIs / ⸫ not standard format – do for next TB
36	MI	Q	- other style – don't take time now / MI went through everything she did / - no defects – showed RK+SM something / on paper – don't change for now
38	MI → RK, SM	Q	
40	RK → M	Q	re DB filename
41	SM	A	nothing on category
42	SM → RK	G/D	null instead of O – had trouble finding it
44	SM → RK, MI	D	Parameter Error exception – trying to figure out where it's thrown
46	SM → RK	U	similar to above / "This leads me to my BIG QUESTION" – SM
47	SM → RK, MI	U (RK+SM)	RK catching error that will never happen / MI: you're making it a lot more complex than you need to – too much error checking / - discussion of meanings of various parameters / - MI: "action item for the 2 of you to battle out"
53	RK → SM	Q	why is certain error generated by classgen?
55	RK → MI, SM	Q	clarification
56	SM → RK, MI	D	Parameter Error – handle differently from the way classgen does it

Margin notes:
"Ken already gave you his stuff, correct?" – SM to RK / yes
"I'm having a hard time concentrating"
CA standing up by door
MI gave RK marked up copy of test plan
EV3
EVS.1 / 43 CA leaves
printout very small – hard to read – SM + AP off blaming their glasses
47 CA comes back

Lots of time for everyone trying to find right place in printout – small print is a factor

Fig. 2 Time log used to document discussions during inspection meetings

to get the greatest advantage from improvements made to data collection procedures as a result of the exercise.

Before the observations in which she participated, the second observer was instructed by the principal observer in the forms used for data collection, the codes used to categorize discussions, the procedure used to time discussions, and some background on the development project and developers. A total of 42 discussions were recorded during the three doubly-observed meetings. Out of those, both observers agreed on the coding for 26, or 62%. Although, to our knowledge, there is no standard acceptable threshold for this agreement percentage, we had hoped to obtain a higher value. However, the two observers were later able to come to an agreement on coding for all discussions on which they initially disagreed. The observers generally agreed on the length of each discussion.

Many of the coding discrepancies were due to the second observer's lack of familiarity with the project and the developers. Others arose from the second observer's lack of experience with the instrument (the form and coding categories), and the subjectivity of the categories. The coding scheme was actually modified slightly due to the problems the second observer had. It should be noted that some of the discrepancies over coding (3 out of 26 discrepancies) were eventually resolved in the second observer's favor. That is, the principal observer had made an error. Another troubling result of this exercise was the number of discussions (five) that one observer had completely missed, but had been recorded by the other. Both the principal and second observers missed discussions. This would imply that a single observer will usually miss some interaction.

The results of a rater agreement exercise, ideally, should confirm that the data collection techniques being used are robust. However, as in the Inspection Study, the exercise often reveals the limitations of the study. This is valuable, however, as many of the limitations revealed in the study design can be overcome if they are discovered early enough. Even if they are not surmountable, they can be reported along with the results and can inform the design of future studies. For example, in the Inspection Study, the results of the rater agreement exercise indicated that the data collected during observations would have been more accurate if more observers had been used for all observations, or if the meetings had been recorded. These procedural changes would have either required prohibitive amounts of effort, or stretched the goodwill of the study's subjects beyond its limits. However, these should be taken into consideration in the design of future studies.

Recording of observations, either with audio or video, is another issue to be considered when planning a study involving observation. The main advantage of electronically recording observations is in ensuring accuracy of the data. Usually, the field notes are written after the observation while listening to or watching the recording. In this way, the notes are much less likely to introduce inaccuracies due to the observer's faulty memory or even bias.

2.2. Interviewing

Another commonly used technique for collecting qualitative data is the interview. Interviews are conducted with a variety of objectives. Often they are used to collect historical data from the memories of interviewees (Lutters and Seaman, 2007), to collect opinions or impressions about something, or to help identify the terminology used in a particular setting. In software engineering, they are often used to elicit software processes (Parra et al., 1997). They are sometimes used in combination with observations to clarify things that happened or were said during an observation, to elicit impressions of the meeting or other event that was observed, or to collect information on relevant events that were not observed.

Interviews come in several types. In Lincoln and Guba (1985), a structured interview is described as one in which "the questions are in the hands of the interviewer and the response rests with the interviewee," as opposed to an unstructured interview in which the interviewee is the source of both questions and answers. In an unstructured interview, the object is to elicit as much information as possible on a broadly defined topic. The interviewer does not know the form of this information ahead of time, so the questions asked must be as open-ended as possible. In the extreme, the interviewer doesn't even ask questions, but just mentions the topic to be discussed and allows the interviewee to expound.

In a structured interview, on the other hand, the interviewer has very specific objectives for the type of information sought in the interview, so the questions can be fairly specific. The more structured an interview, the more likely it is to be focused on quantitative, rather than qualitative data. The extreme of a structured interview is one in which no qualitative information is gained at all, i.e. all responses can be quantified (e.g. yes/no, high/medium/low, etc.). If the study is qualitative, however, the interview must be flexible enough to allow unforeseen types of information to be recorded. A purely unstructured interview is often too costly to be used extensively. Therefore, many studies employ semi-structured interviews. These interviews include a mixture of open-ended and specific questions, designed to elicit not only the information foreseen, but also unexpected types of information. A good example of a software engineering study based on semi-structured interviews is that conducted by Singer (1998), in which software maintainers were asked about their practices. Some of the more structured questions from this study include:

• How many years have you been programming?
• What languages have you had extensive experience programming in?
• How long have you worked on this project?

More open-ended questions included:

• When you get a maintenance request, how do you go about fulfilling it?
• What do you see as the biggest problem in maintaining programmes?

Again, as in the previous section on observation, the advice given here about interviewing is based in part on the literature [in particular Taylor and Bogdan (1984)] and partly on the experience and reflection of this author.

The interviewer should begin each interview with a short explanation of the research being conducted. Just how much information the interviewer should give about the study should be carefully considered. Interviewees may be less likely to fully participate if they do not understand the goals of the study or agree that they are worthy. However, if interviewees are told too much about it, they may filter their responses, leaving out information that they think the interviewer is not interested in.

Another judgement that the interviewer must often make is when to cut off the interviewee when the conversation has wandered too far. On one hand, interview time is usually valuable and shouldn't be wasted. However, in a qualitative study, all data is potentially useful and the usefulness of a particular piece of data often is not known until long after it is collected. Of course, interviewees should never be cut off abruptly or rudely. Steering them back to the subject at hand must be done gently. In general, it is better to err on the side of letting the interviewee ramble. Often the ramblings make more sense in hindsight. The opposite problem, of course, is that of an interviewee who says the barest minimum. One strategy is to ask questions that cannot possibly be answered with a "yes" or a "no." Another is to feign ignorance, i.e. to ask for details that are already well known to the interviewer. This may get the interviewee talking, as well as help dispel any perception they might have of the interviewer as an "expert." It is also important to make it clear that there are no "right" answers. Software developers sometimes mistakenly believe that anyone coming to interview them is really there to evaluate them.

Like observational data, interview data are ultimately recorded in field notes, which are governed by the same guidelines as described in the previous section. Also, as described earlier, forms can be used and filled out by the interviewer in order to facilitate the gathering of specific pieces of information. Another tool that is very useful during an interview is an interview guide (Taylor and Bogdan, 1984). An interview guide is not as formal as a data form, but it helps the interviewer to organize the interview. It serves a purpose similar to a script. It usually consists of a list of questions, possibly with some notes about the direction in which to steer the interview under different circumstances. In a structured interview, the questions are fairly straightforward, and they might be arranged in an "if-then" structure that leads the interviewer along one of several paths depending on the answers to previous questions. In an unstructured interview, there might not be an interview guide, or it may simply be a short list of topics to be touched on. Interview guides are purely for the use of the interviewer; they are never shown to the interviewee.

The interviewer may make some notes on the guide to help him or her remember how to steer the interview, but the guide should not be used for taking notes of the interview. In general, it is difficult for an interviewer to take notes and conduct the interview at the same time, unless the interviewer is very skilled. It is useful, if the interviewee consents, to audiotape the interview. The tape can then be used to aid the writing of the field notes later. Recording has the added advantage that the interviewer can hear him/herself on the tape and assess his or her interviewing skills. Another way to facilitate the taking of notes is to use a scribe. A scribe is present at the interview only to take notes and does not normally participate in any other way. Using a scribe takes the note-writing responsibilities from the interviewer completely, which can be an advantage for the researcher. However, verbatim notes are not possible this way, and the scribe does not always share the interviewer's ideas about what is important to record. The use of a scribe is also often prohibitively expensive or intimidating to the interviewee.

Another study that we will use as a detailed example is Parra et al. (1997), a study of Commercial-Off-The-Shelf (COTS) integration (hereafter referred to as the COTS Study). The objective of the study was to document the process that NASA software project teams were following to produce software systems largely constructed from COTS components. This type of system development, or "integration," was fairly new in the NASA group studied at that time. Consequently, there was no documented process for it and it was suspected that a number of different processes were being followed. The COTS Study team was tasked with building a process model general enough to apply to all of the different ways that COTS integration was being done. The model would then be used as a baseline to design process measures, to plan improvements to the process, and to make recommendations for process support. Interviews with developers on projects that involved a large amount of COTS integration provided the bulk of the data used to build the process model. Scribes, as described above, were used to record these interviews. Many interviewees were interviewed multiple times, at increasing levels of detail. These interviews were semi-structured because each interview started with a specific set of questions, the answers to which were the objective of the interview. However, many of these questions were open-ended and were intended for (and successful in) soliciting other information not foreseen by the interviewer. For example, one question on the COTS Study interview guide was:

What are the disadvantages of [COTS integration] in comparison with traditional development?

The study team had expected that answers to this question would describe technical difficulties such as incompatible file formats, interface problems, or low COTS product quality. However, much of the data gathered through this question had to do with the administrative difficulties of COTS integration, e.g. procurement, finding information on current licences, negotiating maintenance agreements, etc. As a result, a major portion of the study's recommendations to NASA had to do with more administrative support of various kinds for COTS integration projects.

Semi-structured interviews were also used in the Inspection Study (Seaman and Basili, 1998). After each inspection meeting, an interview guide was constructed to include the information missing from the data form for that inspection, as well as several questions that were asked of all interviewees. The questions asked also varied somewhat depending on the role that the interviewee played in the inspection. An example of such a form is shown in Fig. 3. Most interviews in this study were audio taped in their entirety. Extensive field notes were written immediately after each interview. The tapes were used during the writing of field notes, but they were not transcribed verbatim.

3. Data Analysis Methods

Collection of qualitative data is often a very satisfying experience for the researcher. Although it is often more labor-intensive, it is also more enjoyable to collect than quantitative data. It is interesting and engaging and it often gives the researcher the sense that they are closer to reality than when dealing with quantitative abstractions. The analysis of qualitative data, on the other hand, is not always as pleasant. Although the discovery of new knowledge is always motivating, the mechanics of

Interview Guide

Logistical info: record name, office#, date, time

Organization:

How long have you worked on [project]?   At [company]?

Have you work with any of the [project] members before on other projects?

Who on the [project] team do you interact with most?

To whom do you report?

To whom are you responsible for your progress on [project]?

Inspection process:

Who chose the inspectors?

How long did it take?

Why were those ones chosen in particular?

Which inspectors inspected what?

Who took care of scheduling?

Was it done via email or face-to-face?

How much time did it take?

What steps were involved in putting together the inspection package?

How much time did that take?

How are [project] inspections different from inspections in other [company] projects you've been on?

How was this inspection different from other [project] inspections you've been involved with?

Reviewed material:

How much was inspected?

How is that measure?

Were the inspected classes more or less complex then average?

Fig. 3 An interview guide used in the Inspection Study

qualitative analysis are sometimes boring, often tedious, and always more time-consuming than expected. It is tempting to take shortcuts in the analysis process, but rigorous analysis is necessary for the integrity of the research, and results in more insightful, useful, and valid conclusions.

As in quantitative studies, data analysis should be planned up front, before data collection begins. However, the difference is that qualitative researchers collect and analyse data nearly in parallel, or at least alternate between the two. Qualitative analysis begins as soon as some significant amount of data has been collected. Preliminary analysis results also can modify subsequent data collection.

In the next two sections, we present several analysis techniques, roughly divided into two categories, although the line between them is not well delineated. The first set of methods (Sect. 3.1) is used to generate hypotheses that fit the data (or are "grounded" in the data), normally used in exploratory, or grounded theory studies (Glaser and Strauss, 1967). Section 3.2 describes some methods used to build up the "weight of evidence" necessary to confirm hypotheses in confirmatory studies. Following, in Sect. 3.3, we discuss the use of visualization of qualitative data, which is useful in conjunction with any analysis approach, and for presenting results. Finally, Sect. 3.4 presents some basic techniques for transforming qualitative data for subsequent quantitative analysis. The methods presented in these sections represent only a small sample of the methods, techniques, and approaches available for analysing qualitative data. Yin (1994) and Miles and Huberman (1994) are excellent sources for other data analysis approaches.

3.1. Generation of Theory

Theory generation methods are generally used to extract from a set of field notes a statement or proposition that is supported in multiple ways by the data. The statement or proposition is first constructed from some passage in the notes, and then refined, modified, and elaborated upon as other related passages are found and incorporated. The end result is a statement or proposition that insightfully and richly describes a phenomenon. Often these propositions are used as hypotheses to be tested in a future study or in some later stage of the same study. These methods are often referred to as grounded theory methods because the theories, or propositions, are "grounded" in the data (Glaser and Strauss, 1967). Two grounded theory techniques, the constant comparison method and cross-case analysis, are briefly described below. See Seaman (1999) for a fuller description of these techniques as applied to software engineering studies.

3.1.1. Constant Comparison Method

There are a number of methods for conducting and analysing single case studies. An excellent reference for this type of research design is Yin (1994). Here, we will explore a classic theory generation method, the constant comparison method. This method was originally presented by Glaser and Strauss (1967), but has been more clearly and practically explained by others since (e.g. Miles and Huberman, 1994).

The process begins with open coding of the field notes, which involves attaching codes, or labels, to pieces of text that are relevant to a particular theme or idea of interest in the study. Codes can be either preformed or postformed. When the objectives of the study are clear ahead of time, a set of preformed codes [a "start list" (Miles and Huberman, 1994)] can be constructed before data collection begins and then used to code the data. Postformed codes (codes created during the coding process) are used when the study objectives are very open and unfocused. In either case, the set of codes often develops a structure, with subcodes and categories emerging as the analysis proceeds. Coding a section of notes involves reading through it once, then going back and assigning codes to "chunks" of text (which vary widely in size) and then reading through it again to make sure that the codes are being used consistently. Not everything in the notes needs to be assigned a code, and differently coded chunks often overlap. In the section of coded notes from the Inspection Study, below, the codes T, CG, and S correspond to passages about testing, the core group, and functional specifications, respectively. The numbers simply number the passages chronologically within each code.

(*T4*) These classes had already been extensively tested, and this was cited as the reason that very few defects were found. [Moderator] said: "must have done some really exhaustive testing on this class"

(*CG18*) [Inspector2] said very little in the inspection, despite the fact that twice [Moderator] asked him specifically if he had any questions or issues. Once he said that he had had a whole bunch of questions, but he had already talked to [Author] and resolved them all.

OC: Find out how much time was spent when [Author] and [Inspector2] met.

(*S4*) Several discussions had to do with the fact that the specs had not been updated. [Author] had worked from a set of updated specs that she had gotten from her officemate (who is not on the [project] team, as far as I know). I think these were updated [previous project] specs. The [project] specs did not reflect the updates. [Team lead] was given an action item to work with [Spec guru] to make sure that the specs were updated.

Then passages of text are grouped into patterns according to the codes and subcodes they've been assigned. These groupings are examined for underlying themes and explanations of phenomena in the next step of the process, called axial coding. Axial coding can be thought of as the process of reassembling the data that was broken up into parts (chunks) in open coding. One way to do this is to search for a particular code, moving to each passage assigned that code and reading it in context. It is not recommended to cut and paste similarly coded passages into one long passage so that they can be read together. The context of each passage is important and must be included in consideration of each group of passages. This is where the intensive, or "constant" comparison comes in. The coded data is reviewed and re-reviewed in order to identify relationships among categories and codes. The focus is on unifying explanations of underlying phenomenon, in particular the how's and why's.

The next step, selective coding or "sense making," culminates in the writing of a field memo that articulates a proposition (a preliminary hypothesis to be considered) or an observation synthesized from the coded data. Because qualitative data collection and analysis occur concurrently, the feasibility of the new proposition is then checked in the next round of data collection. Field memos can take a number of forms, from a bulleted list of related themes, to a reminder to go back to check a particular idea later, to several pages outlining a more complex proposition. Field memos also provide a way to capture possibly incomplete thoughts before they get lost in the next interesting idea. More detailed memos can also show how strong or weak the support for a particular proposition is thus far. According to Miles and Huberman, field memos are "one of the most useful and powerful sense-making tools at hand." (Miles and Huberman, 1994, p. 72)

Ideally, after every round of coding and analysis, there is more data collection to be done, which provides an opportunity to check any propositions that have been formed. This can happen in several ways. In particular, intermediate propositions can be checked by focusing the next round of data collection in an effort to collect data that might support or refute the proposition. In this way, opportunities may arise for refining the proposition Also, if the proposition holds in different situations, then further evidence is gathered to support its representativeness. This approach may offend the sensibilities of researchers who are accustomed to performing quantitative analyses that rely on random sampling to help ensure representativeness. The qualitative researcher, on the other hand, typically uses methods to ensure representativeness later in the study by choosing cases accordingly during the course of the study. This is sometimes called theoretical sampling, which we will not discuss in detail here, but the reader is referred to Miles and Huberman (1994) for a good explanation of its use and justification.

3.1.2. Cross-Case Analysis

In many software engineering studies, the data can be divided into "cases," which in quantitative studies might be referred to as "data points" or "trials." When this is possible, cross-case analysis is appropriate. For example, in the Inspection Study, all data were collected from the same development project, so they could be viewed as a single case study. Some of the analysis was done with this perspective (e.g. the analysis described in the previous section). However, some cross-case analysis was also performed by treating each inspection as a "case."

Eisenhardt (1989) suggests several useful strategies for cross-case analysis, all based on the goal of looking at the data in many different ways. For example, the cases can be partitioned into two groups based on some attribute (e.g. number of people involved, type of product, etc.), and then examined to see what similarities hold within each group, and what differences exist between the two groups. Another strategy is to compare pairs of cases to determine variations and similarities. A third strategy presented by Eisenhardt is to divide the data based on data source (e.g. interviews, observations, etc.).

In the Inspection Study (Seaman and Basili, 1998), we used a comparison method that progressed as follows. The field notes corresponding to the first two inspections observed were reviewed and a list of short descriptors (e.g. aggressive author; discussion dominated by one inspector; really long meeting, etc.) was compiled for each inspection. Then these two lists were compared to determine the similarities and differences. The next step was to list, in the form of propositions, conclusions one would draw if these two inspections were the only two in the data set (e.g. really long meetings are generally dominated by one inspector). Each proposition had associated with it a list of inspections that supported it (beginning with the first two inspections compared). Then the third inspection was examined, a list of its descriptors was compiled, and it was determined whether this third inspection supported or refuted any of the propositions formulated from the first two. If a proposition was supported, then this third inspection was added to its list of supporting evidence. If it contradicted a proposition then either the proposition was modified (e.g. really long meetings are generally dominated by one inspector when the other inspectors are inexperienced) or the inspection was noted as refuting that proposition. Any additional propositions suggested by the third inspection were added to the list. This process was repeated with each subsequent inspection. The end result was a list of propositions (most very rich in detail), each with a set of supporting and refuting evidence.

A different approach to cross-case analysis was used in the COTS Study (Parra et al., 1997). Each development project that was studied was treated as a separate case. The objective of the analysis was to document the COTS integration process by building an abstraction, or model, of the process that was flexible enough to accommodate all of the different variations that existed in the different projects. This model-building exercise was carried out iteratively by a team of researchers. The first step was to group all of the field notes by development project. Then, for each project, the notes were used to build a preliminary process model for that project's COTS integration process. These preliminary models were built by different researchers. Then the study team came together to study the models, identify similarities and differences, and resolve discrepancies in terminology. From this, one single model was built that encompassed the models for the different projects. This aggregate model went through numerous cycles of review and modification by different members of the study team. Finally, an extensive member checking process (see Sect. 3.2) was conducted through individual interviews with project members, a large group interview with a number of project personnel, and some email reviews of the model. The resulting model can be found in Parra et al. (1997).

Cross-case analysis was also used in the Orlikowski study of CASE tool adoption (Orlikowski, 1993). Data from the first case was collected and coded, then the second case's data was collected and an attempt was made to use the same set of codes to analyse it. Of course, some codes were inappropriate or inadequate and so new or modified codes resulted. These were then taken back to the first case, whose data was re-sorted and re-analysed to incorporate the new concepts. This type of back-and-forth analysis [sometimes referred to as "controlled opportunism" (Eisenhardt, 1989)] is a unique and valuable property of grounded theory research.

3.2. Confirmation of Theory

Most qualitative data analysis methods are aimed at generating theory, as described in the previous section, but there are a number of methods and approaches to strengthening, or "confirming" a proposition after it has been generated from the data. The goal is to build up the "weight of evidence" in support of a particular proposition, not to prove it. The emphasis is on addressing various threats to the validity of the proposition. Although quantitative hypothesis testing methods seem more conclusive than the methods we will present in this section, they really do not provide any stronger evidence of a proposition's truth. A hypothesis cannot be proven, it can only be supported or refuted, and this is true using either quantitative or qualitative evidence, or both. Qualitative methods have the added advantage of providing more explanatory information, and help in refining a proposition to better fit the data.

Negative case analysis (Judd et al., 1991) is a very important qualitative tool for helping to confirm hypotheses. Judd et al. even go so far as to say that "negative case analysis is what the field-worker uses in place of statistical analysis." The idea is incorporated into each of the analysis methods described in Sect. 3.1. When performed rigorously, the process involves an exhaustive search for evidence that might logically contradict a generated proposition, revision of the proposition to cover the negative evidence, re-checking the new proposition against existing and newly collected data, and then continuing the search for contradictory evidence. The search for contradictory evidence can include purposely selecting new cases for study that increase representativeness, as explained earlier, as well as seeking new sources and types of data to help triangulate the findings.

Triangulation (Jick, 1979) is another important tool for confirming the validity of conclusions. The concept is not limited to qualitative studies. The basic idea is to gather different types of evidence to support a proposition. The evidence might come from different sources, be collected using different methods, be analysed using different methods, have different forms (interviews, observations, documents, etc.), or come from a different study altogether. This last point means that triangulation also includes what we normally call replication. It also includes the combining of quantitative and qualitative methods. A classic combination is the statistical testing of a hypothesis that has been generated qualitatively. In the Inspection Study (Seaman and Basili, 1998), triangulation occurred at the data source level. Certain types of data (e.g. size and complexity of the code inspected, the roles of different participants, etc.) were gathered multiple times, from observations, from interviews, and from the inspection data forms that each inspection moderator filled out.

Anomalies in the data (including outliers, extreme cases, and surprises) are treated very differently in qualitative research than in quantitative research. In quantitative analysis, there are statistical methods for identifying and eliminating outliers from the analysis. Extreme cases can be effectively ignored in statistical tests if they are outweighed by more average cases. But in qualitative analysis, these anomalies play an important role in explaining, shaping, and even supporting a proposition.

As Miles and Huberman (1994) explain, "the outlier is your friend." The Inspection Study has a good outlier example. There were few cases in the study that illustrated what happens when the group of inspection participants is organizationally distant (i.e. include members from disparate parts of the organization). However, one case could easily be identified as an outlier in terms of both its long duration and the high number of defects reported in the meeting. This case also involved a set of organizationally distant inspection participants. The unusual values for meeting length and number of defects could not be explained by any of the other variables that had been determined to affect these factors. Thus, we could hypothesize that organizational distance had an effect on length and number of defects. In addition, the case provided a lot of explanatory data on why that effect existed.

Replication, as with quantitative studies, is a powerful but expensive tool for confirming findings. Replication in the qualitative arena, however, has a slightly looser meaning than in quantitative research. While a quantitative study, to be called a replication of another study, is expected to employ to some degree the same instruments, measures, and procedures as the original study [see the discussion by Andy Brooks et al. (2007), this volume], a qualitative replication must only preserve the conditions set forth in the theory being tested. That is, if the proposition to be tested is something like

Gilb-type inspections of C++ code involving two inspectors and a moderator will take longer but reveal more defects if the inspection participants have not worked together before

then the replicating study must be of Gilb-type inspections of C++ code involving two inspectors and a moderator, some of which have participants who have worked together before and some who have participants who have not worked together before. Data do not necessarily have to be collected or analysed in the same way that they were in the original study.

One last method for helping to confirm findings, which is particularly well suited to most studies of software engineering, is getting feedback on the findings from the subjects who provided the data in the first place. This strategy is sometimes called *member checking* (Lincoln and Guba, 1985). Presenting findings to subjects, either formally or informally, has the added benefits of making subjects feel part of the process, helping them to understand how the results were derived, and gaining their support for final conclusions. This is especially important when the results of the study may change the way the subjects will be expected to do their jobs. This is usually what we, as empirical software engineering researchers, hope will happen. Researchers in our area often have a marketing role as well, trying to promote the importance and usefulness of empirical study in software engineering. Member checking helps to accomplish this at the grass roots. Miles and Huberman (1994) give several guidelines on how and when to best present intermediate findings to subjects, including taking care that the results presented are couched in local terminology, explaining the findings from the raw data up, and taking into account a subject's possible personal reaction to a finding (e.g. if it is threatening or critical).

Member checking was used extensively in the Inspection Study. An entire round of scheduled interviews was devoted to this exercise, and it yielded a great deal of insight. For example, a finding emerged that indicated that, as the project progressed, inspection participants were spending less and less time discussing unresolved issues in inspection meetings, i.e. issues that eventually had to be referred to someone not at the meeting. One subject, when presented with this finding, explained that this was because developers were getting better at recognizing issues and problems that were best referred to others, and were less likely now than at the beginning of the project to waste time trying to resolve any issues they were not equipped to resolve. This was an important insight, and in particular one that had not occurred to the researcher.

One of the most important ways to help confirm a qualitatively generated proposition is to ensure the validity of the methods used to generate it. In previous sections, we have briefly addressed some of the validity concerns in qualitative studies. One is representativeness, which has to do with the people and events chosen to be interviewed or observed. In Sect. 3.1, there is a discussion of how, after initial propositions are generated, cases for further study can be specifically chosen to increase or ensure representativeness. Another validity concern is the possibility of researcher effects on the study. Miles and Huberman warn of two types of researcher effects and present some techniques for countering them. The first is that the presence of the researcher may affect the behavior of the subjects. This type of effect is discussed earlier in Sect. 2.1. The second is that the researchers may lose their objectivity by becoming too close to the setting being observed. A quote from one researcher (Whyte, 1984) illustrates the second type of bias: "I began as a nonparticipating observer and ended up as a nonobserving participant." In studies of software engineering, it is unlikely that the researcher will be permitted to become involved technically in the work being studied, unless that was part of the study plan from the beginning, but it is possible for the researcher to become part of the political and organizational context of the project without realizing it.

In summary, many qualitative methods for confirming theory are also employed during theory generation. That is, as propositions are being generated, they are immediately subjected to some testing before they are even reported as findings. The idea is to build up a "weight of evidence" that supports the hypothesis, where the evidence is as diverse as possible. This is not so different from the aim of quantitative research, in which a hypothesis is never "proven," but evidence, in the form of statistically significant results from different settings and different researchers, is built up to support it. It could be said that some qualitative methods used to test propositions are actually stronger than statistical tests because they do not allow any contradictory evidence. Any data that contradict the proposition are used to modify it so that the resulting proposition fits all the data. Ideally, any proposition, no matter how generated, is best supported by both qualitative and quantitative evidence.

3.3. Data Modelling and Visualization

In theory, qualitative data can take a number of forms, including pictures and images. However, in practice, most raw qualitative data is in the form of text. While text has the advantage of being able to fully capture the richness and complexity of the phenomena being studied, it also has some drawbacks. First, text is linear in the sense that only one passage can be read at a time, so concepts that are non-linear or spatial can be difficult, cognitively, to capture by reading. Second, text is often more voluminous than is necessary to express a concept. "A picture is worth a thousand words" is sometimes very, very true. Finally, it can be difficult to visually identify what parts of a textual dataset might be related to other parts without some visual clues.

For all these reasons, visual modelling is often used in qualitative analysis for several purposes. Diagrams of different types are often used as a mechanism for presenting and explaining findings. In writing up qualitative work, using a diagram can often save a lot of space when a concept is more succinctly summarized graphically than textually. But diagrams also serve as a useful mechanism for the analysis task itself. Graphical representations of data often help the researcher to organize concepts and to reveal relationships and patterns that are obscured by volumes of textual data. This is similar and analogous to the use of graphs and charts when presenting quantitative results and data. Although there are numerous types of diagrams that can be useful in various ways in qualitative analysis, we will discuss two: matrices and maps (Dey, 1993) [called "networks" in Miles and Huberman (1994)].

Matrices are especially useful when the data comes from a series of distinct cases (i.e. sites, interviewees, episodes, etc.). In such a study, the researcher creates a matrix in which the rows are cases and the columns are variables of interest. For example, suppose a study has been conducted consisting of interviews with managers of a variety of software development projects. One useful technique to check the representativeness of the data is to create a matrix of characterization information on the cases from which data has been collected. The columns of the matrix would include such characteristics as project size, application domain, experience of the development team, etc. Filling in the cells of such a matrix for each case studied is a useful exercise and gives the reader feedback on what background information is missing, and what types of projects are missing from the sample.

Augmenting such a matrix with more columns representing emerging constructs (i.e. codes or categories) is also a useful analysis technique. For example, suppose in the previous example that many of the interviewees talked about development team meetings, and this topic emerged as an important issue in the study. In the (very simplified) matrix excerpt shown in Fig. 4 (from a fictitious study), we see that the first few columns contain characterizing information on the cases, while the last column contains passages that have been coded under "meetings." Organizing the data in this way clearly shows that the implications of development meetings are very different for small projects than for medium projects. This insight might not have been evident if the data analysis had relied solely on coding the textual data. It's usually advisable to use an electronic spreadsheet to create analysis matrices in order to take advantage of searching and sorting capabilities.

Maps, or basic shapes-and-lines diagrams, are also useful for sorting out concepts and relationships during qualitative analysis (Dey, 1993). Such maps are

Case	Project Size	Application Domain	Experience of Developers	Meetings
1	huge	banquing	mixed	"We spend way too much time in meetings"
2	small	banquing		"We try to touch base with the whole team as often as we can"
3	small	aerospace	low	"The daily briefings are really useful, although some people say it interrupts their 'real' work"
4	large		high	"We would all be so much more productive if we could somehow get rid of meetings"
5	medium	communications	high	"People don't like to come to meetings, but I guess most of them are useful"

Fig. 4 An example matrix

particularly effective at expressing complex concepts in much less space than one is able to do with text alone. The format and symbols used in maps are limited only by imagination; there are no rules governing them. There are, however, a few guidelines that help make maps meaningful to the reader and useful to the researcher. First, maps quickly lose their effectiveness if they become too complicated. If it takes more space to explain how to read and interpret the map than it would have to textually explain the concept depicted in the map, then the map is not useful. While shapes and lines can be uninspiring, their simplicity makes them ideal as a tool to illuminate complex concepts. On the other hand, the researcher must take care to clearly and consistently define the meanings of both the shapes and lines (and any other symbols used in the map). Because these symbols are so simple, they can also be used in multiple ways, and it is tempting to use them in multiple ways in the same diagram. So one must define, for a particular map, whether the lines connecting shapes (i.e. concepts) signify causal relationships (e.g. the presence of one concept causes the presence of the other), or temporal relationships (e.g. one concept precedes another), or contextual relationships (e.g. the two concepts tend to occur in similar contexts), etc.

Despite the need for simplicity, it is possible to include more than simple shapes and lines in a map. Of course, different shapes can be used to denote different types of concepts (e.g. aggregate concepts) (Dey, 1993). The thickness of a line can denote the strength of a relationship, or the weight of evidence supporting it. Colours and patterns can also be used to convey different meanings. Textual annotations, within reason, are also usually needed to label elements on a map.

Miles and Huberman (1994) devote much of their book on analysis to the development of different types of diagrams, and a very large number of examples and variations are explained there. Many of them are similar in appearance and concept

Fig. 5 A causal network
showing hypothesized
causal relationships

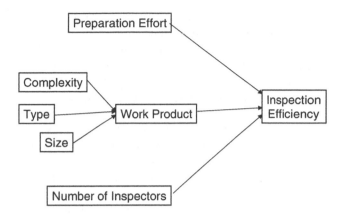

to diagramming techniques used in software development (e.g. control flow diagrams, statecharts, process models, class diagrams). These are especially appealing for software engineering studies because they are already familiar to our community.

While maps can be used for a variety of analysis tasks, one specific use is particularly handy when the qualitative work is exploratory, and intended to lay the groundwork for further empirical work. A good map of concepts and relationships can serve as a research plan for follow-up studies by defining the concepts (i.e. shapes) that need to be developed in further exploratory studies, and the hypotheses (i.e. relationships represented as lines) upon which further confirmatory work can be based. One version of this type of map is the causal network (Miles and Huberman, 1994), a simple example of which is shown in Fig. 5, which identifies factors affecting the efficiency of a software inspection. Such a map can be annotated to show the hypothesized (or tested) strength of the relationships and references to supporting evidence (e.g. identifiers for informants or coded segments).

Creating visual models of qualitative data, and the findings resulting from that data, is a very useful tool for qualitative researchers. Modelling is useful in two ways: during analysis to sort out ideas and relationships; and during presentation as a way to convey findings to the reader. Modelling can be seen as a form of data reduction because diagrams simply take up less space, and are more quickly scanned and digested, than text. They also depict insights arising from the data that are difficult to express succinctly in words.

3.4. Quantification of Qualitative Data

In many studies, it is appropriate to allow the analysis to iterate between quantitative and qualitative approaches. There are several ways to quantify some parts of a body of qualitative data. Such quantification is usually preceded by some preliminary qualitative analysis in order to make sense of the main categories in the data. It is often also followed by further qualitative analysis to make sense of the quantitative findings, which then leads to further quantitative analysis or re-analysis, and so on.

The most straightforward way to quantify qualitative data is simply to extract quantifiable pieces of information from the text. This is often also called coding, but must be distinguished from the types of coding related to the grounded theory approach, discussed in Sect. 3.1.

To understand the data transformation that takes place during this type of coding, we need to address a common misconception about the difference between quantitative and qualitative data. Qualitative data is often assumed to be subjective, but that is not necessarily the case. On the other hand, quantitative data is often assumed to be objective, but neither is that necessarily the case. In fact, the objectivity or subjectivity of data is orthogonal to whether it is qualitative or quantitative. The process of coding transforms qualitative data into quantitative data, but it does not affect its subjectivity or objectivity. For example, consider the following text, which constitutes a fragment of qualitative data:

Tom, Shirley, and Fred were the only participants in the meeting.

Now consider the following quantitative data, which was generated by coding the above qualitative data:

num_participants = 3

The fact that the information is objective was not changed by the coding process. Note also that the process of coding has resulted in some lost information (the names of the participants). This is frequently the case, as qualitative information often carries more content than is easily quantified. Consider another example:

[Respondent] said that this particular C++ class was really very easy to understand, and not very complex at all, especially compared to other classes in the system.

And the resulting coded quantitative data:

complexity = low

Again, the process of coding this subjective data did not make it more objective, although the quantitative form may appear less subjective.

When coding is performed on a set of qualitative data, the measurement scale of the resulting quantitative data is determined by the nature of the data itself, and is not restricted by the fact that it was derived from qualitative data. For example, in the "num_participants" example, above, the quantitative variable turned out to be on an absolute scale. But in the "complexity" example, the variable is ordinal.

Coding results in more reliably accurate quantitative data when it is restricted to straightforward, objective information, as in the first example above. However, it is often desirable to quantify subjective information as well in order to perform statistical analysis. This must be done with care in order to minimize the amount of information lost in the transformation and to ensure the accuracy of the resulting quantitative data as much as possible. Often subjects use different words to describe the same phenomenon, and the same words to describe different phenomena. In describing a subjective concept (e.g. the complexity of a C++ class), a subject may use straightforward words (e.g. low, medium, high), that mask underlying ambiguities. For example, if a subject says that a particular class has "low complexity," does that mean that it was easy to read and understand, or easy to write, or unlikely to contain defects, or just small? This is why, as mentioned earlier, preliminary qualitative analysis of the data to be coded is important in order to sort out the use of language and the nuances of the concept being described.

Another situation that complicates coding is when something is rated differently by different subjects. There were eight inspections in the Inspection Study in which the complexity of the inspected material was rated differently by different participants in the inspection. In all but one of these cases, the ratings differed by only one level (e.g. "average" and "high," or "high" and "very high," etc.). One way to resolve such discrepancies is to decide that one subject (or data source) is more reliable than another. Miles and Huberman (1994) discuss a number of factors that affect the reliability of one data source as compared with another, and the process of weighting data with respect to its source. In the Inspection Study, it was decided that an inspector was a more reliable judge of the complexity of the code than the author, since we were interested in how complexity might affect the inspection of that code. This assumption was used to resolve most of the discrepancies.

Another approach to quantification of qualitative data is content analysis (Holsti, 1969). Content analysis, originally developed for the analysis of human communication in the social sciences, is defined in various ways, but for our purposes can be described as an analysis method based on counting the frequency of occurrence of some meaningful lexical phenomenon in a textual data set. This technique is applicable when the textual data can be divided into cases along some criteria (e.g. different sites or respondents). In any particular application of content analysis, counting rules must be defined that make sense given the nature of the data and the research goals. This is why preliminary qualitative analysis is necessary, to determine the "nature of the data." Counting rules can take several forms, e.g.:

- Counting the occurrence of particular keywords in each case and then correlating (statistically or more informally) the counts with other attributes of the cases
- Counting the number of cases in which certain keywords occur and then comparing the counts of different keywords, or comparing the set of cases containing the keyword to those that do not
- Counting the occurrence of one keyword in proximity to a second keyword, and then comparing that count to the number of occurrences of the first keyword without the second keyword

There are numerous other variations on this theme. Note that the first example above only yields meaningful results if one can assume that the frequency of use of a particular word or phrase somehow indicates its importance, or the strength of opinion about it or some other relevant characteristic. This is often not a reasonable assumption because it depends too much on the speaking and writing style of the sources of the case data. A good example of the use of content analysis is Hall and Rainer's work (with others), in particular (Rainer et al., 2003) and (Rainer and Hall, 2003). Holsti (1969) provides a good reference on content analysis as used in the social sciences.

4. Conclusions

The focus of this chapter has been to provide guidance on using qualitative research methods, particularly in studies in which they are combined with quantitative methods, in empirical studies of software engineering. Nearly any software engineering issue is best investigated using a combination of qualitative and quantitative methods. Some of the more common mixed method research designs include the following:

- Qualitative data can be used to illuminate the statistical results employed to test a hypothesis. This allows the researcher to go beyond the statistics to help explain the causal relationships revealed by the quantitative results.
- When differences between subjects are an important part of the study design, quantitative measures of individual performance can be augmented with qualitative interview data that helps explain differences in performance, as well as may identify other relevant differences that were not measured.
- In studying a new process or technique, qualitative data from an early observation study of groups using the technique can be used to identify relevant variables to be measured in a subsequent experiment to evaluate the performance of the process or technique.
- Initial qualitative data, from interviews or document analysis, can serve as a starting point for a case study by both setting the context for the researchers as well as identifying important issues and variables for the study.

Finally, it should be noted that there are software packages on the market that facilitate coding and other types of qualitative analysis [see Miles and Huberman (1994), appendix, for an overview of qualitative analysis software]. Space does not permit a full discussion of software tools, but one commonly used application is NVivo™ from QSR International.[2] NVivo aids the researcher in organizing, coding, and grouping textual data, in defining and maintaining links between different pieces of data, and in developing visual models of the data and of findings.

Empiricists in software engineering often complain about the lack of opportunities to study software development and maintenance in real settings. This really implies that we must exploit to the fullest every opportunity we do have, by collecting and analysing as much data of as many different types as possible. Qualitative data is richer than quantitative data, so using qualitative methods increases the

---

[2] http://www.qsrinternational.com/

amount of information contained in the data collected. It also increases the diversity of the data and thus increases confidence in the results through triangulation, multiple analyses, and greater interpretive ability.

References

Barley SR (1990) The Alignment of Technology and Structure through Roles and Networks. Administrative Science Quarterly 35:61–103.

Brooks A, Roper M, Wood M, Daly J, Miller J (2007) Replication's Role in Software Engineering, this volume.

Creswell JW (1998) Qualitative Inquiry and Research Design: Choosing Among Five Traditions. Sage Publications, Thousand Oaks.

Dey I (1993) Qualitative Analysis: A User-Friendly Guide. Routledge, New York.

Eisenhardt KM (1989) Building Theories from Case Study Research. Academy of Management Review 14:532–550.

Gilgun JF (1992) Definitions, Methodologies, and Methods in Qualitative Family Research, in *Qualitative Methods in Family Research*. Sage Publications, Thousand Oaks.

Glaser BG, Strauss AL (1967) The Discovery of Grounded Theory: Strategies for Qualitative Research. Aldine Publishing Company, Somerset, NJ, USA.

Guindon R, Krasner H, Curtis B (1987) Breakdowns and Processes During the Early Activities of Software Design by Professionals, in *Empirical Studies of Programmers*, second workshop, Gary Olsen, Sylvia Sheppard, and Elliot Soloway, eds., 65–82, Ablex Publishing, Greenwich, CT, USA.

Hackos JT, Redish JD (1998) User and Task Analysis for Interface Design. Wiley, New York.

Holsti OR (1969) Content Analysis for the Social Sciences and Humanities. Addison-Wesley, Menlo Park.

Jick T (1979) Mixing Qualitative and Quantitative Methods: Triangulation in Action. Administrative Science Quarterly 24(4):602–611.

Judd CM, Smith ER, Kidder LH (1991) Research Methods in Social Relations, sixth edition. Harcourt Brace Jovanovich, Fort Worth.

Kontio J, Bragge J, Lehtola L (2007) The Focus Group Method as an Empirical Tool in Software Engineering, this volume.

Lethbridge T, Sim SE, Singer J (2005) Studying Software Engineers: Data Collection Techniques for Software Field Studies. Empirical Software Engineering: An International Journal 10(3):311–341.

Lincoln YS, Guba EG (1985) Naturalistic Inquiry. Sage Publishing, Thousand Oaks.

Lutters WG, Seaman CB (2007) The Value of War Stories in Debunking the Myths of Documentation in Software Maintenance. Information and Software Technology 49(6): 576–587.

Miles MB, Huberman AM (1994) Qualitative Data Analysis: An Expanded Sourcebook, second edition. Sage Publishing, Thousand Oaks.

Orlikowski WJ (1993) CASE Tools as Organizational Change: Investigating Incremental and Radical Changes in Systems Development. MIS Quarterly 17(3):309–340.

Orlikowski WJ, Baroudi JJ (1991) Studying Information Technology in Organizations: Research Approaches and Assumptions. Information Systems Research 2(1):1–28.

Parra A, Seaman C, Basili V, Kraft S, Condon S, Burke S, Yakimovich D (1997) The Package-Based Development Process in the Flight Dynamics Division. Proceedings of the Twenty-second Software Engineering Workshop, NASA/Goddard Space Flight Center Software Engineering Laboratory (SEL), Greenbelt, MD, USA.

Perry DE, Staudenmayer NA, Votta LG (1994) People, Organizations, and Process Improvement. IEEE Software 11(July): 36–45.

Rainer A, Hall T (2003) A Quantitative and Qualitative Analysis of Factors Affecting Software Processes. Journal of Systems and Software 66:7–21.

Rainer A, Hall T, Baddoo N (2003) Persuading Developers to 'Buy Into' Software Process Improvement: Local Opinion and Empirical Evidence. Proceedings of the International Symposium on Empirical Software Engineering (ISESE), IEEE, Los Alamitos, CA, USA.

Seaman CB (1999) Qualitative Methods in Empirical Studies of Software Engineering. IEEE Transactions on Software Engineering 25(4):557–572.

Seaman CB, Basili VR (1998) Communication and Organization: An Empirical Study of Discussion in Inspection Meetings. IEEE Transactions on Software Engineering 24(7):559–572.

Sharp H, Robinson H (2004) An Ethnographic Study of XP Practice. Empirical Software Engineering 9:353–375.

Shneiderman B (1998) Designing the User Interface: Strategies for Effective Human-Computer Interaction, third edition. Addison-Wesley, Reading, MA, USA.

Singer J (1998) Practices of Software Maintenance. Proceedings of the International Conference on Software Maintenance, IEEE Computer Society Press, Los Alamitos, CA, pp. 139–145.

Taylor SJ, Bogdan R (1984) Introduction to Qualitative Research Methods. Wiley, New York.

von Mayrhauser A, Vans AM (1996) Identification of Dynamic Comprehension Processes During Large Scale Maintenance. IEEE Transactions on Software Engineering 22(6):424–437.

Whyte WF (1984) Learning from the Field: A Guide from Experience. Sage Publications, Beverly Hills.

Yin RK (1994) Case Study Research: Design and Methods. Sage Publications, Newbury Park, CA, USA.

Chapter 3
Personal Opinion Surveys

Barbara A. Kitchenham and Shari L. Pfleeger

Abstract Although surveys are an extremely common research method, survey-based research is not an easy option. In this chapter, we use examples of three software engineering surveys to illustrate the advantages and pitfalls of using surveys. We discuss the six most important stages in survey-based research: setting the survey's objectives; selecting the most appropriate survey design; constructing the survey instrument (concentrating on self-administered questionnaires); assessing the reliability and validity of the survey instrument; administering the instrument; and, finally, analysing the collected data. This chapter provides only an introduction to survey-based research; readers should consult the referenced literature for more detailed advice.

1. Introduction

Surveys are probably the most commonly used research method worldwide. Survey work is visible because we are often asked to participate in surveys in our private capacity, as electors, consumers, or service users. This widespread use of surveys may give the impression that survey-based research is straightforward, an easy option for researchers to gather important information about products, context, processes, workers and more. However, in our experience this is not the case. In this chapter, we will use actual survey examples to illustrate the attractions and pitfalls of the survey technique.

The three surveys we will use as our examples will be discussed in the next section. After that we will define what we mean by a survey. Then we will discuss the main activities that need to be considered when you undertake a survey:

- Setting the objectives
- Survey design
- Developing the survey instrument (i.e. the questionnaire)
- Evaluating the survey instrument
- Obtaining valid data
- Analysing the data

F. Shull et al. (eds.), *Guide to Advanced Empirical Software Engineering.*
© Springer 2008

2. Example Surveys

In this section we describe three software engineering surveys that will be used as examples throughout this chapter.

2.1. Technology Evaluation Survey

Recently we were involved in far from successful survey. A few years ago, Zelkowitz et al. (1998) surveyed practitioners to determine their confidence in different types of empirical evaluations as the basis for technology adoption decisions. Their findings indicated that the evidence produced by the research community to support technology adoption is not the kind of evidence being sought by practitioners. To build on Zelkowitz et al.'s work, a group of researchers, including ourselves, wanted to do a follow-up survey of managers, to find out what kinds of evaluations they make of proposed technologies, and what kinds of evidence they rely on for their technology decisions.

We had noticed that many newsletters often include reader survey forms, some of whose questions and answers could provide useful insight into managers' decision-making processes. We approached the publisher of *Applied Software Development*; he was eager to cooperate with the research community, and he agreed to insert a one-page survey in the newsletter and gather the responses. As a result, we took the following steps:

1. We designed a survey form and asked several of colleagues to critique it. The survey asked respondents to examine a list of technologies and tell us if the technology had been evaluated and if it had been used. If it had been evaluated, the respondents were asked to distinguish between a "soft" evaluation, such as a survey or feature analysis, and a "hard" evaluation, such as formal experiment or case study.
2. We "tested" the resulting survey form on a colleague at Lucent Technologies. We asked him to fill out the survey form and give feedback on the clarity of the questions and responses, and on the time it took him to complete the form. Based on his very positive reaction to the questionnaire, we submitted a slightly revised survey to the newsletter publisher.
3. The publisher then revised the survey, subject to our approval, so that it would fit on one page of his newsletter. The questionnaire was formatted as a table with four questions for each of 23 different software technologies (see Table 1).
4. The survey form was included in all copies of a summer 1999 issue of Applied Software Development.

Of the several thousand possible recipients of *Applied Software Development*, only 171 responded by sending their survey form back; thus, the response rate was low, which is typical in this type of survey. The staff at *Applied Software Development*

Table 1 Format of technology survey questionnaire

Technology/ technique	Did your company evaluate this technology?	Soft Evaluation techniques: read case studies, articles, talking with peers, lessons learned, or other more anecdotal evidence?	Hard Evaluation techniques: feature comparisons, performance benchmark, or other more quantitative evidence?	Are you now using the technique in some production work or most production work?
Specific software technology	Yes/No	Yes/No	Yes/No	Some/Most/None

transferred the data from the survey sheets to a spreadsheet. However, when the results of the survey were analyzed, it appeared that we had made errors in survey design, construction, administration and analysis that rendered any results inconclusive at best.

2.2. Software Education Survey

Lethbridge (1998, 2000) conducted surveys to help him understand those areas where practitioners feel they need more or better education. The goal of the surveys was to provide information to educational institutions and companies as they plan curricula and training programs. A secondary goal involved providing data that will assist educators and practitioners in evaluating existing and proposed curricula.

Lethbridge and his team recruited participants for the surveys in two ways: by approaching companies directly and asking them to participate, and by advertising for participants on the Web. To determine the effects of formal education, Lethbridge presented the respondents with a list of topics related to computer science, mathematics and business. For each topic, the respondent was asked "How much did you learn about this in your formal education?" The choices for answers ranged on a six-point ordinal scale from "learned nothing" to "learned in depth." Other questions included

- What is your current knowledge about this considering what you have learned on the job as well as forgotten?
- How useful has this specific material been to you in your career?
- How useful would it be (or have been) to learn more about this (e.g. additional courses)? (This question appeared in the first version of the survey.)
- How much influence has learning the material had on your thinking (i.e. your approach to problems and your general maturity), whether or not you have directly used the details of the material? Please consider influence on both your

career and other aspects of you life. (This question appeared in the second version of the survey.)

2.3. Software Risk Management Survey

Ropponen and Lyytinen (2000) described an examination of risk management practices. They administered a survey addressing two overall questions:

- What are the components of software development risk?
- What risk management practices and environmental contingencies help to address these components?

To find out the answers, the researchers mailed a questionnaire to each of a pre-selected sample of members of the Finnish Information Processing Association whose job title was "manager" or equivalent. They sent the questionnaire to at most two managers in the same company.

Ropponen and Lyytinen asked twenty questions about risk by presenting scenarios and asking the respondents to rate their occurrence with a five-point ordinal scale, ranging from "hardly ever" to "almost always." For example, the scenarios included:

Your project is cancelled before completing it
and
Subcontracted tasks in the project are performed as expected.

The researchers posed additional questions relating to organizational characteristics, such as the organization's size, industry, type of systems developed, and contractual arrangement. They also sought technology characteristics, such as the newness of the technology, the complexity and novelty of technological solutions, and the process technologies used. Finally, they asked questions about the respondents themselves: their experience with different sizes of projects, their education, their experience with project management, and the software used.

3. What is a Survey?

To begin, let us review exactly what a survey is. A survey is not just the instrument (the questionnaire or checklist) for gathering information. It is a comprehensive research method for collecting information to describe, compare or explain knowledge, attitudes and behavior (Fink, 1995). Fowler (2002) defines a quantitative survey in the following way:

- The purpose of a survey is to produce statistics, that is, quantitative or numerical descriptions of some aspects of the study population.

- The main way of collecting information is by asking questions; their answers constitute the data to be analysed.
- Generally information is to be collected from only a fraction of the population, that is a sample, rather than from every member of the population.

In this chapter we will concentrate on surveys of this type where data is collected by means of a questionnaire completed by the subject. This excludes surveys that use a semi-structured interview schedule administered by the researcher. We will also exclude surveys using mainly open-ended questions, surveys based on observing participant behaviour and data mining exercises. Thus, we restrict ourselves to surveys that collect quantitative but subjective data (concerning individual's opinions, attitudes and preferences) and objective data such as demographic information for example a subject's age and educational level.

4. Setting Objectives

The first step in any survey research (or any research, for that matter!) is setting objectives otherwise referred to as problem definition. Each objective is simply a statement of the survey's expected outcomes or a question that the survey is intended to answer. For instance, a survey may hope to identify the most useful features of a front-end development tool, or the most common training needs for new hires.

There are three common type of objective:

- To evaluate the rate or frequency of some characteristic that occurs in a population, for example, we might be interested in the frequency of failing projects (Standish Group, 2003).
- To assess the severity of some characteristic or condition that occurs in a population, for example, we might be interested in the average overrun of software projects (Moløkken-Østvold et al., 2004).
- To identify factors that influence a characteristic or condition, for example, we might be interested in factors that predispose a process improvement activity towards failure or towards success Dybå (2005).

The first two types of survey objective are descriptive: they describe some condition or factor found in a population in terms of its frequency and impact. The second type of survey looks at the relationship existing among factors and conditions within a population.

As the objectives are defined in more detail, you should be able to specify:

- The hypotheses to be tested
- What alterative explanations are to be investigated or excluded
- What scope of survey project is appropriate to address the objectives
- What resources are necessary to achieve the objectives

At this stage it is important to decide whether a survey is an appropriate research method to address the stated objectives. You need to be able to answer questions of the type:

- Is it clear what population can answer the survey questions reliably?
- Is there a method of obtaining a representative sample of that population?
- Does the project have sufficient the resources to collect a sample large enough to answer the study questions?
- Is it clear what variables need to be measured?
- Is it clear how to measure the variables?

If you cannot answer all these questions positively, you need to consider whether a survey is an appropriate means to address your research objectives.

5. Survey Design

Two common types of survey design are:

- *Cross sectional:* In this type of study, participants are asked for information at one fixed point in time. For example, we may poll all the members of a software development organization at 10 AM on a particular Monday, to find out what activities they are working on that morning. This information gives us a snapshot of what is going on in the organization.
- *Longitudinal:* This type of study is forward-looking, providing information about changes in a specific population over time. There are two main variants of longitudinal designs, you can survey the same people at each time period or you can survey different people.

Recall the three survey examples we introduced in Sect. 2. The Lethbridge survey asked respondents about their levels of training and education (see Lethbridge, 1998, 2000). The Ropponen and Lyytinen (2000) study requested information about risk management practices from Finnish software projects. The Pfleeger-Kitchenham study sought to determine what kinds of evidence were used to support technology adoption decisions. All three surveys were all cross-sectional studies, in which participants were asked about their past experiences at a particular fixed point in time. It is not simply coincidence that all our examples are of this type; in our experience, most surveys in software engineering have this kind of design.

There are other more complex forms of survey design, for example designs that compare different populations, or designs that aim to assess the impact of a change. For information on such designs see, for example, Shaddish et al. 2002).

The other issue to decide is the way in which the survey will be administered. Options include:

- Self-administered questionnaires (usually postal but increasingly Internet).
- Telephone surveys.
- One-to-one interviews.

The questions that can be addressed are influenced by this factor. In addition, strategies for obtaining reliable data such as question ordering and wording differ according to the administration method. Fowler provides a detailed examination of the pros and cons of different administration methods (Fowler, 2002). In this chapter we concentrate primarily on self-administered questionnaires.

6. Developing a Survey Instrument

In this section, we turn to how to develop a survey instrument. Survey instruments, which are usually questionnaires, are developed using the following steps:

- Search the relevant literature.
- Construct an instrument.
- Evaluate the instrument.
- Document the instrument.

We discuss instrument construction in this section and instrument validation and documentation in Sect. 7, using the three surveys described in Sect. 2 to illustrate good and bad practice.

6.1. Searching the Literature

As with any good investigative study, we must begin our work by looking through the literature. We need such searches to:

- Identify what other studies have been done on the topic.
- Determine how the previous studies' researchers collected their data. In particular, we want to find out what questionnaires or other data collection mechanisms were used.

There are many reasons for knowing what has come before. First, we do not want *unknowingly* to duplicate someone else's research. Second, we want to learn from and improve upon previous studies. For example, if previous studies have developed relevant validated instruments or questions that we can adopt, it makes our own survey easier to administer and validate. Similarly, if other researchers had problems with response rates, we will be aware of the need to adopt measures to address this problem. Finally, other studies may give us ideas about variables and issues we need to consider in designing our own studies.

6.2. Creating or Re-Using an Instrument

In software engineering, we often start from scratch, building models of a problem and designing survey instruments specifically for the problem at hand. However, in other disciplines, it is rare to develop a new survey instrument. Researchers usually rely on using existing instruments, perhaps tailored slightly to accommodate variations on a common theme. This reliance on standard instrumentation has two important advantages.

1. The existing instruments have already been assessed for validity and reliability.
2. By using common instruments, it is easy to compare new results with the results of other studies.

When researchers in other disciplines cannot use an existing instrument, they are often able to amend existing instruments. An instrument might be amended if:

- It is too long to be used in entirety.
- A different population is being studied from the one for which the original instrument was designed.
- It needs to be translated.
- The data collection method is different in some way from the original instrument's data collection.

However, we must take care when considering amending an instrument. Our changes may introduce complications that make the research more difficult. For example:

- If the original instrument is copyrighted, we may need permission to change it.
- We must repeat pilot testing of the instrument.
- The new instrument must be assessed for validity and reliability.

Unfortunately, because most survey instruments in software engineering research are developed from scratch, we introduce many practical problems. In particular, software engineering research instruments are seldom properly validated.

6.3. Creating a New Questionnaire

A survey asks the respondents to answer questions for a reason, so the starting point in designing the survey instrument should always be the survey's purpose and objectives. However, simply converting a list of objectives into a set of questions seldom leads to a successful survey instrument. The type of question and wording of the questions and answers need to be carefully designed.

6.3.1. Question Types

When formulating questions for a survey instrument, you can express them in one of two ways: open or closed. A question is *open* when the respondents are asked to frame their own reply. Conversely, a question is *closed* when the respondents are asked to select an answer from a list of predefined choices.

There are advantages and disadvantages to each type of question. Open questions avoid imposing any restrictions on the respondent. However, there are many different ways respondents may choose to answer a question. Moreover, no matter how carefully we word the question, open questions may leave room for misinterpretation and provision of an irrelevant or confusing answer. Thus, open questions can be difficult to code and analyze.

6.3.2. Designing Questions

Once we have an idea of what we want to ask, we must give some thought to how we want to pose the questions. Questions need to be precise, unambiguous and understandable to respondents. In order to achieve that we need to ensure that:

- The language used is appropriate for the intended respondents and any possibly ambiguous terms are fully defined.
- We use standard grammar, punctuation and spelling.
- Each question expresses one and only one concept so we need to keep questions short but complete and avoid double-barrelled questions.
- Questions do not included vague or ambiguous qualifiers.
- Colloquialisms and jargon are avoided.
- We use negative as well as positive questions but avoid simply negating a question or using a double negative.
- We avoid asking question about events that occurred a long time in the past.
- We avoid asking sensitive questions that respondents may not be willing to answer in a self-administered questionnaire.

It is also important to make sure that respondents have sufficient knowledge to answer the questions. It can be extremely frustrating to be asked questions you are not in a position to answer. For example, of the three surveys described in Sect. 2, two of the surveys (Lethbridge's survey and the Finnish survey) asked respondents about their personal experiences. In contrast, the survey of technology adoption asked respondents to answer questions such as

Did your company evaluate this technology? Yes/No
Are you now using the technique in some production work or most production work? Yes/No

In this case, we were asking people to answer questions on behalf of their company. The questions may have caused difficulties for respondents working in large companies or respondents who had worked for the company only for a relatively short period of time.

To see how wording can affect results, consider the two Lethbridge surveys. Each was on the same topic, but he changed the wording of his last question. In the first survey Lethbridge, 1998, question 4 was:

How useful would it be (or have been) to learn more about this (e.g. additional courses)?

In his second survey (Lethbridge, 2000), question 4 was:

> How much influence has learning the material had on your thinking (i.e. your approach to problems and your general maturity), whether or not you have directly used the details of the material? Please consider influence on both your career and other aspects of your life.

The first version of the question is considerably better than the second version, because the second version is more complex and thus more difficult to interpret and understand. In particular, the second version appears to be two-edged (referring both to approach to problems and to general maturity) and rather imprecise (since it may not be clear what "general maturity" really means). However, further reflection indicates that even the first version of the question is ambiguous. Is the respondent supposed to answer in terms of whether (s)he would have benefited from more courses at university, or in terms of whether (s)he would benefit from industrial courses at the present time?

The survey of technologies posed questions about evaluation procedures in terms of how the respondent's company performed its evaluation studies. In particular, it asked questions about soft and hard evaluation techniques by defining them at the top of two of the columns:

> Soft evaluation techniques: Read case studies, articles, talking with peers, lessons learned or other more anecdotal evidence? Yes/No
> Hard evaluation techniques: feature comparison, performance benchmark, or other more quantitative evidence? Yes/No

These questions include jargon terms related to evaluation that may not be well understood by the potential respondents. Similarly, the researchers used jargon when defining the technology types as well: CASE tools, Rapid Application Development, 4GLs, and more. Were the questions to be redesigned, they should spell out each technology and include a glossary to describe each one. Such information ensures that the respondents have a common understanding of the terminology.

6.3.3. Designing Answers to Questions

Answers are usually of one of four types:

1. Numerical values (e.g. Age)
2. Response categories (e.g. Job type)
3. Yes/No answers
4. Ordinal scales.

Numerical values are usually straightforward but other types of answer may cause difficulties.

Response categories require all respondents to choose from a set of possible categories. They should be:

- Exhaustive but not too long
- Mutually exclusive

- Allow for multiple selections if required
- Include an "Other" category if the categories are not known to be exhaustive

Yes/No answers are particularly problematic. They suffer from acquiescence bias (Krosnick, 1990) as well as problems with lack of reliability (because people do not give the same answer on different occasions), imprecision (because the restrict measurement to only two levels) and many characteristics are broad in scope and not easily expressed as a single question (Spector 1992). Consider the question in the technology evaluation survey:

Are you now using the technique in some production work or most production work?

In this case our question about technology use doesn't suit a two point Yes/No scale very well. The question needs an ordinal scale answer.

Generally it is better to use an ordinal scale for attitudes and preferences. There are three types of scale:

1. Agreement scales e.g. a response choice of the form: Strongly Disagree, Disagree, Neither Agree nor Disagree, Agree, Strongly Agree.
2. Frequency scales e.g. a response choice of the form: Never, Rarely, Seldom, Sometimes, Occasionally, Most of the time.
3 Evaluation scales e.g. a response choice of the form: Terrible, Inferior, Passable, Good, Excellent.

Like response categories, ordinal scales need to be exhaustive but not too long. Researchers usually restrict them to seven points. In addition, Krosnick recommended points on a scale be labeled with words (to assist reliability and validity) but not numbered (because numbers can be interpreted in unanticipated ways by respondents) (Krosnick, 1990).

However, understanding (and hence reliability) may also be increased if we define each point on a scale. For example, Lethbridge gives some indication of the detail needed to define an ordinal scale in his survey. Each of his four main questions has its own associated ordinal scale with responses defined in the context of the question. For instance, the question "How much did you learn about this at university or college" had the following scale:

Score	Definition
1	Learned nothing at all
2	Became vaguely familiar
3	Learned the basics
4	Became functional (moderate working knowledge)
5	Learned a lot
6	Learned in depth, became expert (learned almost everything)

Although the intermediate points on the scale are a little vague, the end points are clear and unambiguous. Lethbridge's scale conforms to the normal standard of using between 5 and 7 choices along an ordinal scale. Lethbridge's scale is also a reasonably balanced one. A scale is *balanced* when the two endpoints mean the opposite of one another *and* the intervals between the scale points appear to be about equal. Creating equal distances between the scale points is called anchoring the instrument. It is difficult to create an anchored scale and even more difficult to validate that a scale is properly anchored.

A final issue that applies to ordinal scale categories is whether to include a "Don't know" category. There is some disagreement in the social science community about this issue. Some researchers feel that such choices allow respondents to avoid answering a question. However, it may be counter-productive to force people to answer questions they don't want to, or to force them to make a choice about which they feel ambivalent. The usual approach is to consider whether the respondents have been selected because they are in a position to answer the question. If that is the case a "Don't Know" category is usually not permitted.

6.3.4. Measuring Complex Concepts

Spector points out some concepts are difficult to map to single self-standing questions (Spector 1992). This may result in one (or both) of two type of unreliability

1. If people answer in different ways at different time
2. If people make mistakes in their responses.

He proposes measures based on *summated rating scales* to address this problem. A summated rating scale is a set of two or more items (i.e. questions) that address a specific topic or aspect of interest. Having multiple items improves reliability by reducing the chance of respondents making an error in their response and increases the precision with which a concept is measured.

6.4. Questionnaire Format

For self-administered questionnaires, it is important to consider both the format of the questionnaire and the questionnaire instructions. For formatting printed questionnaires, use the following checklist (much of which applies to Web-based questionnaires, too):

- Leave a space for the respondents to comment on the questionnaire.
- Use space between questions.
- Use vertical format, spaces, boxes, arrows, etc. to maximize the clarity of questions. However, do not overwhelm the respondent with "clever" formatting techniques (particularly for Web Questionnaires).
- Consider the use of simple grids.
- Consider the use of a booklet format.

- Have a good contrast between print and paper.
- Stick to a font size of 10–12.
- Use a font that is easy to read.
- Avoid italics.
- Use bolding, underlining or capitals judiciously and consistently for emphasis and instructions.
- Do not split instructions, questions and associated responses between pages.

The order in which questions are placed is also be important. Bourque and Fielder (1995) recommend questions be asked in a logical order, starting with easy questions first. However, although most questionnaires include demographic questions (that is, questions that describe the respondent) at the front of the questionnaire, Bourque and Fielder suggest putting them at the end instead. They point out that demographic details may be off-putting at the start of the questionnaire and so may discourage respondents.

The questionnaire must be accompanied by various administrative information including:

- An explanation of the purpose of the study.
- A description of who is sponsoring the study (and perhaps why).
- A cover letter using letterhead paper, dated to be consistent with the mail shot, providing a contact name and phone number. Personalize the salutation if possible.
- An explanation of how the respondents were chosen and why.
- An explanation of how to return the questionnaire.
- A realistic estimate of the time required to complete the questionnaire. Note that an unrealistic estimate will be counter-productive.

6.5. Response Rates and Motivation

It is often very difficult to motivate people to answer an unsolicited survey. Survey researchers can use inducements such as small monetary rewards or gifts, but these are not usually very successful. In general, people will be more motivated to provide complete and accurate responses if they can see that the results of the study are likely to be useful to them. For this reason, we should be sure that the survey instrument is accompanied by several key pieces of information supplied to participants:

- What the purpose of the study is.
- Why it should be of relevance to them.
- Why each individual's participation is important.
- How and why each participant was chosen.
- How confidentiality will be preserved.

Lethbridge (1998) attempted to motivate response with the following statement:

> The questionnaire is designed to discover what aspects of your educational background have been useful to you in your career. The results of the survey will be used to help improve curricula. All the information you provide will be kept confidential. In particular we have no intention of judging you as a person–we are merely interested in learning about the relevance of certain topics to your work.

By contrast, the technology adoption survey attempted to motivate response with the statement:

> Dear Executive, We are sponsoring a study for the University of X, and Professors Y and Z. It is only through our cooperative efforts with the academic community that we bring our commercial experiences to the classroom. Thank you for your help.

It fairly clear that Lethbridge's statement is likely to be more motivating although neither is compelling.

6.6. Questionnaire Length

Although we all know that we should strive for the shortest questionnaire that will answer our research questions, there is always a temptation to add a few extra questions "while we are going to all the trouble of organising a survey". This is usually a mistake. You should use pre-tests (see Sect. 7) to assess how long it takes to answer your questionnaire and whether the length (in time and number of questions) will de-motivate respondents.

If you have too many questions, you may need to remove some. Questions can usually be grouped together into topics, where each topic addresses a specific objective. One way to prune questions is to identify a topic that is addressed by many questions, and then remove some of the less vital ones. Another way is to remove some groups of questions. Keep in mind, though, that such pruning sometimes means reducing the objectives that the questionnaire addresses. In other words, you must maintain a balance between what you want to accomplish and what the respondents are willing to tell you. Validity and reliability assessments undertaken during pre-tests can help you decide which questions can be omitted with least impact on your survey objectives.

One way to reduce the time taken to complete a survey is to have standardized response formats. For example, in attitude surveys, responses are usually standardized to an ordinal scale of the form:

> Strongly Agree, Agree, Disagree, Strongly Disagree.

If all responses are standardized, respondents know their choices for each question and do not have to take time to read the choices carefully, question by question. Thus, respondents can usually answer more standard-format questions in a given time than non-standard ones.

6.7. *Researcher Bias*

An important consideration throughout questionnaire construction is the impact of our own bias. We often have some idea of what we are seeking, and the way we build the survey instrument can inadvertently reveal our biases. For example, if we create a new tool and distribute it free to a variety of users, we may decide to send out a follow-up questionnaire to see if the users find the tool helpful. If we do not take great care in the way we design our survey, we may word our questions in a way that is sure to confirm our desired result. For instance, we can influence replies by:

- The way a question is asked.
- The number of questions asked.
- The range and type of response categories.
- The instructions to respondents.

To avoid bias, we need to:

- Develop neutral questions. In other words, take care to use wording that does not influence the way the respondent thinks about the problem.
- Ask enough questions to adequately cover the topic.
- Pay attention to the order of questions (so that the answer to one does not influence the response to the next).
- Provide exhaustive, unbiased and mutually exclusive response categories.
- Write clear, unbiased instructions.

We need to consider the impact of our own prejudices throughout questionnaire construction. However, we also need to evaluate our questionnaire more formally, using methods discussed in Sect. 7.

7. Survey Instrument Evaluation

We often think that once we have defined the questions for our survey, we can administer it and gather the resulting data. But we tend to forget that creating a set of questions is only the start of instrument construction. Once we have created the instrument, it is essential that we evaluate it (Litwin, 1995). Evaluation is often called *pre-testing*, and it has several different goals:

- To check that the questions are understandable.
- To assess the likely response rate and the effectiveness of the follow-up procedures.
- To evaluate the reliability and validity of the instrument.
- To ensure that our data analysis techniques match our expected responses.

The two most common ways to organize an evaluation are focus groups and pilot studies. Focus groups are mediated discussion groups. We assemble a group of people representing either those who will use the results of the survey or those who will be asked to complete the survey (or perhaps a mixture of the two groups). The group members are asked to fill in the questionnaire and to identify any potential problems. Thus, focus groups are expected to help identify missing or unnecessary questions, and ambiguous questions or instructions. As we will see below, focus groups also contribute to the evaluation of instrument validity.

Pilot studies of surveys are performed using the same procedures as the survey, but the survey instrument is administered to a smaller sample. Pilot studies are intended to identify any problems with the questionnaire itself, as well as with the response rate and follow-up procedures. They may also contribute to reliability assessment.

The most important goal of pre-testing is to assess the reliability and validity of the instrument. Reliability is concerned with how well we can reproduce the survey data, as well as the extent of measurement error. That is, a survey is reliable if we get the same kinds and distribution of answers when we administer the survey to two similar groups of respondents. By contrast, validity is concerned with how well the instrument measures what it is supposed to measure. The various types of validity and reliability are described below.

Instrument evaluation is extremely important and can absorb a large amount of time and effort. Straub presents a demonstration exercise for instrument validation in MIS that included a Pretest, Technical Validation and Pilot Project (Straub, 1989). The Pretest involved 37 participants, the Technical Validation involved 44 people using a paper and pencil instrument and an equal number of people being interviewed; finally the Pilot test analysed 170 questionnaires. All this took place before the questionnaire was administered to the target population.

7.1. Types of Reliability

In software, we tend to think of reliability in terms of lack of failure; software is reliable if it runs for a very long time without failing. But survey reliability has a very different meaning. The basic idea is that a survey is reliable if we administer it many times and get roughly the same distribution of results each time.

Test-Retest (Intra-observer) Reliability is based on the idea that if the same person responds to a survey twice, we would like to get the same answers each time. We can evaluate this kind of reliability by asking the same respondents to complete the survey questions at different times. If the correlation between the first set of answers and the second is greater than 0.7, we can assume that test-retest reliability is good. However, test-retest will not work well if:

- Variables naturally change over time.
- Answering the questionnaire may change the respondents' attitudes and hence their answers.
- Respondents remember what they said previously, so they answer the same way in an effort to be consistent (even if new information in the intervening time makes a second, different answer more correct).

Alternate form reliability is based on rewording or re-ordering questions in different versions of the questionnaire. This reduces the practice effect and recall problems associated with a simple test-retest reliability study. However, alternative form reliability has its own problems. Rewording is difficult because it is important to ensure that the meaning of the questions is not changed and that the questions are not made more difficult to understand. For example, changing questions into a negative format is usually inappropriate because negatively framed questions are more difficult to understand than positively framed questions. In addition, re-ordering results can be problematic, because some responses may be affected by previous questions.

Inter-observer (inter-rater) reliability is used to assess the reliability of non-administered surveys that involve a trained person completing a survey instrument based on their own observations. In this case, we need to check whether or not different observers give similar answers when they assess the same situation. Clearly inter-rater reliability cannot be used for self-administered surveys that measure personal behaviors or attitudes. It is used where there is a subjective component in the measurement of an external variable, such as with process or tool evaluation. There are standard statistical techniques available to measure how well two or more evaluators agree. To obtain more information about inter-rater reliability, you should review papers by El Emam and his colleagues who were responsible for assessing ISO/IEC 15504 Software Process Capability Scale, also known as SPICE (see for example El Emam et al., 1996, 1998).

Two reliability measures are particularly important for summated rating scales: the Cronbach alpha coefficient (Cronbach, 1951) and the Item-remainder coefficient. These measures assess the *internal consistency* of a set of items (questions) that are intended to measure a single concept. The item-remainder coefficient is the correlation between the answer for one item and sum of the answers of the other items. Items with the highest item-remainder are important to the consistency of the scale. The Cronbach alpha is calculated as

$$\alpha = \frac{k}{k-1} \times \frac{s_T^2 - \sum s_I^2}{s_T^2} \tag{1}$$

Where S_T^2 is the total variance of the sum of all the items for a specific construct and S_I^2 is the variance of an individual item and k is the number of items.

If variables are independent the variance of their sum is equal to the sum of each individual variance. If variables are not independent the variance of their sum is inflated by the covariance among the variables. Thus if the Cronbach alpha is small we would assume that the variables were independent and did not together contribute to the measurement of a single construct. If the Cronbach alpha is large (conventionally >0.7), we assume that the items are highly inter-correlated and together measure a single construct.

7.2. Types of Validity

As noted above, we also want to make sure that our survey instrument is measuring what we want it to measure. This called survey validity. Four types of validity are discussed below.

Face validity is a cursory review of items by untrained judges. It hardly counts as a measure of validity at all, because it is so subjective and ill-defined.

Content validity is a subjective assessment of how appropriate the instrument seems to a group of reviewers (i.e. a focus group) with knowledge of the subject matter. It typically involves a systematic review of the survey's contents to ensure that it includes everything it should and nothing that it shouldn't. The focus group should include subject domain experts as well as members of the target population.

There is no content validity statistic. Thus, it is not a scientific measure of a survey instrument's validity. Nonetheless, it provides a good foundation on which to base a rigorous assessment of validity. Furthermore if we are developing a new survey instrument in a topic area that has not previously been researched, it is the only form of preliminary validation available.

Criterion validity is the ability of a measurement instrument to distinguish respondents belonging to different groups. This requires a theoretical framework to determine which groups an instrument is intended to distinguish. Criterion validity is similar to *concurrent* validity and *predictive* validity. Concurrent validity is based on confirming that an instrument is highly correlated to an already validated measure or instrument that it is meant to be related to. Predictive validity is based on confirming that the instruments predicts a future measure or outcome that it is intended to predict.

Construct validity concerns how well an instrument measures the construct it is designed to measure. This form of validity is very important for validating summated measurement scales (Spector 1992). *Convergent* construct validity assesses the extent to which different questions which are intended to measure the same concept give similar results. *Divergent* construct validity assesses the extent to which concepts *do not correlate* with similar but distinct concepts. Like criterion validity, divergent and convergent construct validity can be assessed by correlating a new instrument with an already validated instrument. Dybå (2000) presents a software engineering example of the validation process for a software survey using summated measurement scales.

7.3. Validity and Reliability in Software Engineering Surveys

Generally, software engineering surveys are weak in the area of validity and reliability. For example, for many years, in the extensive literature relating to the CMM, there was only one reference to a reliability coefficient (the Cronbach's alpha) and that concerned the 1987 version of the Maturity Questionnaire (Humphrey, 1991).

Of the three surveys we discussed in Sect. 1.2, only the Finnish Survey (Ropponen and Lyytinen, 2000) made a concerted effort to undertake reliability and validity studies. The technology adoption survey used face validity only. Lethbridge discusses the basis for his questions, but his discussion of validity is based only on a post-hoc assessment of possible responder bias (Lethbridge, 1998, 2000). In contrast, the Finnish researchers used a panel of experts to judge the content validity of the questions. They also attempted to assess the internal reliability of their instrument. Unfortunately, they did not perform an independent pilot study. They analyzed their survey responses using principal components to identify strategies for managing risks. They then derived Cronbach alpha statistics (Cronbach, 1951) from the same responses. They found high values and concluded that their survey instrument had good reliability. However, Cronbach alpha values were bound to be high, because they measure the structure already detected by the principal component analysis.

7.4. Survey Documentation

After the instrument is finalized, Bourque and Fielder (1995) recommend starting to document the survey. If the survey is self-administered, you should consider writing an initial descriptive document, called a *questionnaire specification*. It should include:

- The objective(s) of the study.
- A description the rationale for each question.
- The rationale for any questions adopted or adapted from other sources, with appropriate citations.
- A description of the evaluation process.

Furthermore, once the questionnaire is administered, the documentation should be updated to record information about:

- Who the respondents were.
- How it was administered.
- How the follow-up procedure was conducted.
- How completed questionnaires were processed.

One of the major reasons for preparing documentation during the survey is that surveys can take a long time. It may be many months between first distributing a questionnaire and when we are able to analyze results. It takes time for respondents to reply and for the researchers to undertake all necessary follow-up procedures. This time lag means that it is easy to forget the details of instrument creation and administration, especially if documentation is left to the end of the study. In general, it is good research practice to keep an experimental diary or log book for any type of empirical studies.

When questionnaires are administered by interview, specifications are referred to as *interviewer specifications* and can be used to train interviewers as well as for reference in the field.

Once all possible responses have been received and all follow-up actions have been completed, we are in a position to analyze the survey data. This is discussed in the following sections. However before tackling analysis we look at the problem of obtaining a data set that is suitable for statistical analysis.

8. Obtaining Valid Data

When we administer a survey, it is not usually cost-effective (and sometimes not even possible) to survey the entire population. Instead, we survey a subset of the population, called a *sample*, in the hope that the responses of the smaller group represent what would have been the responses of the entire group. When choosing the sample to survey, we must keep in mind three aspects of survey design: avoidance of bias, appropriateness, and cost-effectiveness. That is, we want to select a sample that is truly representative of the larger population, is appropriate to involve in our survey, and is not prohibitively expensive to query. If we take these sample characteristics into account, we are more likely to get precise and reliable findings.

In this section, we describe how to obtain a valid survey sample from a target population. We discuss why a proper approach to sampling is necessary and how to obtain a valid sample. We also identify some of the sampling problems that affect software engineering surveys.

The main point to understand is that a valid sample is not simply the set of responses we get when we administer a questionnaire. A set of responses is only a valid sample, in statistical terms, if has been obtained by a random sampling process.

8.1. Samples and Populations

To obtain a sample, you must begin by defining a *target population*. The target population is the group or the individuals to whom the survey applies. In other words, you seek those groups or individuals who are in a position to answer the questions and to whom the results of the survey apply. Ideally, a target population should be represented as a finite list of all its members called a *sampling frame*. For example, when pollsters survey members of the public about their voting preferences, they use the electoral list as their sampling frame.

A valid sample is a *representative subset* of the target population. The critical word in our definition of a sample is the word "representative." If we do not have a representative sample, we cannot claim that our results generalize to the target population. If our results do not generalize, they have little more value than a personal anecdote. Thus, a major concern when we sample a population is to ensure that our sample is representative.

Before we discuss how to obtain a valid sample, let us consider our three survey examples. In Lethbridge's case, he had no defined target population. He might have meant his target population to be every working software developer in the world, but this is simply another way of saying the population was undefined. Furthermore, he had no concept of sampling even his notional population. He merely obtained a set of responses from the group of people motivated to respond. Thus, Lethbridge's target population was vague and his sampling method non-existent. So although he described the demographic properties of his respondents (age, highest education qualification, nationality etc.), no generalization of his results is possible.

With respect to the Pfleeger-Kitchenham survey, we noted previously that we were probably targeting the wrong population because we were asking individuals to answer questions on behalf of their companies. However, even if our target population was all readers of *Applied Software Development*, we did not have any sampling method, so our responses could not be said to constitute a valid sample.

In contrast, in the Finnish survey, Ropponen and Lyytinen had a list of all members of the Finnish Information Processing Association whose title was manager. Thus, they had a defined sampling frame. Then, they sent their questionnaires to a pre-selected subset of the target population. If their subset was obtained by a valid sampling method (surprisingly, no sampling method is reported in their article), their subset constituted a valid sample. As we will see later, this situation is not sufficient to claim that the actual responses were a valid sample, but it is a good starting point.

8.2. Obtaining a Valid Sample

We begin by understanding the target population. We cannot sample a population if we cannot specify what that population is. Our initial assessment of the target population should arise from the survey objectives, not from a sense of who is available to answer our questions. The more precisely the objectives are stated, the easier it will be to define the target population. The specific target population may itself be a subset of a larger population. It may be specified by the use of *inclusion* or *exclusion* criteria.

It is often instructive to consider the target population and sampling procedure from the viewpoint of data analysis. We can do this during questionnaire design but we should also re-assess the situation after any pretests or pilot tests of the survey instrument. At this point we will have some actual responses, so we can try out our analysis procedures. We need to consider whether the analyses will lead to any meaningful conclusions, in particular:

- Will the analysis results address the study objectives?
- Can the target population answer our research questions?

Considering the first question, Lethbridge's objectives were to provide information to educational institutions and companies as they plan curricula and training programs. This goal raises obvious questions: which educational institutions and which companies? Lethbridge's target population was poorly defined but can be characterized as any practising software engineer. Thus, we must ask ourselves whether replies from software engineers who would have attended different education institutions, worked in different companies or had different roles and responsibilities would indicate clearly how curricula and training courses could be improved. At the very least, general conclusions may be difficult. The results would need to be interpreted by people responsible for curricula or training courses in the light of their specific situation.

The next question concerns the target population. Will the target population provide useful answers? Lethbridge did not apply any inclusion or exclusion criteria to his respondents. Thus, the respondents may include people who graduated a very long time ago or graduated in non-computer science-related disciplines and migrated to software engineering. It seems unlikely that such respondents could offer useful information about current computer science- related curricula or training programs.

Consider now the survey of technology adoption practices. We have already pointed that the Pfleeger-Kitchenham target population was the set of organizations (or organizational decision-makers) making decisions about technology adoption. However, our sample population solicits information from individuals. Thus, our *sampling unit* (i.e. an individual) did not match their *experimental unit* (i.e. an organization). This mismatch between the population sampled and the true target population is a common problem in many surveys, not just in software engineering. If the problem is not spotted, it can result in spurious positive results, since the number of responses may be unfairly inflated by having many responses from organizations instead of one per organization. Furthermore if there are a disproportionate number of responses from one company or one type of company, results will also be biased.

The general target population of the Finnish survey of project risk was Finnish IT project managers. The actual sampling frame was specified as members of Finnish Information Processing Association whose job title was "manager" or equivalent. People were asked about their personal experiences as project managers. In general, it would seem that the sample adequately represents the target population, and the target population should be in a position to answer the survey's questions.

The only weakness is that the Finnish survey did not have any experience-related exclusion criteria. For instance, respondents were asked questions about how frequently they faced different types of project problems. It may be that respondents with very limited management experience cannot give very reliable answers to such questions. Ropponen and Lyytinen did consider experience (in terms of the number of projects managed) in their analysis of the how well different risks were managed. However, they did not consider the effect of lack of experience on the initial analysis of risk factors.

8.3. Sampling Methods

Once we are confident that our target population is appropriate, we must use a rigorous sampling method. If we want to make strong inferences to the target population, we need a probabilistic sampling method. We describe below a variety of sampling methods, both probabilistic and non-probabilistic.

8.3.1. Probabilistic Sampling Methods

A probabilistic sample is one in which every member of a target population has a *known, non-zero probability* of being included in the sample. The aim of a probabilistic sample is to eliminate subjectivity and obtain a sample that is both unbiased and representative of the target population. It is important to remember that we cannot make any statistical inferences from our data unless we have a probabilistic sample.

A *simple random sample* is one in which every member of the target population has the *same* probability of being included in the sample. There are a variety of ways of selecting a random sample from a population list. One way is to use a random number generator to assign a random number to each member of the target population, order the members on the list according to the random number and choose the first *n* members on the list, where *n* is the required sample size.

A *stratified random sample* is obtained by dividing the target population into subgroups called strata. Each stratum is sampled separately. Strata are used when we expect different sections of the target population to respond differently to our questions, or when we expect different sections of the target population to be of different sizes. For example, we may stratify a target population on the basis of sex, because men and women often respond differently to questionnaires. The number of members selected from each stratum is usually proportional to the size of the stratum. In a software engineering survey, we often have far fewer women than men in our target population, so we may want to sample within strata to ensure we have an appropriate number of responses from women. Stratified random samples are useful for non-homogeneous populations, but they are more complicated to analyze than simple random samples.

Systematic sampling involves selecting every *n*th member of the sampling frame. If the list is random, then selecting every *n*th member is another method of obtaining a simple random sample. However, if the list is not random, this procedure can introduce bias. Non-random order would include alphabetical order or date of birth order.

8.3.2. Cluster-Based Sampling

Cluster–based sampling is the term given to surveying individuals that belong to defined groups. For example, we may want to survey all members of a family group, or all patients at specific hospitals. Randomization procedures are based on the cluster, not the individual. We would expect members of each cluster to give more similar answers than we would expect from members of different clusters. That is, answers are expected to be correlated within a cluster. There are well-defined methods for analyzing cluster data, but the analysis is more complex than that of a simple random sample (for example, see Levy and Lemeshow, 1999).

8.3.3. Non-Probabilistic Sampling Methods

Non-probability samples are created when respondents are chosen because the are easily accessible or the researchers have some justification for believing that they are representative of the population. This type of sample runs the risk of being biased (that is, not being representative of the target population), so it is dangerous to draw any strong inferences from them. Certainly it is not possible to draw any statistical inferences from such samples.

Nevertheless, there are three reasons for using non-probability samples:

- The target population is hard to identify. For example, if we want to survey software hackers, they may be difficult to find.
- The target population is very specific and of limited availability. For example if we want to survey senior executives in companies employing more than 5000 software engineers, it may not be possible to rely on a random sample. We may be forced to survey only those executives who are willing to participate.
- The sample is a pilot study, not the final survey, and a non-random group is readily available. For example, participants in a training program might be surveyed to investigate whether a formal trial of the training program is worthwhile.

Three methods of non-probabilistic sampling are discussed below.

Convenience sampling involves obtaining responses from those people who are available and willing to take part. The main problem with this approach is that the people who are willing to participate may differ in important ways from those who are not willing. For example, people who have complaints are more likely to provide feedback than those who are satisfied with a product or service We often see this kind of sampling in software engineering surveys.

Snowball sampling involves asking people who have participated in a survey to nominate other people they believe would be willing to take part. Sampling continues until the required number of responses is obtained. This technique is often used when the population is difficult for the researchers to identify. For example, we might expect software hackers to be known to one another, so if we found one to take part in our survey, we could ask him/her to identify other possible participants.

Quota sampling is the non-probabilistic version of stratified random sampling. The target population is spit into appropriate strata based on know subgroups (e.g. sex, educational achievement, company size etc.). Each stratum is sampled (using convenience or snowball techniques) so that number of respondents in each subgroup is proportional to the proportion in the population.

8.4. Sample Size

A major issue of concern when sampling is determining the appropriate sample size. There are two reasons why sample size is important. First, an inadequate sample size may lead to results that are not significant statistically. In other words, if the sample size is not big enough, we cannot come to a reasonable conclusion, and we cannot generalize to the target population. Second, inadequate sampling of clusters or strata disables our ability to compare and contrast different subsets of the population.

However, Fowler points out that there is no simple equation that can tell you exactly how large your sample ought to be (Fowler, 2002). In particular, he rejects sample size strategies based on a proportion of the population, typical sizes found in other studies, or statistical methods based on expected error levels. His suggestion is to consider your analysis plan and ensure that you have adequate sample sizes of the smallest important subgroups in your population.

8.5. Response Rates

It is not enough to decide how many people to survey. We must also take steps to be sure that enough people return the survey to yield meaningful results. Thus, any reliable survey should measure and report its *response rate*, that is, the proportion of participants who responded compared to the number who were approached.

The validity of survey results is severely compromised if there is a significant level of non-response. If we have a large amount of non-response but we can understand why and can still be sure that our pool of respondents is representative of the larger population, we can proceed with our analysis. But if there is large non-response and we have no idea why people have not responded, we have no way of being sure that our sample truly represents the target population. It is even worse to have no idea what the response rate is. For example, we had 171 responses to our survey, but we did not know exactly how many people subscribed to *Applied Software Development*, so we could not calculate response rate. Similarly, because Lethbridge solicited responses from companies via the Web, the size of the target population was unknown; therefore, he could not calculate the response rate. Thus, in both these cases the cost savings obtained by avoiding a direct mailing may have compromised the validity of the surveys.

It is not obvious what a sort of response rate we should expect. Baruch (1999) reviewed 175 IS surveys and found a median response rate was 60%, but it may be that conditions are different in SE than in IS. Currently, we have relatively few surveys in SE and many of those do not publish response rates.

There are several strategies that can be used to improve response rates. Some were discussed in Sect. 6.5, others include:

- If we expect an initial low response rate, we can plan for *over-sampling*. That is, when we identify the sample size we require, we then sample more than the minimum required to allow for the expected non-response.
- We should have follow-up plans to send reminders to participants.
- We should approach individuals personally, if necessary. One-to-one approaches are particularly important if we want to assess the reason for non-response. For example, the researchers in Finland phoned a random sample of people who did not reply to their survey to ask them why they did not respond. This activity allowed them to confirm that non-response was not likely to have a systematic bias on their results.
- It may be possible to perform statistical adjustments to correct for non-response.

However, recent research has suggested that achieving higher response rates do not necessarily mean more accurate results (Krosnick, 1990). If we have used probability sampling, low response rates may not imply lower representativeness.

9. Analysing Survey Data

In this section, we assume that you have designed and administered your survey, and now you are ready to analyze the data you have collected. If you have designed your survey properly, you should have already identified the main analysis procedures. Furthermore, if you have undertaken any pre-tests or pilot studies, you should have already tested the analysis procedures.

We discuss some general issues involved in analyzing survey data. However, we cannot describe in detail how to analyze all types of survey data, so we concentrate on discussing some of the most common analysis issues.

9.1. Data Validation

Before undertaking any detailed analysis, responses should be vetted for consistency and completeness. It is important to have a policy for handling inconsistent and or incomplete questionnaires. If we find that most respondents answered all questions, we may decide to reject incomplete questionnaires. However, we must investigate the characteristics of rejected questionnaires in the same way that we investigate non-response to ensure that we do not introduce any systematic bias. Alternatively, we may find that most respondents have omitted a few specific questions. In this case, it is more appropriate to remove those questions from the analysis.

Sometimes we can use all the questionnaires, even if some are incomplete. In this case we will have different sample sizes for each question we analyze and we must remember to report that actual sample size for each sample statistic. This approach is suitable for analyses such as calculating sample statistics or comparing mean values, but not for correlation or regression studies. Whenever analysis involves two or more questions you need an agreed procedure for handling missing values.

In some cases, it is possible to use statistical techniques to "impute" the values of missing data (Little and Rubin, 1987). However, such techniques are usually inappropriate when the amount of missing data is excessive and/or the values are categorical rather than numerical.

It is important to reduce the chance of incomplete questionnaires when we design and test our instruments. A very strong justification for pilot surveys is that misleading questions and/or poor instructions may be detected before the main survey takes place.

The questionnaire related to the technology adoption survey (shown in Appendix 1) suffered badly in terms of incomplete answers. A review of the instructions to respondents made it clear why this had happened. The instructions said:

> If you are not sure or don't know an answer just leave the line blank; otherwise it is important to answer YES or NO to the first section of every Technique/Technology section.

With these instructions, perhaps it is not surprising that most of the questionnaires had missing values. However, replies were not just incomplete; they were also inconsistent. For example, some respondents left blank question 1 (Did your company evaluate this technology?) while replying YES to question 2, about the type of evaluation undertaken. Thus, blanks did not just mean "Don't know"; sometimes they also meant YES. Ambiguities of this sort make data analysis extremely difficult and the results dubious.

9.2. Partitioning the Responses

We often need to partition our responses into more homogeneous sub-groups before analysis. Partitioning is usually done on the basis of demographic information. We may want to compare the responses obtained from different subgroups or simply report the results for different subgroup separately. In some cases, partitioning can be used to alleviate some initial design errors. Partitioning the responses is related to data validation since it may lead to some replies being omitted from the analysis.

For example, we noted that Lethbridge did not exclude graduates from non-IT related subjects from his population nor did he exclude people who graduated many years previously. However, he knew a considerable amount about his respondents, because he obtained demographic information from them. In his first paper, he reported that 50% of the respondents had degrees in computer science or software engineering, 30% had degrees in computer engineering or electrical engineering, and 20% had degrees in other disciplines. He also noted that the average time since the first degree was awarded was 11.7 years and 9.6 years since the last degree. Thus, he was in a position to partition the replies and concentrate his analysis on recent IT graduates. However, since he did not partition his data, his results are extremely difficult to interpret.

9.3. Analyzing Ordinal and Nominal Data

Analyzing numerical data is relatively straightforward. However, there are additional problems if your data is ordinal or nominal.

A large number of surveys ask people to respond to questions on an ordinal scale, such a five-point agreement scale. The Finnish survey and Lethbridge's survey both requested answers of this sort. It is common practice to convert the ordinal scale to its numerical equivalent (e.g. the numbers 1–5) and to analyze the data as if they were simple numerical data. There are occasions when this approach is reasonable, but it violates the mathematical rules for analyzing ordinal data. Using a conversion from ordinal to numerical entails a risk that subsequent analysis will give misleading results.

In general, if our data are single peaked and approximately Normal, our risks of misanalysis are low if we convert to numerical values. However, we should also consider whether such a conversion is necessary. There are three approaches that can be used if we want to avoid scale violations:

1. We can use the properties of the multinomial distribution to estimate the proportion of the population in each category and then determine the standard error of the estimate. For example, Moses uses a Bayesian probability model of the multinomial distribution to assess the consistency of subjective ratings of ordinal scale cohesion measures (Moses, 2000).
2. We may be able to convert an ordinal scale to a dichotomous variable. For example, if we are interested in comparing whether the proportion who agree or strongly agree is greater in one group than another, we can re-code our responses into a dichotomous variable (for example, we can code "strongly agree" or "agree" as 1 and all other responses as 0) and use the properties of the binomial distribution. This technique is also useful if we want to assess the impact of other variables on an ordinal scale variable. If we can convert to a dichotomous scale, we can use logistic regression.
3. We can use Spearman's rank correlation or Kendall's tau (Siegel and Castellan, 1998) to measure association among ordinal scale variables.

There are two occasions where there is no real alternative to scale violations:

1. If we want to assess the reliability of our survey instrument using Cronbach's alpha statistic (Cronbach, 1951)..
2. If we want to add together ordinal scale measures of related variables to give overall scores for a concept.

The second case is not a major problem since the central limit theory confirms that the sum of a number of random variables will be approximately Normal even if the individual variables are not themselves Normal.

However, we believe it is important to understand the scale type of our data and analyze it appropriately. Thus, we do not agree with Lethbridge's request for respondents to interpolate between his scale points as they saw fit (e.g. to give a reply of 3.4 if they wanted to).

10. Conclusions

This chapter has discussed the issues involved in undertaking survey-based research, in particular surveys based on self-administered questionnaires. The main message of this chapter is that, in spite of its ubiquity, survey-based research is not a simple research method. It requires time and effort to understand the basic methodology as well as time and effort to create, validate and administer a survey instrument.

We have only scratched the surface of survey methodology in this chapter. We hope this chapter provides a useful starting point but we strongly advise that you consult the text books and research referenced in this chapter before undertaking a survey for the first time.

References

Bourque, L. and Fielder, E. *How to Conduct Self-administered and Mail Surveys*, Sage Publications, Thousand Oaks, CA, 1995.

Baruch, Y. Response rate in academic studies – a comparative analysis. *Human Relations*, 52(4), 1999, pp. 412–438.

Cronbach, L.J. Coefficient alpha and internal structure of tests. *Psychometrika*, 16(3), 1951, pp. 297–334.

Dybå, T. An empirical investigation of the key factors for success in software process improvement. *IEEE Transactions on Software Engineering*, 31(5), 2005, pp. 410–424.

Dybå, T. An instrument for measuring the key factors of success in software process improvement. *Empirical Software Engineering*, 5(4), 2000, pp. 357–390.

El Emam, K., Goldenson, D., Briand, L., and Marshall, P. Interrater Agreement in SPICE Based Assessments. *Proceedings 4th International Software Metrics Conference*, IEEE Computer Society Press, 1996, pp. 149–156.

El Emam, K., Simon, J.-M., Rousseau, S., and Jacquet. E. Cost Implications of Interrater Agreement for Software Process Assignments. *Proceedings 5th International Software Metrics Conference*, IEEE Computer Society Press, 1998, pp. 38–51.

Fowler, F.J. Jr. *Survey Research Methods*, Third Edition, Sage Publications, Thousand Oaks, CA, 2002.

Fink, A. *The Survey Handbook*, Sage Publications, Thousand Oaks, CA, 1995.

Humphrey, W. and Curtis, B. Comments on 'a critical look', *IEEE Software*, 8:4, July, 1991, pp. 42–46.

Krosnick, J.A. Survey research. *Annual Review of Psychology*, 50, 1990, pp. 537–567.

Lethbridge, T. A Survey of the Relevance of Computer Science and Software Engineering Education. *Proceedings of the 11th International Conference on Software Engineering Education*, IEEE Computer Society Press, 1998.

Levy, P.S. and Lemeshow, S. *Sampling of Populations: Methods and Applications*, Third Edition, Wiley Series in Probability and Statistics, Wiley, New York, 1999.

Lethbridge, T. What knowledge is important to a software professional. *IEEE Computer*, 33(5), 2000, pp. 44–50.

Little, R.J.A. and Rubin, D.B. *Statistical Analysis with Missing Data*, Wiley, New York, 1987.

Litwin, M. *How to Measure Survey Reliability and Validity*, Sage Publications, Thousand Oaks, CA, 1995.

Moses, J. Bayesian probability distributions for assessing measurement of subjective software attributes. *Information and Software Technology*, 42(8), 2000, pp. 533–546.

Moløkken-Østvold, K., Jørgensen, M., Tanilkan, S.S., Gallis, H., Lien, A. and Hove, S. A Survey on Software Estimation in the Norwegian Industry. *Proceedings 10th International Symposium on Software metrics. Metrics 2004*, IEEE Computer Society, 2004, pp. 208–219.

Ropponen, J. and Lyytinen, K. Components of software development risk: how to address them. A project manager survey. *IEEE Transactions on Software Engineering*, 26(2), 2000, pp. 98–112.

Shaddish, W.R., Cook, T.D., and Campbell, D.T. *Experimental and Quasi-Experimental Designs for Generalized Causal Inference*, Houghton Mifflin Company, New York, 2002.

Siegel, S. and Castellan, N.J. *Nonparametric Statistics for the Behavioral Sciences*, Second Edition, McGraw-Hill Book Company, New York, 1998.

Spector, P.E. *Summated Rating Scale Construction. An Introduction*, Sage Publications, Thousand Oaks, CA, 1992.

Standish Group. *Chaos Chronicles*, Version 3.0, West Yarmouth, MA, 2003.

Straub, D.W. Validating instruments in MIS research. *MIS Quarterly*, 13 (2), 1989, pp. 147–169.

Zelkowitz, M.V., Dolores, R.W., and Binkley, D. Understanding the culture clash in software engineering technology transfer. University of Maryland technical report, 2 June 1998.

Chapter 4
The Focus Group Method
as an Empirical Tool
in Software Engineering[1]

Jyrki Kontio, Johanna Bragge, and Laura Lehtola

Abstract This chapter presents the focus group method and discusses its use for empirical research in the software engineering context. The background, process and main characteristics of the method are presented, as well as guidelines for its use. Moreover, the traditional as well computer-mediated focus group variations are compared to each other. The chapter concludes in with a discussion of the applicability of the method for software engineering research. In summary, the focus group method is a cost-effective and quick empirical research approach for obtaining qualitative insights and feedback from practitioners. It can be used in several phases and types of research. However, a major limitation of the method is that it is useful only in studying concepts that can be understood by knowledgeable participants in a limited time. We also emphasize the importance of empirical rigor when the method is used in scholarly work.

1. Introduction

The software engineering community has begun to emphasize empirical research methods to improve the validity and generalizability of research results (Basili et al., 1986; Tichy, 1998; Wohlin et al., 2003; Zelkowitz and Wallace, 1998). The community has also recognized the need to improve the amount and quality of empirical research in the field (Buhrer, 2007; Kitchenham et al., 2004; Tichy et al., 1995). Experimentation, in particular, has received much attention in software engineering literature (Juristo and Moreno, 2001; Wohlin et al., 1999) and the community has clearly matured in its use of empirical methods, as evidenced by an increasing number of empirical research papers, textbooks, and emergence of conferences focusing on empirical research.

Increased attention in empirical methods has also interested software engineering researchers in having a broader range of empirical methods in their arsenal so that appropriate methods can be selected and used for each research problem. Similar conclusions have been drawn in related fields of information systems (Benbasat, 1996; Galliers, 1991) and business studies (Ghauri et al., 1995).

---

[1] Based on Kontio, J., Lehtola, L., and Bragge, J. (2004). Using the focus group method in software engineering: obtaining practitioner and user experiences, *International Symposium on Empirical Software Engineering*, pp. 271–280, Redondo Beach, CA.

F. Shull et al. (eds.), *Guide to Advanced Empirical Software Engineering*.
© Springer 2008

This chapter presents a specific qualitative research method, the focus group method. We supplement current research by providing guidelines for the method's use in software engineering research. This chapter is largely based on our earlier paper (Kontio et al., 2004), with extensions to the guidelines on the use of the method, and on the comparison of traditional and three computer-mediated focus group variations.

2. The Focus Group Method

This section gives an overview of the focus group method in general, whereas the next section presents experiences from the software engineering context.

2.1. Background and Definition

Focus groups emerged as a research method in the 1950s in the social sciences. The open-ended interview format was extended to group discussion (Templeton, 1994), hence becoming the focus group method. Morgan defines focus groups as a "research technique that collects data through group interaction on a topic determined by the researcher" (Morgan, 1996). Focus groups are thus carefully planned discussions, designed to obtain personal perceptions of the group members on a defined area of research interest. There are typically between 3 and 12 participants and the discussion is guided and facilitated by a moderator-researcher, who follows a predefined questioning structure so that the discussion stays focused. Members are selected based on their individual characteristics as related to the session topic (so-called purposive sampling). The group setting enables the participants to build on the responses and ideas of other participants, which increases the richness of the information gained (Langford and McDonaugh, 2003).

Focus group sessions produce mainly qualitative information about the objects of study. The benefits of focus groups are that they produce candid, sometimes insightful information, and the method is fairly inexpensive and fast to perform (Widdows et al., 1991). However, the method shares the weaknesses of many other qualitative methods. Results may be biased by group dynamics and sample sizes are often small. Therefore, it may be difficult to generalize the results (Judd et al., 1991). Poorly conducted focus group sessions may, therefore, be particularly prone to producing unreliable results.

Currently, the method is widely used, e.g., in sociological studies, market research, product planning, political campaigning, defining business services, and in system usability studies (Baker, 1991; Edmunds, 1991; Morgan, 1997; Neter and Waksberg, 1964; Stewart and Shamdasani, 1990; Rubin, 1994; Widdows et al., 1991). Focus groups can be used either as a stand-alone research method or in combination with other research methods, e.g. with individual interviews or quantitative surveys (Morgan, 1996).

There are several textbooks and detailed guidelines available on how to plan and run focus groups (Anon., 1997; Feig, 1989; Krueger and Casey, 2000; Nielsen, 1997; Templeton, 1994; Langford and McDonaugh, 2003), making the method that is relatively easy to adopt and use consistently. McQuarrie (1994, 2001), for instance, offers extremely useful focus group book reviews which can direct the reader, a researcher, an industry practitioner, or moderator, to an appropriate approach.

2.2. Steps in Focus Group Research

Based on several sources (Anon., 1997; Edmunds, 1991; Krueger and Casey, 2000; Morgan, 1996; 1997), we have summarized the main steps of focus group research as follows.

2.2.1. Planning the Research

Defining the research problem. The focus group method is best suited to obtaining initial feedback on new concepts, developing questionnaires, generating ideas, collecting or prioritizing potential problems, obtaining feedback on how models or concepts are presented or documented, and discovering underlying motivations (Edmunds, 1991). According to Morgan (1996), among others, survey researchers have increased their use of focus groups to provide valuable data on how the respondents themselves talk about the topic of subsequent surveys, as the questions posed in surveys are inherently limited.

The method is not suitable for all situations. Focus groups can seldom be used to test hypotheses as samples are too small and group dynamics create an uncontrollable variable. In verbally conducted settings it is not easy to obtain subjective quantitative assessments, as opinion leaders or group behaviour may influence the results. It may be also hard to explore political or otherwise sensitive issues as people may not reveal their true opinions in a public setting. Also, it is difficult to study complex issues that are difficult to grasp in a short session, as people have limited mental capacity to grasp complexity and interact simultaneously. Finally, there is the issue of team dynamics and interaction wherein team members may be reluctant to reveal their true subjective preferences. Such limitations might arise in defining prices or cost preferences, for example (Edmunds, 1991).

Typically focus groups are not the only research method used in a study. Morgan's (1997) content analysis of abstracts revealed that a majority of the published research articles using focus groups combined them with other research methods. The most frequent pairings were with either in-depth, individual interviews or subsequent surveys (Morgan, 1997). When focus groups are used in combination with other research methods, they can serve either as a primary research method or as the secondary method in the study (Morgan, 1996). The role of focus groups in the research process should be carefully defined in the planning phase of research.

In some cases, it might be a good idea to use focus groups instead of other similar research methods. For example, Fern's (1982) results suggest that two 8-person focus groups produce as many ideas as ten individual interviews. Thus, in case it is more cost-efficient to arrange two group sessions instead of ten individual meetings, focus groups are worth considering.

2.2.2. Designing focus groups

Typically focus group research should consist of 4–6 focus groups (Morgan, 1997). The size of an individual focus group can vary from 3 to 12, but more typically there are between 4 and 8 participants. Smaller groups seem to be more appropriate with emotionally charged topics that generate high levels of participant involvement, while larger groups work better with more neutral topics that generate lower levels of involvement (Morgan, 1992).

Selecting participants. The value of the method is that it is very sensitive to the experience and insight of participants. Thus, recruiting representative, insightful and motivated participants is critical to the success of the focus group study. Depending on the research question, participants may not have much experience in the topic of the focus group – or they may be seasoned experts who can rely on their years of experience when interacting in the group. However, when discussing novel and innovative concepts or products to be launched, participants seldom have much expertise on the topic.

Segmentation refers to strategies that consciously vary the composition of groups. The most obvious kinds of segmentation captures something about the research topic itself (Morgan, 1997). For example, if age differences are of interest, it might be a good idea to separate groups based on the participants' age.

Morgan (1997) argues that segmentation offers two basic advantages. These are:

1. Building comparative dimension into the entire research project.
2. Facilitating discussions by making the participants more similar to each other.

In practice, it is generally recommended that some over-recruiting take place as last minute cancellations usually happen. It may also be useful to use pre-session questionnaires so that session time is used most effectively for discussions.

2.2.3. Conducting the focus group sessions

Basic sequence. An individual focus group event usually lasts 2–3 h and has a pre-defined schedule and structure. The number of issues to be covered needs to be limited so that sufficient time can be allocated for the participants to comprehend the issue and have meaningful discussion and interaction. Limited time also places a constraint on the complexity of the issues selected.

The focus group session needs to be carefully managed for time while still making sure that all main contributions can be made during the allocated time. The moderator should thus be determined and have adequate skills in guiding group dynamics. The session needs to be initiated by an introduction where the goals and ground rules of the session are explained to participants. Each of the topics is usually presented one after another.

The discussion and interaction in a focus group session can take many forms. It can be a structured discussion, where the moderator acts as a chair; it can involve brainstorming techniques, such as affinity grouping or teamwork methods; polling and voting using preference votes or the Delphi method (Adler and Ziglio, 1996); comparison games; or even role plays (Edmunds, 1991). Some researchers are very strict in defining what constitutes a genuine, interactive focus group discussion, while others are more inclusive in this [see discussion in Morgan (1996)]. For example Langford and McDonaugh (2003) are proponents of the more liberal view, and they present 38 different tools and techniques that can be used to supplement a traditional focus group discussion.

Data capturing. There are several alternatives for data capture during a session. There can be additional observers taking notes during the session. Audio, video or keyboard recording can be used, and artifacts used during the session can be captured if the session involves techniques producing such artifacts. It may also be useful to arrange a debriefing session with some of the participants immediately after the session so that fresh observations and interpretations from the session are captured as fully as possible. It is obvious that relying on moderator notes will not be sufficient because being a moderator is a full-time job in a focus group session. It can even interrupt the discussion if the moderator starts making notes (Langford and McDonaugh, 2003).

The role of the moderator. The role of the moderator is critical in a focus group session. The moderator should facilitate discussion but not allow his or her own opinions to influence the discussion. His or her main task is to listen and probe deeper when necessary, requiring the moderator to be able to grasp substantial discussions quickly. It is often necessary to paraphrase participant points to ensure that the contribution was correctly understood.

2.2.4. Analyzing the data and reporting the results

The *data analysis and reporting* of focus group studies can use the methods used in qualitative data analysis (Bogdan and Biklen, 1982; Miles and Huberman, 1984; Patton, 1990; Taylor and Bogdan, 1984; Myers, 2004). Quantitative data, if gathered, can be analyzed using descriptive statistics and other standard quantitative methods.

3. Experiences in the Software Engineering Context

We collected experiences from three focus group studies we have conducted (Kontio, 2001; Lehtola et al., 2004; Sunikka, 2004). We provide here only short summaries of the studies, as detailed reports on each of them are available elsewhere [see broader account also in Kontio et al. (2004)].

The objective of the first study (Kontio, 2001) was to provide insights into why and how organizations seek to improve their risk management (RM) practices, what they intend to achieve with better RM, and what impediments preventing more effective RM approaches from being used. Furthermore, we also wanted to obtain feedback on specific characteristics of a RM method called Riskit (Kontio, 1997) and the corresponding software tool ("eRiskit"). The study included three focus groups having 12 participants altogether from several organizations.

The objective of the second study (Lehtola et al., 2004) was to clarify the practical challenges in requirements prioritization. We wanted to find out how and in which phases of development work companies prioritize requirements, and who performs the prioritization. We also clarified which factors have an effect on priorities, and from which sources practitioners gather information on which they base their priority decisions. In this study, one focus group with four participants from two organizations was conducted.

Regarding the third study (Sunikka, 2004), the aim was to collect user opinions about the usability of a university's website. This information was used mainly in planning the actual usability testing to follow, but the focus group results also offered additional insights. The usability study as a whole consisted of several phases: focus group discussion, web survey questionnaire, usability tests, and heuristic evaluations. The focus group was computer-mediated, and it had nine participants invited from the personnel of the case university one of the main end-user groups of the website under study.

We reviewed experiences from each study and constructed a mind map of the experiences and lessons learned. These mind maps were compared and discussed between authors, and the synthesized lessons learned are reported in the following sections. In addition, we collected original focus group participants' feedback in informal discussions or in feedback surveys.

We did not track the effort spent during the studies but estimated it afterwards using the Delphi method (Adler and Ziglio, 1996). These estimates are presented in Table 1 by the main tasks.

3.1. Suitability

Our studies showed that the focus group method is suitable for gathering experience: all of the studies resulted in relevant and usable findings that were used to

Table 1 Estimated effort in the studies (person hours)

Task	Risk study (3 groups)	RE study	Usability study
Research problem formulation	15	5	3
Planning and preparation (including rehearsing)	25	10	10
Selecting and recruiting the participants	8	3	2
Conducting the sessions	9	3	2
Transcribing the data	11	6	0[*]
Analysis	15	6	10
Total	83	33	27

[*]Reports of computer-mediated discussion were generated automatically

guide or complement the research projects in which the focus group studies were conducted. We believe that the types of issues that can be addressed by focus groups include, among others, the following:

- Identifying relevant research questions
- Obtaining practitioner feedback on research questions
- Recognizing past experience that can be studied in more detail by other methods
- Initial evaluation of potential solutions, based on practitioner or user feedback
- Collecting "lessons learned" recommendations
- Identifying potential root causes of phenomena

Such issues can be relevant in all the main phases of a research life cycle. We illustrate this here using the general research phases defined by Glass (1995) and extended by Kontio (2001). This research life cycle is divided into the informational, propositional, analytical, evaluative, and technology transfer phases. It should be noted that not every phase is found in each research study, and the last phase especially is typical only in constructive or design research.

In the *informational phase* the focus group method can be used to collect characterizing information about current practices, experiences, or problems. In the *propositional phase* the initial constructs, i.e., models, theories or prototypes, can be subjected to practitioner and user opinions to provide early feedback. In the *analytical phase* user feedback can be used to evaluate the operationalization of constructs or to test their initial feasibility. In the *evaluative phase* focus groups can be used to refine research questions, provide some of the empirical feedback, and support the interpretation of empirical data.

Finally, in the *technology transfer phase* the focus group can help researchers to package their contributions into a form that is more easily deployable by users. In addition, a focus group session can also act as a "sales session" for research results. We have included examples of potential research questions in Table 2 that are relevant in this research framework.

Table 2 Research question examples for the focus group method in different research phases

Phase of research	Description of the phase	Suitable issues for focus groups
Informational phase	Observing the current state-of-art and practice to identify problems and potential solutions	– What are most urgent or relevant research questions? – What kind of problems are common in industry? – Why are some problems relevant or urgent? – What practices currently exist in industry?
Propositional phase	Constructs are formulated, models are built, theories proposed or formulated	– What are possible solutions or hypotheses? – What similar experiences exist in industry (has someone already tried or tested it?)? – Are the assumptions made realistic from practitioner and user perspectives?
Analytical phase	Operationalization of the constructs or models and their analytical evaluation and improvement	– Is the model understandable? – How can it be deployed into practice? – What are the potential problems in using or understanding the model? – Are there any omissions or gaps in the model?
Evaluative phase	Testing and evaluating the constructs or models	– Is there any data available, can data be obtained? – Is the empirical study design sound and practical? – What does the data mean?
Technology transfer phase	Transferring constructs, models and/or new knowledge into practice	– Is the model packaged well for operational use? – What are the potential challenges in selling or using it? – How it could be packaged better?

McQuarrie and McIntyre (1986) offer guidelines on how to utilize focus groups in the evaluation of new product concepts developed by technologically driven companies. They distinguish six stages through which the discussions could evolve. These stages are comparable to the actual adoption and diffusion processes regarding new products (orientation, exposure, evaluation, pricing, extensions, product modification). Nambisan and Wilemon (2000) and Nambisan (2003), among others, have recently discussed how software development and IS in general could benefit from the research done in the field of new product development (NPD), and vice versa. Thus, the framework provided by McQuarrie and McIntyre could well adapt to software NPD processes as well, especially to those software products that are targeted to normal consumers (e.g., software embedded in mobile phones).

3.2. Strengths

Discovery of new insights. The interactive nature of the group setting and participants' different backgrounds seem to encourage and prompt participants to react to points during discussion, reflecting and building on each other's experiences. This may lead to discovery of issues that researchers might not have been able to plan in advance, as happened in our risk management and requirements prioritization studies.

Aided recall. On several occasions in the example studies, the points made by participants resulted in other participants confirming similar, almost similar and opposite incidents or events. These insights might have been hidden in personal interviews.

Cost-efficiency. For the researchers the focus group method is a cost-efficient way of obtaining practitioner and user experience as several participants can be "interviewed" at the same time. In addition, many current research projects are conducted with industrial companies and access to practitioners is limited due to their business responsibilities. Practitioners find the method cost-effective as well.

Depth of interview. Focus group discussions allow in-depth exploration of the reasons why the participants think the way they do. For instance, questionnaire results usually reveal only what people think, not why.

Business benefits to participants. The practitioners in our studies gave positive feedback for having participated in the interactions during the session and found them valuable even before receiving any reports or summaries. In informal feedback sessions they indicated two main reasons that provided immediate benefits to them:

- *Benchmarking.* The participants in our studies indicated that the sessions already provided valuable information to them during the sessions. This seems to have resulted from two factors. First, the discussions resulted in benchmarking experiences and practices between the members of participating organizations. Second, they seemed to value other participants' experiences and insights. This seemed to be a substantial advantage to participants.
- *Networking.* The focus group event seems to increase networking contacts and incentives to increase cooperation between participants.

3.3. Weaknesses

Group dynamics. As the focus group discussion within a topic often takes place without a predefined format, it is possible that the group dynamics or communication styles influence the level of activity. In addition, compared to a personal interview, it is not as easy for the moderator to have control over the flow and style of the discussion. This weakness can be compensated for by using structured discussion techniques or by the moderator balancing the discussion and activating the less active participants.

Social acceptability. In group situations, social acceptability can influence the points made during discussion. For example, it is possible that a participant can volunteer incorrect information and disagreement may take place. Such situations may be perceived as embarrassing by some participants, resulting in selective contributions and volunteering of information. This weakness can be mitigated by laying out appropriate ground rules at the beginning and by the moderator taking an active role in conducting the discussion in those situations.

Hidden agendas. Some participants may have hidden agendas in the session, e.g., due to business relationships between them, a motivation to appear in a favorable light because of the potential publication of the results, or their company's internal politics. Such hidden agendas may bias the results of the session. This can be mitigated by selecting participants into sessions such that business relationships are not present, by emphasizing the importance of open information, and by guaranteeing or agreeing to the anonymity or confidentiality of results.

Secrecy. Some relevant information may be withheld because of proprietary or business reasons. This can be avoided by the same procedures as mentioned above.

Limited comprehension. The time available for discussions in a focus group session is limited and communication happens mostly only verbally during the discussion. This means that complex issues or points are not necessarily understood by all participants – nor by the researchers. However, if the participants are all experts in their area, the discussion may be surprisingly complex and deep for an outsider. Nevertheless, there is an obvious limit to how complex an issue can be discussed. This potential weakness can be mitigated by selecting participants of equal expertise in the session, by providing more thorough briefings to participants, by providing advance reading material to participants, and by partitioning complex issues in to more "digestible" pieces.

4. Computer-Mediated Focus Groups

This section describes and evaluates the application of computer-support in the conduct of focus groups. In particular, the emphasis here is on face-to-face focus groups mediated by Group Support Systems (GSS) technology (Nunamaker et al., 1991). The benefits and drawbacks of GSS-mediated face-to-face focus groups are compared to traditional focus groups, and also to online (distributed) focus groups that have recently gained popularity with increased use of the Internet. Figure 1 illustrates the framework of our analysis (cells with patterned background are analysed). Examples of software engineering research applications are also mentioned in this section.

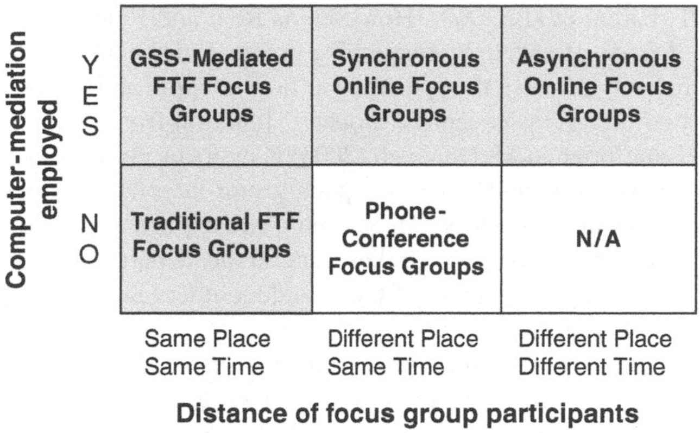

		Same Place Same Time	Different Place Same Time	Different Place Different Time
Computer-mediation employed	**YES**	**GSS-Mediated FTF Focus Groups**	**Synchronous Online Focus Groups**	**Asynchronous Online Focus Groups**
	NO	**Traditional FTF Focus Groups**	**Phone-Conference Focus Groups**	**N/A**

Distance of focus group participants

Fig. 1 Framework of the focus group analysis

As early as in the late 1980s, Management Information Systems researchers developed so-called Group Support Systems (also called Electronic Meeting Systems), to alleviate the common process problems caused by task-oriented group work, such as brainstorming (Nunamaker et al., 1991). These process problems result from, for example, the need to wait for one's own turn to speak, or the dominance of one or a few participants. The strengths of computer-mediated GSS-sessions are built on:

1. Simultaneous and anonymous contribution via computers
2. Structured agenda
3. Real-time voting and multi-criteria analysis possibilities
4. Group memory during and after the sessions
5. Complete records of the electronic discussions

GSS technology is conventionally employed in a same-time same-place mode, where the interaction between the participants is for the most part conducted via personal computers. The majority of the meeting time may be used in deliberating why participants think the way they do, and what to do about it. This is due to the fact that finding out what people are thinking can be conducted in a few minutes due to the parallel input mode – even with large groups of more than 15 participants. Field research results on GSS show savings up to 50% of individual work hours and 90% of project time when compared to regular meetings and group work (Fjermestad and Hiltz, 2000).

Extensive research on GSS usage exists, see for example the laboratory, case and field research reviews (Fjermestad and Hiltz, 1999, 2000), or a recent study profiling 2,000 GSS research articles (Bragge et al., 2007b). Despite the vast amount of research studies on GSS, only a few of them have touched explicitly how the application of GSS may benefit the conduct of focus group studies (Clapper and Massey, 1996; Easton et al., 2003; Klein et al., 2007; Kontio et al., 2004; Massey and

Wallace, 1991; Parent et al., 2000). However, as Reid and Reid (2005) state, "the resemblance of focus groups to brainstorming groups is no accident – focus groups are popular precisely because they generate a 'flow of input and interaction related to the topics that the group is centred around' " [citation from (Edmunds, 1999)]. Furthermore, Langford and McDonaugh (2003) view focus groups as a method that encompasses many tools, and not just a plain group interviewing technique [see discussion also in Morgan (1996)]. Thus, even if not explicitly mentioned, numerous GSS-mediated brainstorming studies centred on a particular topic may be regarded as focus groups, especially if their conduct otherwise follows the steps of the focus group method.

There exists a few commercial GSS software systems on the market today. GroupSystems is the most well known. Others are Facilitate.Pro, WebIQ, MeetingWorks and Grouputer (Austin et al., 2006). Some of these tools provide templates for the conduct of focus groups, which normally follow a structured interview approach [see e.g. (Morgan, 1996)] with predefined questions. However, utilizing the versatile features of the GSS technology it is also possible to use different brainstorming rules, scenario-based discussions, cognitive maps and a variety of other techniques (Langford and McDonaugh, 2003; Morgan, 1996) in a focus group.

Many of the applications in GSS studies concern software engineering or information systems development (see e.g. Boehm et al., 2001; Bragge et al., 2005b; Chen and Nunamaker, 1991; De Vreede et al., 2005; Elfvengren et al., 2004; Gruenbacher et al., 2003; Halling et al., 2001; Liou and Chen, 1993; Rodgers et al., 2004; Van Genuchten et al., 1997, 2001; Vitharana and Ramamurthy, 2003). This may be partially due to the fact that IT professionals are naturally attracted to using various ICT tools to support their work. Processes have been developed especially for requirements engineering (needs assessment, requirements elicitation or requirements negotiation), code inspections and usability studies.

The participants in software engineering related studies may involve people designing and developing a system, people interested in the system's use (e.g., end-users or customers), people having a financial interest, or people responsible for system introduction and maintenance (Gruenbacher et al., 2003). User-centric approaches, which are currently growing in popularity, come closest to focus group studies. End-users are often nowadays widely geographically dispersed, and not within traditional organizational boundaries (Bragge et al., 2005b; Tuunanen and Rossi, 2004). Their inclusion in the software engineering process calls for novel approaches.

The above-mentioned user-centric development, along with the commercialization of the Internet, has brought yet another variation of focus groups to the researcher's toolkit: *online (or virtual) focus groups*. Several authors provide case descriptions or useful practical advice to researchers conducting online focus group studies (Fraunhofer, 2002; Hansen and Hansen, 2006; Klein et al., 2007; Montoya-Weiss et al., 1998; Newby et al., 2003; O'Connor and Madge, 2003; Oringderff, 2004; Reid and Reid, 2005; Sweet, 2001; Ten Pow, 2003; Turney and Pocknee, 2004; Wellner, 2003; Zinchiak, 2001).

The online focus groups can either be conducted in the form of synchronous inter-active groups, or in the form of asynchronous discussion boards. The information systems that may be utilized in online focus groups encompass web-based versions of GSS software, commercial focus group platforms, discussion groups, listservs, chatrooms, bulletin boards, mailing lists, instant messaging systems and so forth. Although these online forms provide many advantages over traditionally conducted focus groups (e.g., anonymity, larger group size, savings in travelling and venue costs), they also have distinct drawbacks, too. For example, the task of the moderator can be much more demanding in online than in face-to-face settings. This is due to the lower richness of the media used (Daft and Lengel, 1986). Media richness is determined by a medium's ability to provide immediate feedback, utilize multiple cues and channels, and enable language variety (Montoya-Weiss et al., 1998).

5. Comparing the Benefits and Drawbacks of Different Focus Group Variations

The literature offers several studies that thoroughly discuss a single type of focus group or compare selected variations with each other (Clapper and Massey, 1996; Easton et al., 2003; Hansen and Hansen, 2006; Klein et al., 2007; Massey and Wallace, 1991; Montoya-Weiss et al., 1998; Morgan, 1996; Newby et al., 2003; Parent et al., 2000; Reid and Reid, 2005; O'Connor and Madge, 2003; Oringderff, 2004; Sweet, 2001; Ten Pow, 2003; Turney and Pocknee, 2004; Wellner, 2003; Zinchiak, 2001). Based on this literature and also on our own experiences of conducting all main types of focus groups (e.g., Bragge et al., 2005a, c, 2007a), we have gathered compara-tive information on traditional, GSS-mediated face-to-face, as well as online focus groups (synchronous and asynchronous). The results of these comparisons are presented in Tables 3–5. Moreover, we will discuss the comparison data with respect to four issues: people, technology, process and costs. We have not cited the above reference sources in the tables or in the discussion to keep them more concise.

5.1. Traditional focus groups

Regarding *people issues*, the moderator's task in traditional focus groups is easier than with computer-mediated groups (that are lower in media richness, especially in different-place settings), although the moderator must possess excellent social skills. The participants may feel more satisfied with a familiar verbal and more social proc-ess, and they do not have to possess typing skills (e.g., elderly people). However, the participants can be recruited from a limited geographical distance, and they may be shy about talking, especially about sensitive or controversial issues.

The media-rich interaction in the verbal *process* is high, and it can result in the deepest insights. The process usually stays focused without any external distractions, and if they happen, the facilitator can respond immediately. However, group thinking, domineering, communication apprehension, getting off-the-track, and social rank related issues are common problems.

Concerning *technology*, the audio or even video recording of the session is quite usual and routine. The latter is needed in case it is important to know afterwards who said what. In traditional settings, it is possible to present handheld prototypes or models. The travelling, venue, and transcribing *costs* are high. Traditional focus groups can accommodate the lowest number of participants due to "serial" communication mode, thus more groups with relatively homogeneous participants are needed (see Table 3 for a summary).

Table 3 Benefits and drawbacks of traditional focus groups

Benefits	Drawbacks
+ Richer media, researchers may observe nonverbal communication, such as body language, facial expressions, tones of voice etc.	− High travelling costs (participants and moderators)
+ Moderator's task is easier than with computer-mediated communications (especially those in different-place settings)	− High rental costs venue
+ Participants may feel more satisfied with a verbal/social process (especially older people)	− High transcribing costs and long delay in reporting
+ The process usually stays focused without any external distractions (and if they happen, the facilitator can respond immediately)	− Limited time to speak per person (e.g. with ten participants 6 min/ person in 1 h)
+ FTF discussion is a familiar form of communication to the participants	− Possible dominance of some persons
+ Participants don't have to have typing skills (e.g. children, old people)	− Group thinking (pressure to conform) and communication apprehension (e.g. with sensitive issues) may occur
+ Possibility to utilize 3D-models, prototypes, highly confidential material etc.	− Comments and ideas evaluated based on the presenter, not the idea itself
+ Smaller probability for technical problems (audio and video recording technologies needed in FTF sessions are more mature than computer-mediated communication technologies)	− Max. 12 participants per group
	− The more people, the more process losses due to the "serial communication" mode
	− The discussion might easily get off track; thus the moderator must be determined and knowledgeable about how to guide the group dynamics
	− Moderator must have excellent social skills
	− Requires homogeneity between participants, and thus often several groups
	− Need for videotaping if vital to know who said what

5.2. GSS-mediated face-to-face focus groups

Concerning *people* issues, the moderator must be an expert in the GSS technology, but his or her task is easier than in different-place settings due to the possibility of giving verbal instructions and seeing the participants' reactions. The moderator must be mentally prepared for back-up plans due to technology breakdowns, although they are rare. The participants can be recruited from a limited geographical distance as in traditional groups, but the groups can accommodate a larger number and more heterogeneous participants due to the parallel communication mode. The participants must possess fluent typing skills and they should be willing to use computers. However, no other technology usage skills than simple e-mail applications are needed.

The *process* must be planned carefully in advance, but several advantages accrue from the anonymous computer-mediated mode: domineering and group thinking are alleviated, confidential and honest sharing of opinions is encouraged, also negative or controversial feedback is easy to give, there are no social-rank related problems due to the equal process, and comments are easily retrievable from the written "group memory" also during the session. However, free-riding and flaming may appear due to anonymity, and the first comments might be overtly influential (anchoring effect). It is possible to include quick electronic polls or surveys in the sessions, and discuss the results immediately. Due to the pre-planned and structured process, it is easy to repeat the same agenda for several focus groups.

There is a need for dedicated room facilities with GSS *technology* (computers for all participants, special group software, and a common white screen, at the minimum). The equipment may however be rented from a service provider. The *costs* are high due to travelling and the need for technology and GSS expertise, but these costs are partially or even completely compensated for as there are no transcribing costs, and more participants can be included in groups at the same time. Accurate reports are immediately available with all computer-mediated communication (see Table 4 for a summary).

5.3. Online (distributed) focus groups

Many of the benefits and drawbacks of GSS-mediated face-to-face focus groups apply to online focus groups, too. Thus, we will mainly concentrate here on issues that are specific to different-place settings. Regarding *people*, the moderator must be an expert in the chosen technology platform, and her task is quite challenging in synchronous settings in case no additional audio or video conferencing systems are used in parallel. "Techies" might be inclined to conduct online groups although they may lack important qualifications needed for guiding group dynamics. The moderator should be able to handle technology problems, which are quite possible as the participants use their own computers with a variety of internet browsers. There are no limits to the geographical participation, although in synchronous

Table 4 Benefits and drawbacks of GSS-mediated, face-to-face focus groups

Benefits	Drawbacks
+ Possibility to contribute simultaneously: efficiency increased, everybody's answers collected for memory	– The medium is less rich (lack of body language, facial expressions etc.), text may be misunderstood
+ Supports larger groups (e.g. 15–25) and more heterogeneous groups	– High travelling costs (participants and moderators)
+ Possibility for anonymous contributions: encourages confidential and honest sharing of opinions. The comments can however be tagged to enable identification of the same person's comments	– High rental costs of venue with GSS
+ Group thinking (social conformity) as well as domineering are alleviated	– Moderator must have expertise on GSS technology
+ Participants feel more comfortable giving negative or controversial feedback	– Not everybody is willing to use computers
+ Ideas are not evaluated based on the presenter	– A backup plan needed in case of technology breakdown
+ The process usually stays focused without any external distractions (and if they happen, the facilitator can respond immediately)	– Fluent typing skills are needed; varying typing speeds may have unfavourable effects on the process
+ Possibility to include quick electronic surveys and polls, also discuss results and pinpoint disagreements	– Anonymity might induce free-riding or flaming (less discretion and tact)
+ Transcription expenses are eliminated, the transcripts are complete and immediately available	– Not suitable if capturing body language is vital
+ Structured agenda aids in keeping time and replicating several groups with different participants	– Possibility for an anchoring effect (first comment may be overtly influential)
+ Moderator may give instructions verbally	

settings separate groups are needed when time zone differences are too large. The number of participants in asynchronous settings can be larger than in same-time settings, and the participants do not need as fluent typing skills. There is no need to dress-up, and people who are normally hard to recruit can participate more flexibly in their own homes or offices and even at the time that is the most suitable for them. Youth, especially, is very accustomed to communicating via the Internet.

The *process* needs to be even more carefully planned and administered than in face-to-face situations, and instructions need to be extremely clear and simple. The process advantages of the anonymous communication mode are practically the same as mentioned in the GSS section above. Clients may easily view the group discussion without participants being aware of their presence. However, the process is more exposed to external distractions, e.g. from family members or colleagues. Also, faster typists and those with faster Internet connections may have more influence on the discussion.

There is a no need for dedicated facilities, and in the simplest form, online focus groups can be conducted using freely available discussion board or similar *technology*. With synchronous settings, it is necessary for the participants to test their connection to the dedicated forum in good time before the session starts. The *costs* are relatively low as there are neither travelling nor transcribing costs involved (see Table 5 for a summary).

Many market researchers recommend that topics related to web-based systems, information technology or the Internet are especially suitable for the

Table 5 Benefits and drawbacks of online focus groups (S or A in parenthesis if specific for synchronous or asynchronous)

Benefits	Drawbacks
+ No geographical limits for participation (except that separate groups may be needed for different time zones in S), also rural areas reached	− The medium is less rich (lack of body language, facial expressions etc.), text may be misunderstood
+ No travelling costs	− Not everybody is willing to use computers
+ Possibility to contribute simultaneously: efficiency increased, everybody's answers collected for memory	− Basic (A) or fluent (S) typing skills are needed for both participants and the moderator
+ Also suitable for heterogeneous groups	− Moderator must have expertise on the technology
+ Possibility for anonymous contributions: encourages confidential and honest sharing of opinions. The comments can however be tagged to enable identification of the same person's comments	− Need for an Internet connection
+ Group thinking (social conformity) as well as domineering are alleviated	− Online information security risks involved
+ Participants also feel more comfortable giving negative or controversial feedback	− Participants should pre-test the forum to eliminate technical difficulties (S)
+ Ideas are not evaluated based on the presenter	− Max. ten participants/group for effective management of online group dynamics (S)
+ Supports large groups of 25–40 participants (A)	− Faster typers and those with faster Internet connections may have too much influence (S)
+ Transcription expenses are eliminated	− More difficult to verify participant identity
+ Transcripts are complete and immediately available	− Moderators need to know how to assure that all participants are contributing
+ Convenient as there is no need to dress up, and participation is possible from home, office etc.	− Larger probability for outside distractions (S)
+ Possibility to contribute at a time that suits best (A)	− Youth audience requires that the moderator knows their "chat" vocabulary and use of emoticons etc.
+ Possibility to come back and continue discussion (A)	− Anonymity might induce free-riding or flaming (less discretion and tact)
+ Reaches groups that are hard to recruit otherwise (e.g. parents, business professionals with limited time)	− Not suitable if capturing body language is vital
+ Incentive costs are smaller for participants	− Not suitable if there is a need to show prototypes or 3D-models, or products need to be handheld

(continued)

Table 5 (continued)

Benefits	Drawbacks
+ Youth is already more accustomed to computer-mediated-communication than verbal discussions	− Not suitable if client material is highly confidential
+ Suitable for studying technology-related topics	− Show rates are lower than in FTF sessions, as participation requires a high level of motivation and interest. More over-recruitment is thus needed
+ Clients may view the group without participants being aware of their presence	− Developing rapport and gaining the trust of the participants is demanding
+ Provides social equalization and egalitarian data collection method as socio-economic status, ethnicity, nationality or gender may be unknown	− Physically demanding to type and read for 60–90 min virtually (S)
	− "Techies" may attempt to conduct groups, although they might lack important moderator qualifications
	− Bulletin boards may be too exhaustive too read, and participants may just answer their own opinions (A)
	− Bulletin boards may generate an enormous amount of text that requires extra reading and analysis time (A)
	− "Pair friendships" may develop (participants engage in their own dialogue and alienate the rest)

online environment. Thus, software engineering researchers should consider online focus group studies, too. Sweet (2001) concludes that the future promises many advancements for online groups including sophisticated visual aids, real-time video and sound, accurate voice recognition, and videoconferencing. We expect that the recent developments in IP-based multi-party video and audio conferencing tools will bring online practice forward in the next 5 years. Many end-users are already more familiar than business people with the utilization of web-cameras, Skype and Messenger conversations and conferences.

5.4. Summary of focus group comparisons

Researchers utilizing focus groups should weigh the benefits and drawbacks of these four main variations presented in Tables 3–5, and come to a conclusion as to which variation is best for their particular study. As Sweet (2001), Montoya-Weiss et al. (1998) and Zinchiak (2001) state, online (or other computer-mediated) focus groups are not going to replace traditional focus groups – merely the research arena is expanding as new tools are added to the pool of research techniques.

6. Discussion

The focus group method is, by its very nature, prone to problems associated with qualitative data. As the developers of models and theories may also act as the researchers responsible for the focus group session, there is an obvious danger of researcher bias influencing the results, either during the planning, during the sessions themselves, or during the analysis. However, e.g. Langford and McDonaugh (2003) mention that it is usually better to use a moderator who is an expert in the subject matter and not in professional facilitation. Thus, we recommend that disciplined, objective and rigorous instrumentation and data analysis methods are used in focus group studies and that all findings be based on traceable data.

We found the affinity grouping method to be a useful and effective tool in obtaining inputs from practitioners and users. While we do recognize the limitations posed by the short time available for discussions, we believe that it is also possible to address more complex issues with focus groups. Compared to consumer studies, the software engineering field contains some well-defined methods and standards that are used fairly consistently across the industry, such as the UML, CMMI, and FPA. Thus, it is possible to select a group of experts who are familiar with a given, complex technology and use the focus group session to elicit these experts' insights.

It is also possible to use brainstorming, scenario-based discussion, cognitive maps and a variety of other methods in a focus group. Langford and McDonaugh (2003) discuss these and 35 other tools and techniques that can be utilized especially regarding ergonomics and human factors design, but also regarding information systems. They posit a view of focus groups as a method that encompasses many tools, and not just a simple group interviewing technique. We also recommend the use of other stimulating techniques that fit the characteristics of the situation.

As our effort data indicates (see Table 1), the actual sessions constitute only a small share of total effort. Yet, these sessions provide more data and are perceived as value-adding sessions to participants as well. Thus, we recommend that more than one session be held when possible.

The role of the moderator is central in focus group sessions and is a particularly challenging task in the software engineering domain, due to the complexity of the technology and issues involved. The moderator should have experience or be trained in non-intrusive, neutral facilitation techniques and be cautious about his or her own bias in the session. A practice session should be mandatory for all focus group studies.

We wanted to include the electronic focus group comparison in this chapter as we believe that the computer-mediated technology is naturally prone to studies in the field of software engineering, as well as in IS studies in general. It is easier to get software users and developers to employ the technology than for example carpenters or other craftsmen. Moreover, the future users of software are more and more used to communicating via electronic media.

Our studies indicate that focus groups can provide valuable, complementary empirical data quickly at low cost. However, there are potential sources for unwanted bias. The method should be used properly and the sessions should be planned and executed well and with appropriate rigor.

Due to its apparent ease of use and low cost, some researchers may be tempted to use focus groups without proper planning and instrumentation. Such studies are likely to contain biases and ignore much of the experience available. Therefore we recommend that researchers take a closer look at the extensive variety of books on focus group research, e.g., by starting with the valuable book reviews by McQuarrie (1994, 2001). Langford and McDonaugh (2003) is also a valuable source to start with.

We hope that the empirical researchers in the research community and in industry learn to use the method with appropriate rigor. As the method is not frequently used in the software engineering domain, we hope that the community develops sound practices for applying the method so that it could establish itself as a reliable research method in the field.

We ourselves plan to continue using the method in our future studies and in addition we aim to develop repeatable focus group processes in the spirit of the newly established field of collaboration engineering (Briggs et al., 2003).

References

Anon., *Focus Group Kit*, Vol. 1–6, Sage Publications, Thousand Oaks, CA, 1997.

Adler, M., Ziglio, E., *Gazing into the Oracle: The Delphi Method and Its Application to Social Policy and Public Health*, Jessica Kingsley Pub, 1996.

Austin, T., Drakos, N., Mann, J., Web Conferencing Amplifies Dysfunctional Meeting Practices. Gartner Research Report Nr. G00138101, Gartner Inc., 2006.

Baker, S.L., Improving Business Services through the Use of Focus Groups, *Reference Quarterly*, 30(Spring):377–385, 1991.

Basili, V.R., Selby, R.W., Hutchens, D.H., Experimentation in Software Engineering, *IEEE Transactions on Software Engineering*, 12(7):758–773, 1986.

Benbasat, I., Rethinking Diversity in Information Systems Research, *Information Systems Research*, 7(4):389–399, 1996.

Boehm, B., Gruenbacher, P., Briggs, R.O., Developing Groupware for Requirements Negotiation: Lessons Learned, *IEEE Software*, 18(3):46–55, 2001.

Bogdan, R.C., Biklen, S.K., *Qualitative Research for Education: An Introduction to Theory and Methods*, Allyn and Bacon Inc., Boston, MA, 1982.

Bragge, J., den Hengst, M., Tuunanen, T., Virtanen, V., A Repeatable Collaboration Process for Developing a Road Map for Mobile Marketing. In Proceedings of the 11th Americas Conference on Information Systems AMCIS, 2005a.

Bragge, J., Marttiin, P., Tuunanen, T., Developing Innovative IS Services Together with Wide Audience End-Users, In Proceedings of the 38th Annual Hawaii International Conference on System Sciences, Los Alamitos, CA, pp. 1–10, 2005b.

Bragge, J., Merisalo-Rantanen, H., Hallikainen, P., Gathering Innovative End-User Feedback for Continuous Development of Information Systems: A Repeatable and Transferable E-Collaboration Process, *IEEE Transactions on Professional Communication*, 48(1):55–67, 2005c.

Bragge, J., Merisalo-Rantanen, H., Nurmi, A., Tanner, L., A Repeatable E-Collaboration Process Based on ThinkLets for Multi-Organization Strategy Development, *Group Decision and Negotiation*, 16(4):363–379, 2007a.

Bragge, J., Relander, S., Sunikka, A., Mannonen, P., Enriching Literature Reviews with Computer-Assisted Research Mining. Case: Profiling Group Support Systems Research. In Proceedings of the 40th Annual Hawaii International Conference on System Sciences (HICSS'07), IEEE, Los Alamitos, CA, pp. 1–10, 2007b.

Briggs, R.O., De Vreede, G.J., Nunamaker, J.F., Collaboration Engineering with ThinkLets to Pursue Sustained Success with Group Support Systems, *Journal of Management Information Systems*, 19(4):31–64, 2003.

Buhrer, H.K., Software Development: What It is, What It should be, and How to get There, *ACM SIGSOFT Software Engineering Notes*, 28(2):1–4, 2007.

Chen, M., Nunamaker, J.F., The Architecture and Design of a Collaborative Environment for Systems Definition, *Data-Base*, 22(1–2):22–29, 1991.

Clapper, D.L., Massey, A.P., Electronic Focus Groups: A Framework for Exploration, *Information and Management*, 30(1):43–50, 1996.

Daft, R., Lengel, R., Organizational Information Requirements, Media Richness, and Structural Design, *Management Science*, 32(5):554–570, 1986.

De Vreede, G.J., Fruhling, A., Chakrapani, A., A Repeatable Collaboration Process for Usability Testing, In Proceedings of the 38th Annual Hawaii International Conference on System Sciences, Los Alamitos, CA, pp. 1–10, 2005.

Easton, G., Easton, A., Belch, M., An Experimental Investigation of Electronic Focus Groups, *Information and Management*, 40:717–727, 2003.

Edmunds, H., *The Focus Group Research Handbook*, NTC Business Books, Lincolnwood, IL, 1991.

Edmunds, H., *The Focus Group Research Handbook*, NTC Business Books and American Marketing Association, Lincolnwood, IL, 1999.

Elfvengren, K., Karkkainen, H., Torkkeli, M., Tuominen, M., A GDSS Based Approach for the Assessment of Customer Needs in Industrial Markets, *International Journal of Production Economics*, 89(3):272–292, 2004.

Feig, B., How to Run a Focus Group, *American Demographics*, 11(December):36–37, 1989.

Fern, E.F., The Use of Focus Groups for Idea Generation: The Effects of Group Size, Acquaintanceship, and Moderator on Response Quantity and Quality, *Journal of Marketing Research*, 19(1):1–13, 1982.

Fjermestad, J., Hiltz, S.R., An Assessment of Group Support Systems Experimental Research: Methodology and Results, *Journal of Management Information Systems*, 15(3):7–150, 1999.

Fjermestad, J., Hiltz, S.R., Group Support Systems: A Descriptive Evaluation of Case and Field Studies, *Journal of Management Information Systems*, 17(3):112–157, 2000.

Fraunhofer USA Inc., Summary of the Third eWorkshop on Agile Methods, Center for Experimental Software Engineering, http://fc-md.umd.edu/projects/Agile/3rd-eWorkshop/summary3rdeWorksh.htm, 2002.

Galliers, R.D., Choosing Appropriate Information Systems Research Approaches: A Revised Taxonomy, in: *Information Systems Research: Contemporary Approaches and Emerging Traditions*, H.-E. Nissen, H.K. Klein and R. Hirschheim, eds. Elsevier Science Publishers, Amsterdam, pp. 327–345, 1991.

Ghauri, P., Grønhaug, K., Kristianslund, I., *Research Methods in Business Studies*, Prentice-Hall, Englewood Cliffs, NJ, 1995.

Glass, R.A., A Structure-Based Critique of Contemporary Computing Research, *Journal of Systems and Software*, 28(1):3–7, 1995.

Gruenbacher, P., Halling, M., Biffl, S., Kitapci, H., Boehm, B.W., Repeatable Quality Assurance Techniques for Requirements Negotiation, In Proceedings of the 36th Annual Hawaii International Conference on System Sciences, Los Alamitos, CA, pp. 1–9, 2003.

Halling, M., Gruenbacher, P., Biffl, S., Tailoring a COTS Group Support System for Software Requirements Inspection, In Proceedings of the 16th Annual International Conference on Automated Software Engineering, IEEE, Los Alamitos, CA 201–208, 2001.

Hansen, K., Hansen, R.S., Using an Asynchronous Discussion Board for Online Focus Groups: A Protocol and Lessons Learned, In Proceedings of the College Teaching and Learning Conference, Clute Institute for Academic Research, Littleton, Colorado 1–8, 2006.

Judd, C.M., Smith, E.R., Kidder, L.H., *Research Methods in Social Relations*, Harcourt Brace Jovanovich College Publishers, New York, 1991.

Juristo, N., Moreno, A.M., *Basics of Software Engineering Experimentation*, Kluwer Academic Publishers, Boston, MA, 2001.

Kitchenham, B., Dyba, T., Jorgensen, M., Evidence-Based Software Engineering. In Proceedings of 26th International Conference on Software Engineering, IEEE, Los Alamitos, CA, pp. 273–281, 2004.

Klein, E.E., Tellefsen, T., Herskovitz, P.J., The Use of Group Support Systems in Focus Groups: Information Technology Meets Qualitative Research, *Computers in Human Behavior*, 23(5):2113–2132, 2007.

Kontio, J., The Riskit Method for Software Risk Management, version 1.00. (College Park, MD, University of Maryland, 1997) CS-TR-3782/UMIACS-TR-97-38, Computer Science Technical Reports.

Kontio, J., Software Engineering Risk Management: A Method, Improvement Framework, and Empirical Evaluation. Doctoral dissertation. (2001), Helsinki University of Technology, publisher: Center of Excellence, ISBN: 952-5136-22-1.

Kontio, J., Bragge, J., Lehtola, L., Using the Focus Group Method in Software Engineering: Obtaining Practitioner and User Experiences. In Proceedings of the International Symposium on Empirical Software Engineering (ISESE), ACM-IEEE, Los Alamitos, CA pp. 271–280, 2004.

Krueger, R.A., Casey, M.A., *Focus Groups: A Practical Guide for Applied Research*, Sage Publications, Thousand Oaks, CA, 2000.

Langford, J., McDonaugh, D., *Focus Groups. Supporting Effective Product Development*, Taylor and Francis, London, 2003.

Lehtola, L., Kauppinen, M., Kujala, S., Requirements-Prioritization-Challenges-in-Practice. In Fifth International Conference on Product Focused Software Process Improvement, 2004.

Liou, Y.I., Chen, M., Using Group Support Systems and Joint Application Development for Requirements Specification, *Journal of Management Information Systems*, 10(3):25–41, 1993.

Massey, A.P., Wallace, W.A., Focus Groups as a Knowledge Elicitation Technique, *IEEE Transactions on Knowledge and Data Engineering*, 3(2):193–200, 1991.

McQuarrie, E.F., New Books in Review: The Handbook for Focus Group Research & Successful Focus Groups: Advancing the State of the Art, *Journal of Marketing Research*, 31:377–380, 1994.

McQuarrie, E.F., New Books in Review: The Mirrored Window: Focus Groups from a Moderator's Point of View & Advanced Focus Group Research, *Journal of Marketing Research*, 38(November):515–516, 2001.

McQuarrie, E.F., McIntyre, S.H., Focus Groups and the Development of New Products by Technologically Driven Companies: Some Guidelines, *Journal of Product Innovation Management*, 1:40–47, 1986.

Miles, M.B., Huberman, A.M., *Qualitative Data Analysis: A Sourcebook of New Methods*, Sage Publications, Thousand Oaks, CA, 1984.

Montoya-Weiss, M.M., Massey, A.P., Clapper, D.L., On-line Focus Groups: Conceptual Issues and a Research Tool, *European Journal of Marketing*, 32(7/8):713–723, 1998.

Morgan, D.L., Designing Focus Group Research, in: *Tools for Primary Care Research. Volume 2: Research Methods for Primary Care*, M. Stewart, F. Tudiver, M.J. Bass, E.V. Dunn and P.G. Norton, eds. Sage Publications, Thousand Oaks, CA, 1992.

Morgan, D.L., Focus Groups, *Annual Review of Sociology*, 22(August):129–152, 1996.

Morgan, D.L., *Focus Groups as Qualitative Research*, Sage Publications, Thousand Oaks, CA, 1997.

Myers, M., Qualitative Research in Information Systems, http://www.qual.auckland.ac.nz/, 2004.

Nambisan, S., Information Systems as a Reference Discipline for New Product Development, *MIS Quarterly*, 27(1):1–18, 2003.

Nambisan, S., Wilemon, D., Software Development and New Product Development: Potentials for Cross-Domain Knowledge Sharing, *IEEE Transactions on Engineering Management*, 47(2):211–220, 2000.

Neter, J., Waksberg, J., A Study of Response Errors in Expenditure Data from Household Interviews, *Journal of the American Statistical Association*, 59:18–55, 1964.

Newby, R., Soutar, G., Watson, J., Comparing Traditional Focus Groups with a Group Support Systems (GSS) Approach for Use in SME Research, *International Small Business Journal*, 21(4):421–433, 2003.

Nielsen, J., The Use and Misuse of Focus Groups, *IEEE Software*, 14(January):94–95, 1997.

Nunamaker, J.F., Dennis, A.R., Valacich, J.S., Vogel, D.R., George, J.F., Electronic Meeting Systems to Support Group Work, *Communications of the ACM*, 34(7):40–61, 1991.

O'Connor, H., Madge, C., "Focus Groups in Cyberspace": Using the Internet for Qualitative Research, *Qualitative Market Research*, 6(2):133–143, 2003.

Oringderff, J., 'My Way': Piloting and Online Focus Group, *International Journal of Qualitative Methods*, 3(3):1–10, 2004.

Parent, M., Gallupe, R.B., Salisbury, W.D., Handelman, J.M., Knowledge Creation in Focus Groups: Can Group Technologies Help?, *Information and Management*, 38(1):47–58, 2000.

Patton, M.Q., *Qualitative Evaluation and Research Methods*, Sage Publications, Thousand Oaks, CA, 1990.

Reid, D.J., Reid, F.J.M., Online Focus Groups. An In-Depth Comparison of Computer-Mediated and Conventional Focus Group Discussions, *International Journal of Market Research*, 47(2):131–162, 2005.

Rodgers, T.L., Dean, D.L., Nunamaker, J.F., Increasing Inspection Efficiency through Group Support Systems, In Proceedings of the 37th Annual Hawaii International Conference on System Sciences, Los Alamitos, CA, pp. 1–10, 2004.

Rubin, J., *Handbook of Usability Testing: How to Plan, Design, and Conduct Effective Tests*, Wiley, New York, 1994.

Stewart, D.W., Shamdasani, P.N., *Focus Groups: Theory and Practice*, Sage Publications, Thousand Oaks, CA, 1990.

Sunikka, A., Usability evaluation of the Helsinki School of Economics Website. Master's thesis, Helsinki School of Economics, 2004.

Sweet, C., Designing and Conducting Virtual Focus Groups, *Qualitative Market Research*, 4(3):130–135, 2001.

Taylor, S.J., Bogdan, R., *Introduction to Qualitative Research Methods*, Wiley, New York, 1984.

Templeton, J.F., *The Focus Group: A Strategic Guide to Organizing, Conducting and Analyzing the Focus Group Interview*, McGraw-Hill Professional Publishing, New York, 1994.

Ten-Pow, J., Fundamentals for Those Considering Online Focus Groups, On Survey Research Intelligence, http://www.onsurvey.ca/supplemental/onfocus.pdf, 2003.

Tichy, W.F., Should Computer Scientists Experiment More?, *IEEE Computer*, 31(5):32–40, 1998.

Tichy, W.F., Lukowicz, P., Prechelt, L., Heinz, E.A., Experimental Evaluation in Computer Science: A Quantitative Study, *Journal of Systems and Software*, 28(1):9–18, 1995.

Turney, L., Pocknee, C., Virtual focus groups: New technologies, new opportunities, new learning environments, Proceedings of the 21st ASCILITE Conference, University of Wollongong, New South Wales, Australia, pp. 905–912.

Tuunanen, T., Rossi, M., Engineering a Method for Wide Audience Requirements Elicitatation and Integrating It to Software Development, In Proceedings of the 37th Annual Hawaii International Conference on System Sciences, Los Alamitos, CA, 2004.

Van Genuchten, M., Cornelissen, W., Van Dijk, C., Supporting Inspections with an Electronic Meeting System, *Journal of Management Information Systems*, 14(3):165–178, 1997.

Van Genuchten, M., Van Dijk, C., Scholten, H., Using Group Support Systems for Software Inspections, *IEEE Software*, 18(3):60–65, 2001.

Vitharana, P., Ramamurthy, K., Computer-Mediated Group Support, Anonymity, and the Software Inspection Process: An Empirical Investigation, *IEEE Transactions on Software Management*, 29(2):167–180, 2003.

Wellner, A.S., The New Science of Focus Groups, American Demographics, March 1 29–33, 2003.

Widdows, R., Hensler, T.A., Wyncott, M.H., The Focus Group Interview: A Method for Assessing User's Evaluation of Library Service, *College and Research Libraries*, 52(July):352–359, 1991.

Wohlin, C., Runeson, P., Host, M., Ohlsson, M.C., *Experimentation in Software Engineering: An Introduction*, Kluwer Academic Publishers, Boston, MA, 1999.

Wohlin, C., Höst, M., Henningsson, K., Empirical Research Methods in Software Engineering, Lecture Notes in Computer Science, Vol. 2765 7–23, 2003.

Zelkowitz, M.V., Wallace, D.R., Experimental Models for Validating Technology, *IEEE Computer*, 31(5):23–31, 1998.

Zinchiak, M., Online Focus Group FAQs, Quirk's Marketing Research Review, http://www.quirks.com/articles/a2001/20010712.aspx?searchID=2619905, July/August 2001.

Chapter 5
Simulation Methods

Mark Müller and Dietmar Pfahl

Abstract This chapter aims to raise awareness about the usefulness and importance of simulation in support of software engineering. Simulation is applied in many critical engineering areas and enables one to address issues before they become problems. Simulation – in particular process simulation – is a state of the art technology to analyze process behaviour, risks and complex systems with their inherent uncertainties. Simulation provides insights into the designs of development processes and projects before significant time and cost has been invested, and can be of great benefit in support of training. The systematic combination of simulation methods with empirical research has the potential for becoming a powerful tool in applied software engineering research. The creation of virtual software engineering laboratories helps to allocate available resources of both industry and academia more effectively.

1. Simulation in the Context of Software Engineering

This chapter aims to raise awareness about the usefulness and importance of simulation in support of software engineering. Simulation is a standard technology in many engineering disciplines and has been successfully applied in manufacturing, economics, biology, and social science. Why can simulation enhance traditional software engineering, too? Simulation models are means to analyze the behaviour of complex processes. In the software process literature, according to our understanding, there is a general agreement that people who understand the static process (i.e., process activities, artefacts, resources, roles, and their relationships), and have data, still have difficulties to anticipate the actual process behaviour. This is due to the inherent (dynamic) complexity of software development processes. Software processes can contain iterations, such as rework loops associated with correction of defects. This can lead to delays which may range from minutes to years. As a consequence it is almost impossible for human (mental) analysis to predict the outcome.

Traditionally, process analysis in software engineering research uses static process descriptions like flow charts. This approach does not shed much light on

F. Shull et al. (eds.), *Guide to Advanced Empirical Software Engineering.*

the behaviour of a process over time. Therefore, the usual way to analyze process behaviour is to perform the actual process in a case study and observe the results. This is a very costly way to perform process analysis, because it involves the active participation of engineers. Furthermore, results from a particular case study cannot necessarily be generalized to other contexts. Another way of analyzing processes is to simulate them. Simulation models help to clarify assumptions – often referred to as mental models, on how a process works. They visualize and quantify the implicit mental models about the causes that govern the observed process behaviour and thus support understanding, analysis, prediction, and decision-support.

Simulation models are like virtual laboratories where hypotheses about observed problems can be tested, and corrective policies can be experimented with before they are implemented in the real system. Experience from applications in other fields than software engineering indicates that significant benefits can be drawn from introducing the use of simulation for management decision support. Furthermore, systematic experimentation with simulation models and the integration of simulation-based experiments with empirical research (i.e., case studies and controlled experiments) can support the building of a software development theory (Rus et al., 2002). Simulation-based virtual software engineering laboratories (Münch et al., 2003, 2005) can help focus experimentation in both industry and academia for this purpose, while saving effort by avoiding experiments in real-world settings that have little chances of generating significant new knowledge.

In practice, process simulation models are frequently used to support project planning and estimation. In a competitive world, accurate predictions of cost, quality and schedule provide a significant advantage. For example, if cost estimates are too high, bids are lost, if too low, organizations find themselves in a difficult financial situation. In this context, simulation is a risk management method. It offers not only estimates of cost, but also estimates of cost uncertainty. Simulation also allows for detailed analysis of process costs (Activity Based Costing).

Simulation is effective only if both the model, and the data used to drive the model, accurately reflect the real world. If quantitative output is expected, a simulation can only be executed if it is supplied with quantitative expert estimates or measurement data. Simulation may use industry data or results of quantitative experiments. In order to limit data collection effort, the simulation modeller has to focus on key variables, such as the percentage of design documents which pass or fail review. Thus, as a side effect, simulation modelling supports the focusing of measurement programs on relevant factors of an engineering process.

This chapter is structured as follows: Section 2 explains how simulation models are developed. Section 3 summarizes the variety of application areas and provides references to relevant publications. Sections 4 and 5 describe the simulation techniques and tools used in software engineering. Section 6 provides a simulation reference model which helps to design process simulation models. Section 7 covers practical aspects of simulation modelling. Finally, the chapter concludes with an outlook for trends in future simulation modelling research.

2. The Process of Simulation Modelling in Software Engineering

This chapter provides an overview of the design and implementation of simulation models. Additional information about process simulation paradigms and general introductions can also be found in (Banks et al., 2000; Cellier, 1991; Law and Kelton, 1999). Detailed descriptions of process simulation modelling methods specialized to instances of the event-driven and continuous simulation modelling paradigms can be found in (Rus et al., 2003) and (Pfahl and Ruhe, 2002), respectively.

Any process simulation modelling process consists of at least five steps (cf. Fig. 1):

1. Formulation of the Problem Statement (modelling goal)
2. Specification of the Reference Behaviour (based on observation or hypothetical)
3. Identification of Model Concepts (physical processes, information flows, decision rules)
4. Implementation of Executable Model (formal, executable representation)
5. Model Experimentation

The starting point of any simulation modelling project is the identification and explicit formulation of a *problem statement*. The problem statement defines the modelling goal and helps to focus the modelling activities. In particular, it determines

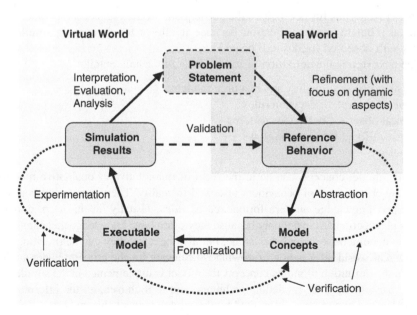

Fig. 1 Iterative process of simulation modelling

the model purpose and scope. For software process simulation models, Kellner et al. (1999) propose the following categories for model purpose and scope:

1. Purpose:
   (a) strategic management
   (b) planning, control and operational management
   (c) process improvement and technology adoption
   (d) understanding
   (e) training and learning
2. Scope:
   (a) a portion of the life cycle (e.g. design phase, code inspection, some or all of testing, requirements management)
   (b) a development project (e.g. single product development life cycle)
   (c) multiple, concurrent projects (e.g., across a department or division)
   (d) long-term product evolution (e.g. multiple, successive releases of a single product)
   (e) long-term organization (e.g., strategic organizational considerations spanning successive releases of multiple products over a substantial time period)

In order to make the problem statement suitable for simulation-based problem-solving, it is helpful to specify the *reference behaviour*. Reference behaviour captures the dynamic (i.e., time-dependent) variation of key attributes of real-world entities. The reference behaviour can be both observed problematic behaviour (e.g., of quality, effort, or cost), which are to be analyzed and improved, and/or a desired behaviour that is to be achieved. The importance of the reference behaviour for the modelling process is twofold. Firstly, it helps identify important model (output) parameters and thus further focuses the subsequent modelling steps. Secondly, it is a crucial input to model validation because it allows for comparing simulation results with observed (or desired) behaviour.

The next step is the definition of *model concepts*, which entail:

1. Existing process, quality, and resource models
2. Implicit or explicit decision rules
3. Typical observed behaviour patterns
4. Organizational information flows
5. Policies

Typically, model concepts can be in the form of quantitative or qualitative models, which are abstractions of behaviours observed in reality. They capture implicit and tacit expert knowledge and are formalized as rules. Usually, in this step, domain experts play a crucial role not only because they often have knowledge that cannot be found in documents or data bases alone, but also because they can help distinguish relevant real-world information from what is irrelevant for the problem under study.

After the definition of model concepts the model is implemented in the simulation tool. Consistent with the modelling technique and tool chosen, all the information, knowledge and experience represented by the model concepts has to be transformed into a computer executable language. The result is an *executable model*. Technical simulation modelling expertise is crucial in the transformation of model concepts into the formal model representation which eventually will be executed on a computer.

The last step is model calibration and experimentation with the executable model, producing *simulation results*. Simulation experiments are performed to understand the system's behaviour. Experimentation goes hand in hand with model calibration. Model calibration refers to the adjustment of simulation model parameters until the model output corresponds to real word data. Model calibration can be done based on expert estimates or through parameter fitting based on historic data. The calibration step is important in order to ensure that the model accurately reflects real-world behaviour and is required to build confidence in simulation results. After a model is calibrated, simulation experiments are performed to understand observed behaviour, to evaluate planning alternatives, or to explore improvement opportunities. At this stage, iteration is likely in model execution and modification as variables and model structures are changed and the simulation model results are compared against each other. Thus, experimentation not only provides simulation results, but also validates the simulation model. Guidance on how to design simulation experiments in general can be found in (Banks et al., 2000) and (Law and Kelton, 1999), and specifically for software processes in (Wakeland et al., 2003).

Like software development projects, simulation modelling involves verification and validation activities. In short, verification can be seen as an activity that ensures that the model fits its intended purpose, while validation can be seen as the activity that ensures that the model appropriately reflects the real-world behaviour. Verification and validation are continuing activities throughout the modelling and simulation life cycle. They help

1. To produce simulation models that represent system behaviour closely enough to be used as a substitute for the actual system when conducting experiments
2. To increase the credibility of simulation models to a level that makes them acceptable for managers and other decision makers

Verification activities check the internal correctness or appropriateness of a simulation model, i.e. they ensure that the model was constructed in the right way. In particular, verification checks whether the transformation steps defined by the simulation modelling process have been conducted correctly. For example, verification ensures that the identified model concepts have properly been implemented in the executable model. For verification activities, expert knowledge on the simulation modelling technique is a major requirement. To some extent, verification is supported by simulation modelling tools. For example, the consistency of units in model equations can be automatically checked by a tool.

Validation activities check the external correctness or appropriateness of a simulation model, i.e. they try to find out whether the right model (with regards to its purpose or application) was constructed. In particular, validation checks whether the model represents the structural and behavioural properties of the real system correctly (appropriately). For example, simulation results can be used to check the robustness or sensitivity of model behaviour for extreme values of input data. Even though validation can be partly supported by simulation modelling tools, expert knowledge about the real world system is needed to interpret the range of results obtained.

The simulation literature offers several proposals for verification and validation of simulation models (Balci, 2003; Banks et al., 2000; Barlas, 1989; Forrester and Senge, 1980; Law and Kelton, 1999; Sargent, 2003). For example, Balci (2003) proposes more than 30 different verification and validation techniques, classified into informal, static, dynamic, and formal. However, full verification and validation of simulation models whilst desirable, are often practically impossible due to cost and time restrictions (Pidd, 2004). Typically, only a subset of the available techniques and methods for model verification and validation are used.

3. Applications of Simulation in Software Engineering

Simulation models have been applied in many technical fields and are increasingly used for problems in business management and software engineering management. This section summarizes applications of simulation and some of the benefits that can be obtained.

Abdel-Hamid and Madnick (1991) were among the first to apply simulation modelling in software project management. They focused on project cost estimation and the effects of project planning on product quality and project performance. During the last decade many new process simulation applications in software engineering have been published, focusing on other specific topics within software project and process management [e.g., Christie (1999a); Kellner et al. (1999); Waeselynck and Pfahl (1994)]. Table 1 lists some significant publications in various application areas.

4. Simulation Techniques

The way in which a simulation model works depends on the modelling technique chosen. Generally, four important distinctions between types of simulation techniques can be made.

4.1. Deterministic Versus Stochastic Simulation

Simulation models that contain probabilistic components are called *stochastic*,[1] those that do not are termed *deterministic*. In the case of a deterministic simulation model, for a fixed set of input parameter values the resulting output parameter values

---

[1] The word "stochastic" is used here in a very broad sense of its meaning, i.e., referring to any type of source of randomness, including, for example, mutation or cross-over generation in genetic algorithms.

Table 1 Simulation applications in software engineering

Application area in software engineering	Selected publications
Project management	Lee and Miller (2004), Lin et al. (1997), Padberg (2006), Pfahl and Lebsanft (2000)
Risk management	Houston et al. (2001), Neu et al. (2002), Pfahl (2005)
Product and requirements engineering	Christie and Staley (2000), Ferreira et al. (2003), Höst et al. (2001), Lerch et al. (1997), Pfahl et al. (2006), Stallinger and Grünbacher (2001)
Process engineering	Bandinelli et al. (1995), Birkhölzer et al. (2004), Christie (1999b), Kuppuswami et al. (2003), Mišic et al. (2004), Powell et al. (1999), Raffo et al. (1999), Tvedt and Collofello (1995)
Strategic planning	Andersson et al. (2002), Pfahl et al. (2006), Williford and Chang (1999)
Quality assurance and management	Aranda et al. (1993), Briand and Pfahl (2000), Briand et al. (2004), Madachy (1996), Müller (2007), Raffo and Kellner (2000), Raffo et al. (2004), Rus (2002), Rus et al. (1999)
Software maintenance and evolution	Cartwright and Shepperd (1999), Smith et al. (2005), Wernick and Hall (2004)
Global software development	Roehling et al. (2000), Setamanit et al. (2006)
Software acquisition management and COTS	Choi and Scacchi (2001), Häberlein (2003), Häberlein and Gantner (2002), Ruiz et al. (2004), Scacchi and Boehm (1998)
Product-lines	Chen et al. (2005)
Training and education	Dantas et al. (2004), Drappa and Ludewig (1999), Madachy and Tarbet (2000), Oh Navarro and van der Hoek (2004), Pfahl et al. (2001)

will always be the same for simulation runs. In the case of a stochastic simulation model, the output parameter values may vary depending on stochastic variation of the values of input parameters or intermediate (internal) model variables. Since the variation of input and intermediate variables is generated by random sampling from given statistical distributions, it is important to repeat stochastic simulation runs for a sufficient number of times in order to be able to observe the statistical distribution of output parameter values. This number depends on limitations to computing power and how much confidence in simulation results is required.

4.2. Static Versus Dynamic Simulation

Static simulation models capture the variation of model parameters at one single point in time, while dynamic simulation models capture the behaviour of model parameters over a specified period of time.

Static simulation in software engineering is often used as a reference to stochastic Monte Carlo simulation which does not investigate behaviour over time. Related examples can be found in (Briand and Pfahl, 2000; Houston, 2003; McCabe, 2003).

4.3. Continuous Versus Event-Driven Simulation

Dynamic simulation models can be either continuous or event-driven. The difference between continuous and event-driven simulation models is the way in which the internal state of the model is calculated.

Continuous simulation models update the values of the model variables representing the model state at equidistant time steps based on a fixed set of well-defined model equations. Essentially, the model equations in continuous simulation models establish a set of time-dependent linear differential equations of first or higher order. Since such mathematical systems usually cannot be solved analytically, the differential equations are transformed into difference equations and solved via numerical integration. The most popular representative of continuous simulation is System Dynamics (SD) (Coyle, 1996). SD was originally invented by Jay Forrester in the late 1950s (Forrester, 1961) and has its roots in cybernetics and servomechanisms (Richardson, 1991). Since the end of the 1980s, when Abdel-Hamid and Madnick published the first SD model for software project management support, more than 100 other SD models in the application domain of software engineering have been published (Pfahl et al., 2006). Thus, SD can be considered the most frequently used dynamic simulation technique in this domain.

Event-driven simulation models update the values of the model variables as new events occur. There exist several types of event-driven simulation techniques. The most frequently used is discrete-event (DE) simulation. DE simulation models are typically represented by a network of activities (sometimes called stations) and items that flow through this network. The set of activities and items represent the model's state. The model's state changes at the occurrence of new events, triggered by combinations of items' attribute values and activities' processing rules. Events are typically generated when an item moves from one activity to another. As this can happen at any point in time, the time between changes in the model state can vary in DE simulations. There exist several other – but less popular – types of event-driven simulation, namely Petri-net based simulation (Bandinelli et al., 1995; Fernström, 1993; Gruhn and Saalmann, 1992; Mizuno et al., 1997), rule-based simulation (Drappa et al., 1995; Mi and Scacchi, 1990), state-based simulation (Humphrey and Kellner, 1989; Kellner and Hansen, 1989), or agent-based simulation (Huang and Madey, 2005; Madey et al., 2002).

4.4. Quantitative Versus Qualitative Simulation

Quantitative simulation requires that the values of model parameters are specified as real or integer numbers. Hence, a major prerequisite of quantitative simulation is either the availability of empirical data of sufficient quality and quantity or the availability of experts that are willing to make quantitative estimates of model parameters. Often, the quantitative modelling approach is costly and time-consuming and might not be appropriate for simulations that aim at delivering simple trend analyses. Qualitative simulation is a useful approach if the goal is to understand general behaviour patterns of dynamic systems, or when conclusions must be drawn from insufficient data.

QUAF (Qualitative Analysis of Causal Feedback) is a qualitative simulation technique for continuous process systems (Rose and Kramer, 1991). The method requires no numerical information beyond the signs and relative values of certain groups of model parameters. QSIM (Qualitative SIMulation) is another well-established qualitative technique for continuous simulation (Kuipers, 1986). Instead of quantifying the parameters of the differential equations underlying the continuous simulation model, it is only required to specify the polarity (i.e., positive or negative) of model functions, indicating whether they represent an increase or decrease of a quantity over time.

In the case of event-driven simulation, for example, Petri-net based and rule-based simulation can be conducted purely qualitatively, if events (e.g., the activation of transitions in Petri-nets, or the execution of a rule in rule-based systems) are triggered exclusively based on the evaluation of non-quantitative conditions.

4.5. Hybrid Simulation

Dynamic simulation models that combine continuous with event-driven or deterministic with stochastic elements are called hybrid simulation models. One benefit of hybrid approaches is the possibility to combine the advantages of stochastic, continuous and event-driven models. In the case of hybrid models that combine continuous and event-driven simulation, however, the drawback is increased model complexity. An example of a hybrid simulation model that combines continuous with event-driven simulation can be found in (Martin and Raffo, 2001).

5. Simulation Tools

Today, many software tools are available to support the various simulation techniques described above. Compared to the first tools available in the 1960s, 1970s, and 1980s, most of today's more popular tools have a user-friendly interface and are inexpensive, making them practical to use for a large variety of decision making situations. Today, most tools

1. Allow for rapid model development through using, for example
   (a) Drag and drop of iconic building blocks
   (b) Graphical element linking
   (c) Syntactic constraints on how elements are linked
2. Are very reliable
3. Require little training
4. Are easy to understand

Because of these features, simulation tools allow modellers to develop large detailed models rapidly. Modern tools have followed the evolution of software languages and software development environments. Now they focus on model design and a proper visualization rather than on programming the simulation logic.

The simulation tools in today's market place are robust and reasonably inexpensive. Most tools cost in the range of $1,000–10,000, and free versions are available for experimentation and evaluation. They run on standard PC hardware, and are therefore affordable even for small organizations with tight budgets.

The number of simulation tools is large, in particular if one counts the ever-growing number of simulation environment research prototypes developed at universities all over the world. In principle, a simulation model based on any of the above mentioned simulation techniques can also be implemented in an ordinary programming languages (e.g., Java®), or by using general purpose simulation languages (e.g., MATLAB®). However, several commercial simulation tools use the most important simulation techniques and are suited to support software engineering problems. Table 2 characterizes three popular examples of simulation tools supporting SD, DE, and Monte Carlo simulation, respectively.

The choice of a simulation tool environment depends on several factors. Since the prices are comparatively low, the most important factor is the appropriateness of the simulation technique that is supported. In a professional simulation environment, in conjunction to the simulation modelling tool, other tools are often used. Professional simulation studies typically involve information systems or data bases which store the input, calibration, and output data, a statistical distribution fitter to analyze the calibration data, and an optimizer. High-end tools such as the more expensive versions of VENSIM® and EXTEND® already include the distribution fitters and optimizers.

Table 2 Examples of commercial simulation tools used in software engineering

Tool name	Main focus	Characterization	Interesting features
VENSIM® (Vensim, 2006)	Support of SD simulation	Dynamic, continuous, deterministic and stochastic, quantitative	Optimization function, calibration support, graphical modelling language (using standard SD symbols), animation, can emulate event-driven simulation to some extend by introducing if-then-else-conditions
EXTEND® (Extend, 2006)	Support of DE and SD simulation	Dynamic, event-driven and continuous, deterministic and stochastic, quantitative	Optimization support, graphical modelling language, strong modularization capability; statistical fitting (StatFit®), library source code available
@RISK® (@Risk, 2007)	Monte Carlo simulation	Static, deterministic, stochastic, quantitative	Can easily be integrated with standard spreadsheet tools (i.e., Microsoft's EXCEL®), provides functionality for distribution fitting (BestFit®)

Next follows a brief introduction into the SD modelling tool VENSIM®, which will be used in the presentation of a process simulation example in Sect. 6 below.

5.1. Essentials of System Dynamics Models

SD models are represented by a set of difference equations, which is resolved by numerical integration. Model variables, which represent the model state are called *levels* and have the following form:

$$\text{Level}\,(t + dt) = \text{Level}(t) + \text{Integral}\,\big[\,\text{Rate\_in}(t)\, - \,\text{Rate\_out}(t)\big]\,dt \qquad (1)$$

The value of a level at a certain point in time[2] depends on its value at the previous discrete point in time plus the integral of the inflows minus the outflows. The initialization of the level happens at the start time of a simulation. In the world of difference equations this would correspond to the starting conditions. In the example given by (1) there is only one inflow, represented by the *rate* variable Rate_in(t) and one outflow, represented by Rate_out(t). Level variables can be considered as containers or reservoirs that accumulate some tangible (e.g., a pile of papers) or intangible (e.g., number of defects in a documents or motivation level of developers) entities, represented by some countable attribute.

In the physical world, the quantities of the accumulated commodities in a reservoir can be regulated through inflow and outflow pipes, each pipe having a valve. In SD models rate variables play the role of valves. Like levels, rates are represented by equations. Rates can depend on levels, e.g., if information feedback concerning the quantity in a level affects the rate of flow elsewhere in the model, on constants, or on auxiliary variables, which are used as abbreviations for intermediate calculations to break up more complex computations. (2) gives an example of a rate variable that represents the development rate (inflow) of a design document (level variable DesignDocSize). If DesignDocSize(t) is less than the estimated expected size of the design document (constant TargetSize), then the daily amount of design documentation added to DesignDocSize equals the product of the number of active designers (Workforce allocated at time t) and the average productivity per person (constant AveragePr oductivityPerPerson). If the design document is complete, i.e., DesignDocSize ≥ TargetSize, then there is nothing to do and the rate variable DesignDevelopment Rate equals 0. Thus no more is added to DesignDocSize unless or until some other activity in the model reduces DesignDocSize or increases TargetSize.

---

[2] "dt" denotes a time step from one discrete point in time to the next.

$$\text{DesignDevelopmentRate}(t) =$$
$$\text{IF THEN ELSE}$$
$$\left(\text{DesignDocSize}(t) < \text{TargetSize},\right. \tag{2}$$
$$\left.\text{Workforce}(t)*\text{AverageProductivityPerPerson, } 0\right)$$

5.2. A System Dynamics Tool: VENSIM®

The VENSIM tool offers a development workbench supporting both textual and graphical model representations. The symbols that are used for the basis model variables and constants follow a de-facto-standard for SD modelling. Level variables are represented as boxes, while rates are represented as valves on pipes (double lines) connected with these boxes. Constants and auxiliary variables are simply represented by their names. Flows of information are represented by single-line arrows.

Figure 2 shows a screen shot of the VENSIM® modelling workbench with a loaded view (sub-model) of a SD model representing the design phase of a software development project. The flow through the pipes attached to level variables (e.g., *design to do size* and *design doc size* in Fig. 3) is regulated by rate variables, represented by valve symbols (e.g., *development activity* in Fig. 3). Auxiliary

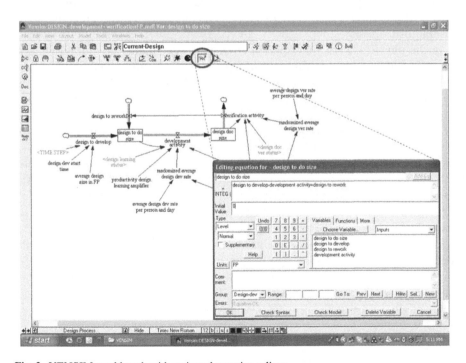

Fig. 2 VENSIM workbench with activated equation editor

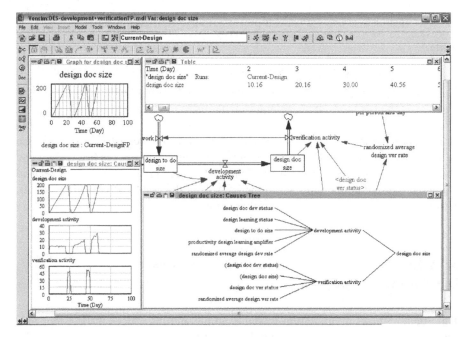

Fig. 3 VENSIM workbench with activated analysis and output tools

variables and constants are represented simply by their names. Values of level, rate, or auxiliary variables are calculated by evaluating functions of the form $y = f (x_1, ..., x_n)$, where $x_1, ..., x_n$ are other variables and constants. The variables and constants involved in such a function are illustrated by a connecting arc (or pipe).

The definition of a function is done through a text-based equation editor. The equation editor window automatically pops up if the details of an equation have not yet been fully defined and the workbench button $[y = x^2]$ is pressed (see Fig. 2). The equation editor not only provides an input window for specifying the exact function but also provides fields for specifying the variable unit and an explanatory comment. The equation editor automatically performs simple syntax and consistency checks. There exists also an equivalent textual representation of the entire model (not shown in Fig. 2). The textual representation of model equations has the advantage that string insertion, deletion, and renaming can easily be performed for the complete model.

The list of buttons directly above the graphical modelling panel offers specialized functionality for adding, deleting, removing, renaming, hiding, and showing of model variables. The column of buttons on the left hand side of the modelling panel provides specialized functionality for model analysis and simulation output presentation in the form of graphs or tables (cf. Fig. 3). For example, the window in the lower right corner of the screen shot presented in Fig. 3 shows two levels of causal dependencies between variables. Values shown in parentheses indicate feedback loops. From the open window within the modelling panel one sees that:

$$\text{design doc size} = f \left(\text{development activity, verification activity}\right) \quad (3)$$

while

$$\text{development activity} = f \text{ (design doc dev status, design learning status,}$$
$$\text{design to do size, productivity design learning amplifier,} \quad (4)$$
$$\text{randomized average design dev rate)}$$

Graphs showing the reverse dependencies, i.e., variable or constant uses, can also be automatically generated (not shown in Fig. 3). Other windows in Fig. 3 show the output of one simulation run (here: Current-Design) in the form of tables and graphs (lower and upper windows in the left half of the graphical modelling panel), as well as information about the model structure.

6. A Reference Simulation Model for Software Development Processes

This section shows a simulation model example and introduces the concept of a simulation reference process. The model is implemented as a stochastic SD model using the VENSIM® tool. Based on the example, a comparison between SD simulation and DE simulation will be made, and the advantages and disadvantages of each technique discussed.

6.1. A Generic Software Development Process

The following example presents a generic – in the sense of re-usable and adaptable – implementation of a standard process typically occurring in any constructive software development phase.

The left-hand side of Fig. 4 shows a typical development and verification work-flow of any type of software-related artefacts. The work-flow presentation uses the following symbols: boxes (for artefacts), ovals (for activities), hexagons (for resources), and arcs (representing *uses*, *produces*, and *consumes* relationships). An artefact may be, for example, a requirements, design, test, or code document. The actual artefact to be developed and verified is positioned in the centre of the work-flow. Before the development of this artefact can start, some input information must be available. For example, a design documents needs to know which requirements have been specified in a previous project stage. The development activity transforms an available artefact input into a new or modified artefact, e.g., a set of requirements into a design document. This artefact is then checked in a verification activity. The result of the verification activity, e.g., an inspection, is a list of defects in the newly created or modified artefact, which in turn is the basis for rework of

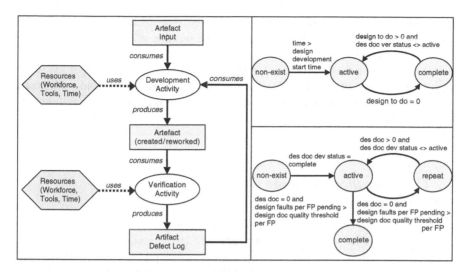

Fig. 4 Generic artefact development/verification process

the artefact. The rework loop is indicated in Fig. 4 by the *consumes*-relationship between the artefact defect log and the development activity. No distinction is made between initial work and rework performed on previous output. Activities use resources, e.g., personnel (implying some cost), tools (also incurring some cost, and supporting certain techniques), techniques (implying a need to quantify productivity), and time.

For larger simulation models, covering more than one stage of the software development process, instances of the generic work-flow shown in Fig. 4 can be combined sequentially by connecting work-flows that create predecessor artefacts with work-flows that create successor artefacts, and concurrently to represent work-flows conducted in parallel that produce separate instances of artefacts of the same type.

The right-hand side of Fig. 4 shows the control of the work-flow, expressed in terms of states that the artefact can assume in relation to its development (upper diagram) and verification activities (lower diagram), and the transitions between states, including the conditions for activating a transition. For example, a development activity related to the artefact "requirements" can either have not yet been started ("non-exist"), be active ("active"), or it can be completed ("complete"). The transition from "non-exist" into "active" is triggered as soon as the elapsed time t is greater than the defined starting time of the related development activity. A transition from "active" to "complete" is triggered, if all of the artefact inputs have been used up in producing the output document (e.g., a design or code document). If rework needs to be done in order to correct defects detected during verification, then a transition from "complete" back to "active" is triggered. The state-transition diagram associated with the verification activity is similar to that of the development activity. The only difference is its fourth state, "repeat." This state signals that a repetition of the verification activity is needed after rework of the defects found in the previous verification round has been completed. The decision as to whether the verification step must be repeated depends on the number of defects found per size unit of the artefact. For example, if requirements size is measured in Function Points (FPs), then a threshold value can be defined in terms of defects per FP. If the number of detected defects per FP is larger then the defined threshold value, then verification has to be repeated, otherwise the document is considered (finally) complete after rework.

6.2. Conceptualization of the Generic Software Development Process

While the work-flow on the left-hand side of **Fig**. 4 is static, the control-flow presented on the right-hand side contains some behavioural information. Both static and behavioural information contained in the generic software development (and verification) process are the basis for the creation of a related simulation model, e. g., using the System Dynamics (SD). As will be shown below, the process shown in Fig. 4 is actually a re-usable pattern that captures the most important aspects of the work-flow, including activities and artefacts, as well as resources that will be used. It also captures some behavioural aspects by specifying the possible states of an activity (or the resulting artefact) and the feasible state transitions. However, for the development of an SD simulation model more information is needed. First, measurement data are needed for model calibration. Second, additional information about managerial decision rules and control policies are needed in order to understand the causal relationships that govern the process behaviour.

Table 3 lists attributes that often characterize the entities of the generic artefact development/verification process (second column), and gives typical examples (third column). The transformation of these attributes into SD model parameters follows a regular pattern (cf. fourth column). The attribute "efficiency" of the entity "activity" always maps to a rate variable. Attributes of artefacts and resources usually map to level variables. However, there are situations where an attribute value of an artefact or resource is considered constant. In particular, this is the case when – for the purpose of the modelling task – it is of no interest to model the variation of an attribute value. An example is the number of designers involved in a design task which may be controlled by processes outside the scope of the activities to be modelled, e.g. senior management policy. The fifth column of Table 3 indicates how the values of model parameters are determined. Level and rate variables are calculated by their defining functions. Constants are either defined by the model user (INPUT) or, in the case that they are used to calibrate the model, based on expert estimates (EST) or derived from available empirical data (EMP). Calibration constants are either deterministic (e.g., by taking the mean) or stochastic (e.g., by triangulation of expert estimates or by statistically fitting the distribution of empirical data).

Table 3 Mapping of generic process attributes to SD model parameters

Process description			System dynamics	
Entity	Attribute	Example	Parameter type	Quantification
Artefact	Size	Design/specification document: – Function points (FP) – Pages	Level Constant	CALC (from flow rates) INPUT or EST or EMP
		Code document: – Lines of code (LOC)	Level Constant	CALC (from flow rates) INPUT or EST or EMP
		Test plan: – Number of test cases	Level Constant	CALC (from flow rates) INPUT or EST or EMP
	Quality	Spec./design/code/test plan: – Defects injected, detected, corrected	Level Constant	CALC (from flow rates) INPUT or EST or EMP
	State	Spec./design/code/test plan: – State values	Level	CALC (flow rates emulate state-transition logic)
Activity	Efficiency	Spec./design/code/test plan: – Development (and rework) volume per time unit – Verification (and validation) volume per time unit – Defect injection, detection, correction ($\rightarrow$ rework) per time unit	Rate	CALC (based on attribute values of used Resources)
Resource	Size	Workforce: – Number of architects, designers, programmers, testers, etc.	Level Constant	CALC (from flow rates) INPUT or EST or EMP
	Quality	Workforce: – Training – Experience	Level Constant	CALC (from flow rates) INPUT or EST or EMP
	Productivity	Development, verification, or validation technique: – Number of pages, FP, LOC, test cases developed, inspected, or tested per person and time unit	Constant	INPUT or EST or EMP

(continued)

Table 3 (continued)

Process description			System dynamics	
Entity	Attribute	Example	Parameter type	Quantification
	Effectiveness	Development, verification, or validation technique: – Number of defects injected per document size unit – Number of defects detected per document size unit	Constant	INPUT or EST or EMP
	Cost	Workforce: – Variable cost (e.g., hourly rate)	Level Constant	CALC (from flow rates) INPUT or EST or EMP
		Development, verification, or validation tools: – Fixed costs (e.g., purchase price) – Variable costs (e.g., leasing cost, storage cost, energy cost)	Level Constant	CALC (from flow rates) INPUT or EST or EMP

CALC calculated by simulation tool; *INPUT* input by model user; *EST* estimated by experts (modelled either deterministic or stochastic); *EMP* derived from empirical data (modelled either deterministic or stochastic)

Figure 5 shows the network of individual cause-effect relationships (so-called base mechanisms) of a SD model of the generic process. The most creative – and difficult – part during simulation model creation is the identification of cause-effect relationships that essentially generate the dynamic behaviour of the system, i.e., the variation of level variables over time. The control flows represented by the state-transition diagrams in Fig. 4 are not sufficient to explain the model behaviour, because they do not specify how relations between model variables change in response to value changes of the entities' attributes. One possible network of base mechanisms that (qualitatively) provides exactly this information is shown in Fig. 5. A base mechanism is represented as a directed graph connecting two nodes (model parameters), e.g., A → (+) B or A → (−) B. The arc that connects the nodes A and B can have a positive or a negative polarity, represented by "+" or "−" respectively. A positive polarity implies that B increases (or decreases), if A increases (or decreases). A negative polarity implies that B increases, if A decreases and vice versa. Using this encoding, the causal diagram in Fig. 5 can be read as follows:

1. If the workforce (e.g., the number of designers) is increased, then both development (or rework) and verification rate increase.

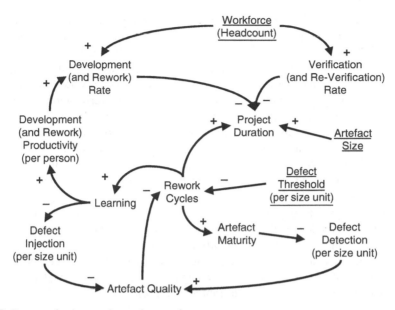

Fig. 5 Base mechanisms and causal network

2. If development and verification rates increase, then project duration decreases (because the artefact is developed faster).
3. If the artefact size is increased, then project duration increases (because a larger artifact has to be developed at a given rate).
4. If the defect threshold is increased (i.e., more defects per size unit have to be found before a re-verification is triggered), then possibly fewer rework cycles (incl. re-verification) have to be performed.
5. If fewer rework cycles (incl. re-verification) are performed, then project duration decreases.
6. If more re-work cycles are performed, then there is more learning and increased product maturity.
7. If there is more learning, then development productivity increases and defect injection (per size unit) decreases.
8. If defect injection (per size unit) decreases, then artefact quality increases.
9. If artefact maturity increases, then defect detection (per size unit) decreases.
10. If defect detection (per size unit) decreases, then artefact quality decreases.

Figure 5 contains three underlined nodes (workforce, artefact size, and defect threshold). These nodes represent either calibration or input parameters of the simulation model. The parameter "Defect Threshold" specifies the number of defects needed to trigger a rework cycle. It determines whether a verification step needs to be repeated (cf. in Fig. 4 the state-transition diagram associated with artefact verification). The importance of the parameter "Defect Threshold" resides in the fact that it not only plays a crucial role in the decision to repeat the verification step, but also because it triggers workforce learning and product maturation. A repetition of the verification (and, as a consequence, the rework) step has multiple effects. First of all, it increases project duration. On the other hand, it speeds up the development (more precisely: rework) rate due to learning. Similarly, due to learning, it reduces the defect injection (per size unit) during rework. Finally, it also decreases the defect detection rate during the subsequent verification step due to product maturation, because most of the defects have already been detected, and there are only a few defects still contained in the artefact which are harder to detect. The last two effects mentioned have a damping effect on the number of rework (and re-verification) cycles, since they both make it more probable that the number of defects detected during re-verification are below the value of model parameter "Defect Threshold." This is an example of negative feedback.

It should be pointed out that the causal network in Fig. 5 is only a subset of the base mechanisms that typically drive the behaviour of a software project. For example, normally one would expect an influence on development rate from defect detection (per size unit). This, and possibly other base mechanisms, have been omitted to keep the example simple and compact. For the same reason, base mechanisms related to project effort consumption have been omitted.

6.3. Implementation of the Generic Process Using a System Dynamics Tool

With the help of the causal network – in addition to the information already contained in Table 3 – the full set of simulation model parameters are determined, and their type and role (from the perspective of the model user) can be defined. In the following, an example SD simulation model implementation for the generic code document development/verification process is presented.

Table 4 lists the complete set of model variables (second column), together with their type (third column) and usage (fourth column). Column one helps to trace back model parameters to the generic process map (cf. Fig. 4 with "artefact" replaced by "code document"). Using the mapping scheme presented in Table 3, the following mappings apply:

1. Size, quality, and state attributes of artefacts (Artefact Input, Artefact, Artefact Defect Log Size) are mapped to level variables
2. Efficiency attributes of activities (Development Activity and Verification Activity) are mapped to rate variables
3. Size, quality, productivity, and effectiveness attributes of resources (for Development and Verification) are mapped to level variables or constants

The list of attributes in Table 4 is very detailed. For example, the quality attribute information related to the code document distinguishes between the number of defects injected, the number of defects detected, the number of defects undetected (equals the difference between injected and detected defects), the number of defects

Table 4 Mapping of static process representation to SD model variables

Process map element	SD model parameter	Type	Usage
Artefact input [Size]	code to do size	Level	Output
initialization	*code dev start time*	*Constant*	*Input(E)*
initialization	*average code size in KLOC*	*Constant*	*Input(E)*
initialization	*code to develop*	*Rate*	*Internal*
Artefact [Size]	code doc size	Level	Output
Artefact [State Devel.]	code doc dev status	Level	Internal
Artefact [State Verif.]	code doc ver status	Level	Internal
initialization	*code doc quality limit per KLOC*	*Constant*	*Input(P)*
Artefact [Quality 1]	code faults generated	Level	Output
Artefact [Quality 2]	code faults detected1 (in one verification round)	Level	Output
re-initialization	*detected code faults flush*	*Rate*	*Internal*
Artefact [Quality 3]	code faults pending	Level	Output
Artefact [Quality 4]	code faults corrected1 (in one rework round)	Level	Output
re-initialization	*corrected code faults flush*	*Rate*	*Internal*
Artefact [Quality 5]	code faults undetected	Level	Output
Artefact Defect Log [Size 1]	code faults detected (total)	Level	Output
Artefact Defect Log [Size 2]	code faults corrected (total)	Level	Output
Devel. Activity [Effic. 1]	development activity	Rate	Internal
calibration	productivity code learning amplifier	Constant	Input (C)
Devel. Activity [Effic. 2]	code fault generation	Rate	Internal
calibration	quality code learning amplifier	Constant	Input (C)
Devel. Activity [Effic. 3]	code fault correction	Rate	Internal
Verif. Activity [Effic. 1]	verification activity (= code to rework)	Rate	Internal
Verif. Activity [Effic. 2]	code fault detection	Rate	Internal
Artefact State Trans. (Dev.)	cdd status change	Rate	Internal
Artefact State Trans. (Ver.)	cdv status change	Rate	Internal
Resources (Devel.) [Size]	Workforce	Constant	Input (E)
Resources (Devel.) [Qual.]	code learning status	Level	Output
Resources (Devel.) [Prod. 1]	average code dev rate per person and day	Constant	Input (C)
Resources (Devel.) [Prod. 2]	average code fault injection per KLOC	Constant	Input (C)
Resources (Verif.) [Size]	Workforce	Constant	Input (E)
Resources (Verif.) [Prod.]	average code ver rate per person and day	Constant	Input (C)
Resources (Verif.) [Effect.]	code ver effectiveness	Constant	Input (C)
Res. State Trans. (Qual.)	cl status change	Rate	Internal

Devel. development; *Effic.* efficiency; *Prod.* productivity; *Qual.* quality; *Res.* resources; *Trans.* transition; *Verif.* verification; *C* calibration; *E* exploration; *P* policy

corrected, and the number of defects pending (equals the difference between detected and not yet corrected defects). Additional distinctions could be made, e.g., between different defect types or severity classes. For the sake of the simplicity of the presentation, these additional distinctions have not been included in the example presented here.

Model parameters that are of purely technical nature are printed in italics. For example, in order to set up a simulation run, certain initializations have to be made, or for the realistic calculation of model attributes, coefficients in the related model equations have to be calibrated.

Typically, level variables play the role of output parameters, since they represent the state of the modelled system. Constants play the role of input parameters. Depending on their purpose, three types of input parameters can be distinguished: policy (P), exploration (E), and calibration parameters (C).

Policy parameters like, for example, the variable *code doc quality limit per KLOC* represent process specific threshold values which are evaluated in managerial decision rules. In the example, the threshold for the number of detected defects per KLOC in a verification step determines whether a re-verification has to be performed.

Calibration parameters like, for example, the variable *productivity code learning amplifier* help to quantify the effects imposed by one or more model variables on another model variable realistic.

Finally, exploration parameters like the variables *average code size in KLOC* or *workforce* represent those model parameters whose effect on the overall behaviour of the system is subject to analysis. In the example, the process completion (i.e., the time when code development is complete) as well as code quality in terms of the density of undetected defects after verification (*code faults undetected/ average code size in KLOC*) are model outputs that depend on other model variables including the size of the artefact to be developed (*average code size in KLOC*) and available resources (*workforce*).

Figures 7–9 show the graphical representations (views) of the complete SD model implementation for the code development and verification process:

1. Figure 6 captures the workflow in terms of size
2. Figure 7 captures the code development and verification states as well as the workforce learning state
3. Figure 8 captures the workflow (or defect co-flow) in terms of quality

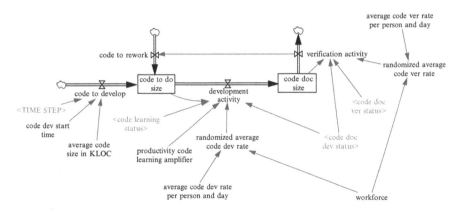

Fig. 6 Implementation of code development and verification work flow (view 1)

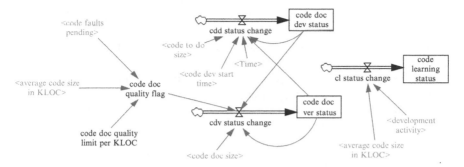

Fig. 7 Implementation of state attributes (view 2)

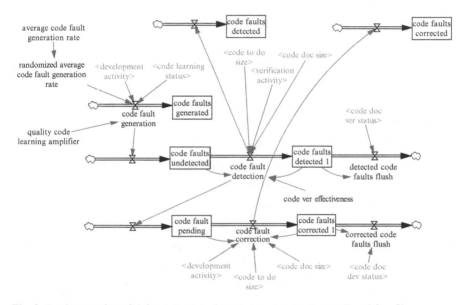

Fig. 8 Implementation of defect injection, detection, and correction co-flow (view 3)

The level variables, represented by boxes, are calculated with the help of inflow and outflow rates as defined by (1) introduced in Sect. 4. For example, level variable *code doc size* increases as a result of development activity and decreases as a result of verification activity (because verified code needs to undergo rework). The rate variables are calculated similarly to (2) introduced in Sect. 4.

In Fig. 6, the inflow rate *code to develop* initializes the level *code to do size*, which otherwise would be equal to zero, and thus no development or verification work has to be performed. At simulation time *code dev start time*, the value of *average code size in KLOC* flows into *code to do size*. In the example implementation, *code dev start time* and *average code size in KLOC* are model inputs. These two model parameters also define an interface to predecessor development and verification processes. For example, if a predecessor process produces a design document, then the completion time and the size of this document can be used to calculate *code dev start time* and *average code size in KLOC*.

Figure 7 shows the part of the model which calculates the states related to code document development and verification as well as resource quality (learning). For example, using the encoding 0, 1, and 2, for the states "non-exist," "active," and "complete," respectively, the rate variable *cdd status change* is calculated as shown in (5) below.

$$
\begin{aligned}
&\text{cdd status change} = \\
&\text{IF THEN ELSE} \\
&\text{(code doc dev status} = 0 \quad \text{/* state} = \text{``non-exist''} \\
&\qquad\qquad :\text{AND:Time} >= \text{code dev start time,} \\
&1, \qquad\qquad\qquad\qquad \text{/* transition ``non-exist''} \rightarrow \text{``active''} \\
&\text{IF THEN ELSE} \\
&\text{(code doc dev status} = 1 \quad \text{/* state} = \text{``active''} \\
&\qquad\qquad :\text{AND:code to do size} <= 0, \\
&1, \qquad\qquad\qquad\qquad \text{/* transition ``active''} \rightarrow \text{``complete''} \\
&\text{IF THEN ELSE} \\
&\text{(code doc dev status} = 2 \quad \text{/* state} = \text{``complete''} \\
&\qquad\qquad :\text{AND:code to do size} > 0 :\text{AND:code doc ver status} <> 1, \\
&-1, \qquad\qquad\qquad\quad \text{/* transition ``complete''} \rightarrow \text{``active''} \\
&0))) \qquad\qquad\qquad\quad \text{/* do nothing}
\end{aligned}
\tag{5}
$$

The first transition, from "non-exist" to "active," executes as soon as development has started, i.e., as soon as the simulation time is greater or equal to the defined development start time. The second transition, from "active" to "complete," executes as soon as there is no code waiting for implementation any more. The third transition, from "complete" back to "active," executes as soon as there is some code waiting for development and code verification is no longer active.

Figure 8 shows the defect co-flow, i.e., the injection (generation), detection, and correction of code faults. Fault generation and correction occur in parallel with code development and rework, while fault detection occurs in parallel with code verification (and re-verification). For example, the rate variable *code fault generation* is directly correlated with the rate variable *development activity*. The actual calculation of code fault generation is shown in (6) below.

$$
\begin{aligned}
&\text{code fault generation} = \text{development activity}* \\
&\text{randomized average code fault injection per KLOC}* \\
&(1/\text{MAX}(1, \text{code learning status}^\wedge\text{quality code learning amplifier}))
\end{aligned}
\tag{6}
$$

From (6) it can be seen that there is only defect injection when *development activity* > 0. The actual number of faults generated per time step depends on the number of KLOC developed per time step and the *randomized average code fault injection per KLOC*, which – in this example – is calculated by multiplying the *average code fault injection per KLOC* with a random number sampled from the triangular distribution triang(0.9, 1, 1.1,), where 1 represents the most probable value, and 0.9 and 1.1 the minimal and maximal values, respectively. The last factor in (6) models the learning effect. As soon as *code learning status* adjusted for the learning amplifier becomes greater than 1, the learning factor is less than 1 and thus the number of injected code faults decreases.

At the start of a simulation run, all model constants are initialized with a default value which can be modified by the user. Figure 9 shows a graphical user interface to the model, built using a Vensim utility, in the form of an input panel with slide bars, default initialization, and admissible value range. For example, variable *code ver effectiveness* is to be initialized with 0.75 (representing a defect detection effectiveness of the code verification technique of 75%), and maximum and minimum values of 0 and 1.

As soon as the simulation has started, the values of all model variables are calculated by Vensim® at each time step, which represents, for example, one work day. When the simulation run is complete the calculated values can be displayed either in tabular form or as graphs showing the time line on the *x*-axis and the variable value on the *y*-axis. Figures 10 and 11 below show example output graphs of the example model.

The upper part of Fig. 10 shows the simulation output for the level variables *code to do size* and *code doc size*. At simulation start (Time = 0), the amount of code work to do, in this case 200 KLOC, flows instantaneously into *code to do size*. This then decreases at a constant rate, caused by the development activity which transforms *code to do size* into *code doc size* (cf. Fig. 6). Consequently, the value of *code doc size* is exactly complementary to the value of *code to do size*, the sum of both always adding up to 200 KLOC. The lower part of Fig. 10 shows the behaviour of the state variables controlling the behaviour of code development, code verification, and learning, respectively. For example, one can see that *code doc dev status* equals 1 ("active") while code is developed. As soon as there is nothing more

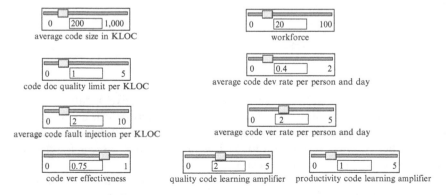

Fig. 9 Simulation input panel

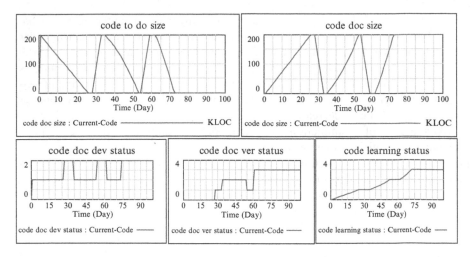

Fig. 10 Simulation output related to model views 1 and 2

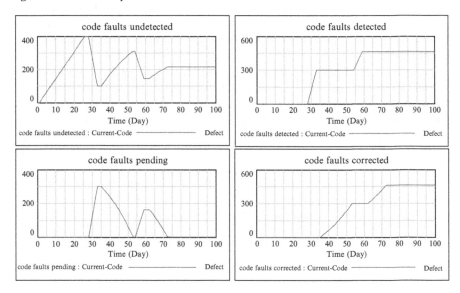

Fig. 11 Simulation output related to model view 3

to develop, i.e., *code to do size* = 0, it switches to 2 ("complete"). At that moment, *code doc ver status* switches from 0 ("non-exist") to 1 ("active"). After some time during which verification is done, depending on how many defects are found, *code doc ver status* switches either to 2 ("repeat") or 3 ("complete"). In Fig. 10, one can see that after the first verification round it is signalled that a second verification round needs to be performed ("repeat").

Figure 11 shows a selection of diagrams related to code fault generation, detection, and correction. The model variable *code faults undetected* represents the difference between the numbers of injected and detected faults, while *code faults pending* represents the difference between detected and corrected code faults. One can see that fault detection occurs when verification is active, and fault correction occurs when development (rework) is active.

6.4. Extension and Reuse of the Reference Simulation Model

The SD model developed in the previous section can be extended and reused in several ways. For example, as mentioned earlier, it is possible to make the model more realistic by adding a causal relationship between the number of errors detected and the fraction (size) of the artefact to be reworked.

The more interesting aspect of reusability is illustrated by Fig. 12. The figure shows the V-model software development process on the right hand side. Simulation models representing the *Design* and *Coding* phases are presented as boxes. For example, the Boxes labelled views 1C to 3C represent the SD model views presented in Figs. 7–9. In Figs. 7–9, the code documents developed and verified in the coding phase are represented by one single level variable. There is no differentiation between code sub-systems or modules. To facilitate a more detailed representation of reality, i.e., explicit modelling of individual subsystems (or even modules), the SD tool VENSIM® offers the possibility of "subscripting," i.e., the possibility of replacing a monolithic entity by an array of entities of the same type. A subscript works like the index of an array. With the help of this mechanism, potentially all variables used in the model views 1C to 3C can be duplicated. For example, if five code sub-systems shall be modelled, they would be represented by level variables *code doc size [1]* to *code doc size [5]*, or, if 100 code modules are to be modelled, the index of *code doc size* would run from 1 to 100, each index representing the *levels* and *rates* associated with each module.

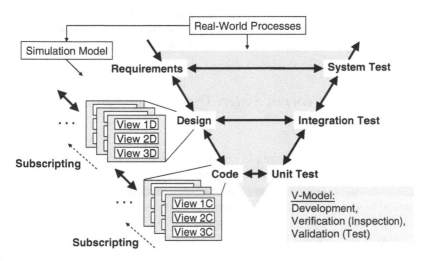

Fig. 12 Reuse-based construction of a simulation model representing a V-Model process

Finally, it is possible to represent the design and requirements specification phases of the V-Model process by simply duplicating the code related views 1C to 3C. This can be done by copying a complete view and replacing the sub-strings "code" by strings "design" in all variable names. Of course, the resulting Views 1D to 3D (and 1R to 3R) have to be re-calibrated based on suitable data or expert estimates. The connection between subsequent views requires only a few information links between variables, e.g., between model variables *design doc size* (which plays in the design phase the role that *code doc size* plays in the coding phase) and *average code size in KLOC*. These connections can be considered similar to "glue code" used to connect reusable software components.

Figure 13 shows several simulation output diagrams for a code development and verification process in which five sub-systems are developed concurrently. The size of each subsystem varies between 35 and 45 KLOC, accumulating to a total of 200 KLOC. One can see the individual traces for each subsystem. The development of one subsystem starts at Time = 0 (begin of coding phase), the others are more or less delayed due to variation in completion of required design documents. Similar graphs are generated for the design and requirements specification phases.

Figure 14 shows for each variable displayed in Fig. 13 the aggregated values of the individual code sub-systems. If compared to the monolithic simulation (i.e., without subscripting) presented in Figs. 11 and 12, one can see that the overall behaviour is similar but that some temporal displacement occurs due to late start of coding of some of the subsystems.

With some additional minor modifications, it is possible to model five subsystems in the design phase and, say, 100 modules in the coding phase. This enhancement requires a mapping of sub-system subscripts (used in the design views 1D to 3D) to module subscripts (used in the code views 1C to 3C). With this modification, the quality views for design (3D) and coding (3C) generate the simulation results shown in Fig. 15 (simulation time $T = 0$ at start of design phase). The Design phase lasts from simulation time $T = 1$ until $T = 140$ days, while the Coding phase starts at time $T = 96$ and ends at time $T = 174$ days. For each phase, the simulated values of injected, detected, pending, and undetected faults are shown.

6.5. Comparison Between System Dynamics and Discrete-Event Simulation

The simulation application example outlined in Sects. 6.2 and 6.3 demonstrated how SD captures complex software process behaviour with a small set of core modelling constructs (i.e., level and rate variables, and constants). This is possible by creation of generic model patterns that are reusable in several ways, either by replicating model variables via subscripting, or by duplicating complete submodels (i.e., model views) by simple text replacement (e.g., replacing the string "code" by the string "design").

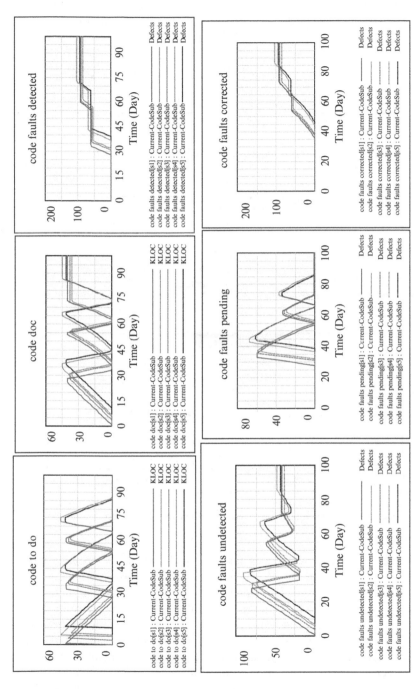

Fig. 13 Simulation outputs for concurrently coding five sub-systems

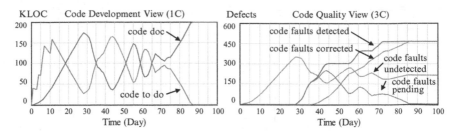

Fig. 14 Aggregated simulation outputs for concurrent coding of five sub-systems

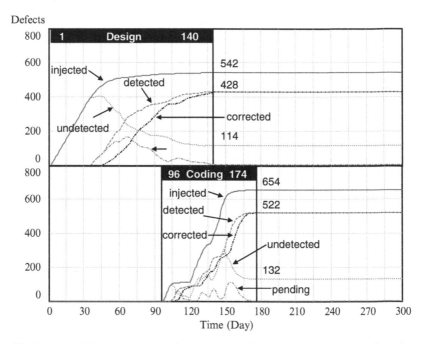

Fig. 15 Aggregated simulation outputs for concurrent sub-system design and module coding

Event-driven simulation techniques take a complementary perspective when modelling the generic artefact development and verification process introduced in Sect. 6.1. For example, instead of modelling the artefact as one monolithic document, e.g., of size 200 KLOC in the case of the code document, event-driven simulation models individual code units as single items which are routed through a sequence of processing stations, e.g., a station for development and a station for verification. These items have several attributes, e.g., size, state, number of defects (injected, detected, corrected), etc. The list of attributes can be extended or refined, e.g., by introducing attributes to distinguish defect types and severity classes. The attribute information determines, for example, the processing time in the development and verification stations, and the routing of an item after leaving a station.

What distinguishes DE simulation from SD simulation is the degree of model detail, the model representation, and the logic underlying the computation of model states. DE simulation modelling is very flexible and easily adaptable when it becomes necessary to add or change attributes of entities. Moreover, in DE simulation it is possible to model the behaviour of distinct real-world entities (e.g., artefacts, resources) of the same type individually, while SD typically models the average behaviour of a large number of entities of the same type. The possibility of subscripting mitigates this limitation of SD only to some extent.

One disadvantage of DE simulation comes as a downside of its ability to capture many details. DE simulation tools like, for example EXTEND®, offer a large number of different modelling constructs, often specifically tailored to manufacturing processes. Although these blocks are reusable in several contexts, more training is needed for the modeller to become familiar with the variety of options and they have to be adapted to capture software development processes. While DE simulation is capable to model production processes in greater detail, SD simulation models can capture not only the "mechanical" aspects of software development processes (which mainly consist of writing and checking different types of documents), but also the cause-effect mechanisms underlying the process behaviour. This includes the flow of information, which is important in software engineering, in contrast to material flows. Typically, information about these cause-effect relationships are part of the (mostly implicit) mental models of managers or decision makers, and contain intangible concepts like learning (cf. variable *code learning state* in the example above), motivation, stress, communication, decision policies, etc.

7. Practical Aspects

As a cautionary note it is well to remember that simulation has limitations and is not a "silver bullet." The predictive power of simulation strongly depends on the degree of model validity. While many scientific and engineering fields base their models on established physical laws, organizational models contain human aspects and intangible processes. This leads to two problems: It is difficult to gather data from human actors and it is very costly and sometimes not feasible to reproduce simulated scenarios in reality for the purpose of model validation.

Simulation is a simplification of the real world, and is thus inherently an approximation. As indicated in (Robertson, 1997) it is impossible to prove a priori the correctness of a simulation model that aims at generating previously unobserved and potentially unexpected behaviour. Thus, model verification and validation must be concerned with creating enough confidence in a model for its results to be accepted. This is done by trying to prove that the model is incorrect. The more tests that are performed in which it cannot be proved that the model is incorrect, the more increases confidence in the model.

Finally, one should not forget that simulation is neither a means in itself (it needs to be followed by action) nor does it generate new ideas. It is still the software manager's and simulation modeler's task to be creative in generating new scenarios for simulation, and in applying the simulation results to improve real-world processes. Simulation does not automatically produce new facts such as knowledge-based expert systems do (e.g., through inference).

8. The Future of Simulation in Software Engineering

The application of simulation techniques, in particular process simulation techniques, offers several interesting perspectives for improving management and learning in software organizations.

Business simulator-type environments (micro-worlds) can confront managers with realistic situations that they may encounter in practice. Simulation allows the rapid exploration of micro-worlds, without the risks associated with real-world interventions and provides visual feedback of the effects of managers' decisions through animation. Simulation increases the effectiveness of the learning process, because trainees quickly gain hands-on experience. The potential of simulation models for the training of managers in other domains than software engineering has long been recognized (Lane, 1995). Simulation-based learning environments also have the potential to play an important role in software management training and education of software engineers, in particular if they are offered as web-based (possibly distributed multi-user) applications.

Analyzing a completed project is a common means for organizations to learn from past experience, and to improve their software development process (Birk et al., 2002). Process simulation can facilitate post-mortem analysis. Models facilitate the replaying of past projects, diagnose management errors that arose, and investigate policies that would have supplied better results. To avoid having a software organization reproduce – and amplify – its past errors, it is possible to identify optimal values for measures of past project performance by simulation, and record these values for future estimation, instead of using actual project outcomes that reflect inefficient policies (Abdel-Hamid, 1993).

To further increase the usage (and usability) of simulation techniques in software engineering, the time and effort needed for model building must further be reduced. One step in this direction is to provide adaptable software process simulation frameworks. Similar to the process simulation reference model described above, these frameworks can be used like a construction kit with reusable model components. Supporting tools and methodological guidance must accompany reuse-based simulation modelling. Furthermore, simulation tools should be connected to popular project planning and tracking tools to decrease the effort of model parameterization and to increase their acceptance by software practitioners. As more and more companies improve their development process maturity, it is also expected that process simulation will gain more attention in industry.

References

Abdel-Hamid TK (1993) Adapting, Correcting and Perfecting Software Estimates: a Maintenance Metaphor. IEEE Computer 20–29.

Abdel-Hamid TK, Madnick SE (1991) Software Projects Dynamics – an Integrated Approach, Prentice-Hall, Englewood Cliffs, NJ.

Andersson C, Karlsson L, Nedstam J, Höst M, Nilsson BI (2002) Understanding Software Processes through System Dynamics Simulation: A Case Study, In: *Proceedings of 9th IEEE International Conference and Workshop on the Engineering of Computer-Based Systems*, pp 41–48.

Aranda RR, Fiddaman T, Oliva R (1993) Quality Microworlds: Modeling the Impact of Quality Initiatives Over the Software Product Life Cycle. American Programmer 52–61.

Balci O (2003) Verification, Validation, and Certification of Modelling and Simulation Applications. In: *Proceedings of the 2003 Winter Simulation Conference*, pp 150–158.

Bandinelli S, Fuggetta A, Lavazza L, Loi M, Picco GP (1995) Modeling and Improving an Industrial Software Process. IEEE Transactions on Software Engineering 21(5): 440–453.

Banks J, Carson JS, Nelson BL (2000) Discrete-Event System Simulation, 3rd edn, MOUS Test Preparation Guides Series, Prentice-Hall, New York.

Barlas Y (1989) Multiple Tests for Validation of System Dynamics Type of Simulation Models. European Journal of Operational Research 42: 59–87.

Birk A, Dingsøyr T, Stålhane T (2002) Postmortem: Never Leave a Project without It. IEEE Software 19(3): 43–45.

Birkhölzer T, Dantas L, Dickmann C, Vaupel J (2004) Interactive Simulation of Software Producing Organization's Operations based on Concepts of CMMI and Balanced Scorecards. In: *Proceedings 5th International Workshop on Software Process Simulation Modeling (ProSim)*, Edinburgh, Scotland, pp 123–132.

Briand LC, Pfahl D (2000) Using Simulation for Assessing the Real Impact of Test-Coverage on Defect-Coverage. IEEE Transactions on Reliability 49(1): 60–70.

Briand LC, Labiche Y, Wang Y (2004) Using Simulation to Empirically Investigate Test Coverage Criteria Based on Statechart. In: *Proceedings of International Conference on Software Engineering (ICSE)*, pp 86–95.

Cartwright M, Shepperd M (1999) On Building Dynamic Models of Maintenance Behavior. In: Kusters R, Cowderoy A, Heemstra F, van Veenendaal E. (eds.) *Project Control for Software Quality*, Shaker Publishing, Maastricht.

Cellier FE (1991) Continuous System Modeling, Springer Press, New York.

Chen Y, Gannod GC, Collofello JS (2005) A Software Product Line Process Simulator. In: *Proceedings of 6th International Workshop on Software Process Simulation and Modeling (ProSim)*, pp 102–109.

Choi SJ, Scacchi W (2001) Modeling and Simulating Software Acquisition Process Architectures. Journal of Systems and Software 59(3): 343–354.

Christie AM (1999a) Simulation: An Enabling Technology in Software Engineering. CROSSTALK – The Journal of Defense Software Engineering 12(4): 25–30.

Christie AM (1999b) Simulation in Support of CMM-Based Process Improvement. Journal of Systems and Software 46(2/3): 107–112.

Christie AM, Staley MJ (2000) Organizational and Social Simulation of a Requirements Development Process. Software Process Improvement and Practice 5: 103–110.

Coyle RG (1996) System Dynamics Modelling – A Practical Approach, Chapman & Hall, London.

Dantas A, de Oliveira Barros M, Lima Werner CM (2004) A Simulation-Based Game for Project Management Experiential Learning. In: *Proceedings of 16th International Conference on Software Engineering & Knowledge Engineering (SEKE)*, pp 19–24.

Drappa A, Ludewig J (1999) Quantitative Modeling for the Interactive Simulation of Software Projects. Journal of Systems and Software 46(2/3): 113–122.

Drappa A, Deininger M, Ludewig J (1995) Modeling and Simulation of Software Projects. In: *Proceedings of 20th Annual Software Engineering Workshop*, Greenbelt, MD, USA, pp 269–275.

Extend (2006) http://www.imaginethatinc.com/ (accessed on March 22, 2006).

Fernström C (1993) PROCESS WEAVER: Adding Process Support to UNIX. In: *Proceedings of 2nd International Conference on the Software Process (ICSP)*, pp 12–26.

Ferreira S, Collofello J, Shunk D, Mackulak G, Wolfe P (2003) Utilization of Process Modeling and Simulation in Understanding the Effects of Requirements Volatility in Software Development. In: *Proceedings 4th Software Process Simulation Modeling Workshop (ProSim)*, Portland, USA.

Forrester JW (1961) Industrial Dynamics. Productivity Press, Cambridge.

Forrester JW, Senge P (1980) Tests for Building Confidence in System Dynamics Models. In: Forrester JW et al. (eds.) *System Dynamics*, North-Holland, New York.

Gruhn V, Saalmann A (1992) Software Process Validation Based on FUNSOFT Nets. In *Proceedings of 2nd European Workshop on Software Process Technology (EWSPT)*, pp 223–226.

Häberlein T (2003) A Framework for System Dynamic Models of Software Acquisition Projects. In: *Proceedings 4th Software Process Simulation Modeling Workshop (ProSim)*, Portland, USA.

Häberlein T, Gantner T (2002) Process-Oriented Interactive Simulation of Software Acquisition Projects. In: *Proceedings of First EurAsian Conference on Information and Communication Technology (EurAsia-ICT)*, LNCS 2510, Shiraz, Iran, pp 806–815.

Höst M, Regnell B, Dag J, Nedstam J, Nyberg C (2001) Exploring Bootlenecks in Market-Driven Requirements Management Processes with Discrete Event Simulation. Journal of Systems and Software 59(3): 323–332.

Houston DX (2003) A Case Study in Software Enhancements as Six Sigma Process Improvements: Simulating Productivity Savings. In: *Proceedings of 4th Software Process Simulation Modeling Workshop (ProSim)*, Portland, USA.

Houston DX, Mackulak GT, Collofello JS (2001) Stochastic Simulation of Risk Factor Potential Effects for Software Development Risk Management. Journal of Systems and Software 59(3): 247–257.

Huang Y, Madey GR (2005) Autonomic Web-Based Simulation. In: *Proceedings of Annual Simulation Symposium 2005*, pp 160–167.

Humphrey WS, Kellner MI (1989) Software Process Modeling: Principles of Entity Process Models. In: *Proceedings of 11th International Conference on Software Engineering (ICSE)*, Pittsburg, PA, USA, pp 331–342.

Kellner MI, Hansen GA (1989) Software Process Modeling: A Case Study. In: *Proceedings of 22nd Annual Hawaii International Conference on System Sciences, Vol. II – Software Track*, pp 175–188.

Kellner MI, Madachy RJ, Raffo DM (1999) Software Process Simulation Modeling: Why? What? How?. Journal of Systems and Software 46(2/3): 91–105.

Kuipers B (1986) Qualitative Simulation. Artificial Intelligence 29(3): 289–338.

Kuppuswami S, Vivekanandan K, Rodrigues P (2003) A System Dynamics Simulation Model to Find the Effects of XP on Cost of Change Curve. In: *Proceedings of 4th International Conference on Extreme Programming and Agile Processes in Software Engineering (XP)*, LNCS 2675, pp 54–62.

Lane DC (1995) On a Resurgence of Management Simulation Games. Journal of the Operational Research Society 46: 604–625.

Law A, Kelton WD (1999) Simulation Modeling and Analysis, 3rd edn, McGraw-Hill, New York.

Lee B, Miller J (2004) Multi-Project Management in Software Engineering Using Simulation Modeling. Software Quality Journal 12: 59–82.

Lerch FJ, Ballou DJ, Harter DE (1997) Using Simulation-Based Experiments for Software Requirements Engineering. Annals of Software Engineering 3: 345–366.

Lin CY, Abdel-Hamid TK, Sherif J (1997) Software-Engineering Process Simulation Model (SEPS). Journal of Systems and Software 38(3): 263–277.

Madachy RJ (1996) System Dynamics Modeling of an Inspection-Based Process. In: *Proceedings 18th International Conference on Software Engineering (ICSE)*, Berlin, Germany, IEEE Computer Society Press, pp 376–386.

Madachy RJ, Tarbet D (2000) Case Studies in Software Process Modeling with System Dynamics. Software Process Improvement and Practice 5: 133–146.

Madey G, Freeh V, Tynan R (2002) Agent-Based Modeling of Open Source using Swarm. In: *Proceedings of Americas Conference on Information Systems (AMCIS)*, Dallas, TX, USA, pp 1472–1475.

Martin R, Raffo D (2001) Application of a Hybrid Process Simulation Model to a Software Development Project. The Journal of Systems and Software 59: 237–246.

McCabe B (2003) Monte Carlo Simulation for Schedule Risks. In: *Proceedings of the 2003 Winter Simulation Conference*, pp 1561–1565.

Mi P, Scacchi W (1990) A Knowledge-Based Environment for Modeling and Simulating Software Engineering Processes. IEEE Trans. Knowledge Data Engineering 2(3): 283–294.

Mišic VB, Gevaert H, Rennie M (2004) Extreme Dynamics: Towards a System Dynamics Model of the Extreme Programming Software Development Process. In: *Proceedings 5th International Workshop on Software Process Simulation Modeling (ProSim)*, Edinburgh, Scotland, pp 237–242.

Mizuno O, Kusumoto S, Kikuno Y, Takagi Y, Sakamoto K (1997) Estimating the Number of Faults Using Simulator Based on Generalized Stochastic Petri-Net Model, In: *Proceedings of the Asian Test Symposium (ATS)*, pp 269–274.

Müller M (2007) Analyzing Software Quality Assurance Strategies through Simulation, Fraunhofer IRB, Stuttgart, pp 262.

Münch J, Rombach HD, Rus I (2003) Creating an Advanced Software Engineering Laboratory by Combining Empirical Studies with Process Simulation. In: *Proceedings 4th Process Simulation Modeling Workshop (ProSim)*, Portland, USA.

Münch J, Pfahl D, Rus I (2005) Virtual Software Engineering Laboratories in Support of Trade-off Analyses. Software Quality Journal 13(4): 407–428.

Neu H, Hanne T, Münch J, Nickel S, Wirsen A (2002) Simulation-Based Risk Reduction for Planning Inspections. In: Oivo M, Komi-Sirviö S (eds.) *Proceedings 4th International Conference on Product Focused Software Process Improvement (PROFES)*, LNCS 2559, Springer Press, Berlin, pp 78–93.

Oh Navarro E, van der Hoek A (2004) SIMSE: An Interactive Simulation Game for Software Engineering Education. In: *Proceedings 7th IASTED International Conference on Computers and Advanced Technology in Education (CATE)*, pp 12–17.

Padberg F (2006) A Study on Optimal Scheduling for Software Projects. Software Process Improvement and Practice 11(1): 77–91.

Pfahl D (2005) ProSim/RA – Software Process Simulation in Support of Risk Assessment. In: Biffl S, Aurum A, Boehm B, Erdogmus H, Grünbacher P (eds.) *Value-based Software Engineering*, Springer Press, Berlin, pp 263–286.

Pfahl D, Lebsanft K (2000) Knowledge Acquisition and Process Guidance for Building System Dynamics Simulation Models: An Experience Report from Software Industry. International Journal of Software Engineering and Knowledge Engineering 10(4): 487–510.

Pfahl D, Ruhe G (2002) IMMoS – A Methodology for Integrated Measurement, Modeling, and Simulation. Software Process Improvement and Practice 7: 189–210.

Pfahl D, Klemm M, Ruhe G (2001) A CBT Module with Integrated Simulation Component for Software Project Management Education and Training. Journal of Systems and Software 59(3): 283–298.

Pfahl D, Ruhe G, Lebsanft K, Stupperich M (2006) Software Process Simulation with System Dynamics – A Tool for Learning and Decision Support. In: Acuña ST, Sánchez-Segura MI (eds.) *New Trends in Software Process Modelling, Series on Software Engineering and Knowledge Engineering*, Vol. 18, World Scientific, Singapore, pp 57–90.

Pidd M (2004) Computer Simulation in Management Science, 5th edn, Wiley, New York, pp 328.

Powell A, Mander K, Brown D (1999) Strategies for Lifecycle Concurrency and Iteration: A System Dynamics Approach. Journal of Systems and Software 46(2/3): 151–162.

Raffo DM, Kellner MI (2000) Analyzing the Unit Test Process Using Software Process Simulation Models: A Case Study. In: *Proceedings 3rd Software Process Simulation Modeling Workshop (ProSim)*, London, UK.

Raffo DM, Vandeville JV, Martin RH (1999) Software Process Simulation to Achieve Higher CMM Levels. Journal of Systems and Software 46(2/3): 163–172.

Raffo DM, Nayak U, Setamanit S, Sullivan P, Wakeland W (2004) Using Software Process Simulation to Assess the Impact of IV&V Activities. In: *Proceedings 5th International Workshop on Software Process Simulation Modeling (ProSim)*, Edinburgh, Scotland, pp 197–205.

Richardson GP (1991) Feedback Thought in Social Science and Systems Theory, University of Pennsylvania Press, Philadelphia, PA, USA.

Robertson S (1997) Simulation Model Verification and Validation: Increase the Users' Confidence. In: *Proceedings of the 1997 Winter Simulation Conference*, pp 53–59.

Roehling ST, Collofello JS, Hermann BG, Smith-Daniels DE (2000) System Dynamics Modeling Applied to Software Outsourcing Decision Support. Software Process Improvement and Practice 5: 169–182.

Rose P, Kramer M (1991) Qualitative Analysis of Causal Feedback. In: *Proceedings of 9th National Conference on Artificial Intelligence (AAAI)*, pp 817–823.

Ruiz M, Ramos I, Toro M (2004) Using Dynamic Modeling and Simulation to Improve the COTS Software Process. In: *Proceedings 5th International Conference on Product Focused Software Process Improvement (PROFES)*, Kyoto, Japan, pp 568–581.

Rus I (2002) Combining Process Simulation and Orthogonal Defect Classification for Improving Software Dependability. In: *Proceedings 13th International Symposium on Software Reliability Engineering (ISSRE)*, Annapolis.

Rus I, Collofello C, Lakey P (1999) Software Process Simulation for Reliability Management. Journal of Systems and Software 46(2/3): 173–182.

Rus I, Biffl S, Hallig M (2002) Systematically Combining Process Simulation and Empirical Data in Support of Decision Analysis in Software Development. In: *Proceedings of the 14th International Conference on Software Engineering and Knowledge Engineering (SEKE)*, Ischia, Italy, pp 827–833.

Rus I, Neu H, Münch J (2003) A Systematic Methodology for Developing Discrete Event Simulation Models of Software Development Processes. In: *Proceedings 4th International Workshop on Software Process Simulation and Modeling (ProSim)*, Portland, Oregon, USA.

@Risk (2007) @Risk Simulation Software: http://www.palisade-europe.com/ (accessed on June 26, 2007).

Sargent R (2003) Verification and Validation of Simulation Models. In: *Proceedings of 2003 Winter Simulation Conference*, pp 37–48.

Scacchi W, Boehm B (1998) Virtual Systems Acquisition: Approach and Transitions, Acquisition Review Quarterly 5(2): 185–216.

Setamanit S, Wakeland W, Raffo DM (2006) Exploring the Impact of Task Allocation Strategies for Global Software Development Using Simulation. In: Wang Q, Pfahl D, Raffo DM, Wernick P (eds.) *Software Process Change – SPW/ProSim 2006, Shanghai, China, May 2006, Proceedings* (LNCS 3966), Springer, Berlin, Heidelberg, pp 274–285.

Smith N, Capiluppi A, Ramil JF (2005) A Study of Open Source Software Evolution Data Using Qualitative Simulation. Software Process: Improvement and Practice 10(3): 287–300.

Stallinger F, Grünbacher P (2001) System Dynamics Modeling and Simulation of Collaborative Requirements Engineering. Journal of Systems and Software 59: 311–321.

Tvedt JD, Collofello JS (1995) Evaluating the Effectiveness of Process Improvements on Development Cycle Time via System Dynamics Modeling. In: *Proceedings Computer Science and Application Conference (COMPSAC)*, pp 318–325.

Vensim (2006) http://www.vensim.com/ (accessed on March 22, 2006).

Waeselynck H, Pfahl D (1994) System Dynamics Applied to the Modeling of Software Projects. Software Concepts and Tools 15(4): 162–176.

Wakeland W, Martin RH, Raffo D (2003) Using Design of Experiments, Sensitivity Analysis, and Hybrid Simulation to Evaluate Changes to a Software Development Process: A Case Study. In: *Proceedings of 4th Process Simulation Modelling Workshop (ProSim)*, Portland, USA.

Wernick P, Hall T (2004) A Policy Investigation Model for Long-Term Software Evolution Processes. In: *Proceedings of 5th International Workshop on Software Process Simulation Modeling (ProSim)*, Edinburgh, Scotland, pp 149–158.

Williford J, Chang A (1999) Modeling the FedEx IT Division: A System Dynamics Approach to Strategic IT Planning. Journal of Systems and Software 46(2/3): 203–211.

Section II
Practical Foundations

Chapter 6
Statistical Methods and Measurement

Jarrett Rosenberg

Abstract   Useful ways of measuring software engineering phenomena have to address two challenges: defining realistic and valid metrics that can feasibly be collected under the constraints and time pressures of real-world software development contexts, and determining valid and accurate ways of analysing the resulting data to guide decisions. Too often, the difficulties of addressing the first challenge mean that the second is given little attention. The purpose of this chapter is to present different techniques for the definition and analysis of metrics such as product quality data. Specifically, statistical issues in the definition and application of metrics are presented with reference to software engineering examples.

1. Introduction

Measurement is ubiquitous in software engineering, whether for management, quality assurance, or research purposes. Effectively creating and using measurements is critical to success in these areas, yet there is much confusion and misunderstanding about the best way in which to define, collect, and utilize them. This chapter discusses the purpose of measurement and statistical analysis in software engineering research and development, and the problems researchers and practitioners face in using these methods effectively; rather than a "how-to," it is a "when-to." Section 2 discusses some fundamental issues in measurement and the context of measurement. A number of the issues in this section are discussed in the ISO/IEC 15939 standard, *Information Technology – Software Measurement Process*. Section 3 discusses two basic aspects of creating effective measures: metric definition and metric evaluation. Sections 4 and 5 covers methods for description, comparison, and prediction for simultaneous and successive measurements, respectively, whether categorical or numeric. Section 6 returns to the context of measurement in discussing the important topic of data quality.

F. Shull et al. (eds.), *Guide to Advanced Empirical Software Engineering*.
© Springer 2008

2. Statistics and Measurement

Measurement is the process of assigning labels (typically numbers) to an attribute of an object or action in such a way that the characteristics of the attribute are mirrored in the characteristics of the labels. The assignment process and the resulting numbers are called a *measurement scale* or *metric*. The reverse process is an interpretive one, and thus if the measurement scale is inappropriate, then the corresponding interpretations of its values will be incorrect. In using the terms "measurement" and "metric", it is usually clear from context whether the process or numerical result is being referred to.

The name "statistics" reflects the origin of the field in the collection of demographic and economic information important to the government of the modern nation state. Such measures as the size of the population, the birth rate, and the annual crop yield became important inputs to decision making. The term *descriptive statistics* applies to such measures, whether simple or complex, that describe some variable quantity of interest. Over the past century and a half, the field of *inferential statistics* has been developed to allow conclusions to be drawn from the comparison of the observed values of descriptive statistics to other real or hypothesized values. These inferential methods require some assumptions in order to work, and much of statistical theory is devoted to making those assumptions as flexible as possible in order to fit real-world situations.

2.1. Statistical Analysis and the Measurement Process

Statistical analysis necessarily assumes some *measurement process* that provides valid and precise measurements of some process of interest, as shown in Fig. 1. The results of the statistical analysis are themselves the prerequisite to a decision-

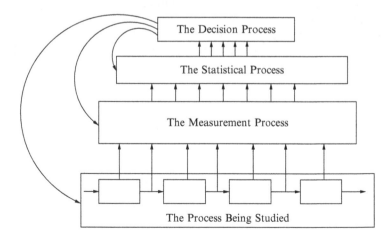

Fig. 1 The roles of the measurement and statistical processes

making process which in turn affects the process of interest, the measurements made on it, and the analyses done on those measurements. It is often the case that too little thought is given to the multi-level nature of this situation: measurements are made because it is possible to do so, statistical analyses are done in a formulaic way, and decisions are made with little data or analysis. In the area of software metrics, Basili et al. (1994) created the "Goal/Question/Metric" framework, which emphasizes that every metric collected must be defined so as to answer some specific question, and every question posed must be relevant to some decision-making goal. This ensures that the entire process depicted in Fig. 1 remains aligned with the overall goal: studying a process in order to make various decisions about it (whether research conclusions or process improvements).

The reason for dwelling on such a banal topic is precisely because it is so often taken for granted; problems with any of these processes or the relations between them become easily lost in the assumption that the overall scheme of things is functioning correctly. Yet if the statistical process is not functioning properly (e.g., incorrect analyses are being performed) decisions will be made on the basis of incorrect analysis and bad outcomes may be misattributed to the decision-making process rather than its statistical inputs. Similarly, it is typically assumed that the measurement process is functioning correctly and that the data it provides are accurate and valid enough to make a statistical analysis worth doing. As Fig. 1 shows, there is no point to a statistical analysis if the data going into it come from a measurement process which is malfunctioning. This involves not only the nature of the measurements involved (discussed in Sect. 3), but also the quality of data obtained.

2.2. The Context of Measurement

While the context of measurement is typically taken for granted and not examined, it nevertheless has a serious impact on the nature and quality of the measurements.

First, the meaning of measurements will vary depending on whether they derive from observation or experiment. If the former, questions of potential bias arise due to various sampling difficulties discussed below. Experiments, on the other hand, while potentially giving precise measurements under controlled conditions, may suffer from a lack of generalizability if they are not carefully designed and interpreted.

Second, it is often the case that the available measurements are not immediately connected with the phenomena of interest: the measures may be what are termed "leading" or "lagging" indicators. The former are highly desirable for forecasting, but the latter are more common; both cases are problematic in steering an organization, because the cause and effect are so separated in time. For example, "number of customer-reported software defects" might seem to be a good metric for evaluating the performance of a software development organization, but it is usually the case that today's customer complaint stems from a defect introduced months or years ago, perhaps by a different set of developers. Similarly, customer satisfaction is typically measured and goaled on an annual or quarterly basis, but it lags a company's products and services typically by several years. Leading/lagging measures are thus difficult to use in managing day-to-day operations.

Third, while measurements are presumably for a purpose, they can often take on a life of their own, produced because someone once decreed they should be produced, but with no-one paying much attention to them because the rationale has been lost, or is no longer meaningful. Worse, the measurement process can have side-effects, where the numbers are "massaged" or the work process altered in order to produce the "right" results.

Finally, good measurements are *actionable*; they can be used to do something. Measurements made for measurement's sake are worse than useless: they divert resources from the real problems. A single global measure of customer satisfaction or product quality may alert management to a problem, but it gives no indication of what to do. Over time, an organization or researcher will sharpen the questions asked and the corresponding metrics used; this process forms the most important context for measurement and analysis.

3. Creating Effective Metrics

Deciding on an appropriate measure or set of measures is neither as easy as it first appears nor as difficult as it later seems. To be effective, a metric must be clearly defined, have appropriate mathematical properties, and be demonstrably reasonable (i.e., precise, reliable, and valid). Above all, however, a metric must be well-motivated. To be well-motivated, a metric must provide at least a partial answer to a specific question, a question which itself is aimed at some particular research or management goal. For example, how one chooses to measure the time to repair a defect depends on the kind of question being asked, which could range from "What is the expected amount of time for a specific class of defects to go from the initial Reported state to the Repaired state?" to "What percent of all customer-reported defects are in the Repaired state within two days of being first reported?" It is usually the case that a single metric is not sufficient to adequately answer even an apparently simple question; this increases the need to make sure that metrics and questions are closely connected.

3.1. Defining a Metric

Metrics can be either simple or compound in definition. Simple metrics include *counts* (e.g., number of units shipped this year), dimensional *measures* (e.g., this year's support costs, in dollars), *categories* (e.g., problem types), and *rankings* (e.g., problem severity). Compound metrics are defined in terms of two or more metrics, typically combined by some simple arithmetic operation such as division (e.g., defects per thousand lines of code). The number and type of metrics combined and the method used to combine them affects how easily understood the compound metric will be. This leads to *ratios* (e.g., defects per thousand units), *rates* (time-based ratios such as number of problem reports per month), *proportions or percentages* (e.g., proportion of customers responding "very satisfied" to a survey question), *linear algebraic combinations* (e.g., mean repair cost – the sum of all repair costs divided by the total number of repairs), and *indices* (dimensionless measures typically based on a sum and then standardized to some baseline value). Whereas simple metrics are always defined in terms of some measurement unit, compound metrics such as percentages and some linear combinations and indices can be dimensionless.

The definition of a metric affects its behavior (i.e., the likelihood of its taking on various values), its possible interpretations, and the kinds of analyses which are suitable for it. This argues for the use of simpler, more easily understood metrics rather than the creative development of new, compound ones with poorly understood behavior. Indices in particular raise serious questions of interpretation and comparison, and are best used for showing long-term trends. The range of values a metric can have does not always follow a bell-shaped Normal curve; for example, durations such as repair times almost always have a highly skewed distribution whose tail values pull the mean far from the median. Investigation of the distribution of a metric's values is one of the first tasks that must be undertaken in a statistical analysis. Furthermore, the range of values a measure can take on can be affected by internal or external limitations; these are referred to as truncation or limitation, and censoring.

Truncation or limitation refers to situations where a measure never takes on a particular value or range of values. For example, repair time in theory can never have a value of zero (if it does, the measurement scale is too coarse). Or one may have results from a survey question which asks for some count, with an "*n* or more" response as the highest value; this means that the upper part of the measure is truncated artificially. These situations can sometimes be problematic, and special statistical methods have been developed to handle them (see Long, 1997; Maddala, 1986). A much more difficult case is that of censoring, which occurs with duration data. If the measure of interest is the time until an event happens (e.g., the time until a defect is repaired), then there necessarily will be cases where the event has not yet happened at the time of measurement. These observations are called "censored" because even though we believe the event will eventually occur and a duration will be defined, we do not know how long that duration will be (only that it has some current lower bound). This problem is often not recognized, and when it is, the typical response is to ignore the missing values. This unfortunately causes the subsequent analysis to be biased. Proper analysis of duration data is an extensive sub-area of statistics usually termed "survival analysis" (because of its use in medical research); its methods are essential for analyzing duration data correctly. See Hosmer and Lemeshow (1999) or Kleinbaum (1996) for a good introduction.

Classical measurement theory (Krantz et al., 1971; Ghiselli et al., 1981) defines four basic types of measurement scale, depending on what kinds of mathematical manipulations make sense for the scale's values. (Additional types have been proposed, but they are typically special cases for mathematical completeness.) The four are

Nominal. The scale values are unordered categories, and no mathematical manipulation makes sense.

Ordinal. The scale values are ordered, but the intervals between the values are not necessarily of the same size, so only order-preserving manipulations such as ranking make sense.

Interval. The scale values are ordered and have equal intervals, but there is no zero point, so only sums and differences make sense.

Ratio. The scale values are ordered and have equal intervals with a zero point, so any mathematical manipulation makes sense.

These scale types determine which kinds of analyses are appropriate for a measurement's values. For example, coding nominal categories as numbers (as with serial numbers, say) does not mean that calculating their mean makes any sense. Similarly, measuring the mean of subjective rating scale values (such as defect severity) is not likely to produce meaningful results, since the rating scale's steps are probably not equal in size.

It is important to realize that the definition, interpretation, and resulting analyses of a metric are not necessarily fixed in advance. Given the complexities shown in Fig. 1, the actual characteristics of a metric are often not entirely clear until after considerable analysis has been done with it. For example, the values on an ostensibly ordinal scale may behave as if they were coming from an underlying ratio scale (as has been shown for many psychometric measures, see Cliff, 1992). It is commonly the case that serial numbers are assigned in a chronologically ordered manner, so that they can be treated as an ordinal, rather than nominal, scale. Velleman (1993) reports the case where branch store number correlated inversely with sales volume, as older stores (with smaller store numbers) had greater sales.

There has been much discussion in the software metrics literature about the implications of measurement theory for software metrics (Zuse, 1990; Shepperd and Ince, 1993; Fenton and Pfleeger, 1997). Much of this discussion has been misguided, as Briand et al. (1996) show. Measurement theory was developed by scientists to aid their empirical research; putting the mathematical theory first and the empirical research after is exactly backwards. The prescriptions of measurement theory apply only after we have understood what sort of scale we are working with, and that is often not the case until we have worked with it extensively.

In practical terms, then, one should initially make conservative assumptions about a scale's type, based on similar scales, and only "promote" it to a higher type when there is good reason to do so. Above all, however, one should avoid uncritically applying measurement theory or any other methodology in doing research.

3.2. Evaluating a Metric's Effectiveness

A measure can have impeccable mathematical credentials and still be totally useless. It order for it to be effective, a measure needs an adequate amount of precision, reliability, and validity. One also has to consider its relationships to other measures, as sometimes misleading results can occur when two related measures are treated as if they were independent.

There are two different concepts sharing the term "measurement precision." One concept is that of the size of a metric's smallest unit (sometimes called its "least count"). Put another way, it is the number of significant digits that can be reported for it. For example, measuring someone's height to the nearest millimeter is absurd, since the typical error in obtaining the measurement would be at least as large. Similarly, measuring someone's height to the nearest meter would be too crude to be of much value. A common mistake is to forget that the precision of any derived measure, including descriptive statistics such as the mean, can not be any greater than that of the original measures, and is almost always less. Thus reporting the average height of a group of people as 178.537 cm implies that the raw measurements were made at the accuracy of 10 µm; this is unlikely. Such a result is better reported as simply 179 cm. The arithmetic combination of measures propagates and magnifies the error inherent in the original values. Thus the sum of two measures has less precision than either alone, and their ratio even less (see Taylor, 1997; Bevington and Robinson, 1992); this should be borne in mind when creating a compound metric.

The other concept of precision is the inverse of variability: the measurements must be consistent across repeated observations in the same circumstances. This property is termed *reliability* in measurement theory. Reliability is usually easy to achieve with physical measurements, but is a major problem in measures with even a small behavioral or subjective component. Rating scales are notorious in this respect, and any research using them needs to report the test-retest reliability of the measures used. Reliability is typically quantified by Cronbach's *coefficient alpha*, which can be viewed as essentially a correlation among repeated measurements; see Ghiselli et al. (1981) for details.

A precise and reliable measure may still be useless for the simple reason that it lacks *validity*, that is, it does not in fact measure what it claims to measure. Validity is a multifaceted concept; while it is conventional to talk about different types of validity, they are all aspects of one underlying concept. (Note that the concepts of internal and external validity apply to *experiments* rather than measurements.)

Content validity is the degree to which the metric reflects the domain it is intended to measure. For example, one would not expect a measure of program complexity to be based on whether the program's identifiers were written in English or French, since that distinction seems unrelated to the domain of programming languages.

Criterion validity is the degree to which a metric reflects the measured object's relationship to some criterion. For example, a complexity metric should assign high values to programs which are known to be highly complex. This idea is sometimes termed *discrimination validity*, i.e., the metric should assign high and low values to objects with high or low degrees of the property in question. In this sense it may be thought of as a kind of "predictive validity."

Construct validity is the degree to which a metric actually measures the conceptual entity of interest. A classical example is the Intelligence Quotient, which attempts to measure the complex and elusive concept of intelligence by a combination of measures of problem-solving ability. Establishing construct validity can be quite difficult, and is usually done by using a variety of convergent means leading to a preponderance of evidence that the metric most likely is measuring the concept. The simpler and more direct the concept, the easier it is to establish construct validity; we have yet to see a generally agreed-upon metric for program complexity, for example, while number of non-commentary source statements is generally accepted as at least one valid metric for program size.

Finally, a metric's effectiveness can vary depending on its context of use, in particular, how it is used in combination with other metrics. There are three pitfalls here. The first is that one can create several ostensibly different metrics, each of which is precise, reliable, and valid, but which all measure the same construct. This becomes a problem when the user of the metrics doesn't realize that they are redundant. Such redundancy can be extremely useful, since a combination of such metrics is usually more accurate that any one of them alone, but if they are assumed to be measuring independent constructs and are entered into a multivariate statistical analysis, disaster will result, since the measures will be highly correlated rather than independent. Therefore one of the first tasks to perform in using a set of metrics is to ascertain if they are measures of the same or different constructs. This is usually done with a factor analysis or principal component analysis (see Comrey and Lee, 1992).

The second pitfall is that if two metrics' definitions contain some component in common, then simple arithmetic will cause their values to not be independent of each other. For example, comparing a pretest score and a difference score (posttest minus pretest) will yield a biased rather than an adjusted result because the difference score contains the pretest score as a term. Another example is the comparison of a ratio with either its numerator or denominator (say, defect density and code size). Such comparisons may be useful, but they cannot be made with the usual null hypothesis of no relationship (see Sect. 4.2), because they are related arithmetically. This problem in the context of measures defined by ratios is discussed by Chayes (1971), who gives formulas for calculating what the *a priori* correlation will be between such metrics.

The third pitfall is failing to realize that some metrics are not of primary interest themselves, but are necessary covariates used for adjusting the values of other metrics. Such measures are known as *exposure factors* since the greater their value, the greater the likelihood of a high value on another measure. For example, in demographics and epidemiology population size is an exposure factor, since the larger the population, the larger the number of criminals, art museums, disease cases, and good Italian restaurants. Similarly, the larger a source module, the larger the value of any of a number of other metrics such as number of defects, complexity, etc., simply because there will be more opportunity for them to be observed. Exposure variables are used in a multivariate analysis such as Analysis of Covariance (ANCOVA) or multiple regression to adjust for ("partial out") the effect of the exposure and show the true effect of the remaining factors.

3.3. *Statistical Analyses*

Having defined appropriate metrics and ensured that data is properly collected, the focus shifts to the question of how to appropriately analyze the data obtained. There are three principal statistical tasks involved: *description, comparison,* and *prediction*. It is useful to discuss separately the analyses appropriate to dynamic or temporal data, i.e., data which have time as a fundamental aspect, from static data, which do not; however, all statistical analyses have some aspects in common.

The prerequisite for any data analysis is *data cleaning*: the auditing of the data for complete and accurate values. This step typically takes at least as much time, if not more, than the application of the statistical techniques themselves. Often data quality problems prevent many of the intended statistical analyses from being carried out, or create so much uncertainty about the validity of their results as to render them useless. It is usually possible to gather some information from even poor quality data, but an initial investment in data quality pays for itself in the ability to do more – and more useful – analyses later. We will return to this issue in Sect. 6.

Statistical analyses are all based on *models of the underlying data-generating process*; these models can be simple or complex, and can make more or fewer assumptions. *Parametric models* assume specific functional forms such as the Normal distribution for univariate data, or a linear regression equation for multivariate data. The parameters of these functional forms are estimated from the data and used in producing descriptive statistics such as the standard error of the mean, or inferential statistics such as the t-statistic used to test for a difference between two means. Because they make stronger assumptions, parametric models can be more useful – if the assumptions are true. If they are not true, biased or even wildly inaccurate results are possible. *Non-parametric models* make few assumptions (typically that the data are unimodal and roughly symmetrical in distribution) and thus can be used in almost any situation. They are also more likely to be accurate at very small sample sizes than parametric methods. The price for this generality is that they are not as efficient as parametric tests when the assumptions for the latter are in fact true, and they are usually not available for multivariate situations.

In the same way that a phenomenon typically cannot be captured by a single metric, a statistical analysis typically cannot be done by conducting one test alone. A good data analyst looks at the data from a variety of different perspectives, with a variety of different methods. From this a picture gradually emerges of what is going on. A word of caution, however: the conventional p-value of 0.05 represents a "false positive" or spurious result rate of 1 in 20. This means that the more statistical tests that are performed, the more likely it is that some of them will be falsely significant (a phenomenon sometimes called "capitalization on chance"). Large correlation matrices are a good example of the phenomenon; to see why, compute the 20×20 correlation matrix among 20 samples of 100 uniform random numbers: of the 190 unique correlations, how many are statistically significant at the 0.05 level? It is thus seriously misleading to do dozens of tests and then report a result with a p-value of 0.05. The usual way of correcting for doing such a large number of tests is to lower the *p*-value to a more stringent level such as 0.01 or even 0.001. The most common way of reducing the false positive rate among multiple tests is called the Bonferroni procedure; it and several improvements on it such as the Scheffé and Tukey methods are described in Keppel (1991). Often preferable to multiple univariate tests is a single multivariate analysis.

4. Analyzing Static Measurement Data

4.1. Description

The first step in any statistical analysis is data description, and the first step of data description is to simply *look at the data*. Figure 2 shows the histograms for two different samples with the same mean and standard deviation; without looking at these histograms, one would think from their descriptive statistics that both samples were from the same population. Looking at the distribution of values for a metric allows one to check for most frequent values (modes), outliers, and overall symmetry of the distribution. If a distribution is skewed by a few extreme values (large or small), many widely used statistics become misleading or invalid. For example, the mean and standard deviation are much more sensitive to extreme values than the median or percentiles, and so the mean of a skewed distribution will be far from the median and therefore a somewhat misleading measure of central tendency. Thus looking at the data allows us to determine which descriptive statistics are most appropriate.

As pointed out above, descriptive statistics such as point estimates are subject to error; it is important to quantify this error so that the precision of the point estimate can be determined. The *standard error* of an estimate is a common way of representing

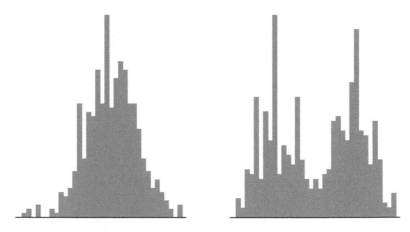

Fig. 2 Two very different samples with the same mean and standard deviation

the precision of an estimate; the range of values two standard errors on either side of the estimate delimit the *95% confidence interval* for that estimate, i.e., the interval within which the true value of the parameter being estimated will fall 95% of the time. A wide confidence interval indicates that the estimate is not very precise, thus knowing the precision is useful for gauging an estimate's value in decision making. The standard error increases as the sample size decreases, and the resulting imprecision in estimates is what makes very small samples so problematic.

4.1.1. Measures of Central Tendency

The main feature of interest in a sample of non-temporal data is its "center of mass". For a roughly symmetric distribution, this will be essentially the same value as its mode (most frequent value) and its median (50th percentile or midpoint). The arithmetic mean is the most commonly used measure of central tendency because of its intuitive definition and mathematical usefulness, but it is seriously affected by extreme values and so is not a good choice for skewed data. The median by definition always lies at the point where half the data are above it and half below, and thus is always an informative measure (indeed, a simple check for skewness in the data is to see how far the mean is from the median). The reason the median is not used more often is that it is more complicated to calculate and much more complicated to devise statistical methods for. When dealing with rates, the geometric mean (the nth root of the product of the n data values) more accurately reflects the average of the observed values.

4.1.2. Measures of Dispersion

Since two entirely different distributions can have the same mean, it is imperative to also include some measure of the data's dispersion in any description of it. The range of the values (the difference between the highest and lowest values) is of little use since it conveys little about the distribution of values in between. The natural measure for distributions characterized by the arithmetic mean is the variance, the sum of the squared deviations about the mean, scaled by the sample size. Since the variance is in squared units, the usual measure reported is its square root, the standard deviation, which is in the same measurement units as the mean. Analogues to the standard deviation when the median rather than the mean is used are the values of the first and third quartiles (i.e., the 25th and 75th percentiles) or the *semi-interquartile range*, which is half the difference between the first and third quartiles. These give a measure of the dispersion that is relatively insensitive to extreme values, just like the median. Another useful measure of dispersion is the *coefficient of variation* (CV), which is simply the standard deviation divided by the mean. This gives some indication of how spread out the values are, adjusted for their overall magnitude. In this sense, the coefficient of variation is a dimensionless statistic which allows direct comparison of the dispersion of samples with different underlying measures (for example, one could compare the CV for cyclomatic complexity with the CV for module length, even though they are measured in totally different units).

4.1.3. Measures of Association

The most common measure of association between two measures is the correlation coefficient, which is a standardized way of describing the amount by which they covary. The correlation coefficient, r, is the square root of the amount of shared covariation between the two measures; thus while r^2 is an easily interpreted ratio measure (an r^2 of 0.4 is half that of an r^2 of 0.8), correlation coefficients are non-linear: an r of 0.4 is *not* half that of an r of 0.8, but only one-quarter as large. Because they are adjusted for the amount of variation present in the variables being correlated, correlation coefficients among different sets of measures can be compared. However, correlation coefficients are sensitive to the range of variation present in each variable; in particular, large differences in the two ranges of variation place an *a priori* limit on the size of r. Thus, special forms of correlation coefficient have been developed for the cases like that of a binary and a continuous variable.

4.1.4. Categorical Data

Categorical data come in two basic kinds: binomial data, where there are only two categories, and multinomial data, where there are more than two. Description of categorical data is typically done by means of the proportion or percentage of the total each category comprises. While pie charts are a common graphical representation, histograms or polar charts (also called Kiviat diagrams or star plots) are more accurately read (Cleveland, 1994). It is important to not report proportions or percentages of small samples to a greater degree of precision than the data warrant: 11 out of 63 cases is not 17.46%, because the smallest percentage that can be observed in a sample of 63 (i.e., one individual) constitutes more than one percent of the sample.

There are a variety of measures of association between two categorical variables (as long as the categories can be considered ordered), see Goodman and Kruskal (1979); all of them can be thought of as special instances of correlation.

4.1.5. Ordinal Data

Ordinal data present special challenges since they contain more information than simple categories, but ostensibly not enough to justify more sophisticated statistical techniques, or even the calculation of the mean and standard deviation. Analysis of ordinal data therefore typically reduces it to the nominal level, or promotes it to the interval or ratio ones. Both of these approaches can frequently be justified on pragmatic grounds.

A prototypical example of ordinal data is the subjective rating scale. The simplest description of such data is simply its distribution, which is done the same way as for multinomial categorical data. Since the number of scale values is limited, simply listing the percentage of cases for each value is more useful than the range or standard deviation. Since such data are often skewed (see Fig. 3 for an example from a satisfaction rating scale), the median is a better measure of central tendency than the mean. Since most responses pile up at one end, this has the effect of making the mean of the scale values most sensitive to changes in values at the other, skewed end (in the case of Fig. 3, at the low-satisfaction end). Thus in Fig. 3 the mean of the satisfaction ratings is paradoxically more sensitive to measuring changes in dissatisfaction than satisfaction.

Correlation of ordinal values is typically done with non-parametric measures such as the Spearman correlation coefficient, Kendall's tau, or the kappa statistic used for inter-rater reliability. Interpretation of such statistics is harder than correlation coefficients because of the lack of equal intervals or ratios in ordinal values; a tau or kappa value of 0.8 is not strictly twice as good as one of 0.4.

4.2. Comparison

Data are rarely collected simply for description; comparison to a real or ideal value is one of the main aims of statistical analysis.

The basic paradigm of statistical comparison is to create a model (the *null hypothesis*) of what we would observe if only chance variation were at play. In the case of comparing two samples, the null hypothesis is that the two samples

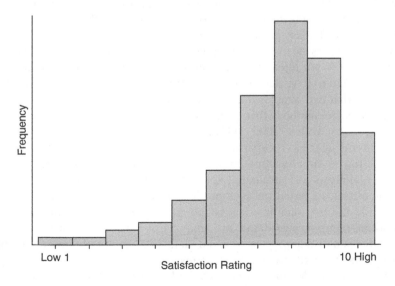

Fig. 3 An example of skewness in ordinal data (from a rating scale)

come from the same underlying population, and thus will have descriptive statistics (e.g., the mean) that differ only by an amount that would be expected by chance, i.e., whose expected difference is zero. If the observed difference is very unlikely to occur just by chance, then we conclude (with some small risk of being wrong) that the two samples are not from the same population, but rather two different ones with different characteristics.

The basic method of statistical comparison is to compare the difference in the average values for two groups with the amount of dispersion in the groups' values. That is, we would judge a difference of 10 units to be more significant if the two groups' values ranged from 30 to 40 than if they ranged from 300 to 400. In the latter case we would easily expect a 10-unit difference to appear in two successive samples drawn from exactly the same population.

Statistical tests of comparison are decisions about whether an observed difference is a real one, and as such, they are subject to two kinds of error:

Type I error (symbolized by α) – incorrectly rejecting the null hypothesis, and deciding that a difference is real when it is not,
Type II error (symbolized by β) – incorrectly not rejecting the null hypothesis, and deciding that a difference is not real when it is.

The probabilities determined for these two types of error affect how a result is to be interpreted. The value for alpha is traditionally set at 0.05; the value for beta is typically not even considered; this is a mistake, because the value of $(1 - \beta)$ determines the *power* of a statistical test, i.e., the probability that it will be able to correctly detect a difference when one is present. The major determinant of statistical power is the size of the sample being analyzed; consequently, an effective use of statistical tests requires determining – before the data are collected – the sample size necessary to provide sufficient power to answer the statistical question being asked. A good introduction to these power analysis/ sample size procedures is given in Cohen (1988).

Because of this issue of statistical power, it is a mistake to assume that, if the null hypothesis is not rejected, then it must be accepted, since the sample size may be too small to have detected the true difference. Demonstrating statistical equivalence (that two samples do, in fact, come from the same population) must be done by special methods that often require even more power than testing for a difference. See Wellek (2002) for an introduction to equivalence testing.

The classic test for comparing two samples is the venerable *t*-test; its generalization to simultaneous comparison of more than two samples is the (one-way) analysis of variance (ANOVA), with its *F*-test. Both of these are parametric tests based on asymptotic approximations to Normal distributions. While the two-sample *t*-test is remarkably resistant to violations of its assumptions (e.g., skewed data), the analysis of variance is not as robust. In general, for small samples or skewed data non-parametric tests are much preferred; most univariate parametric tests have non-parametric analogues (here, the Wilcoxon/Mann-Whitney test and the Kruskal-Wallis test). A good reference is Sprent (1993).

Occasionally, one may wish to compare an observed mean against a hypothesized value rather than another group mean; this can be done by means of a one-sample t-test or equivalently, if the sample is large (>30), by a Z-test.

4.2.1. Categorical Data

Comparison of categorical data between two or more samples is typically done by a chi-squared test on an $n \times m$ table where the rows are the samples and the columns are the categories (see Agresti, 1998; Wickens, 1989). For tables with small cell values (where the standard chi-squared tests are inaccurate), special computationally intensive tests can be used instead (see Good, 1994). Frequently the description and comparison of interest in categorical data is simply a test of whether the proportion of some outcome of interest is the same in two samples; this can be done by a simple binomial test (see Fliess, 1981).

4.2.2. Ordinal Data

Comparison of ordinal data between two or more groups can be done by the same sort of $n \times m$ table methods described above for categorical data (and some ordinal extensions have been developed; see Agresti, 1984). Equally useful are rank-based techniques such as the Wilcoxon/Mann-Whitney and Kruskal-Wallis tests mentioned above.

A common comparative analysis performed on rating scale data is to look for improvements in ratings by comparing the means of two samples taken at different points in time, such as repeated surveys with different respondent samples. Even if calculating the mean for such a scale were reasonable (and it is for some ordinal scales whose behavior appears similar to ratio scales), the mean is sensitive to those few values at the skewed end which are of least interest. Thus any change in the mean at best only indirectly reflects the phenomenon of interest. Using the median does not have this problem, but suffers from the fact that the scale has few values and thus the median is likely to be the same from one sample to the next. There are two ways to compare such samples of rating scale data; both reduce the data to categorical data. The first method is to compare the entire distribution of responses across both samples in a $2 \times n$ table. The second method is to focus just on the category of greatest interest (say, the highest one or two), and compare the proportion of responses in that category in the two samples. While this method loses more information than the first, it focuses on the main area of interest and is easier to report and interpret.

4.3. Prediction

Frequently, measurements are made in order to predict the value of other measurements of interest. Such predictions do not have to be temporal ones; the notion of correlation is at bottom a predictive one: knowing the value of one measurement on a unit, increases one's knowledge of the possible value of other measurements on it. The prototype of such prediction is regression. Originally limited to linear prediction equations and least-squares fitting methods, regression methodology has been extended over the course of the past century to cover an impressive variety of situations and methodologies using the framework of generalized linear models. Good references are Draper and Smith (1998), Rawlings et al. (1998), and Dobson (2001).

The essential method of regression is to fit an equation to pairs of measurements (X, Y) on a sample in such a way as to minimize the error in predicting one of the measures (Y) from the other (X). The simplest such case is where the regression equation is limited to a linear form:

$$Y = a + bX + \text{error}$$

and the total error measure is the sum of squared differences between the predicted and actual observations. The regression coefficient b then reflects the effect on Y of a 1-unit change in X. This notion of regression can then be generalized to prediction of a Y measure by a set of X measures; this is multiple or multivariate regression.

Even an elementary discussion of the method and application of regression is beyond the scope of this chapter (see Rosenberg, 2000 for one oriented toward software metrics), but a number of pitfalls should be mentioned.

First, most regression methods are parametric in nature and thus are sensitive to violations of their assumptions. Even in doing a simple univariate regression, one should always look at the data first. Figure 4 shows a cautionary example from Anscombe (1973); all four datasets have exactly the same regression line.

Second, regression models by definition fit an equation to all and only the data presented to them. In particular, while it is possible to substitute into the regression equation an X value outside the range of those used to originally fit the regression, there is no guarantee that the resulting predicted Y value will be appropriate. In effect, the procedure assumes that the relevant range of X values is present in the sample, and new X values will be within that range. This problem with *out of range* prediction complicates the use of regression methods for temporal predictions where the X value is time, and thus new observations are by definition out of range. For predicting temporal data, other methods must be used (as described in Sect. 5.3).

Third, regression equations have an estimation error attached to them just like any statistical estimate. Plotting the confidence bands around a regression line gives a good indication of how useful the equation really is.

Fourth, multivariate regression assumes that the multiple predictor measures are independent, i.e., uncorrelated with each other, otherwise the results will be incorrect. Since multiple measures are often correlated, it is critical to look at the pattern of correlations among the predictor variables before doing a multivariate regression. If even a moderate amount of correlation is present, something must be done about it, such as dropping or combining predictors.

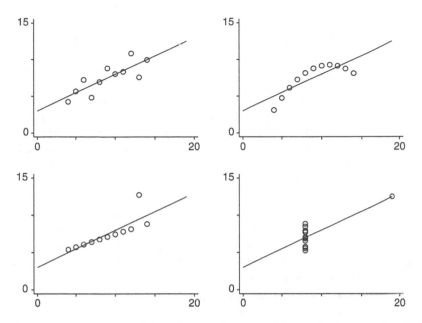

Fig. 4 Anscombe's example of four different data sets with exactly the same best-fitting regression line

4.3.1. Categorical Data

A frequent question of interest is how a binomial or other categorical variable can be predicted from another one, or from one or more ordinal or continuous variables (see El Emam et al., 1999 for an example in the area of software metrics). Such a prediction is sometimes called termed a *classification task*, especially if there are more than two categories; see Hand (1997) for a general discussion. The case of predicting a dichotomous outcome is termed a *diagnostic prediction* from its prototypical example in biostatistics: predicting whether or not a person has a disease based on one or more test outcomes. The accuracy in such a diagnostic situation can be characterized by a 2 × 2 table, as shown in Table 1, where the predictor variable(s) are constrained to make a binomial prediction which is then compared to the "true" value.[1]

Table 1. The structure of a prototypical diagnostic prediction

	Reality	
Prediction	Negative	Positive
Negative	True negative (A)	False negative (B)
Positive	False positive (C)	True positive (D)

---

[1] A known true value in such situations is called a *gold standard*; much work has been done on the problem of assessing predictive accuracy in the absence of such a standard (see, for example, Valenstein, 1990; Phelps and Huston, 1995).

Predictive accuracy in this context can be measured either as *positive predictive accuracy* (D/[C+D]), *negative predictive accuracy* (A/[A+B]), or both together (A+D/[A+B+C+D]). Two other relevant measures are *sensitivity*, the probability of correctly predicting a positive case, (D/[D+B]), and *specificity*, the probability of correctly predicting a negative case, (A/[A+C]).

There is an extensive literature on binomial prediction; much of it has been influenced by the theory of signal detection, which highlights a critical feature of such predictive situations: the prediction is based not only on the amount of information present, but also on some *decision criterion or cutoff point* on the predictor variable where the predicted outcome changes from one binomial value to the other. The choice of where to put the decision criterion inescapably involves a tradeoff between sensitivity and specificity. A consequence of this is that two prediction schemes can share the same data and informational component and yet have very different predictive accuracies if they use different decision criteria. Another way of putting this is that the values in any diagnostic 2 × 2 table are determined by both the data and a decision criterion. The merit of signal detection theory is that it provides an explicit framework for quantifying the effect of different decision criteria, as revealed in the *ROC* curve for a given predictive model, which plots the true-positive rate (sensitivity) and false-positive rate (1 − specificity) of the model for different values of the decision criterion (see Fig. 5). The ROC curve provides two useful pieces of information. First, the area under the curve above the diagonal line is a direct measure of the predictive accuracy of the model (the diagonal line indicates 50% accuracy or chance performance; a curve hugging the upper left

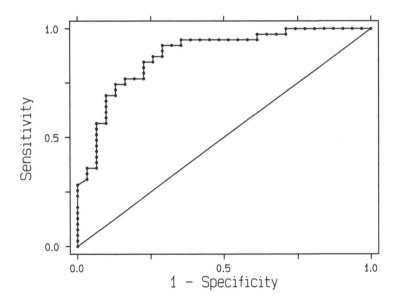

Fig. 5. An example receiver operating characteristic (ROC) curve

corner would indicate 100% accuracy). Second, one can graphically compare the relative accuracy of two models by their ROC curves: if the two curves do not intersect, then one model always dominates the other; if they do intersect, then one model will be more accurate for some values of the predictor variables. A good introduction to signal detection theory is Swets (1996). Zhou et al. (2002) provide a thorough guide to its application.

Regression methodology has been adapted for predicting binomial outcomes; the result is called *logistic regression* because the predictions have to be scaled by the logistic transformation so that they range between 0 and 1 (see Kleinbaum, 1994; Hosmer and Lemeshow, 1989). Coefficients in logistic regression have a somewhat different interpretation than in ordinary regression, due to the different context. The results of a logistic regression are often also expressed in terms of ROC curves.

4.3.2. Ordinal Data

Prediction of ordinal values is rarely done except by assuming that the values reflect an underlying interval or ratio scale, in which case standard regression methods are used.

5. Analyzing Dynamic Measurement Data

One of the most frequent uses of metrics is to track some attribute over time, either to detect or forecast changes in it, or to verify that the value is unchanging apart from unavoidable random variation. Such *time series data*, as they are called, have as their essential characteristic the presence of temporal structure. The chief structural patterns are *trend*, a long-term change in value, typically monotonic but sometimes cyclic in an aperiodic manner, or both; and *seasonal change*, a cycle of change with a fixed period, as with changes over the course of the seasons in a year. While the usual goal is to identify these temporal components, sometimes the goal is to demonstrate that no such components are present; such a time series is said to be *stationary*. It should be noted that analyses of time series data require at least three seasonal cycles worth of data, since estimating the seasonal component require more than one season's worth of data. Having less data seriously restricts the kinds of analyses that can be done, and usually arises in situations more accurately termed *longitudinal* or *repeated measures* analysis, where the goal is to examine relatively large-scale permanent changes such as physical growth or skill-acquisition. See Singer and Willet (2003) and Crowder and Hand (1990) for examples.

In addition to the methods described below, there are a great many other types of dynamic data analysis, such as survival analysis (mentioned briefly above), and state space models. See Gottman (1995) and Haccou and Meelis (1994) for examples.

5.1. Description

As with any analysis, the first step is to look at the data. Figure 6 shows a typical dataset containing a long-term increasing trend, with an additional seasonal component (every 12 months). The top panel shows the observed data, while the lower two panels display the underlying trend and seasonal components, respectively. Methods for such *time-series decomposition* are discussed in Bowerman and O'Connell (1993).

There are a number of ways such data can be used. The first way is simply to describe the history of some process. Rather than summarizing the history by a histogram or descriptive statistics such as the mean or standard deviation (which would miss entirely the temporal aspect of the data), the time chart and its decomposition into trend and seasonal components is the main focus.

Most discussions of time series analysis make the assumption that the observations are made with little or no error, otherwise the variation in the measurements themselves could obscure the temporal patterns. This means that this sort of analysis is best used on continuous measures (or counts) made with high reliability and precision, rather than ordinal measures such as ratings.

It is always important to verify that the temporal measurements in a time series are in fact equivalent. For example, fluctuations in the number of defects reported for each month in a 1-year period might seem to warrant some concern about quality variation, but in that respect they may be illusory. Months may seem equal, but they vary in length by up to 10%, and when the number of actual working days is

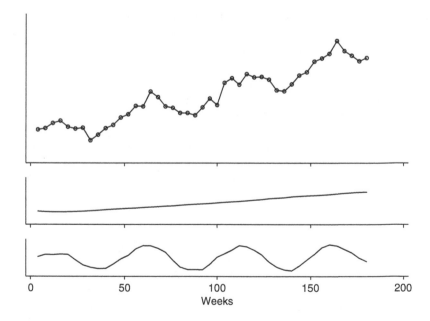

Fig. 6 Time series decomposition chart for data in Fig. 6

taken into account, they can vary by 25% or more. The same data adjusted for the number of work days may show little variation at all. This is not to say that the first approach is "false," merely that it can be seriously misleading if the variation in temporal units is not made clear. Even if the defect submission *rate* is constant from month the month, the actual *number of defects* submitted will vary; the first piece of information may be comforting for the quality manager, but the second piece is more valuable to the support manager.

5.2. Comparison

Often the question of interest is: "Is the latest observation evidence of a change in trend?" Such a question is difficult to answer on the basis of a single observation. Often, however, that observation is actually a summary of a number of observations, for example, the mean of some set of measurements. In that case one can use the same sort of statistical methods used with static data to compare the latest sample with the previous one. Typically, however, the sample sizes involved are too small to detect the small level of change involved. A more common method of looking for a change in trend is to compare the latest observation with the value predicted for it by a forecast.

5.3. Prediction

Another major use of time series data is *forecasting*: predicting one or more future observations based on the data at hand. The larger the amount of data at hand, the better the forecasting that can be done. Even with few data, however, there are some simple techniques that can be used. The simplest forecast technique is the so-called *naive predictor*, which assumes that the future value will be the same as the present value. This actually can be a useful first approximation in many cases, for example, tomorrow's temperature is likely to be similar to today's. Other naive predictors can be defined; for example, if there is a small amount of data beyond one seasonal cycle (say 15 months, January of one year to March of the following year) one can take the average difference between the observations made on the same part of the cycle (January to March for both years) and use that as an increment for forecasting the rest of second cycle based on corresponding values from the first.

Such naive predictors can be useful for first approximations, and can also serve as concrete points of departure for discussions about possible alternative forecasts. Perhaps most importantly, they can be used as baselines for evaluating the predictive accuracy of more sophisticated forecasting techniques.

There are a variety of ways of quantifying the accuracy of forecasts, all of them based on some measure of the difference between forecast and actual values. Chief among these are (here "error" and "deviation" mean the same thing):

Mean absolute deviation (MAD) the average absolute difference between observed and forecasted values (this penalizes errors in direct proportion to their size, and regardless of direction);

Mean squared error (MSE) the average squared difference between observed and forecasted values (this penalizes errors as the square of their size, also regardless of direction);

Mean percentage error (MPE) the average proportional difference between forecast and actual values (i.e., *(actual – forecast/actual)*), expressed as a percentage;

Mean absolute percentage error (MAPE) the average absolute proportional difference, expressed as a percentage.

There are many more possible accuracy measures, each with its advantages and disadvantages; some may not be applicable with some kinds of data (for example, MPE and MAPE do not make sense when the data are not measured on a ratio scale with a zero point). Which to use depends on the purpose of the forecast, and which kinds of errors are considered worse than others (see Makridakis, 1998).[2]

Assessing the overall accuracy of a forecast is more complicated than in the case of static predictions with regression. A common technique is to set a desired standard of absolute or relative accuracy beforehand, and then compare the accuracy of various forecasting methods with that of a naive predictor. Often the choice of forecasting methods comes down to a trade-off between accuracy and difficulty of computation.

An additional issue to consider in forecasting is whether a forecast metric is a *leading*, *lagging*, or *coinciding indicator*, that is, whether changes in the metric occur before, after, or at the same time as changes in some other metric of interest. Leading indicators are highly desirable, but few metrics have that property. The issue is important because a metric cannot be effectively used for process control purposes unless its temporal connection with the process is understood.

5.4. Process Control

The other major use of dynamic, temporally oriented data is in determining that there is *not* change over time. This is the area of *statistical process control*.

A process is performing effectively if its behavior only changes under conscious direction; left alone it should remain stable, and measurements made on it should remain the same apart from the inevitable and unimportant random variation. In the 1920's Walter Shewhart at Western Electric devised a statistical method for quantifying and monitoring the stability of a process, the *control chart*, examples of which are shown in Fig. 7.

As can be seen, the control chart looks very much like a trend chart, except that it is based on a defined *control level* or expected value of the measurements (the

---

[2] These accuracy measures can also be used in assessing the fit of models to static data, of course, but in the latter case there are more useful global goodness-of-fit measures such as R^2 which are used instead. Such measures are not available for forecasting dynamic data.

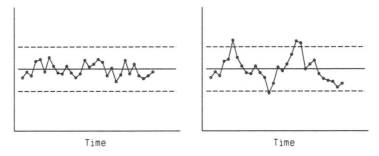

Fig. 7 Control charts showing (**a**) A process which is in control, (**b**) A process which is not in control

solid line), as well as *control limits* (the dashed lines), which define the range of values that are expected to be observed if the process is operating stably at the control level (and thus differences in observed measurements are due simply to random variation). There are different types of control chart, depending on the kind of measurement being tracked, such as continuous measures, counts, or proportions. Multivariate control charts track several measurements jointly. The overall principle is the same in each case: a baseline control level is established by a series of measurements of the process, and control limits are defined in terms of the observed variability of the process (and possibly also the desired variability). One then plots measurements of the process taken at regular intervals and looks either for measurements lying outside the control limits (and thus indicating that the process is operating outside of its normal range, presumably because of some interfering factor), or for patterns in the measurements which suggest that the observed variability is not random, but is due to some factor or factors affecting the process.

Figure 7a illustrates a process that is under statistical control; Fig. 7b shows one that is out of control and Fig. 8a shows one that, while apparently under control (being inside the control limits), shows patterns in the measurements that deserve investigation.

In the decades since they were first developed, there have been many different variations developed to handle the variety of process control situations that arise. One of the most useful variants is the *cumulative sum* or cusum chart, which is more sensitive at detecting changes in the level of process measurements. Cusum charts work by accumulating the deviations from the baseline expected value of the process; if the variation is truly random, the variations in one direction counterbalance those in the opposite direction and the cumulative sum remains close to zero. If, on the other hand, variations in the process are biased even slightly in one direction or the other, then the cumulative sum will advance towards the upper or lower control limit. This accumulation of small biases allows the trend to be detected earlier than would be the case with a standard control chart. Figure 8 shows both a standard chart and a cusum chart for a process that is drifting slowly out of control.

The theory and practice of control charts is highly developed and remains a central part of quality engineering. Good references are Montgomery (1996) and Duncan (1986). More recently, Box and Luceño (1997) have elaborated the relationship between statistical process control and engineering control theory.

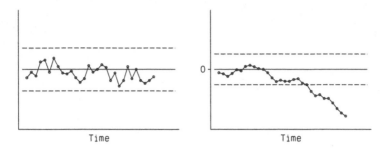

Fig. 8 A Process drifting slowly out of control as shown in (**a**) A standard control chart, (**b**) A cusum chart

There are also statistical methods for the optimization of process metrics, such as Evolutionary Operation (Box and Draper, 1969), response surface methodology (Montgomery and Myers, 2002), and data envelopment analysis/stochastic frontier analysis (Jacobs et al., 2006).

6. Data Quality

At this point, it is appropriate to return to the context of measurement and the dependence of statistical analysis on the quality of the underlying data collection process.

Data quality is a critical problem in industrial management, yet one often only vaguely recognized by decision makers who consume the ultimate endproducts of those data. This problem has come to light with the development of data warehouses, as warehouse developers discover that bad data can turn a data warehouse into a data garbage dump. The first step, then, in using measurements is ensuring that those measurements are of sufficient validity and accuracy to enable conclusions to be drawn from them.

The sources of data quality problems are manifold (apart from the question of bad metrics, dealt with in Sect. 3). Chief among them are

- Organizational problems
- Lack of precise definitions
- Lack of data validation
- Missing data
- Sampling bias

6.1. Organizational Problems

It is common for metrics to be defined and collected by people other than those to whom the metrics apply; this a recipe for trouble. The problem is exacerbated when a process is evaluated by management on the basis of metrics that the people carrying out the process find irrelevant or misguided; the inevitable result is distortion of the work process to produce acceptable numbers, rather than valid or meaningful ones. For a metrics program to be successful, all parts of the organization involved need to be in agreement on the meaningfulness of the metrics and their role in the organization's effective functioning.

6.2. Lack of Precise Definitions

Many problems are caused by lack of a precise definition for a measurement. For example, measuring defects in software for whatever purpose, be it research or quality management, requires a clear definition of what constitutes a defect. This definition may reasonably vary depending on the question being asked (and the goal that question is answering), but whatever the purpose, the definition must address such issues as

- Are feature enhancement requests defects?
- Are usability problems defects?
- Are internally reported problems defects?

Similarly, measuring the time it takes to repair a defect requires addressing such issues as

- When does the clock start?
- Does it start at different times for internally vs. externally reported defects?
- When does the clock stop?
- What time is recorded if the repair of the defect turns out not to be a repair after all?

If these issues are not addressed at the time the metric is defined, then they will have to be addressed by those collecting the data if and when they arise. Not surprisingly, when that happens the results may not be as intended. The problem of vague definition is exacerbated when the measurements must be collected by different groups or individuals who often have, or develop over time, different interpretations of the definition. Such different definitions may go unnoticed for long periods of time until some situation brings it out.

Detecting the lack of precise definitions is done most directly by looking for explicit written documentation of what the definition of each of the measures is. In the frequent case where such information is lacking, it becomes necessary to interrogate those responsible for collecting, processing, and analyzing the data to find out what they have been assuming the measures' definitions to be; their answers will often be conflicting.

6.3. Lack of Data Validation

A precise definition for a metric is no guarantee that the values recorded for it make sense. It is very common to find observations with dubious or outright impossible values, due directly or indirectly to data-entry problems. These range from typing errors to miscalibrated measuring devices to lack of understanding of the metric's definition. The presence of bad values is usually easy to detect if one takes the trouble to look; frequently, as long as the measurement process produces values that seem "reasonable" no-one bothers to audit the process to verify that the measurements are correct. For example, consider measurements of resolution times for customer problems that are derived from recording the dates and times when the service ticket is officially opened and closed. If there is no validation done to ensure that the closing time is chronologically later than the opening time, the derived resolution metric might take on zero or even negative values (perhaps from subtraction of a constant amount from all tickets; this would only become negative in ones with small values). Even if this occurs in only a small percentage of cases, it can seriously bias the estimates of resolution time. Simply dropping anomalous cases when they are found is not a solution until investigation has shown that such cases occur at random rather than for some systematic reason. Any particular case of bad data may have many potential causes which must be investigated; an occasional data entry error might be ignored, but a systematic distortion of entries cannot be.

Validation of data is the essential tedious first step of any data analysis. It can be made much easier and faster if the data are validated as they are collected. There are two difficulties which frequently prevent that from happening. First, those collecting the data are often not the ones who will use it for analysis, and thus have little understanding or interest in making sure that the data are correct. This is not due to maliciousness; it is simply due to different motivation. To take the above example, the people working the service desk have as their main goal the rapid processing of as many service tickets as possible; data validation interferes with this, with little or no visible benefit. Solving this problem requires educating management as well as the workers.

Second, even if validation is intended, it may be impossible to do in real time without degrading process performance. The general solution here is to arrange some way to do it "off line" rather than in real time, for example, validating new database entries overnight.

Detecting problems of data validation is done by performing extensive assertion- and consistency-checking of the dataset. For example, if the dataset contains measures of duration, they should be checked to make sure that each value is greater than zero. Often it is important to ensure that the value of one measure is logically compatible with that of some other measure. For example, a problem resolution of "replaced circuit board" is not consistent with a trouble report classified as "software problem."

6.4. Missing Data

It is rare to find a large dataset without missing values on at least some of its measurements, and care must be taken that missing-value codes (e.g., "99") are not mistakenly interpreted as genuine data values. (A particularly insidious case of this occurs with spreadsheets, which treat missing data as actually having the value "0.") This raises the possibility that an analysis using only the available data may be subject to an unknown amount of error. The issues are therefore how much data can be missing without affecting the quality of the measurements, and what if anything can be done to remedy the situation. There is a large body of literature on this subject, which is discussed in the chapter by Audris Mockus in this volume.

6.5. Sampling Bias

The problems just discussed are easy to observe and understand. More subtle but just as serious is the problem of sampling bias. A precisely defined, thoroughly validated, complete dataset can still be useless if the measurement process only measures a particular subset of the population of interest. This can be for a number of reasons:

6.5.1. Self-selection

It may be that only some units in the population put themselves in the position of being measured. This is a typical problem in surveys, since typically there is little compulsion to respond, and so only those individuals who choose to be measured provide data. Similarly, only those customers with problems are observed by the customer service department.

6.5.2. Observability

Some measurements by definition are selective and can lead to subtle biases. For example, in a study of defect densities, some source modules will have no (known) defects and thus a defect density of zero. If these cases are excluded, then statements about correlates of defect density are true only of modules which have known defects, not all modules, and thus cannot easily be generalized. Another kind of observability problem can occur, not with the units being observed, but with the measuring device. For example, if problem resolutions are measured in days, then resolutions which are done in ten minutes are not accurately observed, since their time must be rounded down to zero or up to one day.

6.5.3. Non-random Sampling

A frequent problem in surveys, this also plagues many other kinds of measurements, including experiments where the selection of experimental units is not properly considered. Lack of information about the population, coupled with a bias to sample those units which are easy to sample, can result in a measured sample which is quite unrepresentative of the population of interest.

Detecting sampling bias can be difficult, because it typically happens before the data are collected. It can sometimes be spotted by the absence of certain kinds of data (customers from one region, service times longer than 1 month, etc.), but usually must be identified by studying the documentation for the data collection process or interrogating the people who carry it out. Correcting sampling bias is extremely difficult, since the basic problem is the complete lack of representation for some part of the population. To the extent that the type and degree of bias is known (also a difficult problem) it may be possible to adjust for it, but generally the only solution is to make it clear just what subset of the population is described in the dataset. A good discussion of detecting and coping with overt and hidden biases can be found in Rosenbaum (2002).

As should be clear from the above, problems of data quality are ubiquitous and difficult to deal with, particularly because there are only general guidelines for what to do, and each case must be handled on its own terms.

7. Summary

This chapter has discussed the role of the measurement process, the need for metrics to be clearly defined, reliable, and valid in order for them to be effective, and various statistical techniques and pitfalls in analyzing measurement data. Understanding measurement is a crucial part in the development of any branch of science (see Hand, 2004); the amount of effort devoted to it in empirical research in software engineering reflects the necessity of answering some of the most fundamental questions facing computer science and engineering. Fortunately, we can take advantage of the experience and knowledge gained by other disciplines, and apply them with advantage in developing effective software measurement.

References

Agresti, A, *Analysis of Ordinal Categorical Data*. New York: Wiley. 1984.
Agresti, A, *An Introduction to Categorical Data Analysis*. New York: Wiley. 1998.
Anscombe, F, Graphs in statistical analysis. *American Statistician*. 27(1):17–21. 1973.
Basili, V, Caldiera, G, and Rombach, D, The goal question metric approach. In: Marciniak, J, ed., *Encyclopedia of Software Engineering*. New York: Wiley. 1994.
Bevington, P, and Robinson, D, *Data Reduction and Error Analysis for the Physical Sciences*, 2nd ed. New York: McGraw-Hill. 1992.
Bowerman, B, and O'Connell, R, *Forecasting and Time Series: An Applied Approach*, 3rd. ed. Belmont, CA: Wadsworth. 1993.
Box, G and Draper, N, *Evolutionary Operation: A Statistical Method for Process Improvement*. New York: Wiley. 1969.
Box, G and Luceño, A, *Statistical Control by Monitoring and Feedback Adjustment*. New York: Wiley. 1997.

Briand, L, El Emam, K, and Morasca, S, On the application of measurement theory to software engineering. *Empirical Software Engineering.* 1(1). 1996.

Chayes, F, *Ratio Correlation.* Chicago: University of Chicago Press. 1971.

Cleveland, W, *The Elements of Graphing Data.* Summit, NJ: Hobart Press. 1994.

Cliff, N, What is and isn't measurement. In: Keren, G and Lewis, C, eds., *A Handbook For Data Analysis in the Behavioral Sciences,* Vol. 1: *Methodological Issues.* Hillsdale, NJ: Erlbaum. 1992.

Cohen, J, *Statistical Power Analysis for the Behavioral Sciences,* 2nd ed. Hillside, NJ: Erlbaum. 1988.

Comrey, A and Lee, H, *A First Course in Factor Analysis,* 2nd ed. Hillsdale, NJ: Erlbaum. 1992.

Crowder, M, and Hand, D, *Analysis of Repeated Measures.* New York: Chapman and Hall. 1990.

Dobson, A, *An Introduction to Generalized Linear Models,* 2nd ed. New York: Chapman and Hall/CRC. 2001.

Draper, N and Smith, H, *Applied Regression Analysis,* 2nd ed. New York: Wiley. 1998.

Duncan, A, *Quality Control and Industrial Statistics,* 5th ed. New York: Irwin. 1986.

El Emam, K, Benlarbi, S, and Goel, N, Comparing case-based reasoning classifiers for predicting high risk software components. National Research Council Canada technical report NRC 43602/ERB-1058. 1999.

Fenton, N and Pfleeger, S, *Software Metrics: A Rigorous and Practical Approach,* 2nd ed. Boston: PWS Publishing. 1997.

Fliess, J, *Statistical Methods for Rates and Proportions,* 2nd ed. New York: Wiley. 1981.

Ghiselli, E, Campbell, J, and Zedeck, S, *Measurement Theory for the Behavioral Sciences.* San Francisco: Freeman. 1981.

Good, P, *Permutation Tests.* New York: Springer. 1994.

Goodman, L and Kruskal, W, *Measures of Association for Cross Classifications.* New York: Springer. 1979.

Gottman, J, ed., *The Analysis of Change.* Hillsdale, NJ: Erlbaum. 1995.

Haccou, P, and Meelis, E, *Statistical Analysis of Behavioural Data: An Approach Based on Time-Structured Models.* Oxford: Oxford University Press. 1994.

Hand, D, *Construction and Assessment of Classification Rules.* New York: Wiley. 1997.

Hand, D, *Measurement Theory and Practice: The World through Quantification.* Oxford: Oxford University Press. 2004.

Hosmer, D and Lemeshow, S, *Applied Logistic Regression.* New York: Wiley. 1989.

Hosmer, D and Lemeshow, S, *Applied Survival Analysis.* New York: Wiley. 1999.

Jacobs, R, Smith, P, and Street, A, *Measuring Efficiency in Health Care: Analytic Techniques and Health Policy.* Cambridge: Cambridge University Press. 2006.

Keppel, G, *Design and Analysis: A Researcher's Handbook,* 3rd ed. New York: Prentice Hall. 1991.

Kleinbaum, D, *Logistic Regression.* New York: Springer. 1994.

Kleinbaum, D, *Survival Analysis.* New York: Springer. 1996.

Krantz, D, Luce, R, Suppes, P, and Tversky, A, *Foundations of Measurement.* New York: Academic. 1971.

Long, J, *Regression Models for Categorical and Limited Dependent Variables.* Thousand Oaks, CA: Sage. 1997.

Maddala, G, *Limited-Dependent and Qualitative Variables in Econometrics.* Cambridge: Cambridge University Press. 1986.

Makridakis, S, Wheelwright, S, and Hyndman, R, *Forecasting: Methods and Applications,* 3rd ed. New York: Wiley. 1998.

Montgomery, D, *Introduction to Statistical Quality Control,* 3rd ed. New York: Wiley. 1996.

Montgomery, D and Myers, R, *Response Surface Methodology: Process and Product Optimization Using Designed Experiments,* 2nd ed. New York: Wiley. 2002.

Phelps, C, and Huston, A, Estimating diagnostic accuracy using a "fuzzy gold standard". *Medical Decision Making* 15:44–57. 1995.

Rawlings, J, Pantula, S, and Dickey, D, *Applied Regression Analysis,* 2nd ed. New York: Springer. 1998.

Rosenbaum, P, *Observational Studies,* 2nd ed. New York: Springer. 2002.

Rosenberg, J, A methodology for evaluating predictive metrics. In: Zelkowitz, M., ed., *Advances in Computers*, Vol. 23. New York: Academic. 2000.

Shepperd, M and Ince, D, *Derivation and Validation of Software Metrics*. Oxford: Clarendon Press. 1993.

Singer, J and Willett, J, *Applied Longitudinal Data Analysis: Modeling Change and Event Occurrence*. Oxford: Oxford University Press. 2003.

Sprent, P, *Applied Non-Parametric Statistical Methods*, 2nd ed. New York: Chapman and Hall. 1993.

Swets, J, *Signal Detection Theory and ROC Analysis in Psychology and Diagnostics*. Hillsdale, NJ: Erlbaum. 1996.

Taylor, J, *An Introduction to Error Analysis*, 2nd ed. Sausalito, CA: University Science Books. 1997.

Valenstein, P, Evaluating diagnostic tests with imperfect standards. *American Journal of Clinical Pathology* 93:252–258. 1990.

Velleman, P, Nominal, ordinal, interval, and ratio typologies are misleading. *American Statistician*. 47:65–72. 1993.

Wellek, S, *Testing Statistical Hypotheses of Equivalence*. New York: Chapman and Hall/CRC Press. 2002.

Wickens, T, *Multiway Contingency Tables Analysis for the Social Sciences*. Hillsdale, NJ: Erlbaum. 1989.

Zhou, X, Obuchowski, N, and McClish, D, *Statistical Methods in Diagnostic Medicine*. New York: Wiley. 2002.

Zuse, H, *Software Complexity: Measures and Methods*. New York: Walter de Gruyter. 1990.

Chapter 7
Missing Data in Software Engineering

Audris Mockus

Abstract The collection of valid software engineering data involves substantial effort and is not a priority in most software production environments. This often leads to missing or otherwise invalid data. This fact tends to be overlooked by most software engineering researchers and may lead to a biased analysis. This chapter reviews missing data methods and applies them on a software engineering data set to illustrate a variety of practical contexts where such techniques are needed and to highlight the pitfalls of ignoring the missing data problem.

1. Introduction

The goal of this chapter is to increase the awareness of missing data techniques among people performing studies in software engineering. Three primary reasons for this presentation are:

1. The "quick-fix" techniques that drop the cases with missing values may yield biased or inconclusive results. Such techniques are still widely (and often implicitly) used in software engineering
2. Dealing with missing values is no longer a burden for a practitioner, because easy to use statistical software is now available on popular platforms
3. Software represents a distinct data source with unique reasons and patterns for missing data. For example, software studies tend not to have the luxury of large sample sizes requiring analysis methods that use all available data, including incomplete cases. Many properties of software can not be measured directly, therefore investigators have to get the necessary information from people who create and maintain a particular piece of software, leading to frequent and complex patterns of missing data

Section 2 discusses sources of software data. The next section introduces an illustrative example evaluating how a software process influences development time. Section 4 presents a general statistical perspective for dealing with missing data with an illustrative example. Section 5 discusses non traditional missing data problems specific to the field of software engineering. A summary is provided in Sect. 6.

F. Shull et al. (eds.), *Guide to Advanced Empirical Software Engineering.*
© Springer 2008

2. Sources of Software Data

Software engineering data come from several distinct sources. The three primary sources are:

- Data collected through experimental, observational, and retrospective studies
- Software metrics or reported project management data including effort, size, and project milestone estimates
- Software artifacts including requirements, design, and inspection documents, source code and its change history, fault tracking, and testing databases

To narrow the scope of the presentation we did not include data sources produced directly by software with little or no human involvement, such as program execution and performance logs or the output of program analysis tools. Such data sources tend to produce tool specific patterns of missing data that are of limited use in other domains.

Surveys in an industrial environment are usually small and expensive to conduct. The primary reasons are the lack of subjects with required knowledge and the minimal availability of expert developers who, it appears, are always working toward a likely-to-be-missed deadline. The small sample size limits the applicability of deletion techniques that reduce the sample size even further. This may lead to an inconclusive analysis, because the sample of complete cases may be too small to detect statistically significant trends. If, on the other hand, the sample sizes are large and only a small percentage of data are missing, a deletion technique (a technique that removes missing observations) may work quite well.

The values in survey data may be missing if a survey respondent declines to fill the survey, ignores a question, or does not know the answer to some of the questions.

Reported data on software metrics often contain the desired measurements on quality and productivity. Unfortunately, the reported data are often not comparable across distinct projects (Herbsleb and Grinter, 1998). The reasons include numerous social and organizational factors related to intended use and potential misuse of metrics, and serious difficulties involved in defining, measuring, and interpreting a conceptual measure in different projects.

Reported data need extensive validation to confirm that it reflects the quantities an analyst is interested in. Data collection is rarely a priority in software organizations (Goldenson et al., 1999). The priority of validating collected data is even lower, often leading to unreliable and misleading software measures. In addition, some software measures are difficult to obtain or have large uncertainty. Examples of such measures include function point estimates or size and effort estimates in the early stages of a project. Frequently data values are missing because some metrics are not collected for the entire period of the study or for a subset of projects.

Software artifacts are large, highly structured, and require substantial effort to interpret. Measures derived from software artifacts tend to be more precise and consistent over time than measures derived from surveys and reported data. They measure the artifact itself, as opposed to the subjective perception of the artifact captured by survey measures. Traditionally, software artifacts are measured based on the properties of source code. Such measures include source code complexity (Halstead, 1977; McCabe, 1976), complexity of an object oriented design (Chidamber and Kemerer, 1994), or functional size (Albrecht and Gaffney, 1983). Instead of measuring the source code, it is possible to measure the properties of changes to the code. This requires analysis of change history data, see, for example, (Mockus, 2007). Artifact data may be missing or difficult to access for older software artifacts because of obsolete storage or backup media. Consequently, software artifacts are usually available or missing in their entirety, reducing the need for the traditional missing data techniques that assume that data are only partially missing. Measuring such artifacts might require substantial effort, especially if they were maintained using obsolete tools.

3. Example Data

To illustrate the application of missing data methods we will use a case study of process improvement in a software organization (Herbsleb et al., 2000). The study involved a medium-size, process-oriented software organization performing contract work. One of the study goals was to determine if the excessive detail of software process had increased the development interval. In particular, the study investigated the relationship of development interval and project tracking measures.

The collected data came from three sources: survey questions, reported project metrics, and the source code change history. The development interval was the response or dependent variable. We model (predict) it using several project tracking measures described below that are used as independent, predictor, or explanatory variables.

3.1. Survey

A total of 68 surveys of 19 individuals evaluating three dimensions of project tracking process for 42 projects were collected.

The three dimensions of project tracking were defined by the following questions.

1. Were the project's actual results (e.g., schedule, size, and cost) compared with estimates in the software plans?
2. Was corrective action taken when actual results deviated significantly from the project's software plans?
3. Were changes in the project's plans agreed to by all affected groups and individuals?

Subjects evaluated three dimensions of project tracking with ordinal ratings: (1) – "Rarely if ever," (2) – "Occasionally," (3) – "About half of the time," (4) – "Frequently," and (5) – "Almost always." When the subject did not have enough knowledge of the project to answer the question, they entered "don't know."

To exemplify missing data techniques we simplify the analysis by treating each survey as an independent observation. In our example several individuals evaluated most projects and several projects were evaluated by a single individual. Therefore, multiple reports on one project (or done by a single person) are not independent. Unfortunately, adjusting for that dependence would distract from the presentation of missing data techniques.

3.2. Software Change Data

The project interval and size data were obtained from change history databases. The project interval was measured in days from the start of the first change until the completion of the last change. The project size was measured in number of logical changes called Maintenance Requests (MRs).

3.3. Reported Project Data

The reported project data included size, staff months, number of faults, and interval. Unfortunately, reported data were not consistent, therefore it was not used in the models. While some projects measured size in function points (FP), other projects measured size in lines of code (LOC). The reported function point and LOC measures did not correlate well with the amount of code developed (as obtained from change history) or with the reported staff months of effort. Furthermore, the reported interval did not correlate with the duration of the development phase measured by the time difference between the last and the first change. These serious validity problems made the reported data unsuitable for further analysis.

3.4. Missing Values

Change history databases for ten of the surveyed projects were moved off line and unavailable for analysis. Because the response variable interval was missing for those projects we excluded them from further consideration (other reasons are given in the discussion of the types of missing data). An additional six cases were dropped because all the project tracking questions were answered "don't know." That left us with 52 cases (corresponding to 34 projects) for the analysis.

The list of data quality problems in this example may seem enormous, but in our experience such data quality is not unusual in a software study.

We used multiple linear regression [see, for example, (Weisberg, 1985)] to model the project development interval. The project size and the three tracking measures were independent variables. We included the project size as a predictor because it affects the project interval.

Inspection of the variables showed increasing variances (a scatterplot with a very large density of points at low values) for the interval and size. A square root transformation was sufficient to stabilize the variance of the interval and size and led to the following final model:

$$\sqrt{\text{Interval}} = b_0 + b_1\sqrt{\text{Size}} + b_2\text{Tracking}_1 + b_3\text{Tracking}_2 + b_4\text{Tracking}_3 + \text{Error}. \quad (1)$$

The following section describes various techniques to fit such models in the presence of missing data.

4. A Statistical Perspective on Missing Data

In statistical analysis the phenomena of interest is commonly represented by a rectangular ($n \times K$) matrix $Y = (y_{ij})$ where rows represent a sample of n observations, cases, or subjects. The columns represent variables measured for each case. Each variable may be continuous, such as size and interval, or categorical like file or project.

Some cells in such a matrix may be missing. It may happen if a measure is not collected, or is not applicable, for example, if a respondent does not answer a question on a survey form.

The mechanism by which some cells are not observed is important to select an appropriate analysis technique. Denote the response indicator

$$R_{ij} = \begin{cases} 1, & y_{ij} \quad \text{observed}, \\ 0, & y_{ij} \quad \text{missing}. \end{cases} \quad (2)$$

Denote all the values of the observations that are missing Y_{mis} as and the rest as Y_{obs}. Let $P(R|Y_{obs}, Y_{mis}, \theta)$ be the probability distribution function of R given a statistical model specified by parameter θ and all the values of Y. The data are *missing at random* (MAR) according to Little and Rubin (1987) if

$$P(R\,|\,Y_{obs}, Y_{mis}, \theta) = P(R\,|\,Y_{obs}, \theta),$$

i.e., the distribution of the response indicator may depend on the observed values but may not depend on the values that are missing. The data are *missing completely at random* (MCAR) if a stronger condition holds:

$$f(R\,|\,Y_{obs}, Y_{mis}, \theta) = f(R\,|\,\theta).$$

The MAR assumption allows the probability that a datum is missing to depend on the datum itself indirectly through quantities that are observed. For example, in the described data, the interviewees might remember less about smaller projects, resulting in higher likelihood that some of the survey's values are missing. The MAR assumption would apply, because the predictor "project size" explains the likelihood that the value will be missing. MCAR assumption would not apply, because the probability that a value is missing depends on project's size. However, if we do not have a measure of project's size or simply do not include project's size in our estimation model, then even the MAR assumption is not satisfied. Such case is referred to as data not missing at random (NMAR). The NMAR data can be made to satisfy the MAR assumption if variables that characterize situations when a value is missing are added. Therefore, it is important to add variables that might predict the missing value mechanism to the dataset.

Personal income obtained via survey represents a typical example where the MAR assumption is not satisfied. It is well known that extreme values of personal income are less likely to be reported. Consequently, the MAR assumption is violated, unless the survey can reliably measure variables that are strongly related to income. When extreme values are more likely to be missing, the probability that a value is missing depends on the value itself and, unless other predictors can fully account for that change in the probability of being missing, the MAR assumption is no longer satisfied.

It is worth pointing out that it is impossible to test the MAR hypothesis based on the dataset itself, since that would require knowing the values for missing observations. It could be tested by gathering additional information, for example, by conducting a repeat survey for the missing cases. However, when the data are missing beyond the control of the investigator one can never be sure whether the MAR assumption holds. It is possible to test the MCAR assumption, [see, e.g. Little (1988); Kim and Curry (1977)]. However, the MCAR assumption rarely needs to be tested, because the MCAR assumption rarely holds in practice and because many easy-to-use MAR methods are available.

Situations where even the MAR assumption does not hold may require an explicit model for the missing data mechanism. Such methods tend to be problem specific and require substantial statistical and domain expertise. A concept related to NMAR data (even though it is treated separately in literature) involves censoring in longitudinal studies where some outcome may not be known at the time the study has ended. For example, in software reliability we want to know the distribution of time until a software outage occurs. However, at any particular moment in time there may be many software systems that have not experienced an outage. Thus, we only know that the time until the first outage is larger than the current system runtime for these systems, but we do not know its value. A common approach to deal with censored data is to estimate a survival curve using Kaplan–Meier Estimate (Kaplan and Meyer, 1958; Fleming and Harrington, 1984). The survival curve is a graph showing the percentage of systems surviving (with no outage) versus system runtime. It has been applied to measure software reliability in, for example, (Mockus, 2006).

Little and Hyonggin (2003) discuss ways to handle undesirable NMAR data and recommend calculating bounds by using all possible values of missing variables (an approach particularly suitable in case of binary values), conducting a sensitivity analysis by considering several models of how the data are missing, or conducting a Bayesian analysis with a prior distribution for missing values. In most practical situations we recommend attempting to measure variables that capture differences between missing and complete cases in order for the missing-data mechanism to satisfy the MAR assumption. Methods that can handle MAR data can then be applied.

In our example, the "don't know" answers in survey questions reflect the lack of knowledge by the subject and have no obvious relationship to the unobserved value. One may argue that even the MCAR assumption might be reasonable in this case. On the other hand, the ten cases for projects without change history present a completely different missing data mechanism. Because the projects are older, they are likely to be different from newer projects in the analyzed sample. Data are missing because these projects are old (and presumably different) and, therefore, the MAR assumption does not apply. Consequently, the conclusions drawn from the analysis of the relationship between project tracking and project interval may not apply to old projects. We removed these projects from further consideration and narrowed conclusions to explicitly exclude them. For simplicity, we also excluded six observations where all tracking measures are missing. One can argue against such a decision, because these observations can still be used to make a more precise regression relationship between project size and project interval.

Many statistical packages deal with missing data by simply dropping the cases that have at least one value missing. Besides being inefficient (fewer observations are used for inference), such a technique may be biased unless the observations are MCAR. The MCAR assumption is rarely a reasonable assumption in practice.

Model based techniques where a statistical model is postulated for complete data provide transparency of assumptions, but other techniques are often simpler to apply in practice. Given that statistical software provides tools to deal with missing data using model based techniques (Schafer, 1999; R Development Core Team, 2005) we would recommend using them instead of the remaining techniques that have limited theoretical justification or require unrealistic assumptions. For completeness, we briefly describe most of traditional techniques as well. The goal of traditional techniques is to produce the sample mean or the covariance matrix to be used for regression, analysis of variance, or simply to calculate correlations. All traditional methods produce correct results under the MCAR assumption.

For more in-depth understanding of the statistical approaches Little and Rubin (1987) summarize statistical models for missing data and Schafer (1997) describes more recent results. Rubin (1987) investigates sampling survey issues. Little and Rubin (1989) and Schafer and Olsen (1998) provide examples with advice for practitioners. Roth (1994) provides a broad review of missing data technique application in many fields.

Various missing data techniques have been evaluated in the software engineering context of cost estimation. Strike et al., (2001) evaluate listwise deletion, mean imputation, and eight different types of hot-deck imputation and find them to have small biases and high precision. This suggests that the simplest technique, listwise deletion, is a reasonable choice. However, it did not have the minimal bias and highest precision obtained by hot-deck imputation. Myrtveit et al. (2001) evaluate listwise deletion, mean imputation, similar response pattern imputation, and full information maximum likelihood (FIML) missing data techniques in the context of software cost modeling. They found bias for non-MCAR data in all but FIML technique and found that listwise deletion performed comparably to the remaining two techniques except in cases where listwise deletion data set was too small to fit a meaningful model. k-Nearest Neighbor Imputation is evaluated by simulating missing data in Jönsson and Wohlin (2004). Authors' find the method to be adequate and recommend to use k equal to the square root of the number of complete cases. More recently, Twala et al. (2006) compare seven missing data techniques using eight datasets and find listwise deletion to be the least efficient and multiple imputation to be the most accurate.

In the following sections we consider several broad classes of missing data techniques. Section 4.1 considers methods that remove cases with missing values. Ways to fill in missing values are considered in Sect. 4.2. Section 4.3 describes techniques that generate multiple complete datasets, each to be analyzed using traditional complete data methods. Results from these analyses are then combined using special rules. We exemplify some of these methods in Sect. 4.4.

4.1. Deletion Techniques

Deletion techniques remove some of the cases in order to compute the mean vector and the covariance matrix. *Casewise deletion, complete case,* or *listwise deletion* method is the simplest technique where all cases missing at least one observation are removed. This approach is applicable only when a small fraction of observations is discarded. If deleted cases do not represent a random sample from the entire population, the inference will be biased. Also, fewer cases result in less efficient inference.

In our example the *complete case* method loses 18 cases (around 34% of the 52 cases that we consider). Table 1 shows output from the multiple regression model in (1).

Table 1 Multiple regression for the *complete case analysis*

Variable	Value	Std. error	t Value	$Pr(>|t|)$
Intercept	3.1060	5.2150	0.5956	0.5561
Sqrt(size)	0.4189	0.1429	2.9315	0.0065
Tracking1	0.9025	0.9885	0.9130	0.3688
Tracking2	0.5363	1.2332	0.4349	0.6669
Tracking3	0.7186	1.1033	0.6513	0.5200

Multiple regression shows that the project size is an important predictor of the interval but none of the process coefficients are significant at the 10% level (although a 5% level is more commonly used, we chose to use a 10% level that is more suitable for the small sample size of our example and, more importantly, to illustrate the differences among missing data methods). It is not too surprising, since more than a third of the observations were removed from the analysis.

Pairwise deletion or *available case* method retains all non missing cases for each pair of variables. We need at least three variables for this approach to be different from listwise deletion. For example, consider the simplest example where the first of three variables are missing in the first case and the remaining cases are complete. Then, the sample covariance matrix would use all cases for the submatrix representing sample covariances of the second and third variables. The entry representing the sample variance of the first variable and sample covariances between the first and the remaining variables would use only complete cases. More generally, the sample covariance matrix is:

$$S_{jk} = \frac{\sum_{jk} R_{ik} R_{ij} (y_j - \overline{y}_i^k)(y_k - \overline{y}_k^j)}{\sum_i R_{ij} R_{ik} - 1},$$

where $\overline{y}_j^k = \sum_i R_{ij} R_{ik} y_{ij} / \sum_i R_{ij} R_{ik}$ and R_{ij} and R_{ik} are indicators of missing values as defined in (2). Although such method uses more observations, it may lead to a covariance matrix that is not positive-definite (positive-definite matrix has positive eigenvalues) and unsuitable for further analysis, i.e., multiple regression.

4.2. Imputation Techniques

The substitution or imputation techniques fill (impute) the values that are missing. Any standard analysis may then be done on the complete dataset. Many such techniques would typically provide underestimated standard errors.

The simplest substitution technique fills in the average value over available cases (*mean substitution*). This underestimates variances and covariances in MCAR case and is likely to introduce bias otherwise. Smaller variances may reduce *p*-values and, therefore, may provide false impressions about the importance of some predictors. Table 2 shows results using *mean substitution*. Table 2 shows that the project size is an

Table 2 Results for the *mean substitution analysis*

Variable	Value	Std. error	t Value	Pr(>|t|)
Intercept	3.1611	2.8054	1.1268	0.2656
Sqrt(size)	0.3904	0.1134	3.4437	0.0012
Tracking1	−0.0871	0.5903	−0.1475	0.8834
Tracking2	0.8557	0.7339	1.1660	0.2495
Tracking3	1.4568	0.7678	1.8975	0.0639

important predictor of the interval and that the third dimension of tracking measure (level of agreement by all affected parties to the changes in the software commitments) might increase the interval. The coefficient is significant at 10% level.

Regression substitution uses multiple linear regression to impute missing values. The regression is done on complete cases. The resulting prediction equation is used for each missing case. *Regression substitution* underestimates the variances less than *mean substitution*. A stochastic variation of *regression substitution* replaces a missing value by the value predicted by regression plus a regression residual from a randomly chosen complete case.

Table 3 shows results based on a basic liner regression substitution. For our example the results are similar to mean substitution.

Other substitution methods include *group mean substitution* that calculates means over groups of cases known to have homogeneous values within the group. A variation of group mean substitution when the group size is one is called *hot-deck* imputation. In *hot-deck* imputation for each case that has a missing value, a similar case is chosen at random. The missing value is then substituted using the value obtained from that case. Similarity may be measured using a Euclidean distance function for numeric variables that are most correlated with the variable that has a missing value.

The following two reasons prevent us from recommending simple deletion and imputation methods when a substantial proportion of cases (more than 10%) are missing:

1. It is not clear when they do not work
2. They give incorrect precision estimates making them unsuitable for interval estimation and hypothesis testing

As the percentage of missing data increases to higher levels, the assumptions and techniques have a more significant impact on results. Consequently, it becomes very important to use a model based technique with a carefully chosen model.

While there is no consensus among all experts about what techniques should be recommended, a fairly detailed set of recommendations is presented in Roth (1994) and Little and Hyonggin (2003), where factors such as proportion of missing data and the type of missing data (MCAR, MAR, NMAR) are considered. Roth (1994) recommends using the simplest techniques, such as pairwise deletion, in the MCAR case and model based techniques when the MAR assumption does not hold or when the percent of missing data exceeds 15%. Because we doubt the validity of the

Table 3 Results for the *regression substitution analysis*

Variable	Value	Std. error	t Value	$Pr(>|t|)$
Intercept	3.5627	3.3068	1.0774	0.2868
Sqrt(Size)	0.3889	0.1242	3.1321	0.0030
Tracking1	0.0339	0.8811	0.0385	0.9695
Tracking2	0.6011	1.0760	0.5586	0.5791
Tracking3	1.5250	0.8518	1.7904	0.0798

MCAR assumption in most practical cases we do not recommend using techniques that rely on it unless the percent of missing data is small.

4.3. Multiple Imputation

Multiple imputation (MI) is a model based technique where a statistical model is postulated for complete data. A multivariate normal model is typically used for continuous data and a log-linear model is used for categorical data. In MI each missing value is replaced (imputed) by $m > 1$ plausible values drawn from their predictive distribution. Consequently, instead of one data table with missing values we get m complete tables. After doing identical analyses on each of the tables the results are combined using simple rules to produce the estimates and standard errors that reflect uncertainty introduced by the missing data.

The possibility of doing an arbitrary statistical analysis for each complete data set and then combining estimates, standard deviations, and *p*-values allows the analyst to use a complete data technique that is the most appropriate for their problem. In our example we chose to use multiple linear regression.

The attractiveness of the MI technique lies in the ability to use any standard statistical package on the imputed datasets. Only a few (3–5) imputations are needed to produce quite accurate results (Schafer and Olsen, 1998). Software to produce the imputed tables is available from several sources, most notably from Schafer (1999) and R Development Core Team (2005). We do not describe the technical details on how the imputations are performed because it is beyond the scope of this presentation and the analyst can use any MI package to perform this step.

After the m MI tables are produced, each table may be analyzed by any statistical package. To combine the results of m analyses the following rules are used (Rubin, 1987). Denote the quantities of interest produced by the analyses as $P_1, \ldots, P_m$ and their estimated variances as $S_1, \ldots, S_m$.

- The overall estimate for P is an average value of P_i's: $\hat{P} = \sum_i P_i / m$

- The overall estimate for S is $\hat{S} = \sum_i S_i / m + \frac{m+1}{m(m-1)} \sum_i (\hat{P} - P_i)^2$

A rough confidence interval for P is $\hat{P} \pm 2\sqrt{\hat{S}}$. This inference is based on a t distribution and is derived under the assumption that complete data have an infinite number of degrees of freedom. A refinement of the rules for small datasets is presented in Barnard and Rubin (1999). There $\hat{P}$ has a t distribution with variance $\hat{S}$ and degrees of freedom given by a fairly involved formula:

$$\left(\frac{1}{v} + \frac{1}{\hat{v}} \right)^{-1},$$

where $v = (m-1)/\gamma^2$, $\hat{v} = n\frac{n+1}{n+3}(1-\gamma)$, n represents degrees of freedom for complete data, and

$$\gamma = \frac{1}{\frac{k(m-1)\sum_i S_i}{(m+1)\sum_i (\hat{P}-P_i)^2} + k}.$$

Sometimes the inference is performed on multiple quantities simultaneously, for example, if we want to compare two nested multiple regression models, where the more general model has one or more extra parameters that are equal to zero in the simpler model. The rules for combining MI results in such a case are quite complicated, [see, e.g., Schafer (1997, pp. 112–118)], however, the MI software (Schafer, 1999) implements required calculations.

4.4. Example

We used the *norm* package (Schafer, 1999) [also available as packages (Novo, 2002) for R system (R Development Core Team, 2005)] for Windows 95/98/NT platform to generate five imputations and ran multiple linear regression on each imputed data table. The estimates and standard errors from the regression were combined using multiple imputation rules. The *norm* package does not perform multiple regression, but it provides the functionality to combine the results from multiple regression analyses. We used this feature and the result is presented in Table 4. The coefficients are not much different from the regression imputation, although the third tracking dimension is now barely significant at the 10% level.

In most practical situations with a medium percentage of missing data there will be relatively small difference between the results obtained using different missing data methods (except for the *complete case* method), as happens to be the case in our example. However, in many examples (like this one), where the conclusions are based on *p*-values that are close to the chosen significance level, the use of MI is essential. In particular, the *mean substitution* method was significant at 0.07 level, but the MI method was not. If we, hypothetically, assume a world where results are judged to be significant at 0.07 significance level (instead of our own world, where the 0.05 significance level is most common), we would have reached different conclusions using different methods.

The example reiterates the fact that the standard deviation is underestimated in imputation methods and, therefore, the significance values are inflated. Although this example does not show large biases introduced by non MI methods, in general

Table 4 Results of *multiple imputation analysis*

Variable	Value	Std. error	t Value	$Pr(>|t|)$
Intercept	3.75	3.686	1.02	0.31
Sqrt(Size)	0.39	0.126	3.12	0.002
Tracking1	0.01	0.787	0.02	0.985
Tracking2	0.56	1.114	0.51	0.614
Tracking3	1.51	0.917	1.65	0.099

it may be a serious issue. The example also illustrates the lack of efficiency of the *complete case* method in line with the studies mentioned above.

5. Other Types of Unavailable Data

Software engineering has its own domain-specific types of missing data that are not present in the general statistical treatment. Here we briefly present specific cases of missing data in software artifacts. The first example deals with missing information on software change purpose, and the second example deals with missing information on software change effort.

5.1. Determining Change Purpose

Three primary driving forces in the evolution of software are: *adaptive* changes introduce new functionality, *corrective* changes eliminate faults, and *perfective* changes restructure code in order to improve understanding and simplify future changes (Swanson, 1976, An et al., 1987). Models of software evolution must take into account the significant differences in purpose and implementation of the three types of changes (Graves et al., 2000, Atkins et al., 1999). However, few change history databases record such information directly. Even if a record exists, it is rarely consistent over time or across organizations. Fortunately, change history databases usually record a short description of the purpose for the change at the maintenance request (MR) or lower level. Such description or abstract is provided by developers who implement the change.

Work in Mockus and Votta (1997) used textual analysis of MR abstracts to impute adaptive, corrective, or perfective labels to the changes. It classified MRs as adaptive, corrective, or perfective depending on which key words appear in these change abstracts. The classification scheme was able to tag around 85% of all MRs.

5.2. Estimating Change Effort

A particularly important quantity related to software is the cost of making changes. Therefore, it is of great interest to understand which factors have historically had strong effects on this cost, which could be approximated by the amount of time developers spend working on the change.

When performing historical studies of cost necessary to make a change, it is important to study changes at a fine level (MRs as opposed to releases). Studying larger units of change, such as releases, may make it impossible to separate the effects of important factors. For example, software releases typically contain a mixture of several types of changes, including new code and bug fixes. Consequently, the relative effort for the different types of changes can not be estimated at the release level. Also, larger change units may involve multiple developers and distinct parts of the code, making it difficult to estimate developer effects.

Measurements of change effort are not recorded in a typical software production environment. Graves and Mockus (1998) describe an iterative imputation algorithm that, in effect, divides a developer's monthly effort across all changes worked on in that month. The algorithm uses several measurements on each change including the size and type of a change. Both measures are related to the amount of effort required to make the change. The effort estimation tools provide valuable cost driver data that could be used in planning and in making decisions on how to reduce expenses in software development.

6. Summary

It should be noted that the quality of collected data will have more influence on the analysis results and the success of a study than a choice of method to deal with missing values. In particular, a successful data collection might result in few or no missing values.

In many realistic scenarios the data quality is low, and some values are missing. In such cases, the first step should be to determine the mechanism by which the data are missing and add observations that may explain why the values are missing. This would make the MAR assumption more plausible. For MAR (and MCAR) data, *multiple imputation* mitigates the effects of missing values. Other research and our case study have shown not only the importance of applying a missing data technique such as imputation, but also the importance of carrying out multiple imputation. In our case study we find that different conclusions may be reached depending on the particular method chosen to handle missing data. This demonstrates that the selection of a proper method to handle missing data is not simply a formal exercise, but it may, in certain circumstances, affect the outcome of an empirical study.

References

Albrecht, A. J. & Gaffney Jr., J. E. (1983), Software function, source lines of code, and development effort prediction: a software science validation, *IEEE Transactions on Software Engineering* **9**(6), 639–648.

An, K. H., Gustafson, D. A. & Melton, A. C. (1987), A model for software maintenance, in *Proceedings of the Conference in Software Maintenance*, Austin, Texas, pp. 57–62.

Atkins, D., Ball, T., Graves, T. & Mockus, A. (1999), Using version control data to evaluate the effectiveness of software tools, in *1999 International Conference on Software Engineering*, ACM Press, Rio de Janeiro, Brazil, pp. 324–333.

Barnard, J. & Rubin, D. B. (1999), Small sample degrees of freedom with multiple imputation, *Biometrika* **86**(4), 948–955.

Chidamber, S. R. & Kemerer, C. F. (1994), A metrics suite for object oriented design, *IEEE Trans. Software Eng.* **20**(6), 476–493.

Fleming, T. H. & Harrington, D. (1984), Nonparametric estimation of the survival distribution in censored data, *Communications in Statistics – Theory and Methods 20* **13**, 2469–2486.

Goldenson, D. R., Gopal, A. & Mukhopadhyay, T. (1999), Determinants of success in software measurement programs, in *Sixth International Symposium on Software Metrics*, IEEE Computer Society Press, Los Alamitos, CA, pp. 10–21.

Graves, T. L. & Mockus, A. (1998), Inferring change effort from configuration management databases, in *Metrics 98: Fifth International Symposium on Software Metrics*, Bethesda, MD, pp. 267–273.

Graves, T. L., Karr, A. F., Marron, J. S. & Siy, H. P. (2000), Predicting fault incidence using software change history, *IEEE Transactions on Software Engineering*, **26**(7), 653–661.

Halstead, M. H. (1977), *Elements of Software Science*, Elsevier North-Holland, New York.

Herbsleb, J. D. & Grinter, R. (1998), Conceptual simplicity meets organizational complexity: Case study of a corporate metrics program, in *20th International Conference on Software Engineering*, IEEE Computer Society Press, Los Alamitos, CA, pp. 271–280.

Herbsleb, J. D., Krishnan, M., Mockus, A., Siy, H. P. & Tucker, G. T. (2000), *Lessons from Ten Years of Software Factory Experience*, Technical Report, Bell Laboratories.

Jönsson, P. & Wohlin, C. (2004), An evaluation of k-nearest neighbour imputation using likert data, in *Proceedings of the 10th International Symposium on Software Metrics*, pp. 108–118.

Kaplan, E. & Meyer, P. (1958), Non-parametric estimation from incomplete observations, *Journal of the American Statistical Association*, 457–481.

Kim, J. & Curry, J. (1977), The treatment of missing data in multivariate analysis, *Social Methods and Research* **6**, 215–240.

Little, R. J. A. (1988), A test of missing completely at random for multivariate data with missing values, *Journal of the American Statistical Association* **83**(404), 1198–1202.

Little, R. & Hyonggin, A. (2003), Robust likelihood-based analysis of multivariate data with missing values, Technical Report Working Paper 5, The University of Michigan Department of Biostatistics Working Paper Series. http://www.bepress.com/umichbiostat/paper5

Little, R. J. A. & Rubin, D. B. (1987), *Statistical Analysis with Missing Data*, Wiley Series in Probability and Mathematical Statistics, Wiley, New York.

Little, R. J. A. & Rubin, D. B. (1989), The analysis of social science data with missing values, *Sociological Methods and Research* **18**(2), 292–326.

McCabe, T. (1976), A complexity measure, *IEEE Transactions on Software Engineering* **2**(4), 308–320.

Mockus, A. (2006), Empirical estimates of software availability of deployed systems, in *2006 International Symposium on Empirical Software Engineering*, ACM Press, Rio de Janeiro, Brazil, pp. 222–231.

Mockus, A. (2007), Software support tools and experimental work, in V. Basili et al., eds, *Empirical Software Engineering Issues*: LNCS 4336, Springer, pp. 91–99.

Mockus, A. & Votta, L. G. (1997), Identifying reasons for software changes using historic databases, Technical Report BL0113590-980410-04, Bell Laboratories.

Myrtveit, I., Stensrud, E. & Olsson, U. (2001), Analyzing data sets with missing data: an empirical evaluation of imputation methods and likelihood-based methods' *IEEE Transactions on Software Engineering* **27**(11), 1999–1013.

Novo, A. (2002), Analysis of multivariate normal datasets with missing values, Ported to R by Alvaro A. Novo. Original by J.L. Schafer.

R Development Core Team (2005), *R: A Language and Environment for Statistical Computing*, R Foundation for Statistical Computing, Vienna, Austria. ISBN 3-900051-07-0. http://www.R-project.org

Roth, P. L. (1994), Missing data: a conceptual review for applied psychologist, *Personnel Psychology* **47**, 537–560.

Rubin, D. B. (1987), *Multiple Imputation for Nonresponse in Surveys*, Wiley, New York.

Schafer, J. L. (1997), *Analysis of Incomplete Data*, Monograph on Statistics and Applied Probability, Chapman & Hall, London.

Schafer, J. S. (1999), Software for multiple imputation. http://www.stat.psu.edu/<jls/misoftwa.html

Schafer, J. L. & Olsen, M. K. (1998), Multiple imputation for multivariate missing data problems, *Multivariate Behavioural Research* **33**(4), 545–571.

Strike, K., Emam, K. E. & Madhavji, N. (2001), Software cost estimation with incomplete data, *IEEE Transactions on Software Engineering* **27**(10), 890–908.

Swanson, E. B. (1976), The dimensions of maintenance, in *Proceedings of the 2nd Conference on Software Engineering*, San Francisco, pp. 492–497.

Twala, B., Cartwright, M. & Shepperd, M. (2006), Ensemble of missing data techniques to improve software prediction accuracy, in *ICSE'06*, ACM, Shanghai, China, pp. 909–912.

Weisberg, S. (1985), *Applied Linear Regression, 2nd Edition*, Wiley, New York, USA.

Chapter 8
Reporting Experiments in Software Engineering

Andreas Jedlitschka, Marcus Ciolkowski, and Dietmar Pfahl

Abstract

Background: One major problem for integrating study results into a common body of knowledge is the heterogeneity of reporting styles: (1) It is difficult to locate relevant information and (2) important information is often missing.

Objective: A guideline for reporting results from controlled experiments is expected to support a systematic, standardized presentation of empirical research, thus improving reporting in order to support readers in (1) finding the information they are looking for, (2) understanding how an experiment is conducted, and (3) assessing the validity of its results.

Method: The guideline for reporting is based on (1) a survey of the most prominent published proposals for reporting guidelines in software engineering and (2) an iterative development incorporating feedback from members of the research community.

Result: This chapter presents the unification of a set of guidelines for reporting experiments in software engineering.

Limitation: The guideline has not been evaluated broadly yet.

Conclusion: The resulting guideline provides detailed guidance on the expected content of the sections and subsections for reporting a specific type of empirical study, i.e., experiments (controlled experiments and quasi-experiments).

1. Introduction

In today's software development organizations, methods and tools are employed that frequently lack sufficient evidence regarding their suitability, limits, qualities, costs, and associated risks. In Communications of the ACM, Robert L. Glass (2004), taking the standpoint of practitioners, asks for help from research: "Here's a message from software practitioners to software researchers: We (practitioners) need your help. We need some better advice on how and when to use methodologies." Therefore, he asks for:

- A taxonomy of available methodologies, based upon their strengths and weaknesses

F. Shull et al. (eds.), *Guide to Advanced Empirical Software Engineering.*
© Springer 2008

- A taxonomy of the spectrum of problem domains, in terms of what practitioners need
- A mapping of the first taxonomy to the second (or the second to the first)

Empirical software engineering (ESE) addresses some of these issues partly by providing a framework for goal-oriented research. The aim of this research is to build an empirically validated body of knowledge and, based on that, comprehensive problem-oriented decision support in the software engineering (SE) domain.

However, one major problem for integrating study results into a body of knowledge is the heterogeneity of study reporting (Jedlitschka and Ciolkowski, 2004). It is often difficult to find relevant information because the same type of information is located in different sections of study reports and important information is also often missing (Wohlin et al., 2003; Sjøberg et al., 2005; Dybå et al., 2006; Kampenes et al., 2007). For example, in study reports, context information is frequently reported differently and without taking into account further generalizability. Furthermore, specific information of interest for practitioners is often missing, like a discussion of the overall impact of the technology on project or business goals.

One way to avoid this heterogeneity of reporting is to introduce and establish reporting guidelines. Specifically, reporting guidelines support a systematic, standardized description of empirical research, thus improving reporting in order to support readers in (1) finding the information they are looking for, (2) understanding how an experiment is conducted, and (3) assessing the validity of its results. This claim is supported by the CONSORT statement (Altman et al., 2001), a research tool in the area of medicine that takes an evidence-based approach to improve the quality of reports of randomized trials to facilitate systematic reuse (e.g., replication, systematic review, and meta analysis).

As identified by Kitchenham et al. (2002, 2004), reporting guidelines are necessary for all relevant kinds of empirical work, but they must address the needs of different stakeholders (i.e., researchers and practitioners). The specific need for standardized reporting of controlled experiments has been mentioned by different authors for a long time, e.g., Lott and Rombach (1996), Pickard et al. (1998), Shull et al. (2003), Vegas et al. (2003), Wohlin et al. (2003), and Sjøberg et al. (2005). At the same time, several more or less comprehensive and demanding reporting guidelines have been proposed, e.g., by Singer (1999), Wohlin et al. (2000), Juristo and Moreno (2001), and Kitchenham et al. (2002). Even though each of these proposals has its merits, none has yet been accepted as a de-facto standard. Moreover, most of the existing guidelines are not explicitly tailored to the specific needs of certain types of empirical studies, e.g., controlled experiments a comprehensive classification of empirical studies is given by Zelkowitz et al. (2003).

The goal of this chapter is to survey the published proposals for reporting guidelines and to derive a unified and – where necessary – enhanced guideline for reporting controlled experiments and quasi-experiments. Nevertheless, many of the elements discussed throughout this chapter will also make sense for reporting other types of empirical work.

2. Background

Empirical software engineering research is not the first research domain to encounter problems with insufficient reporting. Other disciplines, such as medicine and psychology, have experienced similar problems and have achieved various improvements by standardizing and instantiating reporting guidelines, e.g., for randomized controlled trials in biomedical research (Altman et al., 2001; Moher et al., 2001), psychology (Harris, 2002), clinical practice guidelines (Shiffman et al., 2003), and empirical results from psychological research (American Psychological Association, 2001).

In the field of SE research, in 1999, Singer (1999) described how to use the "American Psychological Association (APA) Styleguide" (2001) for publishing experimental results in SE. In 2002, Kitchenham et al. (2002) provided initial guidelines on how to perform, report, and collate results of empirical studies in SE based on medical guidelines as well as on the personal experience of the authors. Shaw (2003) provided a tutorial on how to write scientific papers, including the presentation of empirical research as a special case. Additionally, standard text books on empirical SE, such as Wohlin et al. (2000) and Juristo and Moreno (2001), address the issue of reporting guidelines. Wohlin et al. (2000) suggest an outline for reporting the results of empirical work. Juristo and Moreno (2001) provide a list of the "most important points to be documented for each phase" in the form of "questions to be answered by the experimental documentation."

Jedlitschka et al. presented a first version of a guideline for reporting controlled experiments (2005a) during a workshop on empirical software engineering (Jedlitschka, 2005). Feedback from the workshop participants, as well as from peer reviews, was incorporated into a second version of the guideline (2005b). In parallel, the guideline was evaluated by means of a perspective-based inspection approach (Kitchenham et al., 2006). This evaluation highlighted 42 issues where the guideline would benefit from amendment or clarification and eight defects. The feedback from the perspective-based inspection and discussions with its authors led to a second iteration of the guideline, where the amendments were incorporated if we found them appropriate and defects were removed (Jedlitschka and Ciolkowski, 2006). Additional feedback from individual researchers was also incorporated (Jedlitschka et al., 2007).

Table 1 characterizes the existing proposals for guidelines on reporting empirical work in SE. The first row of the table lists the proposals, arranged with regard to their publication date. The second row of the table describes the focus of the guidelines. The entry "Empirical Research" indicates that the guidelines are not tailored to a specific type of empirical research. Otherwise, the specific type is explicitly mentioned, e.g., "Controlled Experiment" or "Systematic Review." The third row describes the phases of an experiment covered by the guideline. The entry "All" indicates that the guideline covers all phases of a study. The remaining rows list the structuring elements in the proposed guidelines and map them to the structure of our proposal (last column). Elements of existing proposals occurring twice in a column indicate that these elements can be mapped to two different elements of our new proposal.

Table 1 Overview on structuring proposals for reporting controlled experiments

	Singer (1999)	Wohlin et al. (2000)	Kitchenham et al. (2002)	Juristo and Moreno (2001)	Kitchenham (2004)	Jedlitschka et al. (2007)
Type of study	Empirical research	Empirical research	Empirical research	Controlled experiment	Systematic review	Controlled experiment
Phases of study	Reporting	All	All	All	All	Reporting
Structure	*	*	*	*	Title	Title
	*	*	*	*	Authorship	Authorship
	*	*	*	*	Keywords	Keywords
	Abstract	*			Executive summary or structured abstract	Structured abstract
	Introduction	Introduction Problem statement Experiment planning	*	Goal definition	Background	Introduction
	Introduction	Problem statement Experiment planning	Experimental context	Goal definition	Background	Background
	Method	Experiment planning	Experimental context Experimental design	Design	Review questions Review methods	Experiment planning
	Procedure	Experiment operation	Conducting the experiment and data collection	Experiment execution	Included and excluded studies	Deviations from the plan
	Results	Data analysis	Analysis	Experimental analysis	Results	Analysis
	Discussion	Interpretation of results	Interpretation of results	Experimental analysis	Discussion	Discussion
	Discussion	Discussion and conclusion	*	Experimental analysis	Conclusion	Conclusions and future work
	–	–	–	–	Acknowledgments Conflict of interest	Acknowledgements
	References	References	*	*	References	References
	Appendices	Appendix	*	*	Appendices	Appendices

An asterisk (*) indicates that the authors do not explicitly mention or describe details for this element, but it is assumed that the elements are implicitly required.

We investigated the structures of published reports of controlled experiments in empirical software engineering and have concluded that, in general, authors do not use a common set of guidelines in determining what information to include in their report. In other disciplines, such as medicine and psychology, editors have agreed on a common reporting style, not only regarding the layout of the report, but also its content. Given that the first publication of a reporting guideline for empirical SE research by Singer (1999) was over 7 years ago and little has progressed since that time, we conclude that significant effort needs to be invested to make sure that guidelines are widely accepted and used. This is what other communities have already learned (Altman et al., 2001; Harris, 2002).

Because of this, this chapter provides a description of the most common elements in the various reporting guidelines, giving guidance to readers where we have diverged from others suggestions. This guideline should be seen as a means for supporting both authors of a report in providing relevant information in the appropriate place and readers of a report in knowing where to look for a certain type of information.

3. Guideline for Reporting Controlled Experiments

In this section, we discuss what information should be presented in reports of experiments. It some cases, it may be necessary to adapt the length of a report depending on the requirements of the publisher. Therefore, the structure as presented in this section provides several options. For example, for a conference paper (which is usually much shorter than a journal paper) it may be appropriate to combine the description of the experiment planning and the deviations from the plan as well as the description of the analysis procedure and the analysis, whereas for a journal paper, it is generally appropriate to separate the content of these sections.

In all reports, however, generally speaking, enough information has to be provided to enable readers to judge the reliability of the experiment. The need for detailed provision of information is not specific for SE. It is, for example, also pointed out by Harris (2002). We are well aware that due to limitations of pages (e.g., for conferences), this is not possible in all cases, but the author should at least keep this intention in mind while compiling the report.

As indicated in Table 1, our reporting guideline comprises the following elements: Title, Authorship, Structured Abstract, Keywords, Introduction, Background, Experiment Planning, Execution, Analysis, Discussion, Conclusion and Future Work, Acknowledgements, References, and Appendices.

Our proposal reflects the requirements of existing standards, such as APA, but provides more structuring elements and asks for specific details that are not relevant for many experiments in psychology, like a technology's impact on the overall project budget or time and on the product's quality. Furthermore, our guideline incorporates wording as it is common for experiments in empirical SE to also

Table 2 Quick reference

Section	Content	Scope	Priority
3.1 Title		\<title\> + "– A controlled experiment"; Is it informative and does it include the major treatments and the dependent variables?	Required
3.2 Authorship		Does it include contact information, i.e., a valid email?	Required
3.3 Structured abstract	Background	Why is this research important?	Required
	Objective	What is the question addressed with this research?	Required
	Methods	What is the statistical context and methods applied?	Required
	Results	What are the main findings? Practical implications?	Required
	Limitations	What are the weaknesses of this research?	
	Conclusions	What is the conclusion?	Required
3.4 Keywords		Areas of research the treatments, dependent variables, and study type	Might be required by the publisher
3.5 Introduction	Problem statement	What is the problem? Where does it occur? Who has observed it? Why is it important to be solved?	Required
	Research objective	What is the research question to be answered by this study? E.g., by using the GQM goal template: Analyze \<Object(s) of study\> for the purpose of \<purpose\> with respect to their \<Quality Focus\> the point of view of the \<Perspective\> in the context of \<context\>	Required
	Context	What information is necessary to understand whether the research relates to a specific situation (environment)?	Required
3.6 Background	Technology under investigation	What is necessary for a reader to know about the technology to reproduce its application?	Required if not published elsewhere
	Alternative technologies	How does this research relate to alternative technologies? What is the control treatment?	Required
	Related studies	How this research relates to existing research (studies)? What were the results from these studies?	If available
	Relevance to practice	How does it relate to state of the practice?	If available
3.7 Experiment planning	Goals	Formalization of goals, refine the important constructs (e.g., the quality focus) of the experiment's goal	Required

(continued)

Table 2 (continued)

Section	Content	Scope	Priority
	Experimental units	From which population will the sample be drawn? How will the groups be formed (assignment to treatments)? Any kind of randomization and blinding has to be described	Required
	Experimental material	Which objects are selected and why?	Required
	Tasks	Which tasks have to be performed by the subjects?	Required
	Hypotheses, parameters, and variables	What are the constructs and their operationalization? They have to be traceable derived from the research question respectively the goal of the experiment	Required (for an explorative studies there might be no hypothesis defined)
	Design	What type of experimental design has been chosen?	Required
	Procedure	How will the experiment (i.e. data collection) be performed? What instruments, materials, tools will be used and how?	Could be integrated with execution
	Analysis procedure	How will the data be analyzed?	Could be integrated with analysis
3.8 Execution	Preparation	What has been done to prepare the execution of the experiment (i.e., schedule, training)	
	Deviations	Describe any deviations from the plan, e.g., how was the data collection actually performed?	
3.9 Analysis	Descriptive statistics	What are the results from descriptive statistics?	Required
	Data set preparation	What was done to prepare the data set, why, and how?	
	Hypothesis testing	How was the data evaluated and was the analysis model validated?	
3.10 Discussion	Evaluation of results and implications	Explain the results and the relation of the results to earlier research, especially those mentioned in the *Background* section	
	Threats to validity	How is validity of the experimental results assured? How was the data actually validated?	Required

(continued)

Table 2 (continued)

Section	Content	Scope	Priority
		Threats that might have an impact on the validity of the results as such (threats to internal validity, e.g., confounding variables, bias), and, furthermore, on the extent to which the hypothesis captures the objectives and the generalizability of the findings (threats to external validity, e.g., participants, materials) have to be discussed	
	Inferences	Inferences drawn from the data to more general conditions	Required
	Lessons learned	Which experience was collected during the course of the experiment	Nice to have
3.11 Conclusions and future work	Summary	The purpose of this section is to provide a concise summary of the research and its results as presented in the former sections	Required
	Impact	Description of impacts with regard to cost, schedule, and quality, circumstances under which the approach presumably will not yield the expected benefit	
	Future work	What other experiments could be run to further investigate the results yielded or evolve the Body of Knowledge	
3.12 Acknowledgements		Sponsors, participants, and contributors who do not fulfil the requirements for authorship should be mentioned	If appropriate
3.13 References		All cited literature has to be presented in the format requested by the publisher	Absolutely required
3.14 Appendices		Experimental materials, raw data, and detailed analyses, which might be helpful for others to build upon the reported work should be provided	Might be made available trough technical reports or web site

support the reading of already published reports. The structuring elements are discussed in detail in the following subsections. Table 2 shows each element, along with the section it is detailed in, and its particular sub-elements.

3.1. Title

The title of the report has to be informative, because the title (together with the abstract) "alerts potential readers to the existence of an article of interest" (Harris, 2002). To attract readers from industry, it is important to use commonly used industry terms. Harris (2002) suggests avoiding phrases like "A Study of" or "An Experimental Investigation of." This might be true for psychology, but for ESE, where we do not have explicit journals for experiments, we propose adding "– a controlled experiment" (– a replicated controlled experiment, – a quasi-experiment) if there are no limitations with regard to the title length. This helps the reader to easily identify controlled experiments. Furthermore, if possible, it additionally aides the reader if the dependent variables and treatments can be specified in the title.

In fact, where the title length is limited, we believe it is more important to include treatments and the dependent variables than "a controlled experiment." As an example of a succinct meaningful title, consider the following: The title of a publication describing a controlled experiment to investigate technique X compared to technique Y (the treatments) regarding the maintainability of a product (dependent variable) could be "Comparing the Impact of Technique X and Technique Y on Product's Maintainability – A Controlled Experiment." From the perspective of a reader, both from research as well as from industry, this title would allow for easily identifying the main aspects of the publication.

3.2. Authorship

All individuals making a significant contribution should be in the author list or at least acknowledged (c.f. Sect. 3.12).

Most report styles require contact details. If not, provide at least the e-mail address of the responsible author. As authors might change their job, it is sometimes more appropriate to provide the contact information of the more stable author – for example a professor as opposed to a graduate student (Kitchenham, 2004), or, "to be on the safe side," provide contact information for all authors.

3.3. Structured Abstract

The need for a self-contained abstract is beyond any question. It is an important source of information for any reader, as it briefly summarizes the main points of the study and, moreover, is often the only part of a publication that is freely accessible (Kitchenham, 2004). Abstracts should summarize the broad research questions.

Additionally, for a single experiment, regardless of the format of the abstract, authors should ensure that all relevant interventions or conditions (i.e., independent variables) and dependent variables are mentioned. When more than one experiment is reported in a paper, this may be infeasible, and instead authors will need to describe their experiments in more general terms.

The exact format of the abstract needs more discussion. For example, Shaw (2003) found that there is a common structure for the clearest abstracts consisting of the following elements: (a) the current state of the art, identifying a particular problem, (b) the contribution to improving the situation, (c) the specific result and the main idea behind it, and (d) how the result is demonstrated or defended. For reporting experiments in psychology, Harris (2002) suggests that an abstract should describe the following aspects: (1) the problem under investigation, (2) the participants, (3) the empirical method, (4) the findings, and (5) the conclusions.

A large number of journals in medicine and psychology have imposed a special form of the abstract, the structured abstract (Hayward et al., 1993; Bayley and Eldredge, 2003), on authors to improve the clarity of abstracts. The most common elements of structured abstracts are *Background* or *Context*, *Objective* or *Aim*, *Method*, *Results*, and *Conclusion*.

Inspired by the lessons learned from medicine, we propose using a structured abstract consisting of the elements listed below:

Background: Give a brief explanation of the motivation for conducting the study. Example: "Software developers have a plethora of development technologies from which to choose, but often little guidance for making the decision" (Shull et al., 2003).

Objective: Describe the aim of the study, including the object under examination, the focus, and the perspective. Example: "We examined <technique1> vs. <technique2> with regard to fault detection rates from the viewpoint of a quality engineer."

Method: Describe which research method was used to examine the object (e.g., experimental design, number and kind of participants, selection criteria, data collection and analysis procedures). Example: "We conducted a controlled experiment using a 2×2 factorial design with 24 randomly assigned undergraduate students participating. The data were collected with the help of questionnaires and analyzed using ANOVA."

Results: Describe the main findings. Example: "<technique1> was significantly more effective than <technique2> at an alpha level of 0.05."

Limitations: Describe the major limitations of the research, if any. Example: "Generalization of results is limited since the analyzed technique was applied only to specify systems smaller than 10,000 lines of code."

Conclusion: Describe the impact of the results. Example: "The result reinforced existing evidence regarding the superiority of <technique1> over <technique2>."

Furthermore, to address practitioners' information needs, cost, benefits, risks, and transitions should also be described.

Our recommendation to include the element *Limitations* in a structured abstract follows a suggestion made in The Editors of *Annals of Internal Medicine* (2004), since every piece of evidence has its limitations. This additional information helps readers judge the transferability of the results to their context. It also prevents uncritical acceptance by the reader.

It is important to use only a few sentences for each structuring element of the abstract. Hartley (2003) found that the number of words increases by about 30% if structured abstracts are used. But he claims that these "extra costs" pay back because, with the additional information given in the abstract, a wider readership might be encouraged and citation rates improve as do (journal) impact factors. Several researchers who compared the use of structured abstracts to traditional ones found advantages for structured abstracts, but no real disadvantages (Hartley, 2004; Kitchenham, 2004).

From this discussion, we conclude that experimenters should certainly use structured abstracts, but even if the abstract is written as text (without structuring elements), it should still include all of the aforementioned elements. Where publishers limit the length of the abstract by number of words or number of lines, we suggest prioritizing the traditional elements: *background (one sentence), objective, method, results, and conclusion*, but recommend sticking with the structure.

As a final note, to attract readers from industry, authors should use terms that are commonly used in industry in describing their research.

3.4. Keywords

Except for Kitchenham (2004) and Jedlitschka et al. (2007), existing guidelines do not explicitly address keywords. Furthermore, keywords are not necessarily requested by all publications. Nevertheless, if provided (and if free of any predefined characterization, like ACM), keywords should describe the areas of research, the treatments, dependent variables, and study type. The list of keywords should complement the title, as it was described earlier, especially in cases where it was not possible to include all pertinent information in the title. As with the title, keywords help readers to identify relevant publications. This is especially important because publishers use keywords for categorisation, and they are visible even in cases where full access to the publication is restricted. Finally, keywords should not be idiosyncratic, but should instead reflect common terms used in the field.

3.5. Introduction

The purpose of the introduction is to set the scope of the work and give potential readers good reasons for reading the remainder of the publication (motivation). The introduction needs to place the research into a wider context before introducing the specific problem. As can be seen from Table 1, there are several variations with regard to the content of the introduction. In most cases, the introduction starts with a broad description of the research area (Wohlin et al., 2000). With the exception of Wohlin et al. (2000), who recommend a distinct section to describe the problem under study, all of the guidelines include the description of the problem in the introduction. Further, Wohlin et al. (2000) and Kitchenham et al. (2002) suggest the introduction include an explicit description of the context of the study (i.e., the environment in which it is run).

Thus, based on the various guidelines, as a minimum the introduction should include a description of the *Problem Statement*, the *Research Objectives*, and the *Context* of the research.

The problem statement supports readers in comparing their problems with the problem investigated in the reported experiment, thereby judging the relevance of the research to their questions. In general, the problem statement should provide answers to the following questions: What is the problem? Where does it occur? Who has observed it? Why is it important to be solved? In addition, any underlying theory, causal model, or logical model should be specified.

The description of the problem statement should lead directly to the description of the research objective. The research objective starts with a brief description of the solution idea and the (expected) benefits of the solution.

> Example adopted from (Ciolkowski et al. 1997): Recently, it was reported by [...] that defects in a software artefact increase cycle time and development costs. One possible solution would be to start defect detection as early in the development cycle as possible, for example by inspecting requirements documents. The benefit would be that the defects from the requirements phase will not be incorporated in the later phases, which will result in reduced cycle times and development costs.

The description of the research objective (or, as Wohlin et al. (2000) call it, the "Definition of the Experiment"), should be as coherent as possible. One way to achieve this is to use the goal template of the Goal/Question/Metric (GQM) method formulated by Basili et al. (2001). This template includes several elements to be filled in as shown below, with an example underneath.

Analyze <...> for the purpose of <...> with respect to their <...> from the point of view of the <...> in the context of <...>.

The following example is adapted from Ciolkowski et al. (1997):

> Analyze perspective-based reading and ad hoc reading techniques
> For the purpose of evaluation
> With respect to their effectiveness
> From the viewpoint of potential users
> In the context of the software engineering class at the University

For further examples of the use of the goal definition template to describe the research objective, see Wohlin et al. (2000).

The description of the context is essential for practitioners as well as for researchers. Practitioners need context information to see if the technique/process/tool under study would be applicable in their own organization. Researchers need context information to understand the limits of the study (e.g., whether the results are generalizable), to replicate results, and to aggregate results or perform meta-analyses. To describe the context of the research, the CONSORT Statement (Altman et al., 2001; Moher et al., 2001) suggests that the setting and locations of a study are described. In software engineering this could include information about application type (e.g., real-time system), application domain, (e.g., telecommunications), type of company (e.g., small or medium sized), experience of the participants (e.g., professionals with on average 5 years of related practical experience), time constraints (e.g., critical milestones, delivery date), process (e.g., spiral model), tools (e.g., used for capturing requirements), size of project (e.g., 500 person months). Furthermore, it is valuable to know whether there are specific requirements with regard to the environment in which the technique, tool, or method was applied.

A more formal description of context from a researcher's viewpoint comprises context factors that might affect the generality and utility of the conclusions. These are generally detailed when describing the experimental design.

The introduction generally ends with an outline for the remainder of the paper.

3.6. Background

Researchers as well as practitioners need an understanding of the landscape of the reported research, including alternative approaches and relationships between different experiments (Jedlitschka and Ciolkowski, 2004b). Most guidelines require appropriate citation, as described, for example, in the APA style guide (2001).

In contrast to Singer (1999), who includes background information in the Introduction, Wohlin et al. (2000), Juristo and Moreno (2001), Kitchenham et al. (2002), Jedlitschka and Pfahl (2005a, b), and Jedlitschka et al. (2007) suggest presenting background information in a unique section.

At a minimum, the background should present: a description of the *Technology* (or tool, method)[1] *under Investigation*, a description of *Alternative Solutions*, i.e., other reports that address the same problem or are comparable from a technology view point, a *Description of Related Studies*, i.e., empirical studies that have investigated the same or similar treatments, and, if appropriate, levels of *Relevance to Practice*, i.e., how successfully the technique has been applied in industry. In the following, we provide more details on each of these elements.

Because readers need to understand at some level what is being investigated before they can understand how it relates to other work, the background will frequently begin with a brief description of the treatment and control variables of the experiment. The detail of the description depends on the availability of earlier publications and the length of the report. Moreover, for readers who have no specific background in the area, a more general reference, e.g., to a textbook, might be helpful.

---

[1] For ease of reading, we use technology as an umbrella term for technology, method, and tool.

The description of alternative solutions/approaches helps to frame the work within a larger research context. This description should not simply be a list of related research (Shaw, 2003), but rather an objective description of the main findings relevant to the work currently being reported. Alternative solutions should be reported whether they are supportive of or contradictory to the current research approach. Especially in the case of an experiment that compares different approaches, it is crucial to objectively describe the alternative approaches. Note that a comparison of the results of related work and the current results should be done in the discussion section after the results have been presented (c.f. Sect. 3.10).

In the description of related studies, existing evidence (if available), in the form of earlier studies and, especially, experiments, should be described. As with alternative solutions, the relation of the current research to other studies (existing evidence) helps readers understand where this work fits into a larger research context. Moreover, it supports the reuse of this study for replication or systematic review, providing a sound basis for research and improving its value. If the reported study is a replication, the parental study and its findings also have to be described.

In terms of relevance to practice, if applicable, if one of the treatments (technologies) has previously been applied to real software projects or under realistic circumstances, a short summary of the findings and related references should be provided.

3.7. Experiment Planning

This section, sometimes referred to as experimental design or protocol, describes the plan or protocol that is used to perform the experiment and analyze the results. It is important because, as Singer stated, this section is the "recipe for the experiment" (Singer, 1999). Therefore, it should provide all information that is necessary to replicate the study and integrate it into the ESE body of knowledge. In addition, this section allows readers to evaluate the internal validity of the study, which is an important selection criterion for systematic review or meta-analysis (Kitchenham, 2004; Kitchenham et al., 2002).

According to several guidelines (e.g., Harris, 2002), the experiment planning section should describe the *Goals, Participants, Experimental Material, Tasks, Hypotheses, Parameters, and Variables, Experiment Design, Procedure* for conducting the study, as well as the *Analysis Procedure*. Using this order allows for successive refinement of the details of the study. In some cases, however, a different order might be appropriate.

The level of detail regarding the various elements depends on the kind of publication, respecting the required length of the report. Therefore, authors should prioritise the information according to what is most relevant for the particular audience. Alternatively, authors may consider combining several sections into one. For instance, it might be appropriate to integrate the description of the procedure with the description of the execution, or to integrate the description of the analysis procedure with that of the analysis. Furthermore, it might be possible to put all relevant material into an appendix or longer technical report. If this is not possible, archiving the information on a website may be an alternative. To address concerns that arise in sharing protocols, including raw data and material, Basili et al. (2007) propose an initial licensing model.

3.7.1. Goal(s)

Often the original research objective as described in the introduction is not concrete enough. The purpose of this paragraph is, therefore, to define in more concrete terms the main manipulations of the experiment. For example, the GQM template provided in the introduction could be refined into something like:

Example adapted from Ciolkowski et al. (1997):

Goal 1: Analyze perspective-based reading and ad hoc reading techniques
For the purpose of understanding their effectiveness
With respect to the defect detection rate of individual developers

Goal 2: Analyze perspective-based reading perspectives
For the purpose of understanding their effectiveness
With respect to detecting different defect classes

The refinement of the main research question should be described and motivated to allow for traceability down to the hypotheses, which will be described in later in this chapter.

3.7.2. Participants

The participants (often referred to as subjects or, if not humans, experimental units) need to be described in detail. Furthermore, the sampling strategy and the resulting samples need to be described, including the number of participants (per condition), the kind of participants (e.g., computer science students), and the populations from which they were drawn. All measures for randomization have to be reported here, especially the random allocation of participants to treatments. Where a statistical power calculation has been used, assumptions, estimates, and calculations have to be provided.

All participant characteristics that might have an effect on the results or restrict the sample in some way should also be described in this section. This may include experience with the techniques to be applied or mean/range of experience in years, or educational level. For instance, if a certain level of experience is required, the sample might be drawn from fourth-term computer science students (as opposed to first-term students).

A description of the motivation for the participants to participate is mandatory. For instance, it should be stated whether the participants were paid and if so, how much, or whether they earned educational credits for taking part in the experiment. Additionally, the answers to the following questions are of interest (Wohlin et al.,

2000): What was the commitment of the participants? How was consent obtained? How was confidentiality assured? How was participation motivated (induced)?

3.7.3. Experimental Materials

In this section, all experimental materials and equipment should be described. For instance, if the study involves a questionnaire, questions should be described, as should any other characterizations of the questionnaire, e.g., it had five sections focusing on specific topics, with the topics named. As another example, in an experiment looking at different reading techniques, the document used for the application of the reading technique should be described in terms of its length, complexity, seeded faults (number, type, interactions), etc. As with the participant section, all characteristics that might have an impact on the results should be mentioned here as formally as possible. However, in case of conference papers, it is often not possible to present all the materials in detail, so we suggest providing more detail either in the appendix of an associated technical report, or using a website.

Note that in this section, the materials should not be presented verbatim, but rather described with as much detail as necessary for the readers to understand what materials the participants interacted with during the experiment.

3.7.4. Tasks

Here, the tasks performed by the participants should be described in enough detail so that a replication of the experiment is possible without consultation of the authors. Redundancies with regard to the description of the technology in the background section (c.f., Sect. 3.6) should be avoided. If the description requires too much space, the information should be made available in a technical report or as a web resource. When space is a consideration, the task description could be integrated with the description of the procedure. However, separating the two descriptions makes it easier for readers to understand how the hypotheses, parameters, and variables were derived.

3.7.5. Hypotheses, Parameters, and Variables

In this section, hypotheses, parameters, and variables should be described. This description should be linked to the research objective already reported in the introduction.

For each goal stated in the research objective, the null hypotheses, denoted H_{0ij}, and their corresponding alternative hypotheses, denoted H_{1ij}, need to be reported, where i corresponds to the goal identifier, and j is a counter for cases where more than one hypothesis is formulated per goal. The description of both null and alternative hypotheses should be as formal as possible. The main hypotheses should be explicitly separated from ancillary hypotheses and exploratory analyses. In the case of ancillary hypotheses, a hierarchical system is appropriate. Hypotheses need to state the treatments and the control conditions.

Continuing the example for Goal1 from Sect. 3.7.1 (adapted from Ciolkowski et al. (1997)):

The goal of the experiment is to determine:
Q1: Which reading technique produces a higher mean defect detection rate?
One of the possible hypotheses is:
H_{011}: Individuals applying a perspective-based reading (PBR) technique detect more defects than individuals using ad hoc reading.

In the example hypothesis H_{011}, the treatment is perspective-based reading and the control condition is ad hoc reading. A further formalization of H_{011} and the alternative hypothesis H_{111} could be written in the following form (where MDDR stands for mean defect detection rate):

$$H_{011} = MDDR(PBR) > MDDR(ad\,hoc)$$

$$H_{111} = MDDR(PBR) \leq MDDR(ad\,hoc)$$

It is important to differentiate between experimental hypotheses and the specific tests being performed; the tests have to be described in the analysis procedure section.

In addition to the hypotheses, there are two types of variables that need to be described in this section: the dependent variable(s) (aka. response variables) and the independent variable(s) (aka. predictor variables). As with the hypotheses, dependent variables need be defined and justified in terms of their relevance to the goals listed in the *Research Objectives*. Dependent variables are the variables that are measured to ascertain whether the independent variable had an effect on the outcome. Likewise, independent variables are variables that are frequently manipulated in the experiment and may influence the dependent variable(s). Independent variables can include treatments, materials, and some context factors. In this section, only independent variables that are manipulated or controlled through the experimental design (i.e., causal variables) are described. For each independent variable, its corresponding levels (aka. alternatives, treatments) have to be specified in operational form. In the example given above, the dependent variable is the MDDR. The independent variable is the type of reading technique, which has two levels, PBR and ad hoc.

With respect to reporting, authors need to describe their metrics clearly. In particular, if a standardized set of metrics is available, authors have to explain which of them are used. If existing metrics are tailored, the need for the tailoring and the tailored metric have to be explicated. Based on Wohlin et al. (2000), Juristo and Moreno (2001), and Kitchenham et al. (2001), Table 3 gives a schema for the description of variables and related metrics.

Table 3 Schema for the description of variables

Name of the variable	Type of the variable (independent, dependent, moderating)	Abbreviation	Class (product, process, resource, method)	Entity (instance of the class)	Type of attribute (internal, external)	Scale type (nominal, ordinal …)	Unit	Range or, for nominal and restricted ordinal scales, the definition of each scale point	Counting rule in the context of the entity
Type of reading technique	independent	RT	Method	Reading Technique	N.A.	nominal	N.A.	PBR; ad hoc	N.A.
Mean defect detection rate	dependent	MDDR	Process	Inspection process	Internal: efficiency; external: quality	ratio	Number of defects per hour	>= 0	Number of agreed upon defects after review meeting / total effort for inspection process in hours

For subjective metrics, a statistic for inter-rater agreements should be presented, such as the kappa statistics or the intra-class correlation coefficient for continuous metrics (Kitchenham et al., 2002).

3.7.6. Experiment Design

In the *Experiment Design* subsection, the specific design has to be described. Elements in this section that need to be described include whether the experiment was a within – or between-subjects design, or a mixed factors design, with a description of each of the levels of the independent variable. Juristo and Moreno (2001) give a comprehensive description of designs for experiments. Moreover, authors should describe how participants were assigned to levels of the treatments (Kitchenham et al., 2002).

If, for example, an experiment examined the effect of PBR versus ad hoc reading techniques on short and long times spent looking for defects on MDDR, with different sets of subjects using the techniques, it would be reported as a 2 (reading technique) × 2 (time period) between-subjects design with reading technique having two levels: PBR and ad hoc, and time also having two levels (15 min and 30 min).

In addition to this formalization of the design, if any kind of blinding (e.g., blind allocation) has been used, the details need to be provided; this applies to the execution (e.g., blind marking) and the analysis (e.g., blind analysis). If the experiment is a replication, the adjustments and their rationales need to be discussed. If applicable, training provided to the participants has to be described. Any kind of threat mitigation should also be addressed, i.e., what measures were used to manage treats to validity. For example, a typical strategy to reduce learning effects is to have subjects exposed to the various levels of a treatment in a random or ordered fashion.

3.7.7. Procedure

The procedure section should describe precisely what happened to the participants from the moment they arrived to the moment they left (Harris, 2002). This includes a description of any training provided (e.g., the participants received a 2-h lecture introducing perspective-based reading). The procedure section should also include a description of the setting (i.e., where the experiment occurred), and the schedule for the experiment. Furthermore, details of the data collection method have to be described, including when the data was collected, by whom, and with what kind of support (e.g., tool). This is in accordance with Kitchenham et al. (2002), who state that the data collection process describes the "who," the "when," and the "how" of any data collection activity. Any type of transformation of the data (e.g., marking "true" defects in defect lists) and training provided for such should also be described here. If there are limitations with regard to the numbers of pages, the description of the procedure can be integrated with the analysis section.

3.7.8. Analysis Procedure

The statistical tests undertaken depend on the experimental design; therefore, the experimental plan is finalized with a description of the analysis procedure detailing which methods were used to test the hypotheses in analysing the data. If different hypotheses are investigated, information for each hypothesis needs to be provided separately. If any additional influences are expected, their analysis also needs to be described, e.g., see Ciolkowski et al. (1997). If there are page limitations, the analysis procedure can be combined with the analysis section.

3.8. Deviations from the Plan

In an ideal situation, the experiment was conducted exactly as it was planned. Then the description in the procedure section (c.f., Sect. 3.7.7) is both, the representation and the instantiation of the plan. In that case, this section is not needed. However, deviations regarding the original plan are often experienced. Because this might have an impact on both the validity of the results and the replicability of the study, it is necessary to describe those deviations by describing the original plan when deviations occurred. This includes all differences between the instantiated procedure and the plan, for instance, regarding instrumentation and the collection process. Deviations can occur regarding participation (who actually participated), schedule (e.g., the time participants were given for the tasks), or data collection. In addition, information about subjects who do not complete the study should be presented, for example, five subjects did not attend the final session; as recommended by Kitchenham et al. (2002). If possible, reasons for the non-completion should be given; that information is worthwhile when replicating the study.

In the case of a limited number of pages, this description can be integrated with the procedure section (c.f. Sect. 3.7.7). In addition, a general statement confirming the process conformance could be given in the description of the analysis.

3.9. Analysis

According to Singer (1999), the *Analysis* section summarizes the data collected and its treatment. In this section, the results should be described devoid of any interpretation. When there are limited pages, authors might tend to add some interpretation to the analysis section. However, according to existing guidelines, especially from other disciplines, interpretation and results belong to clearly distinct sections. If it is necessary to include interpretation in the analysis section, we strongly favour establishing a clear distinction between the two (e.g., by using textual measures or subsections).

If multiple goals were investigated, separate analysis subsections and an overall (summarizing) analysis are required. Since the analysis procedures are already described in the design section, the purpose of this section is to describe the application of the analysis methods to the data collected. The Analysis section generally contains three types of information: *Descriptive Statistics*, *Data Set Preparation*, and *Hypothesis Testing*. When appropriate, a sensitivity analysis should be reported in the hypothesis testing section.

Presenting the data by using appropriate descriptive statistics, including number of observations, measures for central tendency, and dispersion, gives the reader an overview of the data. Mean, median, and mode are example measures for central tendency. Standard deviation, variance, and range, as well as interval of variation and frequency are example measures for dispersion. To facilitate meta-analysis, it is highly recommended [e.g., by Kitchenham et al. (2002)] to provide raw data in the appendices or to describe where the data can be acquired, e.g., from a website.

Additional processing (or preparation) of the data set may be required. Such preparations should be discussed here. This includes, if appropriate, data transformation, outlier identification and their potential removal, and handling of missing values, as well as the discussion of dropouts (i.e., data from participants who were not present for all experimental sessions). Chap. 7 details methods for dealing with missing values.

For hypothesis testing, special emphasis should be placed on how the data was evaluated (e.g., by an ANOVA) and how the analysis model was validated. The violations of the statistical assumptions underlying the analysis method (e.g., normality, independence, and residuals) should also be described. The values of the resulting statistics also need to be reported. Harris outlines what has to be reported for different kinds of statistical tests (Harris, 2002). Singer (1999) recommends that "inferential statistics are reported with the value of the test (effect size), the probability level, the degrees of freedom, the direction of effect," and the power of the test. To this list, we add the alpha value and the confidence interval where appropriate (Dybå et al., 2006; Kampenes et al., 2007).

3.10. Discussion

The purpose of the discussion section is to interpret the findings presented in the previous section. This includes an overview of the results, threats to validity, generalization (where are the results applicable?), as well as the (potential) impact on cost, time, and quality. Harris (2002) suggests starting this section with a description of what has been found and how well the data fit the predictions. Related to this, authors should discuss whether the hypotheses were confirmed or not. The discussion section should include information about each of the following three elements: *Evaluation of Results and Implications*, *Threats to Validity*, and *Inferences*.

3.10.1. Evaluation of Results and Implications

The purpose of the evaluation of results and implications is to explain the results. All findings, including any unexpected results, should be described in this subsection. Moreover, if the null hypothesis was not rejected, authors may include reasons for why they believe this is the case. Several authors point out that it is important to distinguish between statistical significance and practical importance (Kitchenham et al., 2002) or meaningfulness (Harris, 2002). The results should also be related to both theory and practice.

Although it is still very rare for SE experiments to develop theory, the implications of the findings should be related to the larger theory being developed, and how they further explicate or illuminate that theory (see Chap. 12 for more information about theory). The results should be discussed in the light of the objectives stated in the introduction and also related to the previous work described in the background section. These two together should help to build a broader theoretical foundation for the work.

With respect to practice, the results should be related to current and potential practice, outlining how practice can be improved by applying the results. If the null hypothesis was not rejected, it is not possible to give an interpretation in any direction; in particular, it does not mean that the null hypothesis is true, only that not enough evidence exists to reject it. In some cases, the value of the effect is so small that there may actually be no relevant application to current practice. This has to be explicated as well.

In writing the discussion, it is important to (1) clearly state the results of the analysis separately from any inferences or conclusions based on those results (Kitchenham et al., 2002), (2) to ensure that the conclusions follow from the results (Kitchenham et al., 2002), and (3) that conjectures be made with caution and kept brief, leaving out fanciful speculation (Harris, 2002).

3.10.2. Threats to Validity

All threats that might have an impact on the validity of the results need to be discussed. This includes at least (1) *threats to construct validity*, (2) *threats to internal validity*, (3) *threats to external validity*, and if applicable, and (4) *threats to conclusion validity*. A more comprehensive classification of threats to validity is given in Wohlin et al. (2000). Each of these four types of threats to validity is defined below, and needs to be covered in a research paper. Ignoring the threats can lead to the wrong conclusions regarding the validity of the results. For example, a practitioner might assume that the results would apply to his situation where the external validity could indicate problems regarding generalizability.

Construct validity. Construct validity refers to the degree to which the operationalization of the measures in a study actually represents the constructs in the real world. For instance, in measuring readability, a researcher may look at the time required to read source code. The construct validity of this measure is the extent to which the readability of source code is actually related to the time required to read it. There are a number of threats to construct validity outlined in Wohlin et al. (2000).

Internal validity. Internal validity refers to the extent to which the treatment or independent variable(s) were actually responsible for the effects seen to the dependent variable. Unknown factors may have had an influence on the results and therefore put limitations on the internal validity of the study. Note that it is possible to have internal validity in a study and not have construct validity. For instance, it could be true that the manipulations in the study did actually affect the outcome, and yet the manipulations did not map/represent the desired entity in the real world.

External validity. External validity refers to the degree to which the findings of the study can be generalized to other participant populations or settings. External validity can often be a problem for controlled experiments in artificial environments where the same conditions may not hold in the real world. Wohlin et al. describe three types of threats to internal validity dealing with people, place, and/or time.

Conclusion validity. Conclusion validity refers to whether the conclusions reached in a study are correct. For controlled experiments, conclusion validity is directly related to the application of statistical tests to the data. If the statistical tests are not applied correctly, this is a threat to the conclusion validity. Thus, examples of threats to conclusion validity involve anything that causes a Type I or Type II error.

To facilitate reading, subsections might be appropriate for each threat that has to be discussed. Following the arguments presented by Kitchenham et al. (2002), it is not enough to mention that a threat exists; the implications of the threat with respect to the findings also need to be discussed.

Other threats than those listed above may also need to be discussed, such as personal vested interests or ethical issues regarding the selection of participants (in particular, experimenter-subject dependencies).

3.10.3. Inferences

In this section, the findings can be generalized, within the scope of validity, to broader research questions or settings. This should be done carefully, based on the findings, by incorporating the limitations. All claims need to be supported by the results. For technologies not currently in use, scale-up issues should be discussed.

3.11. Conclusions and Future Work

The final section of the report should describe, based on the results and discussion, the following elements: *Summary, Impact,* and *Future Work.*

The conclusion section begins with a concise summary of the research and its results as presented in the former sections. Unique to the domain of software engineering – in order to enable readers to get the most important findings with regard to the practical impact in one place – in the conclusion we emphasize a description, where possible, of the impact on cost, time, and quality, and a summary of the limitations. Note that these conclusions can only be drawn if they were directly investigated in the experiment.

Impact on Cost: What effort was necessary to introduce and perform the technique (e.g., what are the costs of detecting a defect of a certain type with this technique? Is there any impact on the cost of other steps of the development process, positive or negative ones (e.g., reduced cost for rework)?)

Impact on Time: Is there any positive or negative impact on the time of the proposed solution/technology/technique on other steps of the development process?

Impact on Quality: Is there any impact on the quality of the proposed solution/technology/technique on the quality of other steps of the development process?

Besides the description of the impact, where possible and appropriate, a discussion of the approach's level of maturity, when the investments will pay back, and consequences arising from the implementation will help readers to assess the technology. (Although in most cases artificial, we assume a rough estimate is better than no information.)

If applicable, *limitations* of the approach with regard to its practical implementation should also be described, i.e., circumstances under which the approach presumably will not yield the expected benefits or should not be employed. Furthermore, any risks or side-effects associated with the implementation or application of the approach should also be mentioned.

Finally, an outlook to future work should be given. It should describe what other research (i.e., experiments) could be carried out to further investigate the results yielded or evolve the body of knowledge and theoretical constructs.

3.12. Acknowledgements

In this section, sponsors, participants, and (research) contributors who do not fulfil the requirements for authorship should be mentioned.

3.13. References

In this section, all cited literature has to be presented in the format requested by the publisher.

3.14. Appendices

In this section, material, raw data, and detailed analyses that might be helpful for others to build upon the reported work should be provided (i.e., meta-analysis).

If the raw data is not reported, the authors should specify where and under which conditions the material and the raw data could be made available to other researchers (i.e., technical report, web resource). Here a license model, such as the one proposed by Basili et al. (2007) can be used to ensure to all parties that their contribution is acknowledged and the material is only used for the defined purposes. The licensor can, for example, require that any publication based on the delivered data has to be sent to him.

4. Conclusion

In this chapter, we have motivated the importance of reporting standards for maturing empirical software engineering research. The contribution of this chapter is a guideline for guiding researchers while reporting experiments in software engineering. The presented guideline unifies and extends the most prominent existing guidelines published by various authors (cf. Table 1). In addition to providing a uniform structure of a reporting template, the guideline provides detailed guidance on which information should be provided in the various sections of a report. This guideline was developed for a specific type of empirical study, i.e., controlled experiments and quasi-experiments. Nevertheless, many aspects discussed throughout this chapter have to be reported in other empirical study reports, like case studies.

Thus, this chapter provides researchers with a means for structured and comprehensive documentation of empirical studies, especially experiments. In some cases, due to page limitations (e.g., conference paper), it might not be possible to provide all the proposed information. Although each paper should stand for itself, we have discussed possible shortcuts by integrating certain sections. Furthermore, authors should make use of technical reports or web resources to provide additional information, including material, raw data, and detailed analysis.

During our work on guidelines, we learned that issues are related not only to structure and comprehensiveness, but also to the information needs of stakeholders. In this chapter, we presented, from our perspective, a quite comprehensive model, addressing several stakeholders. To especially attract decision makers in industry, we envisage tailoring this guideline for different audiences (e.g., by providing a guideline for reporting results from empirical research to practitioners). Researchers doing replications or performing a systematic review certainly have different information needs than practitioners looking for candidate techniques for solving their problems. Researchers need more technical information regarding the study as such, whereas practitioners require information regarding the potential of the technique to actually solve their problems; that is, information on development costs, product quality, and development schedule.

An important issue related to the dissemination task is to ensure that the guidelines are used in research practice. One possibility to enforce the usage of reporting guidelines could be that program committees of SE workshops and conferences as well as editorial boards of SE journals make the application of a standard reporting scheme mandatory.

To facilitate the adoption of the guidelines, it would help to stress the benefits that accrue to researchers who apply them. For example, one benefit could be simpler integration of individual results into a common body of knowledge. We also assume that, generally, the SE publication process will become more efficient, since crucial information will be found by reviewers (and other researchers) in the same place every time.

Thus, we would like to conclude this chapter with a call for adherence to guidelines. Whenever reporting results of any kind of empirical studies, it is wise to think about who shall read the publication for what purposes. This way, the report will deliver the information needed for different stakeholder groups and audiences. The guidelines will assist writers to emphasize the right information and the empirical software engineering community to mature.

Acknowledgements While preparing the guidelines, we got valuable feedback from many people. Only the names of some of them can be listed here. We thank Janice Singer for her feedback and support, while finalizing this chapter, the unknown reviewers of the preliminary version of this chapter, Claes Wohlin, who gave valuable insights and comments on an earlier version of the guidelines, Barbara Kitchenham and her team at NICTA for their valuable feedback from the perspective-based reading of an earlier version, which helped to improve the guidelines, and many others from the International Software Engineering Research Network (ISERN) for fruitful discussions. Furthermore, we are grateful to Sonnhild Namingha from Fraunhofer IESE for reviewing a previous version of this chapter.

References

Altman, D.G., Schulz, K.F., Moher, D., Egger, M., Davidoff, F., Elbourne, D., Gøtzsche, P.C., Lang, T. for the CONSORT Group (2001). The Revised CONSORT Statement for Reporting Randomized Trials, Explanation and Elaboration. Annals of Internal Medicine, Vol. 134, No. 8, pp. 663–694.

American Psychological Association (2001). Publication Manual of the American Psychological Association, 5th edn, American Psychological Association, Washington, DC.

Basili, V.R., Caldiera, G., Rombach, H.D. (2001). Goal Question Metric Paradigm, in Marciniak, J.J. (Ed.), *Encyclopedia of Software Engineering*, Vol. 1, Wiley, New York, pp. 528–532.

Basili, V.R., Zelkowitz, M., Sjøberg, D.I.K., Johnson, P., Cowling, T. (2007). Protocols in the use of Empirical Software Engineering Artifacts. Journal of Empirical Software Engineering, 12(1), pp. 107–119.

Bayley, L., Eldredge, J. (2003). The Structured Abstract, An Essential Tool for Researchers, In Hypothesis. The Journal of the Research Section of the Medical Library Association, Vol. 17, No. 1, 4 pp.

Ciolkowski, M., Differding, C., Laitenberger, O., Münch, J. (1997). Empirical Investigation of Perspective-based Reading, A Replicated Experiment, Fraunhofer Institute for Experimental Software Engineering, Germany, ISERN-97-13.

Dybå, T., Kampenes, B.V., Sjøberg, D.I.K. (2006). A Systematic Review of Statistical Power in Software Engineering Experiments, A Survey of Controlled Experiments in Software Engineering. Information and Software Technology, Vol. 48, pp. 745–755.

Glass, R.L. (2004). Matching Methodology to Problem Domain. Communications of the ACM, Vol. 47, No. 5, pp. 19–21.

Harris, P. (2002). Designing and Reporting Experiments in Psychology, 2nd edn, Open University Press, Buckingham.

Hartley, J. (2003). Improving the Clarity of Journal Abstracts in Psychology, The Case for Structure. Science Communication, Vol. 24, No. 3, pp. 366–379.

Hartley, J. (2004). Current Findings from Research on Structured Abstracts. Journal of the Medical Library Association, Vol. 92, No. 3, pp. 368–371.

Hayward, R.S.A., Wilson, M.C., Tunis, S.R., Bass, E.B., Rubin, H.R., Haynes, R.B. (1993). More Informative Abstracts of Articles Describing Clinical Practice Guidelines. Annals of Internal Medicine Vol. 118, No. 9, pp. 731–737.

Jedlitschka, A. (2005). Minutes from Third International Workshop on Empirical Software Engineering "Guidelines for Empirical Work in Software Engineering". IESE-Report 052.05/E, Oulu.

Jedlitschka, A., Ciolkowski, M. (2004). Towards Evidence in Software Engineering, In Proceedings of ACM/IEEE International Symposium on Software Engineering 2004 (ISESE2004). Redondo Beach, California, pp. 261–270.

Jedlitschka, A., Pfahl, D. (2005a). Reporting Guidelines for Controlled Experiments in Software Engineering. IESE-Report IESE-035.5/E.

Jedlitschka, A., Pfahl, D. (2005b). Reporting Guidelines for Controlled Experiments in Software Engineering, In Proceedings of ACM/IEEE International Symposium on Software Engineering 2005 (ISESE2005). Noosa Heads, Australia, pp. 95–104.

Jedlitschka, A., Ciolkowski, M. (2006). Reporting Guidelines for Controlled Experiments in Software Engineering, Fraunhofer Institute for Experimental Software Engineering, Germany, ISERN-06-1.

Jedlitschka, A., Ciolkowski, M. Pfahl, D. (2007). Reporting Guidelines for Controlled Experiments in Software Engineering, Fraunhofer Institute for Experimental Software Engineering, Germany, ISERN-07-1.

Juristo, N., Moreno, A. (2001). Basics of Software Engineering Experimentation, Kluwer Academic Publishers, Boston, MA.

Kampenes, B.V., Dybå, T., Hannay, J., Sjøberg, D.I.K. (2007). A Systematic Review of Effect Size in Software Engineering Experiments. Information and Software Technology, Vol. 49, No. 11–12, pp. 1073–1086.

Kitchenham, B. (2004). Procedures for Performing Systematic Reviews, Keele University Joint Technical Report TR/SE-0401, ISSN,1353–7776 and National ICT Australia Ltd. NICTA Technical Report 0400011T.1.

Kitchenham, B., Al-Khilidar, H., Ali Babar, M., Berry, M., Cox, C., Keung, J., Kurniawati, F., Staples, M., Zhang, H., Zhu, L. (2006). Evaluating Guidelines for Empirical Software Engineering Studies, In Proceedings of ACM/IEEE International Symposium on Software Engineering 2006 (ISESE2006).

Kitchenham, B., Dybå, T., Jørgensen, M. (2004). Evidence-Based Software Engineering, In Proceedings of 26th International Conference on Software Engineering (ICSE'04), pp. 273–281.

Kitchenham, B.A., Hughes, R.T., Linkman, S.G. (2001). Modeling Software Measurement, IEEE Transactions on Software Engineering, Vol. 27, No. 9, pp. 788–804.

Kitchenham, B.A., Pfleeger, S.L., Pickard, L.M., Jones, P.W., Hoaglin, D.C., El Emam, K., Rosenberg, J. (2002). Preliminary Guidelines for Empirical Research in Software Engineering, IEEE Transactions on Software Engineering, Vol. 28, No. 8, pp. 721–734.

Lott, C.M., Rombach, H.D. (1996). Repeatable Software Engineering Experiments for Comparing Defect – Detection Techniques, Empirical Software Engineering Journal, Vol. 3.1, pp. 241–277.

Moher, D., Schulz, K.F., Altman, D. for the CONSORT Group (2001). The CONSORT Statement, Revised Recommendations for Improving the Quality of Reports of Parallel-Group Randomized Trials, Journal of the American Medical Association (JAMA) Vol. 285, No. 15, pp. 1987–1991.

Pickard, L.M., Kitchenham, B.A., Jones, P.W. (1998). Combining Empirical Results in Software Engineering, Information and Software Technology, Vol. 40, No. 14, pp. 811–821.

Shaw, M. (2003). Writing Good Software Engineering Research Papers – Minitutorial, In Proceedings of the 25th International Conference on Software Engineering (ICSE'03). IEEE Computer Society, Portland, Oregon, pp. 726–736.

Shiffman, R.N., Shekelle, P., Overhage, J.M., Slutsky, J., Grimshaw, J., Deshpande, A.M. (2003). Standardized Reporting of Clinical Practice Guidelines, A Proposal from the Conference on Guideline Standardization, Annals of Internal Medicine, Vol. 139, No. 6, pp. 493–498.

Shull, F., Carver, J., Travassos, G.H., Maldonado, J.C., Conradi, R., Basili, V.R. (2003). Replicated Studies, Building a Body of Knowledge about Software Reading Techniques, In Juristo, N., Moreno, A. (Eds.), Lecture Notes on Empirical Software Engineering, World Scientific Publishing, River Edge, NJ, USA, pp. 39–84.

Singer, J. (1999). Using the APA Style Guidelines to Report Experimental Results, In Proceedings of Workshop on Empirical Studies in Software Maintenance, pp. 71–75. (dec.bmth.ac.uk/ESERG/WESS99/singer.ps)

Sjøberg, D.I.K., Hannay, J., Hansen, O., Kampenes, B.V., Karahasanovic, A., Liborg, N.-K., Rekdal, A. (2005). A Survey of Controlled Experiments in Software Engineering. Transactions on Software Engineering, Vol. 31, No. 9, pp. 733–753.

The Editors of Annals of Internal Medicine (2004). Addressing the Limitations of Structured Abstracts (Editorial). Annals of Internal Medicine, Vol. 140, No. 6, pp. 480–481.

Vegas, S., Juristo, N., Basili, V. (2003). A Process for Identifying Relevant Information for a Repository, A Case Study for Testing Techniques. In Aurum, A., Jeffery, R.,Wohlin, C., Handzic, M. (Eds.). Managing Software Engineering Knowledge, Springer-Verlag, Berlin, pp. 199–230.

Wohlin, C., Petersson, H., Aurum, A. (2003). Combining Data from Reading Experiments in Software Inspections, In Juristo, N., Moreno, A. (Eds.), Lecture Notes on Empirical Software Engineering, World Scientific Publishing, River Edge, NJ, USA, pp. 85–132.

Wohlin, C., Runeson, P., Höst, M., Ohlsson, M.C., Regnell, B., Wesslén, A. (2000). Experimentation in Software Engineering – An Introduction, Kluwer Academic Publishers, Boston, MA.

Zelkowitz, M.V., Wallace, D.R., Binkley, D.W. (2003). Experimental Validation of New Software Technology. In Juristo, N., Moreno, A. (Eds.), Lecture Notes on Empirical Software Engineering, World Scientific Publishing, River Edge, NJ, USA, pp. 229–263.

Chapter 9
A Practical Guide to Ethical Research Involving Humans[1]

Norman G. Vinson and Janice Singer

Abstract The popularity of empirical methods in software engineering research is on the rise. Surveys, experiments, metrics, case studies, and field studies are examples of empirical methods used to investigate both software engineering processes and products. The increased application of such methods has also brought about an increase in discussions about adapting these methods to the particularities of software engineering. In contrast, the ethical issues raised by empirical methods have received little attention in the software engineering literature. In this chapter, we introduce four ethics principles of primary importance for conducting ethical research. We additionally discuss and provide examples of applying these principles in the context of ethics review.

1. Introduction

How should an empirical researcher approach subjects?

How should data be collected and stored?

How can a researcher reduce subjects' unease about being observed?[2]

Should a company's name be mentioned in the acknowledgements of a paper?

Each of these real-life issues has an ethical dimension. As such, ethics play a role in the proper management of a research project (Mirvis and Seashore, 1982) which, in turn, affects the project's success. Accordingly, it is important that empirical

---

[1] Based on Singer, J.A. & Vinson, N.G. (2002). Ethical issues in empirical studies of software engineering, *IEEE Transactions on Software Engineering* 28(12), 1171–1180.

[2] Several recent publications (e.g. National Health and Medical Research Council et al., 2007) suggest that it is more appropriate to refer to the people under study as research participants rather than research subjects. However others (e.g. Canadian Institutes of Health Research et al., 2005) note that the term "participant" is ambiguous, as it can refer to virtually anyone involved in the research project. To avoid any such ambiguity we will use the term "subject" to refer to those people who are being studied.

F. Shull et al. (eds.), *Guide to Advanced Empirical Software Engineering.*
© Springer 2008

researchers understand research ethics and their application. In this chapter, we will introduce the major ethical concepts relating to Empirical Software Engineering (ESE) research with human subjects and provide a practical guide to the ethics review process[3].

Because empirical research is relatively new to software engineering, discussion of the ethical issues raised by ESE is still in its early stages (Harrison, 1998; Jeffrey and Votta, 1999; Singer and Vinson, 2001, 2002). Therefore, we will rely on information from other fields to support our discussion. Nonetheless, our examples will focus on situations ESE researchers are likely to face.

It is insufficient to simply expect scientists to behave ethically (Beecher, 1966a; McNeill, 1993). In an attempt to minimize unethical behaviour, governments and scientific communities have developed codes of research ethics (McNeill, 1993). By providing a standard of behaviour for researchers to follow, and by helping them reason about ethical issues in specific situations, it is hoped that these codes of ethics will reduce the incidence of unethical behaviour (Anderson et al., 1993; Frankel, 1989; Gotterbarn et al., 1999; McNeill, 1993). However, it is ultimately up to individual researchers to ensure research practices are ethical. In this regard, experience has shown that to behave ethically, people must understand the ethical principles underlying codes of ethics and spend the time and effort required to intelligently apply them to their own circumstances (Anderson et al., 1993; Canadian Institutes of Health Research et al., 2005). To quote the preamble of the ACM/IEEE-CS SE Code of Ethics and Professional Practice, "the Code is not a simple ethical algorithm that generates ethical decisions" (Gotterbarn et al., 1999, p. 104).

Unfortunately, the ESE community has yet to develop its own code of research ethics (Harrison, 1998; Jeffrey and Votta, 1999; Singer and Vinson, 2002) Researchers must therefore try to apply codes from related disciplines to ESE studies. For ESE research practices similar to those of other disciplines, this does not pose a problem. In this vein, codes from the social sciences and computing sciences are especially relevant. However, for research practices more common or even unique to ESE, such as the use of source code as data (see El-Emam, 2001; Vinson and Singer, 2001), the existing codes are of little value. In these cases, ESE researchers will have to reason from ethical principles to determine an ethical course of action. To support such reasoning, we provide a detailed explanation of the main principles of ethical research in the first section of this chapter. We also describe some common problems in applying these principles to ESE projects and present solutions to those problems.

---

[3] Scientific research raises a host of ethical issues such as the assignment of authorship, the relationship between graduate students and their advisors, and scientific fraud. These issues apply broadly to most research disciplines (Committee on Science, 1992, 1993, 1995). Computer science and software engineering research raises additional issues (Wright, 2006). In this chapter, we will ignore broad issues to instead focus on the ethical issues raised by the researcher/subject relationship in ESE; issues such as those highlighted above.

This chapter also includes a discussion of the role of Ethics Review Boards (ERBs) and research ethics regulations. In the USA, Canada, and Australia most ESE projects receiving government funding and involving human subjects must be reviewed by an ERB to ensure that the project complies with the relevant ethical guidelines (Australian Research Council (ARC), 2007; Canadian Institutes of Health Research et al., 2005; National Health and Medical Research Council et al., 2007; Penslar, 1993). However, because the regulations and guidelines still retain characteristics of their original focus on biomedical research (Canadian Association of University Teachers (CAUT), 1997; Lane, 2006; Sieber, 2001b), it can sometimes be difficult to determine whether and how they apply to ESE (El-Emam, 2001; Lethbridge, 2001; Sieber, 2001a, 2001b; Vinson and Singer, 2001; Vinson and Singer, 2004).

In general, Europe's regulations focus on biomedical research. However, the Research Council of Norway expects institutions to ensure that the necessary ethical precautions are taken (H.H. Simonsen, Senior Adviser, National Research Council of Norway, personal communication (e-mail), July 20, 2006). Similarly in the UK, the Engineering and Physical Sciences Research Council (EPSRC) holds the institution responsible for ensuring that research ethics standards are followed (Engineering and Physical Sciences Research Council (EPSRC), 2007, p. 31), but it does not appear that ESE research need be reviewed by an ERB or comply with a specific set of research ethics guidelines.

Europe does however have personal information privacy laws, as do Canada and Australia (Patrick, 2006). These laws conform in large part to the Organisation for Economic Co-operation and Development (OECD) Guidelines on the Protection of Privacy and Transborder Flows of Personal Data (Organisation for Economic Development and Co-operation (OECD), 1980; Patrick, 2006). While specific implementations will differ from country to country, they will rest on the principles we describe below. Moreover, researchers should note that it is not within the mandate of ERBs to ensure compliance to privacy laws.

In reading this chapter it is important to keep in mind the important distinction between principles and regulations: research practices are rendered ethical primarily by the application of ethics principles. Principles, if they are abstract enough, can be applied to any relevant situation. In contrast, existing regulations are not well suited to all research situations that raise ethical issues (Sieber, 2001a, b; Singer and Vinson, 2002). Consequently, simply complying with regulations can nonetheless result in violations of the principles of ethical research (Beecher, 1966a; McNeill, 1993). The distinction between rules and principles is particularly important for ESE researchers since some of their research practices are not covered by existing regulations (Sieber, 2001a; Singer and Vinson, 2002). In order to conduct research ethically, ESE researchers must not simply rely on complying with the rules but must be able to apply ethical principles to their particular circumstances (Gotterbarn et al., 1999).

Accordingly, our goals in this chapter are to introduce the topic of research ethics, aid researchers with the ethics review process, and foster ethical decision-making in the context of ESE research. In service of these goals we will first focus on ethical principles and then present sample ERB documents. Knowledge of both these components is vital to planning and conducting research projects.

2. Ethical Principles

Singer and Vinson (2002) reviewed codes of ethics from government funding bodies, and biomedical, social science, and computing science professional organizations to determine common principles relevant to ESE research practices. They discovered four such common principles: *informed consent, scientific value, confidentiality,* and *beneficence.* The principle of informed consent stipulates that potential subjects should be informed of all relevant facts about a study before making an explicit, free and well-considered decision about whether to participate. The study should also have some scientific value in order to call upon human subjects to expose themselves to even minimal risks. Researchers must also undertake every effort to maintain the confidentiality of data and sensitive information. Finally, beneficence results from a weighing of the risks, harms, and benefits of the proposed research. Beneficence must be positive in order to proceed.

Note that all of these principles apply whether researchers are observing the subjects' behaviour directly (as in job shadowing (see Singer et al., Chap. 1)), or indirectly (as when collecting command logs), or whether the subjects are simply providing code to be examined. These principles also apply whether the subjects are students, employees, volunteers, or organizations (e.g. companies). Each of these principles is reviewed below, and the implications for ESE researchers are discussed.

2.1. Informed Consent

The principle of full informed consent on the part of research subjects to participate in a study follows from the more abstract principle of respecting an individual's autonomy (Fleuhr-Lobban, 1994). In essence, before the research begins, potential subjects have the right to choose whether they will participate in the project. Ethicists do not agree on the necessary components of full informed consent, but it is clear that it must contain at least some of the following elements: *disclosure, comprehension and competence, voluntariness,* and *the actual consent* or *decision* (Faden and Beauchamp, 1986). Below we provide an abstract description of each of these elements and then we focus more closely on consent in the context of ESE.

Disclosure refers to the information that the researcher must provide to the subjects for them to make an informed decision about whether to participate in the research. This information usually includes, but is not limited to: the purpose of the research, the research procedure, the risks to the subjects, the anticipated benefits to the subjects and the world at large, alternatives to participation (typically for students in a subject pool), the treatment of confidential information, the voluntary nature of participation, and a statement offering to answer the subjects' questions (Sieber, 1992). As well, the disclosure should describe the type of data that will be collected and the uses it will be put to (Patrick, 2006). The intent is to provide potential subjects with all the information necessary to understand how the research will affect them (Faden and Beauchamp, 1986). The need for comprehension compels the researcher to present the information in a manner that the subjects can understand, e.g. eschewing technical jargon that is outside the subjects' repertoire. Competence refers to the subjects' ability to make a rational informed decision to participate in the research. This element is intended to protect vulnerable subjects who may not understand the nature of the research or the risks, such as children or the mentally disabled. Finally, voluntariness specifies that informed consent must be obtained under conditions free of coercion and undue influence, and that the consent must be intentional. The subjects' right to terminate their participation at any time is also a component of voluntariness. Typically, the decision to participate must represent an active authorization on the part of the subject, as opposed to a tacit acceptance or mere formality (Faden and Beauchamp, 1986). In regard to the specific elements of informed consent – disclosure, comprehension and competence, voluntariness, and the actual consent or decision – ESE researchers are *not* likely to have trouble with comprehension and competence.

For field research in companies, it will almost always be necessary to obtain consent from the company first, whether one is interviewing employees or simply obtaining metrics on source code (ACM Executive Council, 1993). The wise researcher will also try to convince the relevant managers to support the project.

When an individual can be identified from the data, consent is usually required, regardless of the way in which the data are collected (Patrick, 2006). Indeed, the ACM code (ACM Executive Council, 1993) explicitly forbids access to an individual's electronic data and communications, such as e-mail, without the individual's prior consent. In contrast, when there is no information in the raw data that could allow a particular individual to be identified, informed consent of individuals will usually not be required (Canadian Institutes of Health Research et al., 2005; Penslar, 1993). For example, measurements of network traffic do not include data identifying individuals, therefore, the informed consent of employees using the network would not be required even though the employees are the source of some of the data.

Obtaining signed informed consent forms in participant observation field research will often pose a problem (Fleuhr-Lobban, 1994; University of Toronto Social Sciences and Humanities Research Ethics Board (SSH REB), 2005). When using participant observation methods, the researcher becomes a member of the community that is the object of study (Singer et al., Chap. 1; University of Toronto Social Sciences and Humanities Research Ethics Board (SSH REB), 2005). In these contexts, consent is an ongoing process. For example, as the research evolves, the participants' (subjects and researchers) roles will change and unforeseen risks may arise (Fleuhr-Lobban, 1994; Mirvis and Seashore, 1982; University of Toronto Social Sciences and Humanities Research Ethics Board (SSH REB), 2005). Given the changing participant roles and the evolution of the research, it is practically impossible to even prepare a consent form as described in the ethics regulations (see 45CFR§46[4]; Canadian Institutes of Health Research et al., 2005).

---

[4] Listed in the references section as: Public Welfare, Protection of Human Subjects, Code of Federal Regulations, Title 45, Pt. 46 (45CFR§46), (2005), http://www.hhs.gov/ohrp/humansubjects/guidance/45cfr46.htm

At the outset of the study, the subjects should receive as much disclosure about the study as possible, perhaps through a general announcement. Subjects should also be made aware that their behaviour might be recorded. In addition, given the evolving nature of the research, the researcher should maintain an ongoing dialog with the subjects, apprising them of relevant changes that can affect their consent (American Anthropological Association, 2004; Fleuhr-Lobban, 1994; University of Toronto Social Sciences and Humanities Research Ethics Board (SSH REB), 2005).

A distinction can be drawn between consent and assent, the latter being more passive, more similar to acquiescence. When giving consent, the subject is required to sign an informed consent document. In contrast, assent is limited to a verbal or tacit agreement to participate. For telephone interviews or surveys, assent (in contrast to consent) is usually acceptable (Fowler, 1993), as long as the study poses no real risk to the subjects and there is no collection of information that could be used to identify the subjects. To give assent, subjects still need all the necessary information to make an informed decision about whether to participate in the research. They simply do not have to sign a form (Fowler, 1993). In a participant observation context, the researcher's primary subjects may sign a consent form at the study's outset, and then maintain their participation through assent as the study evolves. For other participants whose interaction with the researcher is limited, assent may be sufficient (University of Toronto Social Sciences and Humanities Research Ethics Board (SSH REB), 2005).

Many codes of ethics (e.g., Canadian Institutes of Health Research et al., 2005) set full disclosure as the standard for an acceptable informed consent. Full disclosure is defined in contrast to deception, where the true intent and methods of the study are not revealed to the subjects. For example, a social science researcher might be interested in how women and men interact in small spaces. To examine this, the scientist sets up an experiment in which subjects are told that they will process some paperwork with a partner. They are led to believe that the partner, like them, is a subject. However, in reality, the partner is part of the experimenter's team and is only pretending to be a subject. The partner's role is to engage the subject in particular ways. The effects of those different engagement techniques on the subjects' behaviour are the true focus of the experiment. To avoid biasing the subjects' responses, the subjects are told nothing of this, and therein lay the deceit.

Rather than full disclosure or deception, many ESE studies employ some form of partial disclosure. Partial disclosure refers to providing the subjects with a less than complete account of the study's goal or hypotheses. If the subjects knew the hypotheses in detail, they could well modify their behaviour as a function of this knowledge, thus invalidating their data (Sieber, 1992; Worchel and Cooper, 1979). For example, consider an ESE experiment on source code searching. The experimenters could partially disclose the goal of the study by simply telling subjects that their patterns of file access and use will be recorded and examined. The experimenters mask the true goal of the study by formulating it in a more general, abstract, and vague manner. After the subjects have completed the experiment, they are provided with more detailed explanations of the experiment's goals and hypotheses. Since the subjects' data have already been collected, these explanations will not affect the data's validity. This is the least objectionable form of partial disclosure, since it does not affect the subjects' assessments of the risks of participation; full disclosure is provided at the conclusion of the experiment (Smith and Richardson, 1983); and no outright deception is involved.

It is unlikely that research in software engineering will involve any great form of deception. Nonetheless, Sieber (1992) gives excellent guidance, and Smith and Richardson (1983) discuss the crucial role of debriefing in deception experiments.

Perhaps the most important aspect of disclosure is the risks of participation. Many of the risks to subjects in ESE studies result from breaches of confidentiality. When employees serve as subjects, research reports can provide enough information for managers (or other employees) to identify the data of individuals. This can adversely affect the subjects' careers if, for example, it is found that they did not follow company procedures. Companies can also suffer if sensitive information is disclosed (see Sect. 2.2 Beneficence for other examples). It is therefore important to inform the subjects of the limits of confidentiality and the risks resulting from breaches of confidentiality as part of the disclosure process. Note that it is also advisable to minimize these risks by employing the techniques presented below in the section on confidentiality.

An additional difficulty in ESE is that the limited autonomy of many potential subjects raises questions about voluntariness. Namely, employees of a company that has approved a workplace research project and students in the researcher's class may fear a reprisal for not participating or may anticipate a reward for participating. For instance, an employee may fear upsetting his manager who supports the project, and a student may wish to curry her professor's favour. These expectations, even if they are false, taint the consent-giving process (Penslar, 1993). Of course, employees are only vulnerable if their employer has approved (or disapproved) of the research project. Research taking place outside the workplace context does not raise the possibility of employer coercion, even if it calls upon knowledge of software engineering.

Several measures can be taken to reduce the perception of coercion. First, in the case of field studies, researchers should emphasize to the potential subjects, and their managers if applicable, the importance of voluntariness and confidentiality of both participation and data. Second, researchers should establish explicit procedures to protect confidentiality (see Sect. 2.3). If managers and professors do not know who is participating, they can neither punish non-participants nor reward subjects. Consequently, their influence over potential subjects is significantly diminished.

However, it is easy to conceive of cases in which the research project would be carried out regardless of whether individual SEs consented or not (Vinson and Singer, 2004). This is because, as employees of a company, SEs can be directed by their managers to perform certain activities. In short, SEs are not fully autonomous in the context of their employment. Unfortunately, respect of the individual's autonomy is the cornerstone of research ethics guidelines and regulations (Fleuhr-Lobban, 1994). Thus in some cases, ESE field studies can conflict fundamentally with research ethics guidelines and regulations in regard to the subject's autonomy (Vinson and Singer, 2004).

For example a company may want metrics for several modules of code. Since the code belongs to the company, it has a legal right to obtain code metrics, regardless of whether the SEs or development group managers consent to it. In such a case, should a metrics researcher be required to obtain the consent of the individual SEs and their managers before working on the project?

For studies involving students, researchers should avoid recruiting students in the classroom setting and should avoid trying to recruit their own students. For example, an upcoming study could be announced in every class, and interested students would place their names on a list held in a secretary's office. This reduces the possibility and the perception of intimidation. Researchers should also ensure that the study has no impact on the students' grades. This not only reduces the possibility of coercion, it also minimizes the risk of harming subjects through their grades (refer to Sect. 2.2). Finally, students should also be given the opportunity of withholding their data.

In sum, ESE researchers must obtain informed consent from their subjects, whether these are individuals or organizations. However, it is unclear whether consent must be obtained from programmers when the research project is limited to examining source code they do not own. Disclosure is a required component of the consent process since it allows potential subjects to assess the desirability of participation. However, if the risks are clearly stated, partial disclosure that simply masks the precise hypotheses being tested should be acceptable. Perhaps the most serious difficulty for ESE researchers is the requirement of voluntariness. Voluntariness is threatened by the potential for coercion (real or merely perceived) of the employees and students. To limit the effects of coercion, researchers can implement procedures to protect confidentiality and minimize the harm that would result from breaches of confidentially. Techniques to minimize harm and protect confidentiality are discussed in the following sections.

2.2. Beneficence

The degree of beneficence results from a weighted combination of risks, harms, and benefits to the subjects and society from participation in a study (McNeill, 1993). Researchers are required to maximize beneficence, particularly for research subjects. In ESE, benefits tend to arise from the research topic (e.g. better training software), whereas potential harm tends to arise from the research methods (e.g. having some students use the training software instead of coming to class). Consequently, once the research question has been chosen, researchers can usually maximize beneficence by adopting methods that minimize the risk of harm to the subjects.

The principle of beneficence applies not only to the individual subject, but also to groups of subjects, like particular ethnic or socio-economic groups (Canadian Institutes of Health Research et al., 2005), and/or organizations, like companies. Moreover, in the context of minimizing harm, the definition of "harm" is not limited to physical harm. Instead, it is very broadly construed, and contains such diverse elements as stress, the loss of dignity, self-esteem, or personal autonomy, the disruption of day-to-day activities, tedium, and of course financial harm (National Health and Medical Research Council et al., 2007; Sieber, 2001b).

In ESE, the greatest risk for harm often comes from breaches of confidentiality. Imagine, for instance, that a metrics project allows a company to rank its programmers by injected fault rate. An employee's ranking could then affect future promotions. ESE research can also harm organizations through financial loss resulting from the disclosure of sensitive information. For example, a researcher may evaluate source code from several companies and name the companies in an appendix to a published article. Negative evaluations could lead prospective clients to choose competing products. Accordingly, procedures that maintain confidentiality reduce the risks of harm. Such procedures are discussed below in the section on confidentiality.

Social science research methods used in ESE studies also have a potential for harm. For example, job shadowing, wherein a researcher closely observes a subject at work, can cause some people a great deal of stress. The risk of such harm can be minimized by respecting and emphasizing the informed consent provisions discussed earlier. In particular, when a subject shows discomfort, the researcher can ask if anything can be done to alleviate the discomfort and may remind the subject that she can withdraw from the study without penalty. Interview and observation sessions should be scheduled in consultation with the subjects to avoid times of high stress, such as immediately before a software release. Schrier (1992) details several other techniques to reduce the stress that can arise from being observed.

In the context of ESE, researchers may take on the role of software engineers. The activities performed in this applied context can also harm the subjects, raising ethical issues (Lethbridge, 2001). For example, consider a project on source code re-engineering and automated translation. This will have a substantial impact on the software engineers who maintain the code, especially if they do not know the new code's language. At the very least it will increase their stress, and at worse it will place their employment at risk. Procedures can be implemented to minimize the impact of the source changes on the software engineers. For example, researchers can arrange for the software engineers to receive training in the new code's language. Researchers who introduce or modify technology should also avoid any action that might damage the subject's property. To continue our example of code translation, it is the researchers' responsibility to ensure that the translated code functions correctly even though, in practice, testing and debugging will often be carried out jointly by the researchers and the industrial partners. Similar issues arise when introducing new software tools or modifying interfaces (Lethbridge, 2001). When researchers take on the role of information technology provider, as illustrated here, they can find guidance in the ACM and IEEE-CS/ACM SE codes of ethics. It is not clear how and even whether research ethics regulations apply in these kinds of contexts (Lethbridge, 2001; Sieber, 2001a). However, it is clear that the ethical issues that can arise often fall outside the scope of research ethics. Mirvis and Seashore (1982) extensively discuss such ethical issues from the perspective of the various roles a researcher may adopt in an applied field research project.

Beneficence can lead to an ethical quandary when studying an organization and/or its members, or a company and its employees. In these cases, the reduction of harm to individuals may be at odds with the reduction of harm to the organization. For instance, if researchers uncover problematic processes in a company, whose harm should they attempt to minimize? To minimize harm to the company, the researchers should inform management of problems that could harm the company through increased costs and reduced product quality. However this could result in dismissals, thus harming individuals (Becker-Kornstaedt, 2001).

In the case of student subjects, classroom studies have the potential of harming subjects' learning and grades. For example, a classroom study comparing different software development environments, each used by a different group of students for class assignments, may influence the students' grades. In contrast, a 1-h laboratory study involving bug fixing should have no impact on grades. Consequently, a laboratory study is more acceptable from an ethical perspective than a classroom study. If methodological considerations force the researcher to use the classroom setting, several measures can be taken to improve its ethical acceptability. To reduce the effect of the manipulated factor (e.g. type of programming environment) on grades, each group of students could in turn be exposed to each level of factor. Over the course of the semester, each student would have his grade affected by all levels of the factor, rather than just one. Another possibility is to normalize the grades across student groups.

To summarize, in many cases, risks of harm can be minimized by protecting confidentiality. However researchers should use the least harmful yet still methodologically valid procedure. Here, codes of ethics can provide some guidance, but approaching the problem analytically and creatively will likely prove more useful.

2.3. Confidentiality

The principle of confidentiality refers to the subjects' right to expect that any information they share with researchers will remain confidential. In general, researchers should also conceal and protect subjects' identities, whether they are individuals or organizations such as departments in a company or companies themselves. Moreover, even information that is not directly related to the research project should be considered private and kept confidential.

Confidentiality has three components: data privacy, data anonymity, and anonymity of participation. Data privacy refers to the limitations imposed on access to the data collected from the subjects. To maintain data privacy, the data should be securely stored, with password protection and/or under lock and key. Access should be limited to a small number of people, all of whom would normally be part of the research team (Patrick, 2006).

Data anonymity is preserved when an examination of the data cannot reveal the identity of the subjects. There are several means to preserve the anonymity of the data. First, if at all possible, researchers should not collect any personal or organizational information that could lead to the identification of the subjects (ACM Executive Council, 1993; Patrick, 2006). Such information is typically referred to as *personally identifiable information, identifiable private information (45CFR§46.102(f)*[4]) or *identifiers*. Avoiding the collection of personally identifiable information reduces the possibility of breaches of confidentiality, and may even allow researchers to avoid the requirement to obtain informed consent. For example, subject numbers can be used instead of subject names. (However, if the names were needed for a follow-up, a key linking the names to the numbers would be securely stored apart from the data, preserving some degree of data anonymity.) Note that personal characteristics other than names could also serve as identifiers. For example, someone who knows the subjects could use programming experience to associate some of the data to some of the subjects. Another way to anonymize data is to report only aggregated data (such as cross-subject averages, medians, standard deviations, etc.) instead of individual data points. Unfortunately, ESE studies are often conducted with only a small number of subjects so that it may be impossible to anonymize the data by simply aggregating data across subjects. In this case, it is important to disclose the limits of confidentiality to subjects before they decide to participate in the research.

Anonymity of participation is accomplished by hiding the identity of the subjects from their colleagues, managers, professors, competitors, clients, and the public. Protecting the subjects' identities from managers and professors is particularly important since they can have the greatest impact on the subjects' careers. Competitors and clients have the greatest impact on companies and organizations, so researchers should be particularly sensitive to concealing the names and identifying characteristics of companies participating in research.

Recruitment should take place through some means that protects the subjects' identities. For example, e-mail and sign up sheets that are only accessible to the researchers offer some identity protection. Additionally, sampling from a large pool of potential participants can protect the subjects' identities. Therefore if an employee or student is not participating in the research, the manager or professor does not know whether the employee or student declined to participate or simply was not asked to participate (assuming, of course, that neither the professor nor the manager is an experimenter).

For data collection, it is best to see subjects in a private area. However, this cannot always be accomplished, as with observational studies in open office (cubicle) settings. Anonymity could still be maintained through remote observation (e.g. command logs) or observation at a time when confidentiality will not be breached, such as early in the morning, or when a manager has a meeting. If neither of these solutions is feasible, the potential subjects must be informed of the limits of confidentiality before agreeing to participate.

Names of subjects or organizations should not be reported, even in the acknowledgements section. Protecting the subjects' identities in the body of a paper makes little sense if identifying information is provided in the acknowledgements. Where an identifier is necessary for clarity, authors should use misleading pseudonyms. One should also avoid reporting identifying characteristics of companies under study. This is not always possible, particularly with case studies. If identifying characteristics will have to be reported, the executives providing consent should be informed of the resulting limits of confidentiality. Moreover, executives sometimes request that their company by identified. In such a case, researchers should inform them of the potential risks, and proceed with what makes the most sense.

The importance of confidentiality should be emphasized to all of those involved in the study, whether they are researchers, research assistants, subjects, managers or professors. Breaches in confidentiality lead to breakdowns in trust between researchers and subject populations. This loss of trust can leave a researcher without access to a subject population. It is therefore paramount to protect the confidentiality of subjects and their data, and to inform subjects of any limits to confidentiality.

2.4. Scientific Value

Scientific value has two components: the validity of the study, and the importance of the research topic (McNeill, 1993; National Health and Medical Research Council et al., 2007). First, if the study is not methodologically valid, its results will not faithfully reflect reality. Consequently, the study will provide no benefit. A study without benefit should not be undertaken (Freedman, 1987; McNeill, 1993).

In many of the codes of ethics promulgated by professions, the issue of competence is the counterpart to the issue of scientific validity (e.g. American Psychological Association, 2002). In the context of ESE, competence refers to an understanding of the standard research and statistical methodologies. ESE researchers should therefore be familiar with the appropriate and relevant methodologies or consult with other professionals who possess the necessary competence.

Because ESE is a relatively new approach, if not a new field, there is still a great deal of activity in the development of new methodologies, particularly in regard to metrics. Methodological development poses a problem for evaluating scientific value. Since it is difficult to assess a new methodology's validity, precisely because it is new, it is difficult to assess the scientific value of the development of that methodology. One way to validate a new methodology is by using it to replicate well-established results. ESE researchers wishing to develop and use a new methodology should consider validating this methodology through replication as soon as possible.

The previous sections of this chapter reviewed four ethical principles paramount to conducting ethical research in ESE. Researchers should be familiar with these principles and know how to apply them to their research projects. It is not sufficient to simply follow a set of regulations. Each decision regarding ethics should be made in consideration of the underlying principles.

The next section of the chapter introduces project review by summarizing the history of the regulation of research by governments, and defining some common terms associated with ethics review.

3. Project Review

Several governments have mandated that an independent ERB review proposed research involving human subjects to ensure compliance with ethical guidelines. Canada, Australia, and increasingly the UK, are following the lead established by the United States (45CFR§46[4]; Canadian Institutes of Health Research et al., 2005; Economic and Social Research Council (ESRC), undated; McNeill, 1993; National Health and Medical Research Council et al., 2007). In this section, we describe project review and its associated documents primarily from the US perspective since it has the most established process. This section, especially the example documents, provides a very concrete (though limited) illustration of how to apply the ethics principles discussed above. Accordingly, the information presented here is useful for all researchers, including those in Europe who do not yet face project review.

In the United States, regulations requiring ethics review were put into place following the Jewish Chronic Disease Hospital case (McNeill, 1993). This case involved hospital researchers who injected live cancer cells into patients without their consent. Because the study was partially funded by the US federal government, the scandal spurred the government to require ethics review of federally funded research. Subsequent ethical transgressions eventually led to the creation of the Common Rule (45CFR§46[4]), the US federal regulation governing the ethics of research projects involving humans (McNeill, 1993). By 1991, the Common Rule had been adopted by several federal agencies, among them the National Science Foundation, the Department of Education, the Department of Defence, and NASA, which are the government agencies most likely to fund software engineering research. This means that all research funded by these agencies is bound by the Common Rule regulations (Sieber, 2001b).

The Common Rule requires that all research involving human subjects be reviewed by an Institutional Review Board (IRB) (Penslar, 1993) (which we refer to as an Ethics Review Board (ERB), as the specific terms for ERBs differ from country to country). The ERB is an administrative body whose mandate is to protect the rights of research subjects. Generally, each university or government agency has its own ERB to review all human subjects research projects conducted by members of the ERB's institution. Companies whose research is funded by the federal government may also have an ERB or contract the services of private ERBs (Heath, 1998; Penslar, 1993). In the US and Canada, the ERB has the authority to approve, reject, propose modifications to, or *terminate* any proposed or ongoing research involving human subjects under its jurisdiction (Penslar, 1993; 45CFR§46.113[4]; Canadian Institutes of Health Research et al., 2005). In Australia, it is the institution that has the responsibility to ensure compliance with the national ethics statement (National Health and Medical Research Council et al., 2007).

Only projects constituting *research* that involves *human subjects* are subject to ERB review. It is the ERB's responsibility to determine whether the proposed project constitutes research and whether it involves human subjects. Research is defined in the Common Rule as "a systematic investigation, including research, development, testing and evaluation, designed to develop or contribute to generalizable knowledge" (45CFR§46.102(d)[4]). The key phrase here is "generalizable knowledge". Generalisable knowledge is not considered to result from quality assurance or performance reviews undertaken within a specific context. For example, the evaluation of a professor's performance through the use of student questionnaires would not be considered research because it does not contribute to generalisable knowledge in that the knowledge applies only to that professor. On the other hand, collecting student questionnaires to determine the characteristics of excellent professors constitutes research because generalisable knowledge is produced in that the resulting "excellent professor" profile can be compared to the profile of any other professor.

Some forms of human subjects research are typically exempt from ERB review. The two most important exemptions for ESE research are surveys and the development of educational tests and materials. For a project to be exempted from review, the data must not contain any information that can lead to the identification of individual subjects. Additionally, reporting the data must not place the subjects at risk for loss of employment, liability, financial loss or other risks to the subjects' good standing in the community (Penslar, 1993). In general, then, when conducting surveys or collecting evaluative education data, it is best to refrain from collecting any information that could lead to the identification of an individual's data (Patrick, 2006). Researchers should note that there is some confusion over what constitutes research and that some regulations are unclear on the matter (Canadian Institutes of Health Research et al., 2005; Lethbridge, 2001; Sieber, 2001a). Consequently, we recommend that researchers consult with their ERB when in doubt about whether their work constitutes research, and whether it is subject to review.

Besides determining whether a proposal involves research, the ERB must also determine whether it involves human subjects. The Common Rule specifies that, to involve human subjects, the research must involve the collection of identifiable private information or data from living individuals by interacting with them or manipulating their environment. "Identifiable private information" refers to information that is normally not observed, recorded, or made public *and* can be used to identify the subject who is the source of this information (45CFR§46.102(f)[4]). For example, someone's opinion about the utility of design reviews is typically considered private information. In contrast, an opinion about design reviews that is published in an article is considered to be in the public domain, and consequently, does not constitute private information. US and Canadian regulations explicitly exclude the collection of public domain data from the definition of human subjects research (45CFR§46.101(b)(4)[4]; Canadian Institutes of Health Research et al., 2005).

This definition of human subjects research leads to an interesting problem for software engineering research. In particular, when source code is used as a data source and individual programmers' identities can be used as a variable in the analysis, it is not clear whether the research comes under the purview of the ERB (El-Emam, 2001; Vinson and Singer, 2001). It could be argued that when the programmers identified themselves as authors of a certain piece of source code, they had a reasonable expectation that this information would not be made public. Of course, this would probably differ for open-source projects or information collected from internet sources. Nonetheless, it is not entirely clear whether such a project must be reviewed. Again, when in doubt, consult the local ERB.

In summary, projects that receive Canadian, Australian or US federal funding and involve research with human subjects are required, in most cases, to be reviewed by an ERB to ensure that it meets the relevant ethical standards. If investigators are unsure about whether their research must undergo review, they should consult their local ERB. Avoiding ethics review when regulations specify that it is necessary can result in loss of funding, not only for the researchers involved but also for their institution as a whole. Therefore, ethics review and approval protects not only research subjects, but the researchers as well. Finally, whether a project is subject to review or not, it is prudent to adhere to the standards of ethical research. These standards help researchers avoid the type of conflicts that can jeopardize access to the subject population and the validity of the results.

3.1. Planning for Ethics Review

Planning for ethics review should be integral to the human subjects research process. Though approval times vary across institutions, it can take a considerable amount of time for a project to be approved, particularly if it contains controversial elements. For example, one local field study Singer conducted with employees as subjects took over 4 months to be approved. Proper planning can reduce approval time by increasing the odds that the proposal will be approved at the first review meeting. Part of this planning should include talking to colleagues who have already had a proposal approved, as they can provide much information about appropriate forms and the ERB review process.

To aid researchers in this endeavour, in the following sections, we describe the review process and provide examples of documents generally required by ERBs to review research proposals. We also relate the forms' contents to the ethics principles discussed earlier.

3.2. Review Process

Most institutions have their own ERB with its own procedures. However, the process typically begins with the researcher submitting documents describing the proposed project to the ERB. (Note that potential subjects cannot even be approached before the ERB has approved the project.) The ERB chair will then determine whether the project involves more than minimal risk. Minimal risk research is generally defined as research involving the same degree of risk that people normally encounter in their daily lives (Penslar, 1993). Moreover, to be judged of minimal risk, research must not involve vulnerable subject populations, such as students or employees of a sponsoring or collaborating company. Employees and students are considered vulnerable due to the potential for coercion or undue influence from employers or professors (Penslar, 1993). Projects that involve more than minimal risk are generally reviewed by the full board at periodic board meetings. In contrast, minimal risk projects are often given expedited review, wherein only a few board members need review the project. Moreover, since expedited review does not require a board meeting, it is usually faster than full (board) review.

Some ERBs will also require a scientific review to ensure the project has sufficient scientific value. The requirement for scientific review can depend on the project's level of risk.

Departments in which minimal risk human subjects research is a frequent occurrence sometimes have the authority to review and approve projects directly rather than submitting them to the institutional ERB. However, this is unlikely to be the case in computer science or software engineering departments, where few, if any, departmental ERBs exist. Moreover, in Canada, regulations forbid such departmental review boards, except for undergraduate research projects in the context of a specific course (Article 1.4a, Canadian Institutes of Health Research et al., 2005).

Projects are not always approved at first consideration. Moreover, when an ERB requires changes or amendments to the original proposal, the changes or amendments must usually also be reviewed by the ERB before approval can be granted. However, this latter review may be expedited. The number and magnitude of changes required, and therefore the time to final approval, will depend on the researchers' experience with the ethics review process, and on the ERB's experience with ESE research. To help researchers proceed more efficiently through the review process, below we discuss the types of documents usually submitted when seeking ethics approval and relate their contents to the foregoing material.

4. Documents Needed for Review

In the course of preparing documents for a review, it is often helpful to have a set of example documents as a guide, as we provide here. However, it is important to remember that the specific set of documents required will vary from one ERB to another. Consequently, the most important part of preparing for a review is to consult the local ERB, or other department members who have been through the ERB process. We have found that the requirements and filing procedures are often available on the web.

As we cannot specify what individual institutions will require, this section will present generic examples of the type of documents usually required. Our web search showed that most institutions require that a proposal contain a cover letter, a project description, a consent form, and a scientific review (see also Sieber, 1992).

Each of the required documents is detailed below. Where appropriate, the elements of the document are related to the four ethical principles described earlier.

4.1. Cover Letter

The cover letter introduces the project to the ERB. It usually includes the principal investigators' names and contact information. It should be clear who will carry out the research and who will be responsible for its supervision and conduct. It is usually sufficient to provide information about the principal investigators only; the rest of the team need not be profiled. Also included in the cover letter is a note indicating whether the proposal relates to a new project, a changed project, or an annual review of an on-going project. If the project is a changed project or an annual review, the cover letter should also include the project ID, which is usually assigned at the time of initial approval.

The cover letter can include information about the qualifications of the researcher. This is especially useful for a first proposal submitted to the ERB. Including a curriculum vita as an appendix can serve the same purpose. Finally, the cover letter should include any additional information that the researchers believe will help the reviewers assess the proposal, such as experience with the same subject population, eagerness of the industrial site in maintaining subjects' rights, etc.

4.2. Project Description

The project description usually has several specific subheadings. The ERB will often ask researchers to respond to a set of standard questions referring to specific aspects of the research, such as whether deception will be used, or whether subjects will be drawn from a vulnerable population. Depending on the answers, researchers may have to provide additional explanations. The answers will also often determine whether the project is deemed of minimal risk, and so can undergo expedited review (refer to Sect. 3.2).

Figure 1 shows an example of a project description that describes some observational research we conducted at an industrial site. Because the study used employees as subjects (a vulnerable population), it was *not* deemed minimal risk, and was therefore reviewed by the full board. The ERB was particularly interested in recruitment and confidentiality issues.

4.2.1. Project Overview

The primary purpose of the project overview is to satisfy the ERB that the research being embarked upon addresses an important question. It usually begins with a short description of the project and its goals, including a short literature review. The project overview also usually includes a description of the study's design, including the specific procedures, tests, interviews and interview schedules, and samples of any questionnaires that will be used. Not everyone on the ERB will have expertise

STUDIES OF SOFTWARE DEVELOPER WORK PRACTICES
Project Description

Project Overview

In the past, software engineering tools have been designed based on the intuitions of designers and not the real needs of software engineers. The goal of this research is therefore to improve software engineering tools by gathering tool requirements from the software engineering community. Following, Lethbridge and Singer (1998), we will be studying the work practices of software engineers as they go about their daily work. Software engineers will be observed for one hour on one day. Portable computers and paper and pencil will be used to collect data. Additionally subjects will be asked to think out-loud while they perform their tasks. This think out-loud data will be tape-recorded. All subjects will be informed of their rights as subjects before participating. We will be under a non-disclosure agreement with the company pertaining to the results of the study.

Subjects

Ten software engineers involved in the development of a large scale software engineering project will be selected as subjects for this experiment.

Confidentiality and data storage

Because the data involves audiotapes where subjects may identify themselves or colleagues, the data cannot be cleared of identifying features. To ensure security, all tapes, transcripts of tapes, and computer logs will be stored in a locked filing cabinet in a locked office at the university. The only people who will have access to the data are the principal investigators and graduate students working with the team. All graduate students will be required to sign an agreement to not disclose information to anyone outside of the research team. When publishing results, all identifying information will be stripped from the data before it is published. If it is possible for identification to occur, subjects will be shown the paper and asked to give informed consent to the data usage before the paper is published.

Recruitment Procedures

Senior company management have identified the groups for us to contact. Recruitment will occur via email to each group member. If a group member replies, a researcher will contact the group member by phone to give more details of the research. If the group member is still interested, an observation date will be set, at which time the group member will be given the subject information sheet and the consent form. If the member agrees, the observation will commence immediately. One week from the initial message, a reminder message will be sent to all group members who did not respond to the initial message.

Regarding data collection, the researchers will ensure the confidentiality of the research subjects in two ways. First, the managers will not be told who participated in the research. Second, the researchers will randomly sample from those subjects who have indicated a willingness to participate. In this way, the managers will not know whether subjects were simply not chosen to participate or whether they chose not to participate.

Subjects will not be compensated for participating in this research.

(continued)

Benefits, Harms and Inconveniences

There is no direct benefit to the subject for participating in this research. There is a benefit to the software engineering community in the form of improved requirements for tool design to support maintainers. There are no harms to participating in this research. Subjects may feel slightly intimidated at the beginning of observation sessions, but in previous research this has abated quickly.

There is no deception involved in this research

Fig. 1 An example of a project description form. See Sect. 4.2 for greater detail

in software engineering, so the overview and procedures should be written for a layperson.

In general, the project overview allows the ERB to determine the project's scientific importance (although not validity), which in turn helps the ERB estimate scientific value and beneficence. If an ERB finds no scientific value to a project, it is conceivable that the proposal will be rejected. Consequently it is important that researchers fully motivate their research. Note that our example project overview was kept short to save space.

4.2.2. Subjects

The subjects section should contain a description of the subject population. If more than one type of subject is involved (e.g., chemistry students vs. computer science students), all types should be adequately described. In this section, researchers should include any information that helps the ERB understand why this particular subject group is being sought, e.g. computer science students are familiar with a particular language that relates to the study hypothesis.

The subjects section should also subtly convey the subject group's familiarity with the types of risks that will arise from participation in the experiment. The following example illustrates how ethical concerns can change as a function, not of methods, but of subject group. Consider an experiment in which subjects experience a simulated airplane crash. If the subjects are test pilots, we can be sure that they will have the knowledge and experience required to make a reasonable decision about participation. If the subjects are undergraduates, we have to be sure that the risks of participation are clearly disclosed. If the subjects are senior citizens, the risks of injury may be too great for the study to go forward. A description of the subject groups' familiarity with the risks will therefore help the ERB in its evaluation.

Similarly, the subjects' context in regard to coercion or undue influence could be described. One concern in research is that people could agree to participate simply because they perceive the researcher as a trusted authority who should be obeyed (Kelman, 1972). This risk is even greater in medical research when a doctor adopts the role of experimenter (Beecher, 1966b; Canadian Institutes of Health Research et al., 2005; National Health and Medical Research Council et al., 2007). An ERB once raised a similar objection to the author (Singer) recruiting SEs in person. The ERB was concerned that the SEs would be intimidated by Singer's (as the board perceived it) higher social status, and so would feel pressure to volunteer. The ERB felt the SEs would be less intimated (and therefore less pressured) if the request took place through e-mail. While this concern is unwarranted when it comes to North American SEs, it is a legitimate concern in general (Kelman, 1972). Cultural differences could also have an impact, such that social status differences could affect the recruitment of SEs for studies taking place outside North America. Moreover, other social variables, such as age or gender, could also have an impact. Consequently, a short explanation of the role played by social differences between SEs and researchers in recruitment should help the ERB with its assessment of the proposal.

Of course, the real problem for voluntariness in ESE is not social status but the subject's position in the organizational hierarchy, which can lead to undue influence, if not coercion (Kelman, 1972) (refer to our section on informed consent). The subject's position in the organization should be described here. Any mitigations of the undue influence should be described in the relevant project description sections (e.g. Recruitment Procedures).

Finally, ERBs are often concerned that neither the burden nor benefits of research are disproportionally felt by a particular social group (Canadian Institutes of Health Research et al., 2005; National Health and Medical Research Council et al., 2007; Penslar, 1993). In ESE, this concern is most likely to manifest itself in the scrutiny of any inclusion or exclusion criteria proposed by the researcher. For example, researchers may want to exclude experienced SEs from their study. Any such criteria will have to be justified.

4.2.3. Confidentiality and Data Storage

In this section, measures to secure the data should be described. The ERB will want to ensure that data are protected from theft, interception, unauthorized reading and copying. To maintain security, data is often stored in a locked facility that can only be accessed by members of the research team. Some additional means of protecting data are described above in the section on confidentiality.

Since studies with vulnerable subject populations (employees and students) are common in ESE, this section might also include a description of the measures taken to protect the subjects' identities.

4.2.4. Recruitment Procedures

Since our example subjects are employees in an industrial setting (with the prior consent of their managers), there is a possibility of coercion in the recruitment process. Thus, we included a separate section in our project proposal detailing how we would recruit subjects while minimizing the possibility of coercion. An example e-mail message for potential subjects is included so an ERB can ensure that the language is neutral and does not in any way coerce the employees to participate in the study (e.g. by mentioning that their manager thought the information gained would be highly valuable to the company).

There are three important aspects to our recruitment procedures. First, recruitment is conducted via e-mail rather than in person. Second, the recruitment e-mail message emphasizes that participation is voluntary and that no harm can come from a refusal to participate. Finally, the e-mail message is sent to a larger pool of potential volunteers than is necessary given the experimental design to help ensure the anonymity of subjects.

ERBs will want to know whether subjects are being compensated for participation. The ERB wants to ensure that compensation is not so great that it will induce subjects to take risks that they would not normally take. This is easy to understand in the context of a medical study. For example, giving homeless subjects an excessive monetary reward for participating in risky medical research would be deemed highly unethical, because it would be seen as a form of implicit coercion. In software engineering studies, it is unclear what an appropriate compensatory scheme would be. Researchers intending to provide compensation to subjects should provide the ERB with adequate information to understand the compensatory scheme (e.g., software engineers will be paid in line with their salary on an hourly basis).

The ERB will also sometimes require a delay between the time the subject is given information about the study and the time at which the subject actually consents to participate. This is important in medical studies where the ERB needs to make sure that the subjects fully consider the risks of participation, but it can also be required in lower risk studies.

The ERB will also want to ensure that appropriate recruitment measures have been taken to ensure the study's validity.

It is advisable to provide more, rather than less, detail about how subjects will be approached and recruited. Recruitment is at the heart of some very delicate ethical matters (such as confidentiality and voluntariness of informed consent), and therefore the ERB will be quite serious in ensuring that recruitment is conducted appropriately.

4.2.5. Benefits, Harms, and Inconveniences

The degree of acceptable research risk depends on several factors, as mentioned in our section on beneficence. Consequently, the judgment of what constitutes an acceptable risk can vary dramatically depending on the context of the research and the risks to which subjects from a particular group are typically exposed. For example, because of their situation, terminal cancer patients can incur more risk as part of research into a treatment for their cancer than would be acceptable, say, for healthy children. Consequently, when writing a proposal for ethics review, it is advisable to clearly present the risks and benefits subjects will incur through the proposed research. However, we do not recommend that researchers try to antici-pate ERB objections by listing a series of potential risks that will *not* arise out of the proposed research. This exposes researchers to being required to provide addi-tional information on each of the measures put in place to eliminate those risks. It is important to recall that beneficence involves considering the relationship between risks and benefits for the subjects and society. Consequently, it is important to also clearly specify any benefit that may accrue from the research.

4.2.6. Deception

It would be unusual for an ESE study to employ outright deception. The section on deception will therefore typically state that no deception will be employed. It is important to remember that partial disclosure is not deception. Partial disclosure and deception are discussed earlier in the section on informed consent.

4.3. Informed Consent

In order to give fully informed consent, subjects must be given all the information needed to decide whether to participate in the research. In our proposal, we used two forms (see Fig. 2). The first is a subject information sheet providing subjects with an understanding of the research process and their potential involvement. The second form is the actual consent form.

Generally, researchers will bring two copies of the informed consent form to the subject. The subject will keep one copy for his reference, and return a signed copy for the researchers' records.

In participant/observation or ethnographic studies, where the researcher assumes the role of an SE, it is impractical (if not impossible) to obtain written consent from everyone the researcher encounters. Regulations offer some flexibility in the informed consent process (American Anthropological Association, 2004; Canadian Institutes of Health Research et al., 2005; Penslar, 1993) but ERBs have been reluctant to avail themselves of this flexibility (American Anthropological Association, 2004; Fleuhr-Lobban, 1994). Our suggestion to researchers is to attempt to ensure that every subject who is at risk of harm provide written consent, and to emphasize this to the IRB.

4.3.1. Subject Information Sheet

Though some ERBs do not require it, we have found it helpful to group all the important information on one sheet. The subject information sheet contains the information neces-sary for the subjects to decide whether to participate in the research. It should also inform subjects of some of their basic rights, such as the right to withdraw without penalty.

STUDIES OF SOFTWARE DEVELOPER WORK PRACTICES
SUBJECT INFORMATION SHEET

Traditionally, tools for software maintenance engineers are designed without knowing much about the specific circumstances under which software maintenance engineers work. Our research aims to correct this oversight by studying software maintenance engineers as they go about their daily work. We want to know not only where you spend your time, but also how you go about solving problems, what sources of information you consult, how you interact with the software and hardware, and what you find the most enjoyable and the most difficult aspects of your work.

Participants for this project will be selected via their place of employment. As part of the CSER initiative, certain corporations have agreed to allow us access to their employees. Your employer has specified your group as a possible source of participants in our research. The research will occur in your place of employment.

If you consent to participate in our research, we will observe you as you go about your work in one 1 hour sessions. You simply do what you would normally do, and we use a computer or paper and pencil to record your actions. Occasionally, we ask for clarification on a certain procedure, but in general try to be silent observers.

Participation in this research project is voluntary. Participants can withdraw their consent to participate and discontinue participation at any time without any consequences. Your employer will not know whether or not you have participated, or whether or not you have withdrawn participation. All collected data is strictly confidential, it will not be made available to anyone (including your employer) except as aggregate data. In the case that you may be identified in any reports, the researchers will ensure that you consent to the publication. Collected data will only be used by members of this research project as analysis vehicles for understanding the work practices of software maintenance engineers. The data will not be used for any other purpose. All participants can review their own data at any time.

All participants have the right to obtain any publicly available documents that are published about this research. All data collected is stored in a locked office at the National Research Council or the University of Ottawa.

STUDIES OF SOFTWARE DEVELOPER WORK PRACTICES
INFORMED CONSENT

Research Contact:
Dr. Sam Jones
Some University
(800) 555-1212
sam.jones@someuni.edu

Ethics Contact:
Dr. Ellen Good, Ethics Ombudsman
Some University
(888) 555-1212
ellen.good@someuni.edu

I hereby give my consent to participate in the research proposal, Study of Software Maintenance Engineers. I have been given a copy of the Subject Information Sheet. I have read this sheet and understand what it says. I understand that this project involves research. I understand the procedures that will be used.

I understand that my consent can be withdrawn at any time without any consequences.

I understand that I can view the data pertaining to me. I understand that all collected data is strictly confidential and will not be seen by anyone except members of the research team, or as aggregate data. I understand that all data is kept in locked offices at the NRC or University of Ottawa.

(continued)

I understand that this research will be used to better understand the work practices of software maintenance engineers and this in turn will lead to better tool design. I understand that beyond this, there is no personal benefit to me for participating in this research. I also understand that there is no harm to me for participating in this research. There may be minor inconveniences as the researchers set up their equipment. I understand that I will not receive any payment for my participation in this research.

I understand that I may request additional information about this research at any time, but as of now, all of my questions have been answered.

_____

Name (Printed)   Signature Date

Fig. 2 An example of an informed consent form (including the subject information sheet). See Sects. 4.2 and 4.3 for further detail.

It begins with a brief statement of the background, purpose, and goals of the research. The sheet should be comprehensible to the potential subjects. Jargon should be avoided, but if technical terms will help explain the research, and the potential subjects will understand the terms, then it is appropriate to use them.

The subject information sheet contains other pertinent information including how the subjects were chosen; whether their employer has given them permission to participate; the location of the research; and finally what is expected of them and how long the their tasks will take. In observational studies, there is no experiment per se, so subjects are generally told to engage in their normal behaviour but to be aware that they might be observed.

The next section informs the subjects that their participation is voluntary and that they may withdraw consent at any time without any consequences. All informed consent forms will require such a statement to support the voluntariness of the informed consent. The next several statements address confidentiality. Generally these statements describe the confidentiality provisions as well as the limits on confidentiality, if any. In our example, we assure the subjects that their employer will not know whether they participated and will not have the opportunity to look at an individual's data. The subjects are also told that another informed consent will be sought if it turns out that the reports could lead to the identification of individual subjects. The subject information sheet assures subjects that they can look at their data at any time. In some cases, subjects are informed that their data will be destroyed at their asking.

The subject information sheet ends by telling subjects that they have the right to published reports of the research. Additionally, it tells subjects where the data will be stored.

Note that the subject information sheet is written from the perspective of the researcher providing explanations to the potential subject, whereas the informed consent form is written from the perspective of the subject. That is, the statements in the informed consent form begin with "I" and are not simply informational.

4.3.2. Consent Form

Research Project Title. The informed consent form must always include the title of the research project as it appears in the documents submitted to the ethics board, so the subjects can correctly refer to the research should they wish to contact someone about their participation, e.g., to complain about their experience.

Contact Information. The informed consent form should also always provide a research contact and an ethics contact. The research contact is the person the subjects would contact if they have any questions about the research, including obtaining results or papers, scheduling sessions, etc. The ethics contact is usually someone in the researcher's organization who acts as an ethics ombudsman. This is the person whom subjects should contact to voice any concerns about the way they were treated during the research project, such as feeling coerced into participating. It is the responsibility of the ethics contact's office to take complaints, investigate them, and decide upon actions where warranted.

Consent and Comprehension. In this section, the subjects are actually giving their consent to participate in the research project. This section also addresses the subjects' comprehension of the proposed research. The subjects are basically stating that they understand what is required of them, and that they understand that they will be participating in a research project.

Withdrawal. This section states that the subjects' signatures attest to their understanding that they can withdraw from the research project without penalty. All informed consent forms will require such a statement. This feature reinforces the voluntariness of the consent.

Confidentiality. Here the provisions of confidentiality regarding the research project and the data are reiterated.

Risks and Benefits. Here the subjects are asked to consent to the risks and benefits incurred from participating as a subject. Note that the form states that the subjects do not give up any legal rights by signing it.

Clarification. This statement regards the subjects' understanding that they can request additional information at any time. It also ensures that all the subjects' questions have been answered. Remember that in order to give fully informed consent, the subjects must completely understand their role in the research project. This statement just ensures that they have been given the opportunity to do so.

Signature. Finally, in all informed consent forms, the subjects are required to sign and date the form appropriately. The experimenter is often also required to sign. Subjects are then given a copy of the subject information sheet and the informed consent form. In some cases, verbal assent is sufficient. For instance, with surveys or questionnaires, the assent implied by filling out and returning the document may be considered sufficient evidence of consent by the ERB.

5. Conclusion

In this chapter we have presented four ethical principles that form the core of several research ethics guidelines and codes: informed consent, beneficence, confidentiality, and scientific value. How can one ensure that ethics plays a role in a research project? First, and foremost, researchers must educate themselves about ethics, just as they would about methodology or data analysis. This includes educating graduate and undergraduate students about the primary tenets behind ethical research. Ideally, this education should include practical as well as classroom experience. Researchers can also share their experiences with others so that the community as a whole develops its competency in this area.

Researchers also need to plan for ethics in their research, as one cannot always quickly solve problems as they occur. For instance, in conducting a classroom study, researchers need to have a plan for those students who do not wish to participate. Building likely scenarios can help researchers to understand specific issues and have solutions in place to address them.

Finally, researchers need to consult others who can help them to plan and implement ethical research. For instance, ERBs have a great deal of expertise on ethics and research. Researchers can use this important resource early in the planning stages to address potential problems. This has the added advantage of educating local ERBs on topics of importance to ESE researchers.

Ethical research does not happen by chance. Individual researchers must be committed to making their research ethical. By addressing some of the issues surrounding ethics in ESE research, we hope to have given ESE researchers the understanding they need to reason ethically about their own work.

Acknowledgements We would like to thank Paula Desjardins for her assistance in conducting a survey of the types of documents submitted to ERBs.

References

ACM Executive Council. (1993). ACM code of ethics and professional conduct. *Communications of the ACM, 36*(2), 99–105. http://www.acm.org/constitution/code.html

American Anthropological Association. (2004). *Statement on Ethnography and Institutional Review Boards.* http://www.aaanet.org/stmts/index.htm

American Psychological Association. (2002). *Ethical Principles of Psychologists and Code of Conduct.* http://www.apa.org/ethics/code2002.html

Anderson, R. E., Johnson, D. G., Gotterbarn, D., & Perrolle, J. (1993). Using the new ACM code of ethics in decision making. *Communications of the ACM, 36*(2), 98–107.

Australian Research Council (ARC). (2007). *Research Ethics*. www.arc.gov.au/about_arc/research_ethics.htm

Becker-Kornstaedt, U. (2001). Descriptive software process modeling – how to deal with sensitive process information. *Empirical Software Engineering*, 6(4), 353–367.

Beecher, H. K. (1966a). Ethics and clinical research. *New England Journal of Medicine*, 274(24), 1354–1360.

Beecher, H. K. (1966b). Consent in clinical experimentation: myth and reality. *Journal of the American Medical Association*, 195(1), 124–125.

Canadian Association of University Teachers (CAUT). (1997, October). CAUT responds to tri-council code. *CAUT Bulletin*. www.caut.ca/en/bulletin/issues/1997_oct/tricouncil.htm

Canadian Institutes of Health Research, Natural Sciences and Engineering Research Council, & Social Sciences and Humanities Research Council. (2005). *Tri-Council Policy Statement: Ethical Conduct for Research Involving Humans*. Public Works and Government Services Canada. www.pre.ethics.gc.ca

Committee on Science, Engineering and Public Policy of the National Academy of Sciences, National Academy of Engineering, and Institute of Medicine. (1992). *Responsible Science: Ensuring the Integrity of the Research Process* (1). Washington DC: National Academy Press.

Committee on Science, Engineering and Public Policy of the National Academy of Sciences, National Academy of Engineering, and Institute of Medicine. (1993). *Responsible Science: Ensuring the Integrity of the Research Process* (2). Washington DC: National Academy Press.

Committee on Science, Engineering and Public Policy of the National Academy of Sciences, National Academy of Engineering, and Institute of Medicine. (1995). *On Being a Scientist: Responsible Conduct in Research* (2nd edn). Washington DC: National Academy Press.

Economic and Social Research Council (ESRC). (undated). *Research Ethics Framework*. Swindon, UK: ESRC. http://www.esrcsocietytoday.ac.uk/ESRCInfoCentre/Images/ESRC_Re_Ethics_Frame_tcm6-11291.pdf

El-Emam, K. (2001). Ethics and open source. *Empirical Software Engineering*, 6(4), 291–292.

Engineering and Physical Sciences Research Council (EPSRC). (2007). *Funding Guide*. Swindon, UK: EPSRC.

Faden, R. R. & Beauchamp, T. L. (1986). *A History and Theory of Informed Consent*. New York: Oxford University Press.

Fleuhr-Lobban, C. (1994). Informed consent in anthropological research: we are not exempt. *Human Organization*, 53(1), 1–10.

Fowler, F. J. Jr. (1993). *Survey Research Methods* (1) (2nd edn). Thousand Oaks, CA: Sage.

Frankel, M. S. (1989). Professional codes: why, how, and with what impact? *Journal of Business Ethics*, 8(2), 109–115.

Freedman, B. (1987). Scientific value and validity as scientific requirements for research: a proposed explication. *IRB: Ethics and Human Research*, 9(6), 7–10.

Gotterbarn, D., Miller, K., & Rogerson, S. (1999). Software engineering code of ethics is approved. *Communications of the ACM*, 42(10), 102–108.

Harrison, W. (1998). An issue of ethics: responsibilities and obligations of empirical software engineering researchers. *Empirical Software Engineering*, 3, 7–9.

Heath, E. (1998). The noninstitutional review board: what distinguishes us from them? *IRB*, 20(5), 8–11.

Jeffrey, D. R. & Votta, L. G. (1999). Guest editor's special section introduction. *IEEE Transactions on Software Engineering*, 25(4), 435–437.

Kelman, H. C. (1972). The rights of the subjects in social research: an analysis in terms of relative power and legitimacy. *American Psychologist*, 27, 989–1016.

Lane, B. (2006, August 16). Ethics draft provokes anger. *The Australian*. http://www.theaustralian.news.com.au/

Lethbridge, T. C. (2001). Mixing software engineering research and development – what needs ethical review and what does not? *Empirical Software Engineering*, 6(4), 319–321.

McNeill, P. (1993). *The Ethics and Politics of Human Experimentation*. New York: Cambridge University Press.

Mirvis, P. H. & Seashore, S. E. (1982). Creating ethical relationships in organizational research. In J. Sieber (Ed.), *The Ethics of Social Research*, New York: Springer-Verlag, (pp. 79–104).

National Health and Medical Research Council, Australian Research Council, & Australian Vice-Chancellors' Committee. (2007). *National Statement on Ethical Conduct in Human Research*. Australian Government.

Organisation for Economic Development and Co-operation (OECD). (1980). *OECD Guidelines on the Protection of Privacy and Transborder Flows of Personal Data*. OECD.

Patrick, A. S. (2006). Privacy practices for HCI research. *HOT Topics!*, *5*(2). http://www.carleton. ca/hotlab/hottopics/Articles/February2006-PrivacyPract.html

Penslar, R. L. (1993). *Protecting Human Research Subjects: Institutional Review Board Guidebook*. Washington DC: National Institutes of Health, U.S. Government Printing Office. www.hhs.gov/ohrp/irb/irb_guidebook.htm

Public Welfare, Protection of Human Subjects, Code of Federal Regulations, Title 45, Pt. 46 (45CFR§46), (2005), http://www.hhs.gov/ohrp/humansubjects/guidance/45cfr46.htm

Schrier, J. (1992). Reducing stress associated with participating in a usability study. In *Proceedings of Human Factors' Society 36th Annual Meeting*, Santa Monica, CA.

Sieber, J. E. (1992). *Planning Ethically Responsible Research: A Guide for Students and Internal Review Boards* (31). Thousand Oaks, CA: Sage.

Sieber, J. E. (2001a). Not your ordinary research. *Empirical Software Engineering*, *6*(4), 323–327.

Sieber, J. E. (2001b). Protecting research subjects, employees and researchers: implications for software engineering. *Empirical Software Engineering*, *6*(4), 329–341.

Singer, J., Sim, S. E., & Lethbridge, T. C. (2008). Software engineering data collection for field studies. In F. Shull et al. (Eds.) *Guide to Advanced Empirical Software Engineering*, Springer.

Singer, J. & Vinson, N. G. (2002). Ethical issues in empirical studies of software engineering. *IEEE Transactions on Software Engineering*, *28*(12), 1171–1180.

Singer, J. & Vinson, N. (2001). Why and how research ethics matters to you. Yes, you!. *Empirical Software Engineering*, *6*(4), 287–290.

Smith, S. & Richardson, D. (1983). Amelioration of deception and harm in psychological research: the important role of debriefing. *Journal of Personality and Social Psychology, 44*(5), 1075–1082.

University of Toronto Social Sciences and Humanities Research Ethics Board (SSH REB). (2005). *Guidelines for Ethical Conduct in Participant Observation*. http://www.research.utoronto.ca/ ethics/eh_policy.html

Vinson, N. & Singer, J. (2001). Getting to the source of ethical issues. *Empirical Software Engineering*, *6*(4), 293–297.

Vinson, N. G. & Singer, J. (2004). Consent issues raised by observational research in organisations. *NCEHR Communiqué, 12*(2), 35–36.

Worchel, S. & Cooper, J. (1979). *Understanding Social Psychology, Revised Edition*. Homewood, IL: The Dorsey Press.

Wright, D. R. (2006). Research ethics and computer science: an unconsummated marriage. In *Proceedings of SIGDOC '06*, Myrtle Beach, SC, USA.

Chapter 10
The Management of University–Industry Collaborations Involving Empirical Studies of Software Engineering

Timothy C. Lethbridge, Steve Lyon, and Peter Perry

Abstract In this chapter we will discuss some of the pragmatic considerations that we believe university researchers and companies should consider when establishing collaborative software engineering research projects; in particular, those involving empirical studies of software engineers. The chapter is illustrated using as a case study a research collaboration in which the authors are involved. We enumerate the costs, benefits, risks and risk-reducing factors that can have an impact on all the parties involved in the collaboration (the company, the faculty members and the graduate student researchers). Understanding this information is needed to help justify the research in the first place, and to manage it effectively. We then discuss many of the activities that will be needed to plan and manage the project, including such issues as attracting students, handling intellectual property, obtaining ethical approval and interacting with participants. The main objective of the chapter is to provoke some thoughts in the minds of those planning empirical research projects in software engineering.

1. Introduction

Most software engineering tools and techniques are aimed at reducing cost, speeding development and/or increasing software quality – all in the context of the pervasive complexity and rapid change one finds in industrial software projects. Researchers must conduct empirical studies in industrial settings in order to properly understand the complexities of commercial software products and processes, and to evaluate new ideas. This paper presents lessons we have learned through a university-industry research collaboration in which the authors participated. The objective of the paper is to help guide others who are considering embarking on similar endeavors.

Empirical studies in companies can take many forms; the discussion in this paper does not presuppose one form in particular. Studies will most often investigate software engineering processes, but may also assess the usefulness of various technologies

F. Shull et al. (eds.), *Guide to Advanced Empirical Software Engineering*.

that software engineers use or develop. Some empirical studies, e.g. learning how much of a typical project's duration or effort is devoted to a certain activity, could stand on their own: Their conclusions would be used for general decision-making. Other empirical studies might enable the researchers to form hypotheses about, or validate, their own research ideas. Examples of the latter include novel testing techniques or programming languages.

Empirical studies can use a variety of techniques ranging from questionnaire-based surveys, structured interviews and observation sessions to controlled experiments (Lethbridge et al., 2005; Sjøberg et al., 2005). Almost all these techniques involve people as research participants. Traditionally students have performed this role, but as emphasized above, it is often essential to use industrial employees in order to obtain accurate and relevant answers to many research questions.

Researchers in empirical studies can take on the role of the indifferent outsider, observing and measuring what goes on in the company. Or they can take on a more participatory role, seeking to improve the industrial environment by conducting *action research* (Potts, 2003; Baskerville and Wood-Harper, 1996; Checkland, 1991; Dittrich, 2002).

Conducting empirical studies in software companies is not easy. In this chapter we will focus on how to plan and manage such projects; we will look at how to justify such projects, find participants and staff, deal with the competing interests of the researchers and company managers, as well as various other issues. Additional challenges, discussed elsewhere in this book, arise from the need to conduct good science. The latter challenges include establishing adequate experimental controls, choosing appropriate metrics, and properly analyzing the resulting data.

Software engineering researchers are normally not trained in management. As more of them recognize the imperative to conduct empirical studies in industry, we expect increasing interest in learning from the experiences of others. In this chapter we present a set of issues that researchers need to consider, illustrated by the case study of a research project in which the authors collaborated.

The authors represent both industry and academia and have each conducted research with several different partners. The academic author has also worked in industry. The issues raised in this chapter are therefore derived from a variety of experiences.

There is some existing literature about industry-university collaboration. Conradi et al. (2003) discuss experiences in Norway in which several small and medium enterprises (SMEs) and several universities jointly worked on process improvement research. Some of the lessons-learned they present are similar to the ones we present here, although our experiences relate more to individual performance improvement rather than company process improvement. Beckman et al. (1997) and Mead et al. (1999) provide some suggestions about another type of industry-university collaboration – working together to design and deliver educational programs. Arisholm et al. (1999) provide a series of small case studies about industrial collaborations, each with their own lessons learned. Finally,

Rombach and Achatz (2007) summarize a variety of issues regarding research collaborations.

In the next section we give a brief overview of the research project that will serve as the case study. We then enumerate the benefits of university-industry research projects and the factors that can lower risks. Following this we discuss the costs and the risks themselves. We conclude by presenting a set of considerations that industrial and university researchers should consider as they plan their projects.

2. An Example Research Project:
The Mitel – University of Ottawa CSER Collaboration

We will illustrate this chapter with examples from our own experiences as University of Ottawa researchers and Mitel managers conducting collaborative research. These results are personal reflections gathered from brainstorming ourselves about what worked, and how we could have conducted our research better.

Mitel is a medium-sized telecommunications company, best known for its PBX hardware and software. As with all telecommunications software, the Mitel systems are very large.

In 1995 the Mitel managers (the second and third authors of this paper) approached University of Ottawa researchers with a general research problem: How to reduce the cost of maintenance of a large software system. As is normally the case when starting such projects, we had particular ideas we wished to test. We believed that one of the biggest difficulties faced by the engineers was an inability to visualize the system's design, due to its complexity and the sheer magnitude of its code and documentation. In earlier research, the first author had developed a knowledge base management system (KBMS) (Lethbridge, 1994) and believed that if we modeled the Mitel system using this KBMS we would be able to help Mitel engineers to understand their system better. Such a KBMS model was expected to be especially helpful in enabling new design staff members to learn the Mitel system, and become productive more quickly.

Since we wanted to apply good scientific method, we decided that an important part of the research would be to study software engineers and their product (Singer and Lethbridge, 1998). The objective of this was to better capture the nature of the problem that the KBMS was supposed to solve, and to develop hypotheses that we would later seek to confirm. Before long, we noticed several patterns in the work of the engineers. In particular, they were spending a large amount of effort searching code, and they were having significant difficulty manipulating and organizing the results of their searches. They were thus finding it hard to effectively use this information. As a result we changed our research direction considerably and focused on designing a tool to solve these immediate and pressing problems. Investigating the KBMS ideas dropped to a lower priority.

In 1996, Mitel joined the Consortium for Software Engineering Research (CSER, www.cser.ca,), and the research project grew to encompass studies of various features that might be appropriate in a software exploration environment. The tool that we developed, *TkSee* (Lethbridge and Anquetil, 1997), saw continuous voluntary use by Mitel engineers from the date it was introduced (1996) until several years after the project concluded in 2002. It also served as a test environment for several aspects of the research. In the rest of this chapter, we will refer to this work as the Mitel-CSER project.

Research on the Mitel-CSER project used many approaches: To gather data from software engineers we measured their use of tools, interviewed them, asked them to draw pictures describing their views of the architecture of some software, and shadowed them. We developed a new shadowing technique called *Synchronized Shadowing*, and a new approach to analyzing the large amount of data that results – representing *work patterns* using use-case maps (www.use casemaps.org). We have conducted usability studies (Herrera, 1999) to ensure our tool is usable. We believe that if the tool has poor usability, this would negatively impact user acceptance, hence we would not be able to tell if its core functionality was useful or not. We also developed techniques for analyzing Mitel software (Somé and Lethbridge, 1998) that are used to build the databases that TkSee uses.

The research involved the academics immersing themselves in the industrial environment – not to the extent of actually working on Mitel products, but rather through being on the premises and actively trying to solve problems faced by the developers. We therefore followed the research paradigm suggested by Potts (2003), in which one 'intertwines research and industry intervention'.

Both the academics and the company benefited from the research. Mitel was pleased with the impact of the tool, and the academics were able to produce many publications, (e.g. Anquetil and Lethbridge, 2003; Anquetil and Lethbridge, 1999; Sayyad Shirabad et al., 2003; Lethbridge and Singer, 2001; Liu and Lethbridge, 2002; Somé and Lethbridge, 1998).

However, there have also been several difficulties that turned the research into a good case study. Most notably, it has not been easy to motivate graduate students and others on the research team to embrace techniques that involve studying work practices and software usability. It has also not been easy to strike a balance between conducting well-designed and focused research on the one hand, and solving difficult-to-characterize industrial problems on the other hand. We sometimes spent excessive effort developing software of sufficient quality so that it can be actually used by the engineers – necessary so we can determine if our ideas are valid. We similarly had difficulty attracting a large enough population of users to scientifically validate our ideas, although several Mitel users have used TkSee extensively.

The Mitel-CSER research project is considered successful despite these difficulties. We hope our accumulated lessons-learned as presented in this chapter will be of value to others who embark on similar research.

3. The Benefits of University-Industry Software Engineering Empirical Studies

In this section and the next we will enumerate the positive and negative sides of empirical software engineering research projects involving companies and university research groups. Before starting any such project we believe it is important to attempt to quantify these factors. The information may be used to help 'sell' research projects to either the company or the researchers, to plan such projects and to manage risk.

In what follows we separately enumerate the benefits to the company, to faculty members and to students involved in the research. These are summarized in Table 1 While many of these benefits might be self-evident, the parties may not necessarily

Table 1 Benefits of industry–company research collaborations

Category of benefit	Benefit type	Typical amount of benefit (impact * probability of occurrence)
To the company		
Direct benefits	• New or improved technology or product	Medium
	• Data and knowledge useful for decision making	High
	• Patents	Low
Indirect benefits	• Potential employees for company	Medium
	• Ideas and expertise of researchers	High
	• Public relations	Medium
Factors lowering risk of research	• Graduate students are often top achievers	Medium
	• Researchers have a personal stake in success	Medium
	• Low cost compared to in-house research	High
	• Government matching funds and tax incentives	High
To researchers		
Direct benefits	• Funding	High
	• Interesting and challenging problems and data	High
	• Test-bed for ideas	High
Indirect benefits	• Exposure to the 'real world': Provides valid and relevant knowledge, consulting and networking.	High
To the public		
Indirect benefits	• Advancement of state-of-the art and state-of-the-practice	High

think of all of them. We believe that systematically analyzing these factors, quantitatively if possible, should be done more frequently when research projects are planned. Knowing the potential benefits we can, a) balance them with the costs to decide whether the project (or an aspect of it) is worth doing and attract adequate funding, and b) make sure we actively work to realize the benefits.

3.1. Potential Benefits to the Company

Benefits to the company fall into three categories: Direct benefits, indirect benefits and risk-reducing factors. The direct benefits are what immediately spring to mind, and result from success of the research. However the indirect benefits might be of considerable value too. The risk-lowering factors are considered as a separate category of 'positive' factors that make it worthwhile doing the research in conjunction with universities as opposed to in-house.

3.1.1. Direct benefits

The most obvious direct benefit to the company is new or improved technology (processes, techniques and tools) and products. Empirical software engineering research does not itself normally directly create such improvements, but provides data and knowledge useful for making management or design decisions.

For example, in the Mitel-CSER project our studies of software engineers gave us design ideas and led to changes in research focus. Similarly, our studies of usability told us what tool improvements were necessary. We used data from an empirical study to develop the TkSee tool, which in turn reduced the elapsed time some new employees took to learn about Mitel software. In fact the training time for designers new to the product was typically halved, and this provided the most readily quantifiable benefit of the project. It is important to note that this kind of benefit requires management of technology transfer, an issue discussed by Zelkowitz (1995) and Pfleeger (1999).

Technology transfer involves taking an idea from laboratory prototype to permanent use of a mature product within a company or industry as a whole. One of the issues often faced is establishing the appropriate intellectual property framework to do this – for us, this was not a challenge because we had a well-written collaborative research agreement from the start, which anticipated close interaction with the company and had clauses clearly describing IP rights. We did, however find three *practical* technology transfer issues challenging: Firstly we needed to make our research software usable enough so that it could be used in daily practice; in other words we had to approach 'product quality'. We were able to achieve this by following rigorous usability engineering techniques, such as usability studies. The second challenge was integrating TkSee with the corporate tools and data infrastructure. Our database needed regular builds, and our server needed to be maintained. We were able to train a Mitel staff person to do this, however, from time to time that person was unavailable, causing some down time. The third challenge was spreading the use of the tool from one focused team to the wider organization or industry as a whole. Although we attempted to do this, we never had any 'takers' beyond the original team. We were not able to make the extra investment of time and effort to broaden the technology transfer. We had quite a lot of requests from outside Mitel to obtain TkSee, but we found it hard to service these requests, since setting up the tool required a lot of time-consuming configuration.

Another possible direct benefit of empirical studies is intellectual property: Such studies might uncover data that could provide competitive advantage or a patentable invention.

3.1.2. Indirect benefits

In today's employment environment, where people with appropriate skills are often hard to find, an important indirect benefit of research collaborations is the exposure to the company of potential highly-skilled employees. Graduate students can learn a considerable amount about the company during their research and develop a desire to work there. It is important, however, for companies to actively recruit such students (as they approach the completion of their degree) in order to realize this benefit – in the Mitel-CSER project we learned this lesson only after the first few years.

A related indirect benefit to the company is exposure to academic researchers who can provide expertise and fresh ideas; this can be achieved through formal presentations or informal discussions. Faculty members will also absorb corporate know-how and the corporate needs for future stills; they will thus be in a better position to educate future employees.

A final indirect benefit is the public relations value resulting from the joint publication of research results.

3.1.3. Risk-lowering factors

Research can be conducted using in-house employees instead of university researchers. In many cases, however, the specialized expertise is not available, and both the uncertainty of the outcome, and the cost of the research are too high for the industrial agenda. There are several benefits from using university researchers: Graduate students tend to be talented individuals with the latest knowledge. They have a personal stake in the project's success and direct power over its success due to their need to complete a thesis – their main reward, graduation, does not come until success is achieved. Graduate students are also paid relatively little, seeing their work as an investment in themselves. Added to this is the benefit of the guidance of experienced faculty members.

Faculty members are also personally motivated to succeed in the research due to their need to publish papers, although this can be a double-edged sword as we will discuss later. Furthermore a faculty member's time may be at least partly 'free' to the company.

Finally, government matching funds that cover part of the cost to the universities and tax incentives for industrial research all reduce the risk to the company.

The lists of direct and indirect benefits are similar to the benefits of industrial collaboration reported by Conradi et al. (2003). Conradi et al. also discuss benefits to individual participants, but don't discuss the risk-lowering factors.

3.2. Potential Benefits to the Faculty Members, Graduate Students, and the Public

Significant benefits also accrue to faculty members and graduate students. Both categories of academic researchers directly benefit from significant amounts of funding for their work, interesting intellectual problems and data to work with, and a test-bed for their ideas. Indirect benefits include exposure to the 'real world'; the knowledge researchers acquire is likely to help the researchers improve other aspects of their research as well as their teaching. Opportunities for networking and consulting will also likely arise: Faculty members might find potential graduate students or other collaborators in the companies, while students might receive job offers.

Finally, as mentioned at the beginning of the chapter, there is one important public benefit to empirical studies in industry: They are necessary to properly understand the complexities of software engineering, and thus advance the state-of-the-practice, resulting in better and cheaper software-intensive products and services in most parts of our society.

4. The Drawbacks of University-Industry Software Engineering Empirical Studies

In this section, we present the drawbacks of university–company collaborations for empirical software engineering research. These factors should be balanced against the benefits discussed in the last section. Awareness of these factors can also suggest ways to manage and reduce them. Table 2 provides a summary.

We divide the sets of drawbacks into those that primarily affect the companies, those that affect the faculty members and graduate students, and those that affect the success of the project as a whole (impacting everybody who is interested in the results).

We also divide the drawbacks into costs and risks. Costs are factors that can be estimated directly, while risks are uncertainty factors for which one can estimate their probability of occurrence and their impact on costs and benefits if they occur.

Table 2 Drawbacks of industry–company research collaborations

Category of drawback	Drawback type	Typical amount of drawback (impact * probability of occurrence)
To the company		
Costs	• Cash funding	Varies from none to medium
	• Consumption of employee time	Varies, normally medium
	• Office space and equipment	Normally low
Risk factors	• Different definitions of success (bottom line for industry vs. scientific results and publication for researchers)	Medium if the company has defined the problem; otherwise low
	• Unknown consumption of employee time	Low to medium
	• Inappropriate release of intellectual property	Normally low for empirical studies
To researchers		
Costs	• Constrained research freedom	High if the company has defined the problem; otherwise low
	• Excess consumption of time	Moderate to high, depending on experience of researchers and research design
Risk factor	• Company-initiated cancellation	Varies from low to high depending on corporate priorities and rapport between researchers and the company
To the project as a whole		
Risk factors	• Different perceptions of the problem	High if the company has defined to the problem for researchers solve; otherwise low
	• Failure to staff the project with sufficient numbers of skilled researchers	Medium
	• Unknown skill level of researchers, including their ability to estimate the required effort	Varies from low to high depending on experience of researchers
	• Failure to find or keep adequate numbers of participants	Varies from low to high; depending on effort needed, management support, and other factors
	• Inconclusive or non-useful results	Low, but higher when the objective is to validate a hypothesis

Note that some projects are initiated by researchers while others are initiated by companies who have an active need to solve to a problem. Some risks are considerably higher in the latter case.

4.1. Potential Drawbacks to the Company

The costs to the company of participation in research projects with universities include direct cash funding of the research, consumption of employee and management time as well as office space, equipment and other supplies devoted to the research. For empirical studies, the time of research participants may be the greatest cost.

The following are risk factors that add uncertainty to the costs and benefits; these are listed starting with the most significant. Note that we enumerate risks to success of the project *as a whole* later in this section.

4.1.1. Different definitions of success

Unless a project is very small and the company is purely expecting indirect benefits (see Sect. 3), then the company will expect some concrete result that will ultimately impact their bottom line. Researchers, on the other hand usually have completely different motivations for participating, the main one being publishing results. This cultural conflict is explored in more detail by Zelkowitz et al. (1998).

This fundamental difference of interest can lead, in the worst case, to researchers not paying any attention to the needs of the company. Normally, with well-intentioned researchers, the impact is more subtle: The researchers might be stressed about their thesis deadlines, paper deadlines or other academic requirements and give priority to them. Or the researchers might deviate from a project plan that interests the company because they find interesting side-problems that will more readily result in publishable results.

This difference of interest is probably the biggest risk factor to companies, and thus must be carefully managed. In the Mitel-CSER project, this risk factor had a major impact – many graduate students wanted to direct their theses to topics that related to, but were not directly central to, the original project plan. The faculty member directing the project was also in the process of achieving tenure and so spent considerable time writing papers – sometimes leaving the project plan to languish at a lower priority for long periods.

4.1.2. Unknown consumption of employee time

In some empirical projects, such as those involving completing surveys, this is not a high risk. However for observational studies or those that involve open-ended investigation the risk is higher.

4.1.3. Difficulty controlling release of intellectual property

Companies tend to worry that publication of research results might cause them to lose competitive advantage. Some also have concerns about source code or design information getting into the hands of competitors. If these issues are discussed during project planning (see Sect. 5), these risks can be minimized.

4.2. Potential Drawbacks to Faculty Members and Graduate Students

There are two clear costs to the academic researchers of collaborating with industry.

The first cost occurs when there are constraints placed on the freedom of researchers to follow their interests. Software engineering is a very rich domain with many potential problems and much data to be gathered. This richness, however, means that some problems will be considerably more interesting and easy to publish about than others. When working on an industrially-sponsored project, the researcher has a responsibility to the company and cannot readily sidetrack to pursue ideas that might prove more publishable.

The second cost to the researchers is the substantial amount of human resources that empirical studies take. Planning and managing an industrial research project can take far more time than many types of work that can be done on campus and with groups of students as participants.

A risk factor with big potential consequences to the researchers is that the company will undergo some form of reorganization or reprioritization, and cancel the research in progress. The academic author has experienced this several times. In fact, subsequent to the time when this paper was initially written, the Mitel-CSER project itself was cancelled, just after an agreement had been reached to continue it. The reason was simply a high-level decision from the corporate executives to cut all possible costs, including all external research.

A contingency plan for such situations is to work with two or three different companies on the same research problem, however this can be excessively time consuming and may not be possible if the companies are competitors. In case of project cancellation, all may not be lost. The data gathered so far can be reported as preliminary results, and can serve as a point of departure for a new study, or it can be combined with data in a later study. A sliver lining from a cancellation is that the researchers then are freer to work with other companies, where they may gain fresh perspectives. Indeed, we were able to replicate some of our work in IBM, who we later worked with, lending increased confidence to our conclusions.

4.3. Risks to the Research as a Whole

The following risk factors are typical of empirical studies at present. They can impact the ability to obtain useful results, or even to complete the project, and therefore affect both parties (although they only affect the company if it is sponsoring the project because it has a problem to solve).

4.3.1 Different perceptions of the problem

Academics without much experience in industry may have very different notions about what software engineering involves and what are the real problems. On the other hand, industry managers tend to vary widely in the software engineering knowledge they possess. This can lead to difficulty communicating, and misunderstandings about the problem that is to be tackled. This issue is very much related to classic difficulties in requirements analysis where, due to inadequate communication and preconceived ideas, customers have one perception of the problem and software engineers another.

4.3.2 Failure to staff project with sufficient numbers of skilled researchers

Empirical research has not customarily been widely performed in the software engineering community, and for some people lacks a certain 'respect' or is considered to be 'soft'. The Mitel-CSER project has certainly suffered from this phenomenon; we have on occasion tried to convince graduate students to become interested in such studies and have found that they don't see it as 'real' engineering. Empirical studies of usability, as performed by human factors experts, are seen to be part of an entirely different culture. For these reasons, it is hard for the project leaders to attract researchers (graduate students, postdoctoral researchers and faculty) who have expertise and interest. Hopefully this book will make a difference.

In addition to having questionable interestingness or respect, empirical projects also often generate profuse volumes of data, which is very time-consuming to analyze. This acts as a deterrent to software engineering researchers who are used to solving engineering problems. In the Mitel-CSER project, we attempted to use administrative assistants to transcribe tapes in interviews, however this failed because the interviews used so much technical jargon that the transcribers could not adequately understand them.

4.3.3 Unknown skill level of researchers

Even if staff can be found, conducting empirical studies is a skill in which not many software engineering researchers have been trained – something this book hopes to alleviate. Therefore the students, and even faculty, may well be on a learning curve and may make mistakes. Of particular importance is the ability of the researchers to estimate how much time empirical studies will take; our own lack of experience meant that this we severely underestimated when we developed our project plan.

4.3.4 Failure to find or keep adequate numbers of participants

It is common for researchers to get a low response rate to surveys; we conducted one mail-out survey as part of our research and obtained only a 2% response rate.

Within companies, it may be possible to interest participants in observational or interview-oriented studies, but it may be very hard to get enough people to use a specific piece of software as part of their work, or to follow a certain methodology. In addition, participants may leave the team or company, or withdraw from the study for personal reasons. In the Mitel-CSER project, we have suffered from all of these difficulties to a considerable extent, although we have been lucky to have a large enough pool from which to draw new participants.

4.3.5 Inconclusive or non-useful results

No research is guaranteed success, otherwise it wouldn't be research. However in software engineering there tends to be a perception that any engineering problem can be solved given enough work. Questions subjected to empirical studies, however, are often not answered by ingenuity, but rather by analysis of data. There might not be enough data for statistical significance, or there might be too many extraneous variables or methodological errors detected that the results are not meaningful. See Trochim (2007) for excellent coverage of threats to validity. Another point to consider is that an otherwise successful study needs to be well-cited, and 'find its place' in the scientific literature if it is to be truly useful. A study will be more likely to have impact if it uses similar measurement scales and methods as other studies of a similar type. Williams et al. (2005) discuss this in more details.

For companies, an answer to a research question might not require 95% confidence. They may be able to base a decision on a 70% probability of something occurring. Also a company may be satisfied with empirical studies that are simply seeking to gather observations and trends. Success criteria therefore need to be separately defined for both parties in a research collaboration.

In the Mitel-CSER project, neither of our two main empirical studies involved controlled experiments. In one (Herrera, 1999) we explored techniques for conducting usability studies, and in the other (Singer and Lethbridge, 1998) we gathered data in order to generate work patterns. Both studies had largely qualitative outcomes, generating tools or tools improvements, and lessons that could be used in subsequent research. A key sign of success for the company was that the tools we developed were useful to them. The key indicator of success for the researchers was that we were able to publish a significant number of papers.

5. Planning Empirical Studies Projects

In this section we discuss the set of issues that need to be discussed and made part of the project plan as a company-industry empirical research project is established. These include: Justifying the project in the first place, issues that must be agreed between the parties, obtaining ethics approval, staffing the project, working with participants, and analyzing the data.

Table 3 Checklist of activities that should be part of the planning and management process of industry–university collaborations involving empirical studies

Activity	Involves or decided by
• Decision: To use university researchers or in-house employees (refer to Tables 1 and 2 for decision-making information)	Company
• Attracting companies	Researchers
• Decision: Level and type of commitment (finances, resources, timetable, deliverables)	Negotiated
• Decision: How on-going management and risk management will be handled?	Negotiated
• Decision: What is the research focus, what are the goals and what are the research questions?	Negotiated, but may be largely determined by either party
• Decision: What participants will be available and when?	Negotiated
• Decision: What information must be confidential?	Negotiated
• Decision: How will publication of results be handled?	Negotiated
• Decision: Who owns intellectual property?	Negotiated
• Obtain ethics approval	Researchers
• Find researcher team members and train them	Researchers
• Plan the details of work with participants	Researchers
• Plan for data analysis	Researchers
• Evaluate the risks and manage changes	Both parties

A checklist of the activities that should be performed during project planning is presented in Table 3.

5.1. If the Company is Considering Initiating Research: Should it Use University Researchers or Corporate Employees?

As discussed in Sects. 3 and 4, there are many benefits that companies can obtain by involving university researchers, but there are also various risks. If the company is initiating the research, it must first decide whether to instead use its own employees for the research. A university research team will normally involve one or more faculty members and at least the same number of graduate students; since the faculty members' time is split divided among several tasks (teaching, administration and other research), the bulk of the research is often performed by graduate students, under the direction of the faculty members.

The main benefits to using university researchers are that they are a valuable pool of talent, and cost less than in-house employees. University researchers often also have very specific knowledge and research skills that cannot be found inside the companies. The cost of this talent might be so low compared to the potential benefits that very little further analysis is needed. In many countries, graduate students are paid significantly less than company employees. Faculty members might be paid consulting fees for some of the research, but they tend to spend much additional time on the research that is just part of their normal university duties, paid by the university.

On the other hand if the research is of the type where the company absolutely must have a rapid answer to a question, then there is a high risk in involving graduate students who are prone to take their time completing courses and might want to focus their thesis on another topic. Furthermore, an advantage of using corporate employees is that they tend to have a greater knowledge of the company's products, needs and environment.

In summary, there is no single answer to whether it is better to perform research in-house or involve university researchers: the decision depends on the type of research to be done. In-house employees can work full time and may focus better on the problem, but are normally much more expensive and may lack specific expertise in the area of the research.

5.2. If the University is Considering Initiating: How does it Make Contacts with Companies?

The biggest practical problem in studying work practices is obtaining a good sample of participants. If a university researcher is initiating the project, it might be possible in some cases to conduct a study using participants who are solicited individually (for example they might be asked to fill out a questionnaire on the web on their own time). However, it is usually necessary to work with teams within a company. Hence, participation needs to be obtained from the management of one or more companies.

Finding suitable organizations is the first hurdle. While many researchers or their institutions may have a few companies that are their perennial 'contacts' in industry, empirical researchers should give thought to involving companies of several different types to avoid introducing bias. The companies most likely to be willing to participate are those already involved in research – particularly medium to large companies whose primary business is software or computer products. Much harder to penetrate are companies in other industries that develop specialized software or in-house software, for example, banking and health care. In the past, we have experienced considerable frustration finding suitable managers to contact. Our only advice is that unbiased research often requires considerable effort of this type. We were lucky with the Mitel-University of Ottawa collaboration since both parties sought out each other.

When the university researchers are the ones seeking the contacts, two levels of management must be convinced to participate: Higher management must agree to the involvement of the company as a whole, while first-level managers must agree to the involvement of their teams. In both cases, obtaining and maintaining commitment can be hard. Management will naturally be concerned about the costs of the research, particularly in terms of time. Researchers have to effectively, but realistically, show that there are benefits to the company, which can balance the costs. The costs and benefits presented in Sects. 3 and 4 can be used to make a case.

It is easier to make a case to a company when establishing a long-term relationship. We have found companies are more open to empirical studies when other members of the research team are tackling the company's engineering problems (perhaps using data from the empirical studies).

5.3. Key Success Factors: Mutual Understanding in a Co-operative Relationship

Empirical studies of software engineering involve people studying people. The fundamental requirement for a successful research project relationship is that the two parties, the company based software engineers, and the academic research-ers get to know and trust each other. A strong positive social relationship of mutual respect and trust must be established and maintained between the company based manager and the principal researcher. As usual in social matters it really helps if people like each other. This relationship takes time to establish and it may take many meetings spread out over several weeks to develop mutual understanding of the research problem and opportunities for solutions. As Conradi et al. (2003) say, it is important that the researchers have a, 'humble attitude ... towards the situation of the practitioners'.

This dialogue must culminate in a research plan that is mutually acceptable to both parties. Since longer-range research work will always play second fiddle to the immediate product development needs of the company, it is vital that the company manager be personally fully committed to supporting and carrying through the project. He or she must see the value and want to carry it forward in order to accept the hindrance to his day-to-day work. At the same time, expectations must be carefully managed. Overly enthusiastic research promises or commitments of company time can lead to fractured relations and harm the project. The project should have a time frame that anticipates research results corresponding to the normal steps in progress of a thesis.

It is also vital that each party understands and respects the agenda and impera-tives of the other. This understanding should develop as the dialogue between the two project leaders goes on.

5.4. Issues that Must Be Agreed Between the Company and the Researchers

Once a company has established its willingness to participate, it is important to reach agreement on a number of issues. The formality of the agreements will vary with the size and duration of the research. A very large project requires more detailed negotiations than a small one, particularly if financial support is involved. A company will be interested in the project, but be more willing to participate if its managers were given a presentation about empirical software engineering and the proposed methods. In such cases, the researcher should treat educating the organization as part of the negotiation process, so they can proceed as partners in the endeavor.

The following are areas where we believe agreements should be established to help ensure the project's success. In the Mitel-CSER project, some of these items were included in a written agreement, but most were just tacit agreements that evolved over time. If we were starting again, we would probably prefer to write down more details, although there is always the danger that developing a more detailed formal agreement (which might have to be approved by lawyers) would cause inflexibility and possibly lengthy delays, thus potentially causing more harm than good.

5.4.1 Level and type of commitment to the project

The first point of mutual agreement should be the level and type of commitment of both parties to the project. Questions to answer are: What is the project's expected duration? How much support (e.g. space, time, equipment) is expected from the company? What kind of results or specific deliverables, if any, are expected from the researchers? Agreement on these issues often forms the basis for agreement on other issues below.

For our project, Mitel has provided financing since its inception, with NSERC (a Canadian Government funding agency) subsequently matching both cash and in-kind contributions. Mitel also provides office space and equipment, although the distance to the company and lack of direct-enough public transportation has meant that graduate students have usually preferred to work on campus. The faculty member has on average spent one morning a week at the company, although at the peak of the research he tended to spent several consecutive days there. Over 80% of the faculty member's research time has been spent analyzing data and writing up the results, an activity not performed at the company site. We have found it important to communicate with the company frequently during these latter activities to ensure that long absences are not interpreted as delays in the research.

In the first year of the project, we established a very ambitious timetable for the research, which later proved to be unrealistic. Project plans developed in subsequent years were somewhat more accurate, but we still had an unrealistic schedule. This was because we did not sufficiently allow for the fact that it might be hard to find appropriate graduate students, that they are delayed by courses, comprehensive exams, and other activities, and that they receive and often accept tempting job offers and therefore drop to part-time status. The main problem with finding graduate students is that most entering graduate students want to create new software, not perform empirical studies. The delays from courses and exams arise because the graduate students feel they have to give 100% of their time to these activities to maximize their marks. We overcame these problems to some extent by hiring people as research associates – such people have a stronger contractual obligation than graduate students who are merely 'supported' in their studies. Unfortunately market conditions make hiring skilled research associates difficult.

The only real deliverables that Mitel expects are features periodically added to the tool, and regular reports about progress. However our plans were always rather ambiguous regarding the level of quality expected, and we rarely met our target dates (the whole software industry, of course, tends to have this problem). One problem we faced was students and research associates implementing just enough software to test their ideas, but not making the quality of the software high enough so that Mitel could use it on a regular basis after their studies were complete. As discussed earlier, the core TkSee tool was made highly usable, but add-on features created for specific student studies were often never used seriously by Mitel employees.

5.4.2 The decision-making and management process

Since empirical research projects, especially long-duration ones, rarely proceed as initially planned, there need to be agreements about how changes to plans will be made. We believe that an active-risk management approach is needed: At the initial stages, the risks (see Sect. 4) need to be identified and their magnitude estimated. When researchers and company managers meet on a semi-regular basis, both progress and the risk profile should be informally reviewed and changes to the plans agreed.

Risk management was something with which the university researchers had little experience at the start of the Mitel-CSER project. As the project progressed and deviated from the original plans (albeit in parallel with significant success), we did not do a good job of ensuring that both parties clearly understood the reasons for the deviations. University researchers may well be able to learn from the managerial expertise of the company in this regard, just as the company can learn from the technological expertise of the researchers.

At one point we went too far in the opposite direction by regularly updating a detailed project plan. That turned out to be far too time-consuming with not enough benefit. We now believe the kind of regular management needed should involve update and discussion of a very brief progress chart, and a short list of successes, problems and risks.

5.4.3 Access to participants

Both sides need to agree on how many employees will participate in the study and how much time is required from each employee. Sometimes an organization will find it difficult to provide the personnel required by the ideal research design and some compromise may be necessary.

In our project, Mitel agreed to a certain number of employee-hours per year to be devoted to our project, but we did not accurately monitor this, and likely used somewhat less time than budgeted. A key point for Mitel was that before the researchers initiated meetings with employees, they would check with management to see who was busy with 'critical' or 'deadline' work, and avoid these employees until they had more time.

5.4.4 Confidentiality of data

Some data needs to be kept confidential for corporate reasons; for example a company may not allow highly sensitive information such as source code or defect logs to be taken off-site. Data about individuals needs to be kept confidential for ethical reasons – we will discuss this further below. Data that are not confidential for either of the above reasons can serve as the basis for discussions of the next point, publication of results.

We had to negotiate with Mitel regarding the confidentiality of certain data that revealed aspects of their software's design that needed to be kept a trade secret. We were not able to take Mitel's source code out of company premises: This proved useful in some ways because it encouraged grad students to spend time at the company. However it was also quite inconvenient at times.

5.4.5 Publication of results

It is difficult to predict which results will be sufficiently interesting to publish, particularly before data collection has begun. Understandably, companies are reluctant to give blanket approval to disclosure of information. One solution is to set some ground rules at the beginning, and deal with publications on a case-by-case basis. Although this approach adds a step to the process of writing a paper, it has the benefit of providing researcher with an opportunity to verify their observations and conclusions.

On our case, our papers are reviewed for publication by the company at the same time that peer review occurs. Officially, Mitel could have asked to approve them before initial submission, however we established a good working relationship so that we did not need to be so rigid: Mitel told us the kinds of things they didn't want made public and we wrote in a style that accounted for Mitel's desires. At the same time Mitel recognized that academics often have very short lead-times to submit papers. They never rejected any papers, although they requested a few changes.

Another decision to be made is whether or not to identify the organization in the publication. A company may want its contributions acknowledged, or it may not want to be associated with 'negative' findings. Also, it may not be possible to publish the identity of the company without compromising the anonymity of the participants. This question can be dealt with in using the same approach described above for results. Realizing that anyone could find out from various sources that funded our research, we realized it would have been pointless to not mention Mitel's name. In some paper, the company employees also took a personal stake by becoming authors.

5.4.6 Other intellectual property issues

In addition to publication of results and protecting trade secrets, the two parties need to agree on what will happen if a patentable invention should arise from the research. Achieving agreement in this area can be very time consuming. The degree of sensitivity on the part of the company will depend on whether research results could provide functionality central to their products. In the case of the Mitel project, the benefits accrue to design efficiency. For these to be most valuable they need to be incorporated in commercially available tools and so Mitel has little concern about patents in this case. On the other hand another member of CSER is a software tools company and it has a much greater interest.

The formal CSER agreement acknowledges inventions as belonging to the inventors. Members have a free license to use any tools and techniques that arise from the research within their individual businesses. If they wish to sell products incorporating any CSER inventions then they must separately negotiate a license with the inventor.

A final comment regarding the co-operation of companies: One should keep in mind the possibility of a long-term relationship with the company. After going through the effort of establishing a relationship it will likely be useful to extend it either by performing a series of different studies, each building on the previous, or by performing longitudinal studies where software engineers are followed over many years.

5.5. *Obtaining Approval of the Research Ethics Board*

It is now considered essential in most countries that any research project involving human subjects should be scrutinized by a Research Ethics Board (REB) before the project gets underway. This is something that social scientists and medical researchers now take for granted, but which is not widely known in engineering. Even projects involving simple questionnaires need to be evaluated.

Research ethics are the subject of Chap. 12 of this book. There are many issues which are particularly important to industrial empirical studies, such as ensuring that management doesn't influence the freedom of participants to not participate or to withdraw, and doesn't see the raw data. Rather than presenting details about the ethical issues themselves here, we will briefly list some points relevant to the management of the ethics approval process.

The most important management issues for the empirical software engineering researcher to do are:

- Become familiar with the REB process at their institution.
- Plan the project with sufficient care that no ethical guidelines are violated. This means writing a proposal document in considerable detail so as to be convincing to the REB – something that might be more time-consuming than anticipated. The most important parts of such a document are the research protocol itself and the informed consent form that must be signed by all participants.

- Plan the project with sufficient time to allow the REB to make its decision, with allowances for possible required changes and resubmission. REBs very often nit-pick about details of proposals.
- Do not start any studies involving people until approval is received.

Long-term projects where the research is opportunistic in the sense that individual studies are planned on an on-going basis, may have to repeat this approval process.

In the early days of the Mitel-CSER project we conducted the work without REB approval out of ignorance, and because there was no formal mechanism for such approval within engineering. That was later rectified; at the same time Canadian research ethics guidelines have been strengthened and harmonized.

5.6. Staffing the Project and Training Researchers

Company-industry empirical research projects will normally involve graduate students and perhaps postdoctoral fellows. As mentioned in Sect. 4, an important difficulty such projects will face is attracting interested researchers.

One technique that may work is involving researchers from the social sciences as collaborators. Many anthropologists and psychologists have developed an interest in, and expertise in, software engineering processes. Such people would not be able to solve engineering problems, and may have a weaker understanding of what they are observing than engineers, but they should know more than the average engineer about human behaviour, work practices, study methodologies and ethics. The work of course is not lessened, but graduate students in these disciplines might be more motivated to perform the detailed data analysis gathered from human subjects involved in empirical studies.

In the Mitel-CSER project we have been fortunate to work with Janice Singer, a scientist at the National Research Council who has a Ph.D. in psychology and has also worked in software development. Our research group has also involved graduate students in psychology from time to time.

It is essential for the entire research team to practice and refine the research methodology before taking it on the road, otherwise many mistakes will be made and data will be lost. Researchers unfamiliar with the techniques discussed in this book will be surprised about how many difficulties can arise. For example the wording of questions must be thoroughly tested to remove ambiguities. Also the process of setting up cameras, recording, transcribing, and coding should be well rehearsed.

In addition to understanding empirical study techniques, researchers should normally spend considerable time in learning about their company. An understanding of corporate culture needs to be established so researchers can effectively interact with the participants and correctly interpret data. The researchers need a basic understanding of key aspects of the participant's work, such as the problem domain, the business context for the application, and the tools and process they are using. Some of this knowledge can be gained during the study itself, but we have found it more effective to have a learning phase in advance of the study.

5.7. Working with Corporate Employees and Managers

After establishing a research relationship with the company, obtaining ethics approval and training the research staff, the next step is to establish relationships with individual participants. Whether potential participants are willing to participate depends on several factors:

- The type of research: Being watched is of more concern to most people than, for example filling out a survey. Also, long-term or time-consuming research might attract fewer participants.

5.7.1 Whether the participants perceive management to be supportive

We have found it essential that management be enthusiastic about the research and make this clear to their employees. Enthusiasm assures employees that they are not at risk of being penalized for not getting their 'regular' job done while taking time out to participate in the research. Since our research continued for a long period of time, and many employees came and went during this period, management periodically arranged meetings with the employees at which the researchers presented a status report and sought input. However, for ethical reasons, managers should make it clear that participation is completely optional and they are not ordering people to participate.

A technique that we find useful is to use two consent forms. One is signed by the manager, consenting to the participation of his or her staff and assuring them that there will not be any management interference or impact whether or not they participate. A copy of this is given to the participants along with their own consent form.

Whether the participant perceives some benefit to participation: Some participants will enjoy taking time away from their daily work; others may be interested in the research for its own sake or because they feel they may gain something from the results. In our research we always tried to make it clear to employees that we were trying to develop tools that would be helpful to them. It was a concern when our work took longer than expected that some participants might feel let down.

The personality and beliefs of the participants: We have found some employees are more willing to participate than others. In fact, we have had situations where participants actively dissuade us by saying that the work they are doing would not be interesting enough for us to study. Leaving out such people might bias the research, so we tried to encourage the employees to participate while continuing to assure them it was optional.

Empirical research in companies can be mentally intense for researcher and participant. In order to get the most out of the work, the pace should not be rushed. Plenty of flexibility should be built into the day's schedule and no more than two sessions should be held in any day.

It is also important to understand that software engineers follow a development cycle. This means that they are doing different activities at different times. Finding what software engineers do during design and coding does not necessarily reflect what they do during bug-fixing or requirements gathering. Therefore, data collection has to focus on one aspect of the development cycle, or must extend over several time points to get an overall view of software engineering work.

Another consideration is software engineers' time constraints. Researchers need to find, to the greatest extent possible, data collection methods that do not affect the software engineers' productivity. Unfortunately, it is not always possible to gather key information unobtrusively. When a time commitment is required from software engineers, researchers need to make sure that they get the largest possible return for that time.

5.8. Maintaining the Relationship

Maintaining an industrial research relationship takes continued work. Some of the tactics we suggest are the following:

- Ensure all researchers (both faculty and students) have a regular presence in the company premises, whether or not they are actively conducting studies. The mere fact of being there, working on papers, theses, etc. shows a commitment. Participating in company meetings social events can also help to solidify the relationship.
- Report regularly on research progress, perhaps once every month. Even if not much has happened (as is often the case when academics are in the midst of teaching courses, and working on other matters), at least find something to say.
- Offer to give presentations on various topics. These could include updating employees on the status of the research, or giving a lecture on some topic that might simply be interesting to the company. The company will therefore reap value-added in terms of expertise that they can use to further justify continuing the relationship.

5.9. Planning for Data Analysis

Data analysis is probably the most time-consuming phase of most empirical studies. We will not discuss techniques here, since that is the topic of other chapters. However, we wish to point out that it should, where possible, be carefully planned at the project's start.

6. Concluding Remarks

In this chapter we have discussed many of the issues we have faced when managing university-industry empirical studies of software engineering. Our goal in presenting this information is to present the lessons we have learned, and hence to provide guidance for others undertaking similar studies for the first time. The issues discussed, such as the benefits and drawbacks to be considered, establishing contact with organizations and participants, staffing, and obtaining ethical approval, can be made to work more smoothly through effective planning. We also strongly believe in on-going evaluation and change management of the project as it progresses, particularly considering the risk factors we identified.

Acknowledgements This work was supported by the Consortium for Software Engineering Research (CSER) and the Natural Sciences and Engineering Research Council of Canada (NSERC). We would like to thank Janice Singer of the National Research Council who participated in many of the discussions as we planned our research, and thus contributed many of the ideas in this chapter. We would also like to thank anonymous reviewers for their valuable suggestions.

References

Anquetil, N. and Lethbridge, T.C. (2003), A Comparative Study of Clustering Algorithms and Abstract Representations for Software Remodularization, *IEE Proceedings – Software*, pp. 185–201. Winner of the Mather Premium award.

Anquetil, N. and Lethbridge, T.C. (1999), Recovering Software Architecture from the Names of Source Files, *Journal of Software Maintenance: Research and Practice*, 11, pp. 201–221.

Arisholm, E., Anda, B., Jørgensen, M., and Sjøberg, D.I.K. (1999), Guidelines on Conducting Software Process Improvement Studies in Industry, *22nd IRIS Conference (Information Systems Research Seminar in Scandinavia)*, Timo K. Kakola (ed.), Computer Science and information Systems Reports, Technical Reports TR-21, University of Jyvaskyla, Keuruu, Finland, pp. 87–102, 7–10.

Baskerville R.L. and Wood-Harper, A.T. (1996), A Critical Perspective on Action Research as a Method for Information Systems Research, *Journal of Information Technology*, (11), pp. 235–246.

Beckman, K., Khajenoori, S., Coulter, N., and Mead, N. (1997), Collaborations: Closing the Industry-Academia Gap, *IEEE Software*, 14(6), pp. 49–57.

Checkland, P. (1991) From framework through experience to learning: the essential nature of action research, in *Information Systems Research: Contemporary Approaches and Emergent Traditions*, H.-E. Nissen, H.K. Klein, and R.A. Hirschheim (eds.), North-Holland, Amsterdam, pp. 397–403.

Conradi, R., Dybå, T., Sjøberg, D.I.K., and Ulsund, T. (2003), Lessons Learned and Recommendations from Two Large Norwegian SPI Programmes, *9th European Workshop on Software Process Technology (EWSPT 2003)*, Helsinki, Finland 1–2 September, Lecture Notes in Computer Science 2786, Springer-Verlag, pp. 32–45.

Dittrich, Y. (2002), Doing Empirical Research on Software Development: Finding a Path Between Understanding, Intervention, and Method Development, *Social Thinking: Software Practice*, MIT Press, Cambridge MA, pp. 243–262.

Herrera, F. (1999), *A Usability Study of the TkSee Software Exploration Tool*, M.Sc. Thesis in Computer Science, University of Ottawa, http://www.site.uottawa.ca/~tcl/gradtheses/

Lethbridge, T.C., Sim, S., and Singer, J. (2005), Studying Software Engineers: Data Collection Methods for Software Field Studies, *Empirical Software Engineering*, 10(3), pp. 311–341.

Lethbridge, T.C. and Singer, J. (2001), Experiences Conducting Studies of the Work Practices of Software Engineers, in *Advances in Software Engineering: Comprehension, Evaluation and Evolution*, H. Erdogmus and O. Tanir (eds.), Springer-Verlag, ISBN 0–387–95109–1, pp. 53–76.

Lethbridge, T.C. (1994), *Practical Techniques for Organizing and Measuring Knowledge*, Ph.D. Thesis, University of Ottawa, http://www.site.uottawa.ca/~tcl/thesis_html/thesis_ToC.html

Lethbridge, T.C. and Anquetil, N. (1997), *Architecture of a Source Code Exploration Tool: A Software Engineering Case Study*, University of Ottawa, Computer Science Technical Report TR-97-07.

Liu, H. and Lethbridge, T.C. (2002), Intelligent Search Methods for Software Maintenance, *Information Systems Frontiers*, 4(4), pp. 409–423.

Mead, N., Beckman, K., Lawrence, J., O'Mary, G., Parish, C., Perla, U., and Walker, H. (1999), Industry/University Collaborations: Different Perspectives Heighten Mutual Opportunities, *Journal of Systems and Software*, 49, pp. 155–162.

Pfleeger, S.L. (1999), Understanding and Improving Technology Transfer in Software Engineering, *Journal of Systems and Software*, 47, pp. 111–124.

Potts, C. (2003), Software-Engineering Research Revisited, *IEEE Software*, 10(56), pp.19–28.

Rombach, D. and Achatz, R. (2007), Research Collaborations between Academia and Industry, *Future of Software Engineering 2007*, L. Briand and A. Wolf (eds.), ICSE 2007, IEEE-CS Press, 2007, pp. 29–36.

Sayyad Shirabad, J., Lethbridge, T.C., and Matwin, S. (2003), Mining the Maintenance History of a Legacy Software System, *International Conference on Software Maintenance (ICSM)*, Amsterdam, IEEE Computer Society, pp. 95–104.

Sjøberg, D.I.K., Hannay, J.E., Hansen, O., Kampenes, V.B., Karahasanovi , A., Liborg, N.-K., and Rekdal, A.C. (2005) A Survey of Controlled Experiments in Software Engineering, *IEEE Transactions on Software Engineering*, 31(9), pp. 733–753.

Singer, J. and Lethbridge T. (1998), Studying Work Practices to Assist Tool Design in Software Engineering, *6th IEEE International Workshop on Program Comprehension*. A longer version appears as: University of Ottawa, Computer Science Technical Report TR-97-08, Italy, pp. 173–179.

Somé, S.S. and Lethbridge T. (1998), Parsing Minimizing when Extracting information from Code in the Presence of Conditional Compilation, *6th IEEE International Workshop on Program Comprehension*. A longer version appears as University of Ottawa Computer Science Technical Report TR-98-01, Italy, June, pp. 118–125.

Trochim, W.M.K. (2007), *Research Methods Knowledge Base: Introduction to Validity*, http://www.socialresearchmethods. net/kb/introval.php, visited April 13, 2007

Williams, L., Layman, L., and Abrahamsson, P. (2005), Establishing the Essential Components of a Technology-Dependent Framework: A Strawman Framework for Industrial Case Study-Based Research, *Workshop on Evidence-Based Software Engineering at the International Conference on Software Engineering (ICSE)* 2005, St. Louis.

Zelkowitz, M. (1995), *Assessing Software Engineering Technology Transfer within NASA, NASA/GSFC Technical Report, NASA-RPT-003–95, NASA/GSFC, January*. http://www.cs.umd.edu/users/mvz/pub/assessment.ps

Zelkowitz, M., Wallace, D., and Binkley, D. (1998), *Culture Conflicts in Software Engineering Technology Transfer*, University of Maryland Technical Report. http://www.cs.umd.edu/users/mvz/pub/expsurvey.pdf.

Section III
Knowledge Creation

Chapter 11
Selecting Empirical Methods
for Software Engineering Research

Steve Easterbrook, Janice Singer, Margaret-Anne Storey,
and Daniela Damian

Abstract Selecting a research method for empirical software engineering research
is problematic because the benefits and challenges to using each method are not yet
well catalogued. Therefore, this chapter describes a number of empirical methods
available. It examines the goals of each and analyzes the types of questions each
best addresses. Theoretical stances behind the methods, practical considerations
in the application of the methods and data collection are also briefly reviewed.
Taken together, this information provides a suitable basis for both understanding and selecting from the variety of methods applicable to empirical software
engineering.

1. Introduction

Despite widespread interest in empirical software engineering, there is little guidance on which research methods are suitable to which research problems, and how
to choose amongst them. Many researchers select inappropriate methods because
they do not understand the goals underlying a method or possess little knowledge
about alternatives. As a first step in helping researchers select an appropriate
method, this chapter discusses key questions to consider in selecting a method,
from philosophical considerations about the nature of knowledge to practical considerations in the application of the method. We characterize key empirical methods
applicable to empirical software engineering, and explain the strengths and weaknesses
of each.

Software engineering is a multi-disciplinary field, crossing many social and
technological boundaries. To understand how software engineers construct and
maintain complex, evolving software systems, we need to investigate not just the
tools and processes they use, but also the social and cognitive processes surrounding them. This requires the study of human activities. We need to understand how
individual software engineers develop software, as well as how teams and organizations
coordinate their efforts.

F. Shull et al. (eds.), *Guide to Advanced Empirical Software Engineering*.
© Springer 2008

Because of the importance of human activities in software development, many of the research methods that are appropriate to software engineering are drawn from disciplines that study human behaviour, both at the individual level (e.g. psychology) and at the team and organizational levels (e.g. sociology).These methods all have known flaws, and each can only provide limited, qualified evidence about the phenomena being studied. However, each method is flawed differently (McGrath, 1995) and viable research strategies use multiple methods, chosen in such a way that the weaknesses of each method are addressed by use of complementary methods (Creswell, 2002).

Describing in detail the wide variety of possible empirical methods and how to apply them is beyond the scope of the chapter. Instead, we identify and compare five classes of research method that we believe are most relevant to software engineering:

- *Controlled Experiments* (including *Quasi-Experiments*)
- *Case Studies* (both *exploratory* and *confirmatory*)
- *Survey Research*
- *Ethnographies*
- *Action Research*

We describe the tradeoffs involved in choosing between these methods, but do not provide a recipe for building research strategies, as we doubt that such recipes exist. The selection of methods for a given research project depends on many local contingencies, including available resources, access to subjects, opportunity to control the variables of interest, and, of course, the skills of the researcher.

To illustrate the steps involved in deciding which method or methods to use, we present two guiding examples. Two fictional software engineering researchers, Joe and Jane, will explore how the various research methods can be applied to their work:

- Jane is a new PhD student interested in the effectiveness of a novel fisheye-view file navigator. Her research is motivated by the fact that navigation is a primary activity of software developers requiring a lot of scrolling and many clicks to find files. "Fisheye-views" use a distortion technique that, if applied correctly, display information in a compact format that could potentially reduce the amount of scrolling required. Jane's intuition is that the fisheye-view file navigator is more efficient for file navigation, but critics argue that the more compact information is difficult to read and that developers will not adopt it over the traditional file navigator. Her research goal, therefore, is to find evidence that supports or refutes her intuition that fisheye-view file navigators are more efficient than traditional file navigators for navigation.
- Joe is a researcher in an industrial lab. His current interests are in understanding how developers in industry use (or not) UML diagrams during software design. This is because, as a student, his professors recommended UML diagrams be used during software design, but his recent exposure to industrial practices indicates that UML is rarely used. His research goal is to explore how widely UML

diagrams are used in industry, and more specifically how these diagrams are used as collaborative shared artefacts during design.

Throughout the remainder of the chapter, we explore how Jane and Joe develop research strategies for their projects. We begin with an analysis of the type of research question(s) they are asking, and the issue of what constitutes valid answers to them. To address the latter question, we tour the main philosophical stances that underpin empirical research. We then describe the five classes of research method, and introduce criteria for distinguishing between them. Along the way, we explore how Jane and Joe might use each method as part of their research strategies. We end the chapter with a look at the practical considerations that affect their choices.

2. What kind of Research Question are You Asking?

One of the first steps in choosing an appropriate research method is to clarify the research question. While Jane and Joe have identified the problems they wish to work on, neither has pinned down a precise question. In each case, they could focus on a number of different research questions, each of which leads to a different direction in developing research strategies. The classification of research questions we use in this section is adapted from Meltzoff (1998).

Often, the most obvious question is not the best choice for a starting point. Jane's first attempt to formulate her research question is *"Is a fisheye-view file navigator more efficient than the traditional view for file navigation?"*, while Joe asks *"how widely are UML diagrams used as collaborative shared artifacts during design?"*. Both questions are vague, because they make assumptions about the phenomena to be studied, and kinds of situation in which these phenomena occur. For example, Jane's question only makes sense if we already know that some people (who?) need to do file navigation (whatever that is?), under some circumstances (which are?), and that efficiency (measured how?) is a relevant goal for these people (how would we know that?). Joe's question presupposes that we know what a "collaborative shared artifact" is, and can reliably identify one, and even reliably say which things are UML diagrams. Defining the precise meaning of terms is a crucial part of empirical research, and is closely tied with the idea of developing (or selecting) an appropriate *theory*.

In the early stages of a research program, we usually need to ask *exploratory* questions, as we attempt to understand the phenomena, and identify useful distinctions that clarify our understanding. Suitable research methods for exploratory questions tend to be those that offer rich, qualitative data, which help us to build tentative theories. Unless they are building on existing work that already offers clear definitions, both Jane and Joe need to formulate exploratory questions, such as:

- **Existence questions** of the form, "Does X exist?" Jane might need to ask, *"Is file navigation something that (certain types of programmers) actually do?"* and, *"Is efficiency actually a problem in file navigation?"* Joe might need to ask, *"Do collaborative shared artifacts actually exist?"*
- **Description and Classification questions** such as, "What is X like?", "What are its properties?", "How can it be categorized?", "How can we measure it?", "What is its purpose?", "What are its components?", "How do the components relate to one another?", and "What are all the types of X?" Jane might ask, *"How can we measure efficiency for file navigation?"* and Joe might ask, *"What are all the types of collaborative shared artifacts?"*
- **Descriptive-Comparative questions** of the form, "How does X differ from Y?" investigate similarities and differences between two or more phenomena. Jane might ask, *"How do fisheye views differ from conventional views?"* and Joe might ask, *"How do UML diagrams differ from other representations of design information?"*

The answers to these questions result in a clearer understanding of the phenomena, including more precise definitions of the theoretical terms, evidence that we can measure them, and evidence that the measures are valid. In exploring these questions, Jane and Joe will refine their ideas about the nature of the phenomena they are studying. It is possible that there are already good answers to these questions in the published literature. Jane and Joe must still ask these questions. But a literature survey, instead of an empirical study, may answer them.

Once we have a clearer understanding of the phenomena, we may need to ask *base-rate* questions about the normal patterns of occurrence of the phenomena. If we fail to ask base-rate questions, then we have no basis for saying whether a particular situation is normal or unusual. Example base-rate questions include:

- **Frequency and distribution questions** such as, "How often does X occur?" and, "What is an average amount of X?" Often, these questions can be answered in terms of a standard distribution of a characteristic within a well-defined population. Joe's original question appears to be a frequency question, but there are many ways for him to formulate it more precisely. For example, he might ask, *"How many distinct UML diagrams are created in software development projects in large software companies?"* and he might discover the results follow some standard statistical distribution.
- **Descriptive-Process questions** of the form, "How does X normally work?", "What is the process by which X happens?", "In what sequence do the events of X occur?", "What are the steps X goes through as it evolves?", "How does X achieve its purpose?". For example, Jane might ask, *"How do programmers navigate files using existing tools?"*

Often, we are interested in the *relationship* between two different phenomena, and specifically whether occurrence of one is related to occurrence of the other. Hence we need to formulate some:

- **Relationship questions** such as, "Are X and Y related?" and, "Do occurrences of X correlate with the occurrences of Y?" For example, Jane might ask, *"Does* *efficiency in file navigation correlate with the programmer's familiarity with the programming environment?"* Joe might ask, *"Do managers' claims about how often they use UML correlate with the actual use of UML?"*

Once we have established that a relationship exists between two phenomena, it is natural to try to explain why the relationship holds by attempting to identify a cause and effect. It is a common mistake to confuse *correlation* with *causality*. In general it is much harder to demonstrate causality than to show that two variables are correlated. If high values of X correlate with high values of Y, it may be because X causes Y, or because Y causes X. But it is also possible that X and Y share some common cause and neither causes the other. Or perhaps they co-evolve in complex ways so that there is no clear cause-and-effect. *Causality* questions include:

- **Causality questions** of the form, "Does X cause Y?" and "Does X prevent Y?" Plus the more general forms: "What causes Y?", "What are all the factors that cause Y?", "What effect does X have on Y?" In software engineering we often ask whether using a particular tool or technique causes an improvement in quality, speed, and so on. Jane's initial question appears to be of this type: *"Do fisheye-views cause an improvement in efficiency for file navigation?"*
- **Causality-Comparative questions** investigate relationships between different causes: "Does X cause more Y than does Z?" or, "Is X better at preventing Y than is Z?" Unless Jane has good base-rate data for existing file navigation tools, Jane's causality question would be better formulated as *"Do fisheye-views cause programmers to be more efficient at file navigation than conventional views?"*
- **Causality-Comparative Interaction** questions investigate how context affects a cause–effect relationship: "Does X or Z cause more Y under one condition but not others?" If Jane's initial studies reveal a factor (e.g., distractions) that affects causality, she might ask *"Do fisheye-views cause programmers to be more efficient at file navigation than conventional views when programmers are distracted, but not otherwise?"*

The classes of research question above are all *knowledge questions* focused on the way the world is. Empirical research in software engineering addresses these types of questions. In contrast, most *non-empirical* research in software engineering focuses on a very different type of question concerned with designing better ways to do software engineering (Simon, 1996):

- **Design questions** of the form, "What's an effective way to achieve X?" or, "What strategies help to achieve X?" For example, Joe's research might lead him to ask, *"What is an effective way for teams to represent design knowledge to improve coordination?"*

These types of question are necessary when the goal is to design better procedures and tools for carrying out some activity or to design suitable social or regulatory policies. Such questions presuppose that the associated knowledge questions have already been addressed so that we have enough information about the nature of the design problem to be solved. In practice, a long term software engineering research program involves a mix of design questions and knowledge questions as the researchers investigate specific problems, how best to solve them, and which solutions work best (Wieringa and Heerkens, 2006).

3. What will You Accept as an Empirical Truth?

Having specified the research question(s), it is worth considering what to accept as *valid* answers. Different people make different assumptions about scientific truth. Take, for example, Jane's causal question: *"Do fisheye-views cause an improvement in efficiency for file navigation?"* Jane's PhD advisor insists that the only trustworthy evidence to answer this question comes from experiments conducted under controlled laboratory conditions, pointing out that the only conclusive way to prove that A causes B is to manipulate A in a controlled setting, and measure the effect on B. However, another member of Jane's thesis committee is an experienced software practitioner and he claims that laboratory experiments are useless, as they ignore the messy complexity of real software projects. He points out that judgments about "improvements" to file navigation are subjective, and contextual factors such as distractions have a major impact. He suggests that Jane should conduct her research *in the field*, investigating what developers actually do on real projects

The different advice Jane receives reflects major differences in opinion over the nature of truth, and how we arrive at it through scientific investigation. The conflicting advice arises from the different *philosophical stances* adopted by members of Jane's committee. To understand the different stances, it helps to know that philosophers make a distinction between *epistemology* (the nature of human knowledge, and how we obtain it) and *ontology* (the nature of the world irrespective of our attempts to understand it). This separation helps us discuss what we accept as scientific knowledge separately from debates about the content of that knowledge (Chalmers, 1999).

Plato originally defined knowledge as *justified true belief.* In other words, to *know* something, you must *believe* it to be true, and have a clear *justification* for believing it to be true. However, epistemologists have argued for centuries about what form that justification should take. Empiricists argue that all knowledge is derived from our experiences and observations of the world, while rationalists argue that some part of our knowledge is innate, hence not derived from experience. Constructivists argue that we cannot separate knowledge from the language we use to express it – because the meanings of words are constructed by social convention, so is our knowledge.

In this chapter we characterize four dominant philosophical stances (Creswell, 2002). The stance you adopt affects which methods you believe lead to acceptable evidence in response to your research question(s). Being explicit about your stance also helps when talking and writing about research. You might not be able to convince other people to change their stance, but you will be able to argue cogently for why you chose the methods you did.

- **Positivitism** states that all knowledge must be based on logical inference from a set of basic observable facts. Positivists are *reductionist*, in that they study things by breaking them into simpler components. This corresponds to their belief that scientific knowledge is built up incrementally from *verifiable* observations, and inferences based on them. Positivism has been much attacked over the past century due to doubts about the reliability of our observations of the world, and the complication that scientific "fact" built up in this manner sometimes turns out to be wrong. While positivism still dominates the natural sciences, most positivists today might more accurately be described as *post-positivists*, in that they tend to accept the idea (due to Popper) that it is more productive to refute theories than to prove them, and we increase our confidence in a theory each time we fail to refute it, without necessarily ever proving it to be true. Positivists prefer methods that start with precise theories from which verifiable hypotheses can be extracted, and tested in isolation. Hence, positivism is most closely associated with the *controlled experiment;* however, *survey research* and *case studies* are also frequently conducted with a positivist stance. Note that a belief in reductionism is needed to accept laboratory experiments as valid in software engineering – you have to convince yourself that the phenomenon you are interested in can be studied in isolation from its context.
- **Constructivism**, also known as *interpretivism* (Klein and Myers, 1999), rejects the idea that scientific knowledge can be separated from its human context. In particular, the meanings of terms used in scientific theories are socially constructed, so interpretations of what a theory means are just as important in judging its truth as the empirical observations on which it is based. Constructivists concentrate less on verifying theories, and more on understanding how different people make sense of the world, and how they assign meaning to actions. Theories may emerge from this process, but they are always tied to the context being studied. For example, an anthropologist studying the culture of a software design team might seek to find out how different members of the team think about and use the tools they have available, and build *local theories* that explain why this particular team uses tools in the way that they do. This stance is often adopted in the social sciences, where positivist/reductionist approaches have little to say about the richness of social interactions. Constructivists prefer methods that collect rich qualitative data about human activities, from which local theories might emerge. Constructivism is most closely associated with *ethnographies*, although constructivists often use *exploratory case studies* and *survey research* too.
- **Critical Theory** judges scientific knowledge by its ability to free people from restrictive systems of thought (Calhoun, 1995). Critical theorists argue that research is a political act, because knowledge empowers different groups within society, or entrenches existing power structures. Critical theorists therefore choose what research to undertake based on whom it helps. They prefer participatory approaches in which the groups they are trying to help are engaged in the research, including helping to set its goals. Critical theorists therefore tend to take emancipatory or advocacy roles. In sociology, critical theory is most

closely associated with Marxist and feminist studies, along with research that seeks to improve the status of various minority groups. In software engineering, it includes research that actively seeks to challenge existing perceptions about software practice, most notably the open source movement, and, arguably, the process improvement community and the agile community. Critical theorists often use *case studies* to draw attention to things that need changing. However it is *action research* that most closely reflects the philosophy of critical theorists.

- **Pragmatism** acknowledges that all knowledge is approximate and incomplete, and its value depends on the methods by which it was obtained (Menand, 1997). For pragmatists, knowledge is judged by how useful it is for solving practical problems. Put simply, truth is whatever works at the time. This stance therefore entails a degree of relativism: what is useful for one person to believe might not be useful for another; therefore truth is relative to the observer. To overcome the obvious criticisms, many pragmatists emphasize the importance of consensus – truth is uncovered in the process of rational discourse, and is judged by the participants as whatever has the better arguments. Pragmatism is less dogmatic than the other three stances described above, as pragmatists tend to think the researcher should be free to use whatever research methods shed light on the research problem. In essence, pragmatism adopts an engineering approach to research – it values practical knowledge over abstract knowledge, and uses whatever methods are appropriate to obtain it. Pragmatists use any available methods, and strongly prefer *mixed methods* research, where several methods are used to shed light on the issue under study.

Although there are examples of research from each of these stances in the software engineering literature, the underlying philosophies are never mentioned. We believe this has contributed to confusion around the selection of empirical methods and appropriate evaluation of empirical research. In particular, it is impossible to avoid some commitment to a particular stance, as you cannot conduct research, and certainly cannot judge its results, without some criteria for judging what constitutes valid knowledge.

4. The Role of Theory Building

A distinguishing feature of scientific study is the development of theories that explain how and why certain phenomena occur, and allow predictions to be made. Theories are therefore the building blocks of scientific knowledge. The different philosophical stances differ in their ideas about the role of theory (Gregor, 2006). To the positivist, science is the process of verifying theories by testing hypotheses derived from them. To the constructivist, science is the process of seeking local theories that emerge from (and explain) the data. To the critical theorist, theories are assertions of knowledge (and therefore power), to be critiqued in terms of how they shape that power. To the pragmatist, theories are the products of a consensual process among a community of researchers, to be judged for their practical utility.

A scientific theory identifies and defines a set of phenomena, and makes assertions about the nature of those phenomena and the relationships between them. A good theory precisely defines the theoretical terms, so that a community of scientists can observe and measure them. A good theory also explains *why* certain relationships occur. Positivists expect their theories to have strong predictive power, and so look for generalized models of cause-and-effect as the basis for theories. In contrast, constructivists expect theories to strengthen their understanding of complex situations, and so tend make more use of categorizations and analogies. Theories are also judged for aesthetic value. Often there is more than one theory that explains empirical observations, so the theories that are simpler, or more elegant are preferred (LittleJohn and Foss, 2004).

As an example, Joe might develop a theory around the use of UML diagrams as a stylized form of external memory. According to his theory, UML diagrams are used to summarize the results of meetings and discussions, to remind participants of a shared understanding that they have already developed. Joe's theory must precisely define the meaning of terms such as "diagram," "participants," "discussions," in order to identify them in any studies performed. Joe's theory should also explain why people choose to use UML in some circumstances but not others, and why they include certain things in their diagrams and exclude others. And finally, it should be able to predict qualities of the diagrams that a software team might produce based on certain factors.

It is important to understand that in any empirical study, theories have a strong impact on how things are observed and interpreted. The theory becomes a "lens" through which the world is observed. This happens whether or not theories are explicitly acknowledged, because real-world phenomena are simply too rich and complex to study without a huge amount of filtering. In *quantitative* research methods, the theoretical lens is used explicitly to decide which variables to isolate and measure, and which to ignore or exclude. In *qualitative* methods, the theoretical lens is often applied after data is collected, to focus the process of labeling and categorizing ("coding") the data.

Few scientists give thought to how theories are created. A notable exception is *Grounded Theory*, a technique for developing theory iteratively from qualitative data (Glaser and Strauss, 1967). In grounded theory, initial analysis of the data begins without any preconceived categories. As interesting patterns emerge, the researcher repeatedly compares these with existing data, and collects more data to support or refute the emerging theory. Despite its close association with the constructivist stance, Grounded Theory probably approximates how most scientists end up developing theories. The difference is that Grounded Theory makes the process explicit and systematic.

Theories also play a role in connecting research to the relevant literature. By defining the key terms, the results of empirical studies can be compared. Furthermore, theories support the process of empirical induction because an individual study can never offer conclusive results. Each study adds more evidence for or against the propositions of the theory. Without the theory, we have no way of making sense of the accumulation of empirical results.

Software Engineering researchers have traditionally been very poor at making theories explicit (Jørgensen and Sjøberg, 2004). Many of the empirical studies conducted over the past few decades fail to relate the collected data to an underlying theory. The net result is that results are hard to interpret, and studies cannot be compared.

5. Selecting Methods

A method is a set of organizing principles around which empirical data is collected and analyzed. A variety of methods can be applied to any research problem, and it is often necessary to use a combination of methods to fully understand the problem. The choice of methods depends upon the theoretical stance of the researcher(s), access to resources (e.g., students or professionals as subjects/participants) and how closely the method aligns with the question(s) that have been posed. Research Design is the process of selecting a method for a particular research problem, tapping into its strengths, while mitigating its weaknesses. The validity of the results depends on how well the research design compensates for the weaknesses of the methods.

Below we describe in more detail the methods most likely to be applied in software engineering contexts. Because these methods are adapted from a number of different fields, there is no consistent terminology to describe them and even a lack of consensus on how to distinguish these methods from one another. We have chosen terms that should be familiar to software engineers and offer definitions and distinctions that capture the spirit of the methods.

5.1. Controlled Experiments

A controlled experiment is an investigation of a testable hypothesis where one or more *independent variables* are manipulated to measure their effect on one or more *dependent variables*. Controlled experiments allow us to determine in precise terms how the variables are related and, specifically, whether a cause–effect relationship exists between them. Each combination of values of the independent variables is a *treatment*. The simplest experiments have just two treatments representing two levels of a single independent variable (e.g. using a tool vs. not using a tool). More complex experimental designs arise when there are more than two levels or more than one independent variable is used. Most software engineering experiments require human *subjects* to perform some task. We measure the effect of the treatments on the subjects.

A precondition for conducting an experiment is a clear hypothesis. The hypothesis (and the theory from which it is drawn) guide all steps of the experimental design, including deciding which variables to include in the study and how to measure them. For example, Jane might decide to run an experiment to test the hypothesis that fish-eye views *cause* more efficient file navigation than traditional file tree explorer views. This hypothesis is drawn from a theory that explains the effect. The theory is that fisheye views correspond well to the way that people see and navigate in the world, by offering more detail of a specific area of focus, together with a less detailed overview of the peripheral regions, and a smooth way of moving the focus of attention. The theory suggests that less time spent scrolling and fewer clicks should reduce navigation time. This suggests the treatments should be the type of file explorer view used: fisheye view versus the traditional scrolled view, and the dependent variable should be the length of time to navigate to a file.

The theory also helps to decide who the subjects are, and what the tasks should be. To ensure the results of the experiment are valid, the subjects should be drawn from a well-defined population – the idea is to demonstrate that the hypothesis applies to the whole population by testing it on a representative sample. For her experiment, Jane recruits computer science grad students as subject programmers, and screens them to select subjects with lots of programming experience. In SE, it is common to recruit students as subjects. This makes it easier to recruit a large group of subjects, but reduces external validity – an analytical argument is needed for why results on students might still apply to software developers in industry.

Control is important – variables other than the chosen independent variables must not be allowed to affect the experiment. In Jane's case, differences in skill levels of her subjects may affect the experiment, so she might first divide her subjects into groups (or *blocks*) according to their skill level, and randomly assign subjects from each block to the two treatments, for a "between subjects design." An alternative is to use a "within subjects design," in which each subject uses all treatments; however this might introduce learning effects from one treatment to the next, so this needs to be accounted for in the design. Jane needs to decide which confounding factor is more important to control.

The experimental method is closely tied to the positivist stance. This is because experiments are essentially reductionist – they reduce complexity by allowing only a few variables of interest to vary in a controlled manner, while controlling all other variables. If critical variables are ignored or controlled, the experimental results might not generalize to real world settings. For example, in choosing to focus on efficiency as a dependent measure, Jane ignores other possible measures, such as awareness of the file structure that may result from other navigation techniques. The reduction can also mask critical interaction effects, such as the interaction between expertise and preferred navigation environment. For these reasons, if Jane's experiment confirms her hypothesis, it means she has evidence that fish-eye views are more efficient (as she defines efficiency), but it doesn't necessarily mean that fisheye views are better suited to navigation!

The fact that experiments are theory-driven is both a strength and a weakness. It is a strength because basing analysis on hypotheses derived from theories reduces problems of "fishing for results": some correlations occur by chance, and if we look for long enough we'll find them. On the other hand, being theory-driven forces us to decide in advance which variables to ignore, and they might turn out to be important outside the laboratory setting.

Variants on experiments are possible and can be used in circumstances where a true experiment is not possible. For example, in *quasi-experiments* the subjects are not assigned randomly to the treatments. Quasi-experiments may be used, for example, when, for ethical reasons, subjects must be allowed to choose their treatment. Quasi-experiments are also used in the field. For example if an experiment is performed in a company, there may be constraints on which employees can work on which tasks. In *time-series experiments*, the effect of a treatment is measured in discrete time steps over a period of time. These variations are less powerful than true experiments, and require more careful interpretation.

5.2. Case Studies

There is much confusion in the SE literature over what constitutes a case study. The term is often used to mean a worked example. As an empirical method, a case study is something very different. Yin (2002) introduces the case study as "an empirical inquiry that investigates a contemporary phenomenon within its real-life context, especially when the boundaries between phenomenon and context are not clearly evident." Case studies offer in-depth understanding of how and why certain phenomena occur, and can reveal the mechanisms by which cause–effect relationships occur Flyvbjerg (2006). *Exploratory case studies* are used as initial investigations of some phenomena to derive new hypotheses and build theories, and *confirmatory case studies* are used to test existing theories. The latter are especially important for refuting theories: a detailed case study of a real situation in which a theory fails may be more convincing than "failed" experiments in the lab. The detailed insights obtained from confirmatory case studies can also be useful for choosing between rival theories.

A precondition for conducting a case study is a clear research question concerned with how or why certain phenomena occur. This is used to derive a *study proposition* that states precisely what the study is intended to show, and to guide the selection of cases and the types of data to collect. As an example, imagine that Jane is upset as her tool is not adopted by developers after her experiment. She noticed in the post-experiment interviews that subjects frequently mentioned using additional advanced features for navigation that do not involve the file explorer (the only navigation tool available in the experiment). Hence, she poses the research question "How do developers use navigation tool support for large systems under development?", and decides to focus on a specific proposition suggested by the post-experiment interviews that "expert developers use many different strategies for navigation, and move between them very rapidly." This leads her to choose a local company with several very experienced developers as her case, and to focus on observational rather than interview data, to find out what the developers actually do at a fine grain of detail.

The selection of cases is a crucial step in case study research. Case study research uses purposive sampling rather than random sampling. The aim is to select cases that are most relevant to the study proposition. Sometimes a single case is sufficient. This might be because it is a *critical case* for testing a well-formulated theory: if the theory holds for this case, it is likely to be true for many others. Or it might be an *extreme* or *unique case* that is expected to yield interesting insights about what happens under extreme conditions, such as a crisis. Sometimes it is sufficient to identify a *typical case* to gain more insight into common situations. However, a multiple case design usually offers greater validity. The different cases are best thought of as replications, rather than members of a sample. For confirmatory case studies, these can be chosen as *literal replications*, where each case is expected to show the same results, or as *theoretical replications*, where cases are expected to show contrasting results for predictable reasons. An example of the latter would be if Jane's theory predicted that experienced developers do file navigation differently from novices. A multiple case study could include both experts and novices, to confirm that the theory adequately explains both.

A variety of different data sources are typically used in case study research. Qualitative data, including interviews and observation, play a central role, as these offer rich insights into the case. Data collection is always performed with respect to a well-defined *unit of analysis*. In software engineering, the unit of analysis might be a company, a project, a team, an individual developer, a particular episode or event, a specific work product, etc. Choosing an appropriate unit of analysis is important, to ensure the study focuses on the intended phenomena. In Jane's case, she chooses the individual developer as her unit of analysis, allowing her to focus on personal style of different developers. Other choices would lead the case study in different directions. For example, choosing a project as the unit of analysis would allow her to identify whether project teams develop shared navigational styles, but would offer less insights into individual styles. Note that Jane's *case* (a company) has multiple embedded *units of analysis* (the developers). In some studies, the case is the same as the unit of analysis.

Case study research is most appropriate for cases where the reductionism of controlled experiments is inappropriate. This includes situations where the context is expected to play a role in the phenomena (for example if the stresses of a real project affect developers' behaviour), or where effects are expected to be wide ranging, or take a long time (e.g. weeks, months, years) to appear.

The major weakness of case studies is that the data collection and analysis is more open to interpretation and researcher bias. For this reason, an explicit framework is needed for selecting cases and collecting data. Although an individual case study often reveals deep insights, the validity of the results depends on a broader framework of empirical induction. For example, in confirmatory case studies, evidence builds when subsequent case studies also support the theory and/or fail to support rival theories.

Case studies can be applied within all four philosophical stances, although different stances affect the way in which cases are selected and the data analysis is performed. For example, confirmatory case studies draw on the positivist perspective of theory-driven research, but positivists also use exploratory case studies to develop new theories [see Kitchenham et al. (1995), for an brief tutorial of software engineering case study research using a primarily positivist perspective]. Constructivists use exploratory case studies to investigate the differences of culture and perspective in various settings. Critical theorists use both types of case study to draw attention to situations that are regarded as problematic, selecting cases that are politically important, or for which the participants themselves can be most expected to benefit. The criteria for assessing the validity of a case study depends on which philosophical stance is taken.

5.3. Survey Research

Survey research is used to identify the characteristics of a broad population of individuals. It is most closely associated with the use of questionnaires for data collection. However, survey research can also be conducted by using structured interviews, or data logging techniques. The defining characteristic of survey research is the selection of a *representative sample* from a well-defined *population*, and the data analysis techniques used to *generalize* from that sample to the population, usually to answer base-rate questions.

A precondition for conducting survey research is a clear research question that asks about the nature of a particular target population. Because it is usually infeasible (and unnecessary) to poll every member of that population, survey research first identifies a representative subset as the sample, and determines how to reach that subset for data collection. Identifying the unit of analysis is important for determining an appropriate sampling technique. For example, if the research question is about software companies, then sampling over individual developers may give a biased sample, with some companies being over-represented because several developers from the same company were included. Furthermore, simple random sampling of the population might also be inadequate. For example, if our unit of analysis is individual developers, a random sampling might end up with most or all of respondents working at a single, dominant company. In such a case, stratified sampling techniques would be used, to identify subgroups within the population, so that we can sample within each subgroup.

As an example, recall that Joe wished to understand more about how UML is used in industrial settings, and how UML supports collaborative design. He conducts a survey of software companies across the country to ask them whether they use UML, and if so how. He decides to use individual developers as his unit of analysis, so that he can focus on how different developers perceive the utility of UML. He posts his survey to a number of carefully selected developer email lists, and has a response rate of 10%. The results from the survey are interesting. He discovers that only about 20% of the respondents use UML, and that the diagrams are rarely used in shared settings. He also learns that class diagrams are the most frequently used diagram, with sequence diagrams a close second.

Joe could choose from a number of different designs for his study. For example, if he just wishes to establish how widely UML is used, then he would use a cross-sectional design to obtain a snapshot of participants' current activities. In contrast, a case-control design asks each participant about several related issues in order to establish whether a correlation exists between them, across the population. Joe might use this design if he wishes to explore whether there is a relationship between, say, how long developers have used UML and how much they use it for information sharing. A cohort study tracks changes over time for a group of participants. Joe might use such a design, for example, to determine whether use of UML changes over the life of development project, perhaps with "projects" as his unit of analysis.

A major challenge in survey research is to control for sampling bias. Sampling bias causes problems in generalizing the survey results, because the respondents to the survey may not be representative of the target population. Low response rates increase the risk of bias. For example, if the 10% who responded to Joe's survey were the least busy of his targeted developers, it may be that the survey missed the most skilled, or most senior developers. Or perhaps only people who are frustrated with UML answered his survey. In general, it is hard to obtain high response rates unless significant inducements can be offered for participation, although it is sometimes possible to contact non-respondents to assess whether a systematic response bias has occurred.

An even harder challenge is to ensure that the questions are designed in a way that yields useful and valid data. It can be hard to phrase the questions such that all participants understand them in the same way, especially if the target population is diverse. Also, it is possible that what people say they do in response to survey questions bears no relationship to what they actually do, because they are unable to introspect reliably on their work practices.

It is instructive to compare survey research with other empirical methods. In Joe's case, the survey research design is concerned with establishing what is true of developers in general. If instead he wishes to gain deeper insights into how developers actually use UML, or why they don't, he might be better off conducting a case study. This would sacrifice claims of representativeness (because case studies do not use representative sampling) in return for deeper insights into what happens in a small number of selected cases. On the other hand, if he's more interested in how UML changes how developers share information, he might design an experiment or quasi-experiment to test for a causal relationship.

Survey research falls almost exclusively into the positivist tradition. The desire to characterize an entire population via sampling techniques requires a belief in reductionism, and a concern with generalizable theories. If Joe is more interested in understanding the *culture* of information sharing within development teams, he might instead adopt a constructivist stance, and use ethnography or action research.

Kitchenham and Pfleeger (Chap. 3) provide more detailed information on conducting surveys.

5.4. Ethnographies

Ethnography is a form of research focusing on the sociology of meaning through field observation. The goal is to study a *community* of people to understand how the members of that community make sense of their social interactions (Robinson et al., 2007). For software engineering, ethnography can help to understand how technical communities build a culture of practices and communication strategies that enables them to perform technical work collaboratively. An ethnography might focus on a broad technical community (e.g. java programmers in general), or a small, closely knit community (e.g. a single development team).

One notable feature of ethnography is that it avoids imposing any pre-existing theories, but instead focuses on how the members of the community themselves make sense of their social and cultural setting. The researcher explicitly considers his/her own pre-conceptions and how they influence understanding of the studied community. For example, the researcher might focus on phrases used by the community that seem strange to him, to discover how community members use language to create categories that are meaningful to them. The result of an ethnographic study is usually a rich description of the community being studied that helps to build a detailed picture of that community's culture.

The preconditions for an ethnographic study include a research question that focuses on the cultural practices of a particular community, and access to members of that community. Because of the focus on "member's own categories," the precise boundaries of the community to be studied might not be known in advance, and indeed the very notion of membership, and the idea of becoming a member, may be important things to investigate. Using chain sampling, informants within the community are asked to identify representative members of the community, who identify other members of the community, and so on.

As an example, consider the results of the survey that Joe conducted in the previous section. One conclusion from his study is that people don't seem to use UML in the way Joe expected. An ethnography would allow Joe to understand more about how developers use and share UML. He identifies a development team that allows him to observe design meetings for several weeks. He supplements his notes on what he observes with a series of individual and group interviews to further explore how well UML tools match the team's design practices, and why some groups in the company do not use UML.

A special form of ethnography is *participant observation*, where the researcher becomes a member of the community being studied for a period of time. Here, the researcher is not trying to understand the community via the observations of an outsider, but rather through the privileged view that comes from membership. For this to work, the researcher must be accepted by the community as one of them, which may require a much longer duration for the study than "just a few weeks." In software engineering research, becoming a member might only be possible if the researcher has the right technical background.

Ethnographic research takes an explicit constructivist stance. Underlying ethnographic research is the idea that members of a community construct their social and cultural practices on the fly, and their perceptions of those structures also define them. Because of that stance, ethnographic researchers don't seek to prove hypotheses and theories, but rather create *local theories* to improve understanding. This philosophical stance distinguishes ethnography from case studies, surveys and field experiments.

The biggest challenge in ethnographic research is to perform detailed observation, data collection and analysis while avoiding preconceptions. The researcher needs a high degree of training in observational and qualitative data analysis techniques. Sociologists have evolved a collection of techniques for recording observations correctly and for systematic data analysis, as well as for iterative research in which clarifications are sought as new information becomes available. Ethnographic studies in software engineering are valuable for discovering what really goes on in particular (technical) communities, and for revealing subtle but important aspects of work practices.

5.5. Action Research

In Action Research, the researchers attempt to solve a real-world problem while simultaneously studying the experience of solving the problem (Davison et al., 2004). While most empirical research methods attempt to observe the world as it currently exists, action researchers aim to intervene in the studied situations for the explicit purpose of improving the situation. Action research has been pioneered in fields such as education, where major changes in educational strategies cannot be studied without implementing them, and where implementation implies a long term commitment, because the effects may take years to emerge. It has also been adopted in information science, where organizational change can sometimes require a long time to have an impact. However, even in these fields, action research is a relatively new idea, and there is widespread discussion about appropriate methodology, and even debate on the validity of action research as an empirical method.

A precondition for action research is to have a *problem owner* willing to collaborate to both identify a problem, and engage in an effort to solve it. In action research, the problem owners become collaborators in the research. In some cases, the researcher and the problem owner may be the same person. Two key criteria for judging the quality of action research are whether the original problem is *authentic* (i.e. whether it is a real and important problem that needs solving), and whether there are authentic *knowledge outcomes* for the participants. It is additionally important for the researcher to engage in a process of critical reflection upon his past, current and planned actions to identify how they actually helped (or not) to solve the problem. Action research is also characterized by a commitment to effect real change, and an iterative approach to problem solving.

For example, in the process of studying the use of UML, imagine that Joe's colleagues discussed with him their difficulty in integrating software components and predicting the effects of such integration. Joe sees this as an opportunity to work with them to try out ideas from model-driven development (MDD), and to study firsthand how UML changes the way that developers collaborate. Joe initiates a project to work with his colleagues to introduce MDD and to record the experiences. Joe and the development team use a series of data collection techniques, including periodic interviews, questionnaires, and focus groups, to ensure that they establish a process of critical reflection over the life of the project. They use the data collected to develop local theories that explain the experiences of the problem-owners, which, with other research, can be generalized for other people interested in adopting MDD. As new information becomes available, they update these theories to reflect the current understanding of the situation.

Action research is most closely associated with *critical theory*. In an action research project, it is normally taken as self-evident that the problem needs to be solved, and that the adopted solution is desirable: knowledge gained from the research empowers particular individuals or groups, and facilitate a wider change. With this philosophical stance, there is effectively a "moral imperative" to intervene to solve the problem. Therefore, no attempt is made to establish a control group: the moral imperative implies that it would be unethical to withhold the intervention from some groups. Instead, the emphasis is on identifying useful lessons that help others who wish to pursue a similar change agenda. However, action research can be linked to other philosophical stances by divorcing it from its emancipatory roots, and focusing instead on practical problem solving. Positivists would add a concern with careful comparison of the "before" and "after" situations, while constructivists would focus on participants' perceptions of the change process. The key characteristic that differentiates action research from longitudinal case studies and ethnographies is that the researcher is also an agent of change.

The biggest challenge for action research is its immaturity as an empirical method. Although frameworks for evaluating action research have been proposed (e.g. Lau, 1999), they tend to be vague or subjective, leading to accusations that action research is ad hoc. Furthermore, organizational change is often inseparable from organizational politics, and there is a danger that the research fails to address this adequately, either by underestimating the importance of the political agendas of the participants, or by overstating the "moral case" for implementing a change. Researcher bias can be reduced through critical reflection, and by validating the lessons learned through replication. Finally, action research may be expensive, given the organizational commitment needed.

It could be argued that a great deal of software engineering research is actually action research in disguise. Certainly, many key ideas in software engineering were originally developed by trying them out on real development projects, and reporting on the experiences. In this vein, Dittrich (2002) describes cooperative systems development as a form of action research ideally suited to empirical software engineering. By adopting the framework of action research more explicitly, it is likely that the design and evaluation of such research can be made more rigorous. Action research is also an appealing framework for mixing research with professional activities, especially for practitioners interested in reflecting on their experiences and passing on their learning outcomes for the benefit of others.

5.6. Mixed-Methods Approaches

Throughout this chapter we have seen how Joe and Jane could have used different methods as they learned more about their research topics. While Jane began with the design of an experiment to test the efficiency of file navigation with the fisheye view, she went on to perform a case study to explore some of the unexpected findings from the experiment. This approach can be characterized as *mixed methods* research – a more complex research strategy that emerged in the recognition that all methods have limitations, and the weaknesses of one method can be compensated for by the strengths of other methods (Creswell, 2002).

Mixed method research employs data collection and analysis techniques associated with both quantitative and qualitative data. The "mixing" might be within one study, by using multiple data collection techniques, or among several studies. Key decisions involve the strategy for data collection, and the sequence in which different methods are employed. While mixed method research is a powerful approach to inquiry, the researcher is challenged with the need for extensive data collection, the time-intensive nature of analyzing multiple sources of data, as well as the requirement to be familiar with both quantitative and qualitative forms of research.

We include here the description of three most familiar strategies described by Creswell (2002):

The *Sequential explanatory strategy* is characterized by the collection and analysis of quantitative data followed by the collection and analysis of qualitative data. The purpose of this strategy is typically to use qualitative results to assist in explaining and interpreting the findings of a quantitative study. It is particularly useful when unexpected results arise from the quantitative phase. Jane's example above follows this strategy. When her experimental data indicated that developers switch rapidly between navigation strategies, she decided to perform a case study for a more in-depth exploration of a few developers and their navigation behavior. Damian et al. (2000) provides another example of this approach.

The *Sequential exploratory strategy* is characterized by the collection and analysis of qualitative data followed by the collection and analysis of quantitative data. Its purpose is to use quantitative data and results to assist in the interpretation of qualitative findings. This strategy is also useful for testing elements of an emerging theory resulting from a qualitative study. For example, as a result of Joe's ethnographic study of collaborative design, he formulates some hypotheses about how UML affects the quality of the source code in shared design tasks. To explore this further, he uses a sequential exploratory approach to explore the impact of shared UML diagrams on code quality. He plans and conducts a survey of many different software development projects, in which he measures the extent to which they use UML for collaboration, and the number of code defects that can be attributed to communication problems. For a published example of this strategy, see Damian and Chisan (2006).

The *Concurrent triangulation strategy* is probably the most familiar and widely used among the mixed-method approaches. This strategy uses different methods concurrently, in an attempt to confirm, cross-validate or corroborate findings. Triangulation is motivated by the fact that often "what people say" could be different than "what people do," and thus collecting data from multiple sources helps improve validity. For example, Joe might incorporate additional data collection techniques into his ethnographic study on the use of UML. He could collect quantitative data from surveys of similar developers to compare against the results of his ethnography. By collecting both types of data simultaneously, rather than sequentially, each analysis can be adapted to explore emerging results from the other. The challenge in this approach is that it may be difficult for the researcher to compare the results of two analyses or to resolve contradictions that arise in the results. In such cases a further source of evidence, or a follow up study might be necessary. For a published example of this strategy, see Bratthall and Jørgensen (2002).

Mixed methods research can be conducted within any of the philosophical stances. For example, a positivist might combine experiments with confirmatory case studies; a constructivist might mix ethnographies with surveys. However, both positivism and constructivism may limit the ability to mix the methods. While positivists strongly prefer quantitative evidence, and constructivists strongly prefer qualitative evidence, mixed methods research emphasizes the use of evidence from both quantitative and qualitative data. Therefore, mixed methods research is more often associated with a pragmatist stance, where the emphasis is on using those methods that most effectively address the research problem.

6. Data Collection Techniques

Once the research method has been selected, the researcher must decide which data collection techniques are the most suitable for gathering data based on the study's *unit of analysis*. Multiple techniques can be used to gather data from different perspectives, as there are advantages and limitations to each technique. Indeed, using multiple techniques allows the researcher to *triangulate* even within a single method. If different kinds of data support the same conclusions, it strengthens the study. Singer et al. (Chap. 1) provide an overview of various potential data collection techniques.

Selecting suitable techniques requires careful consideration of the research design as well as the pragmatics of the research setting. It is important to note the advantages and disadvantages of the different techniques from the perspectives of the experimenter, the participants, the generalizability and reliability of the results.

A careful blend of techniques can help to offset potential bias and leads to a more comprehensive understanding of the research topic (Varkevisser et al., 2003). New researchers should ensure they are familiar with the techniques they select, and that they are aware of the potential pitfalls they may face. For example, it is always advisable to pilot-test the data collection instrument, and to pilot-test not just the collection aspect of the instrument, but also the analysis procedure. Many problems do not arise until some data is analyzed and it is often possible to detect such problems with even a small data set. How to analyze the data collected is a topic beyond the scope of this chapter. Wohlin et al. (2000) provide a summary of quantitative analysis techniques for software engineering, and Seaman (Chap. 2) provides an excellent guide to coding etc for qualitative research.

In the end, Jane chose to use a post-study questionnaire that collected both quantitative and qualitative data (open-ended responses). During the study, she observed and videotaped the users and their interactions with the computer so that she could time how long it took to complete the navigation tasks she set for them. She also instrumented the IDE they were using to count number of scrollbar selection events and number of mouse clicks. These numbers can be used with the start/end times indicated on the annotated videotapes of the users. Interviews and focus groups are used at the end of her field study to gather more ideas on how navigation features could be improved in the IDE and why the fisheye view is or is not used by some developers. Joe used questionnaires at different stages in his research. He also conducted interviews and collected observations as a participant in the observed group.

7. Empirical Validity

For empirical work to be acceptable as a contribution to scientific knowledge, the researcher needs to convince readers that the conclusions drawn from an empirical study are *valid*. Not surprisingly, the criteria by which researchers judge validity depend on their philosophical stance.

For positivists, research is normally theory-driven. The key steps include deriving study propositions from the theory, designing the study to address the propositions, and then drawing more general conclusions from the results. Each of these steps must be shown to be sound. Accordingly, positivists usually identify four criteria for validity:

- *Construct validity* focuses on whether the theoretical constructs are interpreted and measured correctly. For example, if Jane designs an experiment to test her claims about the efficiency of fish eye views, will she interpret "efficiency" in the same way that other researchers have, and does she have an appropriate means for measuring it? Problems with construct validity occur when the measured variables don't correspond to the intended meanings of the theoretical terms.

- *Internal validity* focuses on the study design, and particularly whether the results really do follow from the data. Typical mistakes include the failure to handle confounding variables properly, and misuse of statistical analysis.
- *External validity* focuses on whether claims for the generality of the results are justified. Often, this depends on the nature of the sampling used in a study. For example, if Jane's experiment is conducted with students as her subjects, it might be hard to convince people that the results would apply to practitioners in general.
- *Reliability* focuses on whether the study yields the same results if other researchers replicate it. Problems occur if the researcher introduces bias, perhaps because the tool being evaluated is one that the researcher herself has a stake in.

These criteria are useful for evaluating all positivist studies, including controlled experiments, most case studies and survey research. In reporting positivist empirical studies, it is important to include a section on *threats to validity*, in which potential weaknesses in the study design as well as attempts to mitigate these threats are discussed in terms of these four criteria. This is important because all study designs have flaws. By acknowledging them explicitly, the researchers show that they are aware of the flaws and have taken reasonable steps to minimize their effects.

In the constructivist stance, assessing validity is more complex. Many researchers who adopt this stance believe that the whole concept of validity is too positivist, and does not accurately reflect the nature of qualitative research. That is, as the constructivist stance assumes that reality is "multiple and constructed," then repeatability is simply not possible (Sandelowski, 1993). Assessment of validity requires a level of objectivity that is not possible. Attempts to develop frameworks to evaluate the contribution of constructivist research have met with mixed reactions. For example, Lincoln and Guba (1985) proposed to analyze *trustworthiness* of research results in terms of credibility, transferability, dependability, and confirmability. Morse et al. (2002) criticise this as being too concerned with post hoc evaluation, and argue instead for strategies to establish validity during the research process. Creswell (2002) identifies eight strategies for improving validity of constructivist research, which are well suited to ethnographies and exploratory case studies in software engineering:

1. Triangulation: use different sources of data to confirm results and build a coherent picture.
2. Member checking: go back to research participants to ensure that the interpretations of the data make sense from their perspective.
3. Rich, thick descriptions: where possible, use detailed descriptions to convey the setting and findings of the research.
4. Clarify bias: be honest with respect to the biases brought by the researchers to the study, and use this self-reflection when reporting findings.
5. Report discrepant information: when reporting findings, report not only those results which confirm the emerging theory, but also those which appear to present different perspectives on the findings.

6. Prolonged contact with participants: Make sure that exposure to the subject population is long enough to ensure a reasonable understanding of the issues and phenomenon under study.
7. Peer debriefing: Before reporting findings, locate a peer debriefer who can ask questions about the study and the assumptions present in the reporting of it, so that the final account is as valid as possible.
8. External auditor: The same as peer debriefing, except instead of using a person known to the researcher, find an external auditor to review the research procedure and findings.

Dittrich et al. (2007) define a similar set of criteria specifically concerned with validity of qualitative research for empirical software engineering.

For critical theorists, assessment of research quality must also take into account the utility of the knowledge gained. Researchers adopting the critical stance often seek to bring about a change by redressing a perceived injustice, or challenging existing perspectives. Repeatability is not usually relevant, because the problems tackled are context sensitive. The practical outcome is at least as important as the knowledge gained, and any assessment of validity must balance these. However, there is little consensus yet on how best to do this. Lau (1999) offers one of the few attempts to establish some criteria, specifically for action research. His criteria include that the problem tackled should be authentic, the intended change should be appropriate and adequate, the participants should be authentic, and the researchers should have an appropriate level of access to the organization, along with a planned exit point. Most importantly, there should be clear knowledge outcomes for the participants.

8. Practical Considerations

In addition to the question of how well the methods fit a given type of research question and philosophical stance, the choice of methods also depends on practical considerations. Often these practical considerations force the researcher to change the original research design in terms of the choice of method, data collection and analysis procedures. It is important to document the original planned research protocol, and all subsequent deviations to it, to allow other researchers to understand the study design, interpret the research results, and replicate the study.

Most of the practical challenges relate to time, budget and personnel resources, and access to data. Rather than describe the challenges for each method individually, we summarize the challenges related to groups of methods, according to the type of data they deal with:

Methods that are primarily qualitative include ethnography, case study, and action research. These methods rely on fieldwork, using techniques such as participant observation and interviews. Key challenges include preparing good questions for structured or semi-structured interviews, and finding the time and resources needed to collect and analyze potentially large sets of data. The researcher needs a thorough training in how to observe and record social behaviour. Access to the field situation may require prolonged time in establishing a relationship with the subject organization such that specific project data is made available. For ethnography, the researcher needs to find a community where she is accepted as a member, which might not be possible unless she has appropriate technical experience. For action research, the researcher needs to balance the need to involve the organization in helping to set appropriate goals for the research with the need to remain objective, such that the research does not become merely consulting.

Methods that are primarily quantitative include controlled experiments and survey research. These methods require more significant time in the planning of the research than strictly qualitative methods. To achieve external validity for both experiments and surveys, the researcher needs the time and budget to (1) define, recruit and (if possible) randomly select a sample population that is representative of the target population, (2) design and pilot the questions such that all respondents are presented with questions that they interpret and understand in exactly the same way (therefore careful attention to detail in phrasing the questions is needed), and (3) define statistical tests ahead of time, in order to interpret the collected data. The goal here is to *plan ahead*, for smooth analysis and interpretation of results.

All research conducted in industrial settings brings a number of challenges. It can be very hard to gather data to find out what practitioners actually do, or what needs to be improved in the organization, rather than what practitioners say they do or think require improvement. Data quality can also be an issue (see Chaps. 1 and 7 for more on this issue). In return for access to the organization, the researcher usually has to give up some control. For example, it is hard to observe and document findings without interfering with the observed situation, especially when the industrial partners want to know in advance what the expected outcomes are. It is often difficult to know if changes are made through involvement in the research or would have occurred anyway (c.f., the Hawthorne effect). Finally, obtaining permission to publish the results can be a challenge. Delays in publication are likely if the organization has concerns about inclusion of confidential data or insights in the research. Singer and Vinson (2002) and Vinson and Singer (2004) discuss the unique ethical challenges involved in research in industrial settings.

9. Conclusions

We have presented an overview of the choices involved in selecting appropriate empirical methods for software engineering research. Our aim in this chapter was not provide a thorough description of each method, but rather to cover the issues that a researcher must face when deciding how to address a given research problem. Further study, and possibly some specialized training may be necessary before a researcher can apply a chosen method.

We have described the key elements of empirical research design: A clear research question provides a focus to your study. An explicit philosophical stance helps you understand your research goals, and select an appropriate research method. A research method helps you design a study, and decide what kinds of data to collect and how to collect it. A theory helps you explain the data and relate it to the research question and to previous studies in the literature. An appropriate set of criteria for assessing validity helps improve the study design, and clarify the nature of the conclusions.

We have not addressed a number of related topics, including replication and meta-analysis. As the number of empirical studies in software engineering increases, these become more important. In particular, it is only through empirical induction that we come to trust the results of empirical research – i.e. the results need to hold up across many different studies to be considered reliable. Meta-analysis is the process of systematically comparing the results of multiple studies, taking into account differences in the design and context of each individual study. In current software engineering research, meta-analysis is hard to accomplish because of huge variability in the style and quality of the published reports of empirical work.

A key message throughout the chapter is that empirical research never produces certain knowledge. Each of the methods we have available for empirical investigations help to elucidate the phenomena being studied, but each also has significant flaws. Awareness of the limitations of each method should allow you to design a study that minimizes the weaknesses. Furthermore, the flaws can be overcome by mixing methods, and/or by conducting replications (see Brooks et al., Chap. 14, for more information on replication).

We believe that clearer distinctions between research methods are necessary to facilitate better study designs and clearer criteria for evaluating empirical research. The definitions and distinctions we offer in this chapter are by no means widely agreed upon, neither in the empirical software engineering community, nor in related disciplines. For example, we have avoided the usual distinction between qualitative and quantitative methods, as we believe the distinctions between methods are more subtle than simply the type of data collected. Instead, we have emphasized differences in philosophical stance, and in criteria used for designing studies for each type of method. We hope that this chapter provides a first step towards a consensus on empirical methodology in software engineering.

References

Bratthall, L. and Jørgensen, M. (2002) Can you trust a single data source exploratory software engineering case study? *Journal of Empirical Software Engineering*, 7(1), 9–26.
Calhoun, C. (1995) *Critical Social Theory: Culture, History, and the Challenge of Difference*. Blackwell, Oxford, UK.
Chalmers, A. (1999) *What Is This Thing Called Science?* 3rd Edition, Hackett Publishing Co, Indianapolis.

Creswell, J.W. (2002) *Research Design: Qualitative, Quantitative and Mixed Methods Approaches*. 2nd Edition, Sage Publications, Thousand Oaks, CA.

Damian, D. and Chisan, J. (2006) An empirical study of the complex relationships between requirements engineering processes and other processes that lead to payoffs in productivity, quality and risk management, *IEEE Transactions on Software Engineering*, 32(8), 433–453.

Damian, D.E., Eberlein, A., Shaw, M., and Gaines, B. (2000) Using different communication media in requirements negotiation, *IEEE Software*, 17(3), 28–36.

Davison, R.M., Martinsons, M.G., and Kock, N. (2004) Principles of canonical action research, *Information Systems Journal*, 14(1), 65–86.

Dittrich, Y. (2002) Doing Empirical Research on Software Development: Finding a Path Between Understanding, Intervention, and Method Development. In *Social Thinking: Software Practice*, Y. Dittrich, C. Floyd, and R. Klischewski, Eds. MIT Press.

Dittrich, Y., John, M., Singer, J., and Tessem, B. (2007) Editorial for the Special Issue on Qualitative Software Engineering Research, *Information and Software Technology*, 49(6), 531–539.

Flyvbjerg, B. (2006) Five misunderstandings about case study research, *Qualitative Inquiry*, 12(2), 219–245.

Glaser, B.G. and Strauss, A. (1967) *Discovery of Grounded Theory: Strategies for Qualitative Research*. Sociology Press, Mill Valley, CA.

Gregor, S. (2006) The Nature of Theories in Information Systems, *MIS Quarterly*, 30(3), 611–642

Jørgensen, M. and Sjøberg, D.I.K. (2004) Generalization and Theory-Building in Software Engineering Research. *IEE Proceedings, Workshop on Empirical Assessment in Software Engineering* (EASE'04), at ICSE'04, pp. 29–36.

Kitchenham, B., Pickard, L., and Pfleeger, S.L. (1995) Case studies for method and tool evaluation, *IEEE Software*, 12(4), 52–62.

Klein, H.K. and Myers, M.D. (1999) A set of principles for conducting and evaluating interpretive field studies in information systems, *MIS Quarterly*, 23(1), 67–93.

Lau, F. (1999).Towards a framework for action research in information systems studies, *Information Technology and People*, 12(2), 148–175.

Lincoln, Y.S. and Guba, E.G. (1985) *Naturalistic Inquiry*. Sage, Beverly Hills, CA.

Littlejohn, S.W. and Foss, K.A. (2004) *Theories of Human Communication*. 8th Edition, Wadsworth Publishing, Belmont, CA.

McGrath, J.E. (1995) Methodology matters: doing research in the behavioral and social sciences. In *Human–Computer Interaction: Toward the Year 2000*, R.M. Baecker, J. Grudin, W. Buxton, A., and Greenberg, S., Eds. Morgan Kaufmann Publishers, San Francisco, CA, pp. 152–169.

Meltzoff, J. (1998) *Critical Thinking About Research: Psychology and Related Fields*. American Psychological Association, Washington DC.

Menand, L. (1997) *Pragmatism: A Reader*. Vintage Press, New York.

Morse, J.M., Barrett, M., Mayan, M., Olson, K. and Spiers, J. (2002) Verification strategies for establishing reliability and validity in qualitative research, *International Journal of Qualitative Methods*, 1(2), 1–19.

Robinson, H., Segal, J. and Sharp, H. (2007) Ethnographically-informed empirical studies of software practice, *Information and Software Technology*, 49(6), 540–551.

Sandelowski, M. (1993) Rigor or rigor mortis: the problem of rigor in qualitative research revisited, *Advances in Nursing Science*, 16(2), 1–8.

Simon, H. (1996) *The Sciences of the Artificial*. 3rd Edition, MIT Press, Cambridge, MA.

Singer, J.A. and Vinson, N.G. (2002) Ethical issues in empirical studies of software engineering, *IEEE Transactions on Software Engineering*, 28(12), 1171–1180.

Varkevisser, C.M., Pathmanathan, I., and Brownlee, A. (2003) *Designing and Conducting Health Systems Research Projects: Volume 1 – Proposal Development and Fieldwork*. Chapter 10: Data Collection Techniques. Available online at http://www.idrc.ca/en/ev-56605-201-1-DO_TOPIC.html

Vinson, N.G. and Singer, J.A. (2004) Consent issues raised by observational research in organisations, *NCEHR Communique*, 12(2), 35–36.

Wicringa, R.J. and Heerkens, J.M.G. (2006) The methodological soundness of requirements engineering papers: a conceptual framework and two case studies, *Requirements Engineering Journal*, 11, 295–307.

Wohlin, C., Runesson, P., Höst, M., Ohlsson, M.C., Regnell, B., and Wesslén, A. (2000) *Introduction to Experimentation in Software Engineering*. Kluwer Academic Publishers, Boston, MA.

Yin, R.K. (2002) *Case Study Research: Design and Methods*. Sage, Thousand Oaks, CA.

Chapter 12
Building Theories in Software Engineering

Dag I.K. Sjøberg, Tore Dybå, Bente C.D. Anda, and Jo E. Hannay

Abstract In mature sciences, building theories is the principal method of acquiring and accumulating knowledge that may be used in a wide range of settings. In software engineering, there is relatively little focus on theories. In particular, there is little use and development of empirically-based theories. We propose, and illustrate with examples, an initial framework for describing software engineering theories, and give advice on how to start proposing, testing, modifying and using theories to support both research and practise in software engineering.

1. Introduction

> When should theorizing begin? "Theorizing should begin as soon as possible" What is the bulk of data necessary to begin theorizing? When is it neither too early nor too late to begin? Nobody can tell. It all depends on the novelty of the field and on the existence of theoretically-bent scientists prepared to take the risk of advancing theories that may not account for the data or that may succumb at the first onslaught from fresh information gathered in order to test the theories: this takes moral courage, particularly in an era dominated by the criterion of success, which is best secured by not attacking big problems. Two things, though, seem certain: namely, that premature theorizing is likely to be wrong – but not sterile – and that a long deferred beginning of theorizing is worse than any number of failures, because (1) it encourages the blind accumulation of information that may turn out to be mostly useless, and (2) a large bulk of information may render the beginning of theorizing next to impossible. (Bunge, 1967, p. 384).

In mature sciences, building theories is the way to gain and cumulate general knowledge. Some effort has been made to propose and test theories based on empirical evidence in software engineering (SE) (Hannay et al., 2007), but the use and building of empirically-based theories[1] in SE is still in its infancy.

---

[1] In this chapter, we focus on empirically-based theories; that is, theories that are built or modified on the basis of empirical research. Hence, in the reminder of this chapter, we use "theory" as short for "empirically-based theory" unless otherwise explicitly stated.

F. Shull et al. (eds.), *Guide to Advanced Empirical Software Engineering*.
© Springer 2008

There are many arguments in favour of using theories. They offer common conceptual frameworks that allow the organization and structuring of facts and knowledge in a concise and precise manner, thus facilitating the communication of ideas and knowledge. Theory is the means through which one may generalize *analytically* (Shadish et al., 2002; Yin, 2003), thus enabling generalization from situations in which statistical generalization is not desirable or possible, such as from case studies (Yin, 2003), across populations (Lucas, 2003), and indeed, from experiments in the social and behavioural sciences (Shadish et al., 2002), with which experiments in empirical SE often share essential features.

Our position is that theories should be useful; we are not interested in theories purely as an academic exercise. As such, we adhere to the view of the philosophical school of pragmatism, "both specific beliefs and methods of inquiry in general should be judged primarily by their consequences, by their usefulness in achieving human goals" (Godfrey-Smith, 2001). Since SE is an applied discipline, SE theories should, at least ultimately, be useful to the software industry. Since each SE setting is unique, the theories would need local adaptations to be directly useful in concrete cases. Figure 1 illustrates that both research communities and industry may benefit from using SE theories.

Arguments in favour of theory have been voiced in the SE community by other researchers as well (Basili, 1996; Endres and Rombach, 2003; Herbsleb and Mockus, 2003; Kitchenham et al., 2002; Land et al., 2003; Sauer et al., 2000; Tichy, 1998; Jørgensen and Sjøberg, 2004). However, there has been little focus on what the nature of SE theories should be like, and how they should be described and built. Hence, in this chapter, we suggest that the description of a theory should be divided into four parts: the *constructs* (*what* are the basic elements), *propositions* (*how* do the constructs interact), *explanations* (*why* are the propositions as specified) and *scope* (what is the universe of discourse in which the theory is applicable). Moreover, we propose a diagrammatic notation for

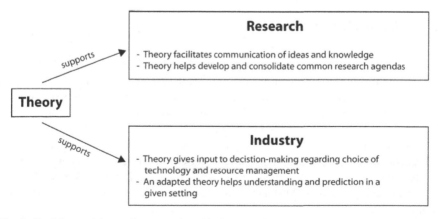

Fig. 1 Usefulness of theory for research and industry

describing the constructs, relationships and scope of a SE theory. In particular, each construct should belong to, or be derived from, one of the four archetype classes *Actor*, *Technology*, *Activity* and *Software System*. We believe that this structure for describing SE theories will support both researchers who propose theories and potential users of such theories.

The remainder of this chapter is organized as follows. Section 2 discusses categories of theories, elements of a theory and how theories may be formed and evaluated. Section 3 presents the framework for describing SE theories. Section 4 illustrates steps in theory building. Section 5 evaluates the example theory according to the criteria given in Sect. 2. Section 6 summarizes and describes topics for future work.

2. What Theories Are

The question of what constitutes a theory is a source of continuing discussion. Answers to this question depend on philosophical issues, practical issues, and not least, the field of study – indeed, the purpose of this chapter is to outline suggestions as to what theories for SE should be like.

There is no universally agreed upon definition of the concept of an empirically-based theory, nor is there any uniform terminology for describing theories. What is agreed is that it is difficult to provide necessary and sufficient conditions that delineate the concept of theory. Nevertheless, it is still possible to get a grasp on what a theory is. In sciences that are relevant to empirical SE, such as information systems, management, and social and behavioral sciences, discussions concerning theory tend to revolve around the following issues: (1) what a theory does, (2) what the elements of a theory are, (3) how theories are formed, and (4) how theories are evaluated. In the following, we summarize some of the answers to these questions.

2.1. What a Theory Does

The focus of this chapter is on theories that relate to observable phenomena, and that are built and modified based on empirical research. According to several accounts, this implies that a theory should offer explanations of why certain phenomena occur in the sense of predicting them. Moreover, the predictions should be testable, so as to render the theory refutable.

This familiar description of what a theory should do is hypothetico-deductive in nature, and would seem particularly suitable for empirical research. However, there are also other relevant modes of empirically-based theory. In the discipline of information systems, Gregor (2006) has classified theories into five types according to what they do.

I. *Analysis*. Theories of this type include descriptions and conceptualizations of "what is." Also included are taxonomies, classifications and ontologies in the sense of Gruber (1993). The lack of explicit explanation and prediction disqualifies this category as theory for many scholars (Bacharach, 1989; Sutton and Staw, 1995; Nagel, 1979).

II. *Explanation*. Theories of this type explicitly explain. What constitutes an explanation is a nontrivial issue. However, a common view is that an explanation answers to a question of *why* something is – or happens (rather than *what* happens) (Van Fraassen, 1980; Sandborg, 1998). Current views insist that explanations include notions of causality and asymmetry (if *A* explains *B*, then *B* should not also be a viable explanation of *A*) (Salmon, 1989).

III. *Prediction*. These theories are geared towards predicting what will happen, without explaining why. Examples are mathematical and probabilistic models of social and natural sciences.

IV. *Explanation and prediction*. Theories of this type combine the traits of II and III, and correspond to what many consider a "standard" conception of empirically-based theories.

V. *Design and action*. These theories describe "how to do" things, that is, they are prescriptive. Design science (Simon, 1996; Hevner et al., 2004; Hevner and March, 2003; March and Smith, 1995) is influential here. Although there is usually an implicit prediction that following the design principles will be beneficial, it is a matter of opinion as to whether this category describes theories (March and Smith, 1995).

These five types illustrate some of the diversity of what may be considered as theories. Our focus is very much on theories that explain phenomena. Thus, Types II and IV are those of primary interest. However, in practice, the explanatory *function* of a theory depends also on how the theory interacts with other theories and the current level of knowledge. For example, many view physical theories as belonging to Type III: Hawking states "that a physical theory is just a mathematical model and that it is meaningless to ask whether it corresponds to reality. All that one can ask is that its predictions should be in agreement with observation" (Hawking and Penrose, 1996, pp. 3–4), a sentiment also expressed by Feynman (1985). However, although they "merely" describe and predict what happens on the quantum level, these theories can thereby also be said to explain phenomena on the macro level (for example, why light refracts off oil films). Also, theories of Type I, that merely describe, may well provide explanations for other theories or phenomena. For example, the text comprehension model of Van Dijk and Kintsch (1983) describes how mental models of increasing complexity form during text comprehension. There are no explicit explanations or predictions, but in conjunction to program comprehension, the model provides an explanation as to why experts and novices follow different strategies when understanding code (Burkhardt et al., 2002). Generally, what constitutes an explanation is very much a pragmatic question.

2.2. What the Elements of Theory are

It seems to be broadly accepted that *constructs* and *relationships* between constructs constitute the basic building blocks of theories, and that it is important to
delineate a theory's area of application by specifying *scope conditions*. Inspired by
Dubin (1978), Whetten (1989) describes these elements as building blocks of theory in the following manner.

- *What* are the entities in terms of which a theory offers description, explanation,
  prediction or prescription? These are the constructs of a theory. Examples are
  "quarks" (quantum physics), "group process" (social science), "cognitive load"
  (cognitive psychology) and "programming skill" (SE). According to some epistemological positions (e.g., logical positivism), constructs must represent directly
  observable entities; while others (scientific realism) allow representations of hith-
  erto unobserved entities ("gravity," "quarks," "feelings") that are postulated to
  exist; while still others (anti-realism, instrumentalism, pragmatism) see constructs
  only as useful instruments to provide descriptions, explanations, etc. In SE, the
  constructs would typically relate to people, organization, technology, activities
  and software system.
- *How* are the constructs related? Relationships between constructs make up a
  theory's propositions, and describe how the constructs interact. Constructs and
  their relationships are the basic constituents of all five types of theory above.
  Describing how things are related may give rise to predictions (Type III and
  Type IV theories).
- *Why* do the relationships hold? Answers to this question are what give the theory
  explanatory power (Type II and Type IV theories). Parts of this may already be
  provided in the propositions established above. Explanatory power may also
  arise from a theory's interaction in a research context.
- *Where, When,* and for *Whom* does the theory apply? *Scope conditions* are
  statements that define the circumstances in which the theory's propositions
  are supposed to be applicable (Cohen, 1989).

2.3. How Theories are Formed

The ways in which theories are built, and from what, say much about what theories are.
Theories in SE may enter the stage in three ways to explain SE phenomena:

1. Theories from other disciplines may be used as they are.
2. Theories from other disciplines may be adapted to SE before use.
3. Theories may be generated from scratch in SE.

Modes (1) and (2) reflect that SE is a multidisciplinary discipline. Examples of the
first mode are the use of theories from cognitive psychology to explain phenomena
in program comprehension (Burkhardt et al., 2002; Abdel-Hamid et al., 1993;

Ramanujan et al., 2000), and theories from social and behavioural sciences to explain group interaction in requirements negotiation and inspection meetings (Land et al., 2003). Examples of the second mode can be found in (Sauer et al., 2000; Land et al., 2003; Herbsleb and Mockus, 2003), while the case described in Sects. 3–5 is an example of the third mode.

This chapter focuses on the concept of "SE theory," that is, theories with constructs and relationships defined from SE entities (Sect. 3). A SE theory thus arises through modes (2) and (3). The latter mode, generating theories from scratch, raises certain methodological issues as to how to build theories, and as a result, what theories are. In the following, we summarize some of these issues.

Referencing (Merton, 1968; Yin, 1984), Carroll and Swatman (2000) give three levels of sophistication or complexity of theories (for information systems):

Level 1. Minor working relationships that are concrete and based directly on observations
Level 2. Theories of the middle range that involve some abstraction but are still closely linked to observations
Level 3. All-embracing theories that seek to explain social behaviour. ("Social behavior" in (Carroll and Swatman, 2000) is here replaced with "SE.")

These levels set milestones in theory generation, but they may also represent full theories, depending on the rationale of the generation process one adheres to and the purpose of one's theory (Sect. 2.1). The development of SE theories from scratch (3) is in early stages, and immediate efforts will probably focus primarily on Levels 1 and 2. The case presented later produces a theory on Level 1.

The formation of theories is a process of continuous refinement and development involving inferences both from practise to theory as well as from theory to practise. Essential elements of this process are conceptual development, operationalization, confirmation or disconfirmation, and application, see Fig. 2.

Inductive methods sample singular observations in an enumerative fashion, in order to generate laws (covering laws) and empirical generalizations ("grounded theory" according to Glaser and Strauss (1967)). The inductive approach admits Levels 1 and 2 as *de facto* theories.

Other approaches view Levels 1 and 2 merely as intermediary steps towards, respectively, Levels 2 and 3. For example, the *abductive* approach to theory generation (Peirce, 1958; Haig, 2005) uses induction only as a first step to define phenomena (relatively stable, recurrent, general features) from observations, and then goes on to generate explanatory theories that explain these phenomena. Abductive inference (Peirce, 1958) introduces a creative aspect to theory generation, in that it transcends observation and is no longer strictly bound by facts (data). Instead, explanations rely on semantic models, i.e., simplified approximations of reality or useful conceptualizations (Franck, 2002; Rosenberg, 2001; Ruse, 1995). Examples are the ideal gas model and the rational choice model in economics that continue to be useful for educational purposes, even though empirical evidence disconfirms the literal interpretation of these models; and various models of the human brain as an information processing unit for explaining human cognition. This independence of

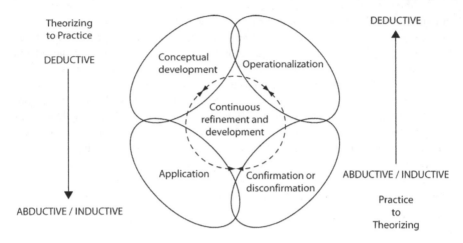

Fig. 2 Theory development consists of inductive and abductive aspects and deductive aspects, and may be initiated from both the practical or from the theoretical realm. Central to forming theory is conceptual development, that is, the conception of pertinent constructs and relationships through inductive and abductive processes. In order for the theory to be confirmed or disconfirmed in a deductive process, the conceptual elements must be operationalized into observable entities and measurable units on the one hand; and on the other hand, they must be applicable in real situations in practical disciplines. (The figure is adapted from (Lynham 2002)).

direct correspondences with reality is favored by aspects in the epistemological directions of anti-realism, instrumentalism and pragmatism. Such models typically constitute Type II and Type IV theories on Level 3. Methods such as induction and abduction are essentials in the conceptual development of theories built from scratch, see Fig. 2.

Deductive methods derive testable hypotheses from a theory and check these for empirical support.

2.4. How Theories are Evaluated

The evaluation of theories involves both logical and empirical standards (Cohen, 1989). However, in order to be able to evaluate the goodness of a theory, we must first establish the criteria by which it is to be evaluated. Several such criteria are described in the literature (Bunge, 1967; Cohen, 1989; Dubin, 1978). Which criteria one adheres to depends on the type of theory one is attempting to generate, as well as on the framework of generation one is adhering to. For the purpose of evaluating empirically-based theories in SE, we believe that the criteria shown in Table 1 are most relevant.

The *hypothetico-deductive* framework sees the criterion of *falsifiability* (Popper, 1959), as the demarcation criterion between science and non-science. It assumes

Table 1 Criteria for evaluating theories

Testability	The degree to which a theory is constructed such that empirical refutation is possible
Empirical support	The degree to which a theory is supported by empirical studies that confirm its validity
Explanatory power	The degree to which a theory accounts for and predicts all known observations within its scope, is simple in that it has few ad hoc assumption, and relates to that which is already well understood
Parsimony	The degree to which a theory is economically constructed with a minimum of concepts and propositions
Generality	The breadth of the scope of a theory and the degree to which the theory is independent of specific settings
Utility	The degree to which a theory supports the relevant areas of the software industry

the presence of a falsifiable theory, which gives rise to hypotheses that are tested by observation. Although this framework as such has been overtaken by other frameworks (Ruse, 1995), the principle of *testability* remains fundamental for empirically-based theories. There are no commonly agreed set of criteria for evaluating testability, but we will emphasize the criteria as follows: (1) The constructs and propositions of a theory should be clear and precise such that they are understandable, internally consistent and free from ambiguities. (2) It must be possible to deduce hypotheses from the theory's propositions, so that the theory may be confirmed or disconfirmed. (3) The theory's scope conditions must be explicitly and clearly specified, so that the domain or situations in which the theory should be (dis-)confirmed and applied is clear.

Note that in social and behavioral sciences, with which empirical SE shares many methodological issues, deeming a theory as false based on its predictions, is rarely feasible (Lindblom, 1987; Weick, 1989). If a prediction is not supported by empirical evidence, alternative theories or refinements of existing theories are sought, rather than theory rejection; or a new phenomenon is defined, which in turn starts the theory generation process for *that* phenomenon. Moreover, several theories may provide descriptions, explanations, etc. for a given phenomenon; all of which may be empirically adequate in the sense of not having been disconfirmed (Rosenberg, 2001; Haig, 2005). One must therefore have criteria that give inferences to *best* descriptions, explanations, predictions, etc. Therefore, in addition to testability, other theory appraisal criteria are equally important.

Related to testability is the degree to which a theory is supported by empirical evidence. Such evidence is also important in choosing among alternative descriptions, explanations, predictions, etc. *Empirical support* requires that the theory is tested in empirical research. Pursuing empirical evidence has the added advantage of treating both confirming and disconfirming evidence as informative. Furthermore, pursuing such evidence clearly points in the direction of designing a series of studies that complement one another (Basili et al., 1999).

Explanatory power can be viewed as a theory's ability to provide explanations of why something happens. Two criteria are (Thagard, 1992): (1) *Analogy*, that is, the degree to which a theory is supported by analogy to well-established theories. Explanatory power is seen as increased if a theory's constructs and relationships are formulated in terms of what is familiar and understood. (2) *Explanatory breadth*, that is, the degree to which a theory accounts for and predicts all known observations within its scope. Some explanations apply to particular events, while others apply to general phenomena or regularities. Nevertheless, if theory *B* can be deduced from theory *A*, then theory *A* has more explanatory breadth than theory *B* (Cohen, 1989). A theory of high explanatory breadth would include all relevant constructs and relationships, and account for all known data in the field to which it applies. Thus, the broader the scope of a theory (i.e., the range of phenomena encompassed by the theory), the greater the explanatory breadth of its propositions.

Parsimony is the extent to which unnecessary constructs and propositions are excluded. It is defined in (Bacharach, 1989) as the ratio of propositions to testable hypotheses; the more hypotheses a proposition accounts for, the better. Thus parsimony interacts with explanatory (and predictive) power. There is a delicate balance with explanatory breadth, i.e., should some factors be deleted because they add little additional value to our understanding? Or as Whetten (1989, p. 490) formulated it: "Sensitivity to the competing virtues of parsimony and comprehensiveness is the hallmark of a good theorist."

Generality pertains to the extent to which a theory has a wide scope and how setting-independent the theory is. A major purpose of generalizing is to increase the explanatory breadth of a theory (Cohen, 1989). However, there is a trade-off here: Higher generality means broader applicability, but may demand more effort in operationalizing constructs and relationships to a given situation; while lesser generality might make a theory immediately applicable, but may compromise its explanatory power by abandoning explanation in terms of basic underlying mechanisms. Nevertheless, sensitivity to context is especially important for empirically-based theories: "Observations are embedded and must be understood within a context. Therefore, authors of inductively generated theories have a particular responsibility for discussing limits of generalizability" (Whetten, 1989, p. 492).

Finally, and of particular importance in an applied field, such as SE, is the *utility* of a theory, which refers to the degree to which the propositions of the theory can be used as input to decision-making, understanding and prediction in a given industrial setting (cf. Fig. 1). A good theory would thus be able to reduce the complexity of the empirical world, or in the words of Kurt Lewin (1945): "There is nothing so practical as a good theory." The utility aspect is far from new; about a century ago, this was also the focus of the pragmatists John Dewey (1899–1924) and William James (1907): "An idea agrees with reality, and is therefore true, if and only if it is successfully employed in human action in pursuit of human goals and interests, that is, if it leads to the resolution of a problematic situation in Dewey's terms."[2]

---

[2] The Internet Encyclopedia of Philosophy, http://www.iep.utm.edu/d/dewey.htm

3. Framework for Describing SE Theories

An SE theory is supposed to explain or predict phenomena occurring in SE. The typical SE situation is that an *actor* applies *technologies* to perform certain activities on an (existing or planned) *software system*. These high-level concepts or "archetype classes" with examples of sub-concepts or subclasses are listed in Table 2. One may also envisage collections of (component) classes for each of the (sub) classes. For example, component classes of a software system may be requirement specifications, design models, source and executable code, test documents, various kinds of documentation, etc.

In addition, appropriate characteristics of the classes, and their relative effect, should also be identified and measured. For example, the usefulness of a technology for a given activity may depend on characteristics of the software engineers, such as their experience, education, mental ability, personality, motivation, and knowledge of a software system, including its application domain and technological environment. Note that contexts or environments are supposed to be part of the descriptions of the respective archetype classes.

Hence, we propose that the constructs of an SE theory should typically be associated with these archetype classes themselves, any subclass specialised from them, possibly successively, or any class that is a component of the archetype classes or subclasses. The constructs could also be any of the attributes of those classes. An SE theory may be defined as a theory that includes at least one construct that is SE specific. For example, if the theory only relates to Actor, then the actor must be a software engineer or an SE team, SE project, etc.

The challenge of selecting or defining appropriate subclasses or component classes that represent constructs of a theory illustrates the need for commonly accepted taxonomies in SE. If the constructs of SE theories do not follow from well-defined and well-understood categories of phenomena, then new theories will frequently require new constructs, and as a consequence theories become difficult to understand and to relate to each other. Hence, development of taxonomies is needed to support theory building.

In the social and behavioural sciences, several scholars argue that theories should be general in the sense of being independent of time and place (Markovsky, 1994; Wagner, 1994; Cohen, 1989). SE theories, being more applied, and at the

Table 2 Framework for SE theories

Archetype class	Subclasses
Actor	Individual, team, project, organisation or industry
Technology	Process model, method, technique, tool or language
Activity	Plan, create, modify or analyze (a software system); see Sjøberg et al. (2005)
Software system	Software systems may be classified along many dimensions, such as size, complexity, application domain, business/scientific/student project or administrative/embedded/real time, etc.

current stage of development, would seem to be somewhat dependent of both time and place. The fact that reality changes also in the SE world means that the validity or usefulness of an SE theory may be temporary. This, in turn, might indicate that *time* should be a factor of an SE theory, for example, change in education, and thus skill, of software engineers may change the validity of a theory. However, we would recommend not including time as part of the theory, but rather attempt to identify the underlying factors that may change over time. In the example of skill above, one should indicate in either the propositions or scope that the theory applies for a certain skill level.

Similarly, *place* is not interesting in SE per se. Place may be a placeholder for cultural, organisational and technological context factors that may affect a theory. However, we would also in this case urge scholars to be explicit on the underlying factors that, we believe, would be associated with one of the four archetype classes.

The constructs, propositions and their explanations, and the scope of a SE theory should be explicitly and clearly presented. We will illustrate how these four parts may be used in a simple example theory. This example is meant to illustrate the main initiating steps of building an SE theory from scratch (Mode (3) at Level 1, Sect. 2.3). Table 3 shows the constructs, the propositions, two examples of explanations, and the scope of an initial theory of the effect of using a development method based on UML (Booch et al., 1999) (in contrast to not using a thorough and systematic method covering all the phases from requirements analysis to testing). The background and steps in the development of the theory will be described in Sect. 4. For space considerations, only explanations E4 and E5, corresponding to, respectively, propositions P4 and P5 are shown in Table 3. The archetype classes associated with the respective constructs are shown in Fig. 3.

We also propose a notation (partly based on UML) to illustrate theories graphically. Figure 3 shows the relationships among the constructs of the UML-based development theory, including what affects what, using this notation. The notation has the following informal semantics:

A construct is represented as a class or an attribute of a class. A class is drawn as a box, and its name is written in the top of the box, e.g., "Distributed project" in Fig. 3). A class may be a subclass (using the UML generalization arrow) or a component class (drawn as a box within another box, e.g., "Team" is a component of "Distributed project"). Typically, if the construct is a particular value of a variable, then the construct is modelled as a subclass or component-class, e.g., the value "Distributed project" of the variable "Actor." On the other hand, if focus is on the variation of values, then the construct is a variable that is modeled as an attribute, e.g., "Costs." An attribute is written as a text in the lower part of a class box (below a horizontal bar).

A relationship is modelled as an arrow; an arrow from A to B means that A affects B, where A is a class or an attribute, and B is an attribute. In a relationship, B may also be a relationship itself, represented by an arrow. A is then called a moderator, e.g., "Training" in Fig. 3. This means that A affects the direction and/or strength of the effect of the relationship B (Baron and Kenny, 1986). The relationships

Table 3 Constructs, propositions, example explanations and scope of the theory of UML-based development

Constructs

C1	*UML-based development method*
C2	*Costs* (total number of person hours in the project)
C3	*Communication* (ease of discussing solutions within development teams and in reviews)
C4	*Design* (perceived structural properties of the code)
C5	*Documentation* (the documentation of the system for the purpose of passing reviews as well as for expected future maintainability)
C6	*Testability* (more efficient development of test cases and better quality, i.e., better coverage)
C7	*Training* (training in the UML-based method before the start of the project)
C8	*Coordination* (of requirements and teams)
C9	*Legacy code* (code that has not been reverse engineered to UML-models)

Propositions

P1	The use of a UML-based development method increases costs
P2	The use of a UML-based development method positively affects communication
P3	The use of a UML-based development method positively affects design
P4	The use of a UML-based development method positively affects documentation
P5	The use of a UML-based development method positively affects testability
P6	The positive effects of UML-based development are reduced if training is not sufficient and adapted
P7	The positive effects of UML-based development are reduced if there is insufficient coordination of modelling activities among distributed teams working on the same project
P8	The positive effects of UML-based development are reduced if the activity includes modification of legacy code

Explanations

E4	The documentation is
	– More complete
	– More consistent due to traceability among models and between models and code
	– More readable, and makes it easier to find specific information, due to a common format
	– More understandable for non-technical people
	– May be viewed from different perspectives due to different types of diagram
E5	Test cases based on UML models
	– Are easier to develop
	– Can be developed earlier
	– Are more complete
	– Have a more a unified format
	Moreover, traceability from requirements to code and test cases makes it is easier to identify which test cases must be run after an update

Scope

	The theory is supposed to be applicable for distributed projects creating and modifying large, embedded, safety-critical subsystems, based on legacy code or new code

are specified further into propositions of the theory, as indicated in Fig. 3; the propositions P6–P8 are examples of moderators.

The scope of the theory is also illustrated in the diagram. Scope conditions are typically modelled as subclasses or component classes. Figure 3 shows that our

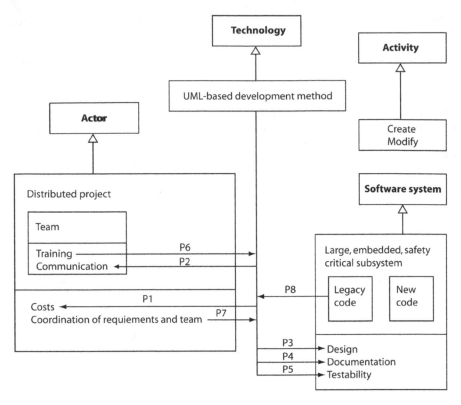

Fig. 3 A theory for the effect of UML-based development

example theory is constrained to "Distributed projects," "Create, modify" activities, and "large, embedded, safety critical subsystems" of a software system. This means, for example, that "Plan" and "Analyse" (two other subclasses of the archetype class "Activity") are outside the scope of this theory. In this example, all the archetype classes are included, but, generally, if any of the archetype classes are not included, then it is assumed that the theory is so general that it is independent of those classes. Note that one purpose of defining the four archetype classes is that we claim that any scholar who propose a SE theory should at least consider whether all of them should be included and specifed. For example, a theory of group performance in software development technical review (Sauer et al., 2000) was perceived by Land et al. (2003) to be too general for a SE context, and was thus specialised to also include, for example, dependencies to various components of a software system, such as requirements documents, designs, codes, test cases/plans and user manuals.

4. Steps in Building SE Theories

The theory-building process in an applied discipline such as SE is a continuous and iterative process of proposing, testing, and modifying theories. We do not always have to start from scratch when proposing a new theory; we can often start the process by adapting and modifying existing theories either from within SE or from related disciplines. However, in many cases, there are no established theories, neither in SE nor in the related disciplines, that are relevant for answering important SE research questions. In these cases, we may attempt to build theories by conducting, for example, case studies and experiments. We may also establish theories by reviewing and synthesizing related research in SE or by reviewing and synthesizing relevant research in related disciplines. Section 4.1 describes five steps in the building of theories. Section 4.2 illustrates each step by an example from an exploratory case study of UML-based development. Note that in practice these steps will often be carried out iteratively and partly in parallel.

4.1. Five Steps in Theory Building

4.1.1. Step 1: Defining the Constructs of the Theory

The first step of the theory-building process involves identifying and defining the constructs of the theory. In the context of this first step, there are five ways in which we might seek to make a theoretical contribution (Weber, 2003):

- Defining new constructs as the basis for building a new theory about some phenomena. These constructs might encompass phenomena that have not been the focus of prior theories. Alternatively, they might conceive phenomena that have been the focus of prior theories, but in a different way. As a result, we need to build a new theory of the phenomena that reflects this conception.
- Introducing new constructs into an existing theory to better account for the phenomena that are the focus of the theory.
- Deleting constructs from an existing theory to provide a more parsimonious account of the phenomena that are the focus of the theory.
- Adding and deleting constructs from an existing theory to provide a different, and hopefully better, account of the phenomena that are the focus of the theory.
- Defining the constructs of an existing theory more precisely or conceptualizing them in somewhat different ways.

4.1.2. Step 2: Defining the Propositions of the Theory

The second step of the theory-building process consists of specifying the propositions of the theory. In the context of this second step, there are four ways in which we might seek to make a theoretical contribution (Weber, 2003):

- Defining new propositions among existing or new constructs in a theory to better account for the phenomena that are the focus of the theory.
- Deleting propositions among the constructs of an existing theory to provide a more parsimonious account of the phenomena that are the focus of the theory.
- Adding and deleting propositions among the constructs of an existing theory to provide a different, and hopefully better, account of the phenomena that are the focus of the theory.
- Define the propositions in an existing theory more precisely or conceptualize them in somewhat different ways, for example, by specifying the functional form of a proposition previously conceived as a simple association between two constructs.

4.1.3. Step 3: Providing Explanations to Justify the Theory

The third step of the theory-building process, providing explanations – the "why" – of the theory, is probably the most challenging. The core issue of this step is to provide explicit assumptions and logical justifications for the constructs and propositions of the theory. In the context of this third step, there are five ways in which we might seek to make a theoretical contribution:

- Explicitly stating the assumptions of the conceptual underpinnings of the constructs and propositions of the theory.
- Challenging or extending existing knowledge of the constructs and propositions of the theory.
- Borrowing perspectives from other disciplines to explain the constructs and propositions of the theory.
- Providing logical justifications based on interpretations of an empirical study.
- Providing logical justifications based on interpretations of a synthesis of all prior empirical evidence within the scope of the theory. Such synthesis, which possibly includes replicated studies, might also expand the scope of a theory:

> Methodological authorities generally regard replication, or what is also referred to as "repeating a study," to be a crucial aspect of the scientific method. ... Heavily differentiated replication leads to extensions of the scope of the result and hence its subsequent practical applicability, that is, to other firms, other industries, different types of executives, other years, or whatever. ... Varying the conditions between different replications not only extends the scope of the generalization and determines its limits, but also tells us about some of the factors that do, or do not, affect the result *causally*.
>
> (Lindsay and Ehrenberg, 1993)

4.1.4. Step 4: Determining the Scope of the Theory

The fourth step of the theory-building process is concerned with determining the scope of the theory, which is especially important for empirically-based SE theories.

In the context of this fourth step, there are two ways in which we might seek to make a theoretical contribution (Weber, 2003):

- Specifying more precisely the values of a construct for which the theory will hold, or conversely, specifying more precisely the values of a construct for which the theory will not hold.
- Specifying more precisely the combinations of values of the constructs for which the theory will hold, or conversely, specifying more precisely the combinations of values of the constructs for which the theory will not hold.

4.1.5. Step 5: Testing the Theory Through Empirical Research

The last step of the theory-building process involves examination of the validity of the theory's predictions through empirical studies. In the context of this last step, different types of empirical studies might be applied, which entails different method-specific sub-steps as well as method-specific strengths and limitations in the theory-building process. For example, the following separates case studies from experiments with respect to theory building:

- In case studies, new insights typically evolve based on the data, while in experiments, previous knowledge must often be applied to explain results.
- In case studies, hypotheses are examined for each case study unit, while in experiments they are examined for an aggregate of the units using statistical hypothesis building/testing.
- Theories derived from case studies tend to become less general than those derived from experiments.
- Theories derived from case studies typically have more focus on explanations than those derived from experiments.

In testing a theory, the following general steps must, nevertheless, be considered:

- Choosing an appropriate research setting and sample. The sample does generally not only include the actors, but also the sample of technologies, activities (tasks) and systems.
- Operationalizing theoretical constructs into empirical variables.
- Operationalizing theoretical propositions into empirically testable hypotheses.

For the purpose of describing the extent to which a theory has been validated, we introduce the two terms *scope of interest* and *scope of validity* of a theory (Fig. 4). "Scope of interest of a theory" is what we have simply denoted "scope of theory" above. In contrast, a theory's scope of validity refers to that part of the scope of interest in which the theory has actually been validated. The scope of validity of a theory is the accumulated scopes of validity of the results of the studies that have tested the theory, or the studies from which the theory has been generated. Figure 4 shows that three studies have been conducted, and the area made up by the three scopes of validity of the three studies corresponds to the scope of validity of the theory (so far). The ultimate goal is that the scope of validity becomes equal

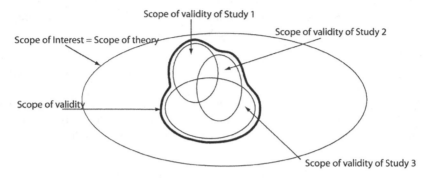

Fig. 4 Scope of interest versus scope of validity

to the scope of interest. The first consideration to make in testing a theory is to make sure that the study fits the theory's scope of interest. Otherwise, the results would be irrelevant to that theory. Moreover, in a given study, typically only a part of the scope of interest can be tested. If that part has not been tested before, and is supported by the study, then the current scope of validity has been extended. However, note that empirical support or inconsistencies between theoretical propositions and empirical observations do not necessarily imply that the theory is validated or disconfirmed, respectively. Judgements regarding the validity of the theory require that the study is well conducted, and not encumbered with, for example,

- Invalid operationalization of theoretical constructs and propositions
- Inappropriate research design
- Inaccuracy in data collection and data analysis
- Misinterpretation of empirical findings

4.2. Example of Generating Theory from an Exploratory Case Study: An Initial Theory for UML-Based Development in Large Projects

The example theory presented in Sect. 3 was derived from an exploratory case study that was conducted in the global company ABB (Anda et al., 2006; Anda and Hansen 2006). The purpose of the case study was to investigate the use of a UML-based method, and in particular to identify benefits and challenges, as well as their causes, of applying such a development method in a large, distributed development project. The goal of the project was to develop a new safety-critical process-control system based on several existing systems. The development took place at four sites in three countries. The total workforce comprised approximately 230 people, and approximately 100 of them were involved in using the UML-based method. This was the first project in ABB with large-scale use of UML. The company consequently wanted to find out whether the UML-based development method improved the quality of the development process and the resulting software product compared with earlier projects that had not used UML.

Data was collected through individual interviews, questionnaires and project documents.

4.2.1. Step 1: Defining the Constructs

In this case study, as is frequently the situation in case studies, much of the data collected was in the form of texts, for example, transcripts of interviews and project documents. These texts were subject to qualitative analysis based on the principles of "grounded theory" (Strauss and Corbin, 1998), which is an established technique for distilling concepts from textual data. Central concepts are candidate constructs for a theory. Hence, the constructs of a theory derived from one or more case studies in this way are well grounded in the data of the case(s).

The interviews of the case study were analyzed using the grounded-theory principles of open, axial and selective coding. In open coding, categories of phenomena are identified; in axial coding, categories are related to each other; and in selective coding, the central categories that are candidates for constructs are identified. The following characteristics of the actors (project, teams and individuals), activities and software system, with corresponding definitions for use in this context, were identified and evolved into the constructs given in Table 3.

4.2.2. Step 2: Defining the Propositions

After identifying the constructs, the next step in text analysis, according to "grounded theory," is to analyze emerging relationships between the constructs. In the ABB case study, relationships were identified from the interviews, for example, relationships were identified between the use of the UML-based development method and several positive aspects of the project documentation such as more documentation, better structured documentation. The identified relationships were checked against each case, that is, against each interview. Relationships that had clear support from the data were candidates for being included in the propositions of the theory. Furthermore, the relationships were validated using questionnaires (although not all relationships could be validated in this way) and compared with literature on UML-based development. Finally, the relationships that were supported by all the data, and that included the candidate constructs identified in Step 1, were aggregated in to the propositions described in Table 3.

Ideally, we would have liked the relationships expressed in the propositions to be more quantitative, in accordance with the view of Dubin (1978, p. 170): "the proposition predicts the specific values that one unit will have in relation to the values of another." Hence, the propositions listed in Table 3 may be regarded as initial propositions. Follow-up studies may help quantify the propositions to some extent, but it seems unrealistic in the near future to provide quantitative propositions in SE. At least, another of magnitude of more empirical studies would then be needed (Sjøberg et al., 2007).

4.2.3. Step 3: Providing Explanations

Explanations for each proposition were identified in the same way as were the propositions. The difference between a proposition and an explanation is that the former is a relationship among constructs, and the latter is a relationship among constructs and other categories, which are not central enough to become constructs (see explanation of "grounded theory"-terminology given under step (1)). This step is typically more elaborate in theories derived from case studies than in theories derived from experiments, because qualitative data, which typically are better at explaining phenomena, are more frequently collected. For two of the propositions, the corresponding explanations were shown in Table 3.

4.2.4. Step 4: Determining the Scope

Since this theory is derived from "grounded theory," the scope of validity of the study would form the starting point for the scope of the theory, which would generally be too narrow to be interesting for a theory. Nevertheless, defining the initial scope is not trivial; the number of potential scope conditions of a case study is large, and there is little guidance in the SE literature regarding how the scope of a case study should be documented, Kitchenham et al. (2002) state: "Be sure to specify as much of the industrial context as possible. In particular, clearly define the entities, attributes and measures that are capturing the contextual information."

In practice, judgment must be exercised in the description of scope conditions and the level of detail of their description. Below we will describe what we consider to be the relevant conditions for the scope of validity of the theory (which is the same as the scope of this case study since the theory is only based on one study so far, see Fig. 3). We will then describe what we think should be the scope of the theory. The scope of validity is too narrow as a scope of a theory, because it would make the theory applicable to very few software projects. This theory is at Level 1 (Sect. 2.3), which indicates a scope of interest relatively similar to the scope of validity of the study, but based on the study and on other work on UML-based development, we propose a wider scope of the theory.

Technology

- *Scope of validity:* In the UML-based development method applied in the study, use case diagrams, sequence diagrams and class diagrams were compulsory, while the use of other UML diagrams was at the discretion of the individual teams.
- *Scope of interest:* UML-based development methods

Actor

- *Scope of validity:* The project was distributed with development at four sites in three countries. Some of the teams were also distributed with team members working at different sites. The teams were medium-sized (typically 8–10 people in each team), the team members mostly had good knowledge of the application domain, their educational background was typically at the level of an MSc, and most were newcomers to the use of UML at the start of the project, but became quite proficient in UML during the project due to it's size.
- *Scope of interest:* Projects with distributed teams

Software system

- *Scope of validity:* The system to be developed was large (approximately 1,000 requirements and 3–4 mill. lines of code), which was divided into approximately ten large subsystems. The software was embedded, C and C++ were used as programming languages, the system was safety-critical and the development followed the requirements of the safety standard IEC61508. Some parts of the system were developed from scratch while others were based on legacy code of existing systems.
- *Scope of interest:* Large, embedded, safety-critical system, possibly based on legacy code.

Activity

Both scope of validity and scope of interest are "create" and "modify."

4.2.5. Step 5: Testing the Theory

This example theory has not yet been tested.

5. Evaluating the Example Theory

This section evaluates the initial theory for UML-based development in large projects described in Sect. 3 according to the criteria presented in Sect. 2.

Testability

The constructs and propositions of the theory are understandable, internally consistent and free from ambiguities, at least from the point of view of developers and practitioners familiar with the topic of the theory. Hypotheses can be derived from the propositions, the scope conditions are clearly defined, although some of the constructs, such as "large" and "distributed," assume the existence of taxonomies of software systems in order to be precisely defined. The theory can be empirically tested in case studies or surveys of development projects that fall within the scope of the theory. Most material for such testing, in the form of interview guides and analysis procedures are available for use, see (Anda et al., 2006). Such empirical testing would consist in testing whether the propositions of the theory are supported in other projects. The scope condition indicating "large subsystems" means that it is difficult, that is, would be very costly, to test this theory in experiments. We consider the testability of this theory as moderate.

Empirical support

There are few other empirical studies on benefits and challenges of UML-based development. Three empirical studies on UML-based development have a similar or wider scope than the scope of our theory (Baker et al., 2005; Petit, 2004; Dobing and Parsons, 2006). These studies all have a slightly different focus than the study on which our theory is based, but they support different propositions of our theory; (Petit, 2004) supports P2 on communications, (Dobing and Parsons, 2006) supports P4 on documentation, and (Baker et al., 2005) supports P5 on testing. Furthermore, two studies on UML-based development have different scope conditions; Arisholm et al. (2006) report a controlled experiment with students performing maintenance activities. The results support P3 on design. MacDonald et al. (2005) report a student project that supports P2 on communication and P8 on legacy development. If more empirical studies are conducted on UML-based development, it may be possible to extend the scope of our theory and in that case those two studies may also be included as part of the empirical support for the theory. Since the example theory is supported or partly supported by all comparable empirical studies on UML-based development, we consider the empirical support for this theory to be moderate.

Explanatory power

Many factors influence the results of software creation and modification activities. Hence, we expect that SE theories will seldom have high explanatory power. This theory is at Level 1 (see Sect. 2) and accounts for some, but far from all aspects of software creation and modification with the use of UML-based development. We consider the explanatory power of the theory as low.

Parsimony

A theory derived from one case and with the use of "grounded theory" will typically be quite complex, with many constructs and propositions, but we have attempted to use a minimum of constructs and propositions in this theory. We consider the parsimony of the theory as moderate.

Generality

The scope of this theory is narrow, something which is typical for theories at Level 1 theories. We consider the generality of the theory as low.

Utility

This theory can be used in the decision making in projects for which it is relevant with little adaptation. We consider the utility of the theory as high.

6. Summary and Future Work

The motivation for the work reported in this chapter is that without a stronger focus on theory building in the empirical SE community, we will probably continue to produce many isolated, exploratory studies, which will limit our ability to aggregate knowledge. Even a weak theory may frequently be better than no theory.

We have described a framework that we believe will benefit the process of proposing, testing and modifying and describing SE theories. We illustrated the framework with an example of how to build theories systematically from an exploratory case study using the technique of "grounded theory." Future work will include describing how to build theories from experiments and from systematic reviews of the SE literature.

The framework suggested above is not intended as "silver bullets" to build and document theories; theory development requires significant reflection and skill regarding study design and argumentation. Hence, there is a need for more systematic teaching of research methods and theory building as part of SE education.

During our work with a survey to identify and describe theories used in SE experiments (Hannay et al., 2007), we experienced that there is no simple way of identifying empirically-based theories that are used or built in SE. There are web sites for collecting and documenting theories in psychology[3] and information systems[4]. In the same manner, Simula Research Laboratory has begun building a site for empirically-based SE theories, see se-theory.simula.no. We believe that this will make it easier for scholars to find relevant theories for their research and that this will stimulate the community to collaborate on building new theories and on improving existing theories.

Acknowledgements We would like to thank Magne Jørgensen and Reidar Conradi for useful discussions and insightful comments, and Chris Wright for proofreading the chapter.

References

Abdel-Hamid, T.K., Sengupta, K. and Ronan, D., Software project control: an experimental investigation of judgement with fallible information, *IEEE Transactions on Software Engineering*, 19(6): 603–612, 1993.

Anda, B.C.D. and Hansen, K., A case study on the application of UML in legacy development. In *ISESE'2006 (Fifth ACM-IEEE International Symposium on Empirical Software Engineering)*, J. Maldonado and C. Wohlin (eds.), Rio de Janeiro, Brasil, ACM Press, September 21–22, pp. 124–133, 2006.

Anda, B.C.D., Hansen, K., Gullesen, I. and Thorsen, H.K., Experiences from using a UML-based development method in a large safety-critical project, *Empirical Software Engineering*, 11(4): 555–581, 2006.

---

[3] http://changingminds.org/explanations/theories/theories.htm

[4] http://www.istheory.yorku.ca/

Arisholm, E., Briand, L.C., Hove, S.E. and Labiche, Y., The impact of UML documentation on software maintenance: an experimental evaluation, *IEEE Transactions on Software Engineering*, 32(6): 365–381, 2006.

Bacharach, S.B., Organizational theories: some criteria for evaluation, *Academy of Management Review*, 14(4): 496–515, 1989.

Baker, P., Loh, S. and Weil, F., Model-driven engineering in a large industrial context – motorola case study. In *MoDELS 2005, LNCS 3713*, L. Briand and C. Williams (eds.), New York, Springer-Verlag, pp. 476–491, 2005.

Baron, R.M. and Kenny, D.A., The moderator-mediator variable distinction in social psychological research: conceptual, strategic, and statistical considerations, *Personality and Social Psychology*, 51(6): 1173–1182, 1986.

Basili, V.R., Editorial, *Empirical Software Engineering*, 1(2), 1996.

Basili, V.R., Shull, F. and Lanubile, F., Building knowledge through families of experiments, *IEEE Transaction on Software Engineering*, 24(4): 456–473, 1999.

Booch, G., Rumbaugh, J. and Jacobson, I. *The Unified Modeling Language User Guide*, Boston, MA, Addison-Wesley, 1999.

Bunge, M., *Scientific Research: The Search for a System*, New York, Springer-Verlag, 1967.

Burkhardt, J.M., Detienne, F. and Wiedenbeck, S., Object-oriented program comprehension: effect of expertise, task and phase, *Empirical Software Engineering*, 7(2): 115–156, 2002.

Carroll, J. and Swatman, P.A., Structured-case: a methodological framework for building theory in information systems research, *European Journal of Information Systems*, 9: 235–242, 2000.

Cohen, B., *Developing Sociological Knowledge: Theory and Method*, 2nd edn, Belmont, CA, Wadsworth Publishing, 1989.

Dobing, B. and Parsons, J., How UML is used, *Communications of the ACM*, 49(5): 109–113, 2006.

Dewey, J., *The Middle Works, 1899–1924*, Vol. 15, J.A. Boydston, (ed.), Carbondale, Southern Illinois University Press, 1976–1983.

Dubin, R., *Theory Building*, Free Press, New York, 1978.

Endres, A. and Rombach, D., *A Handbook of Software and Systems Engineering. Empirical Observations, Laws and Theories. Fraunhofer IESE Series on Software Engineering*, Pearson Education Limited, 2003.

Feynman, R.P., *QED – The Strange Theory of Light and Matter*, Penguin Science, Harmondsworth, 1985.

Franck, R., *The Explanatory Power of Models*, Dordrecht, Kluwer Academic Publishers, 2002.

Glaser H.G. and Strauss A.L., *The Discovery of Grounded Theory: Strategies for Qualitative Research*, Hawthorne, NY, Aldine Publishing Company, 1967.

Godfrey-Smith, P., Pragmatism: philosophical aspects, *International Encyclopedia of the Social & Behavioral Sciences*, 17: 11954–11958, 2001.

Gregor, S., The nature of theory in information systems, *MIS Quarterly*, 30(3): 611–642, 2006.

Gruber, T.R., A translation approach to portable ontology specifications, *Knowledge Acquisition*, 5(2): 199–220, 1993.

Haig, B.D., An abductive theory of scientific method, *Psychological Methods*, 10(4): 371–388, 2005.

Hannay, J.E., Sjøberg, D.I.K. and Dybå, T., A systematic review of theory use in software engineering experiments, *IEEE Transactions on Software Engineering*, 33(2): 87–107, 2007.

Hawking, S. and Penrose R., *The Nature of Space and Time*, Princeton University Press, Princeton, NJ, 1996.

Herbsleb, D.J. and Mockus, A., Formulation and preliminary test of an empirical theory of coordination in software engineering, *ACM SIGSOFT Software Engineering Notes*, 28(5): 138–147, 2003.

Hevner, A.R. and March, S.T., The information systems research cycle, *IEEE Computer Society*, 36(119): 111–113, 2003.

Hevner, A., March, S.T., Park, J., and Ram, S, Design science research in information systems, *MIS Quarterly,* 28(1): 75–105, 2004.

James, W., *Pragmatism: A New Name for Some Old Ways of Thinking*, New York: Longman Green and Co, 1907.

Jørgensen, M. and Sjøberg, D.I.K., Generalization and theory-building in software engineering research. In *Empirical Assessment in Software Engineering (EASE2004), IEE Proceedings,* pp. 29–36, 2004.

Kitchenham, B.A., Pfleeger, S.L., Pickard, L.M., Jones, P.W., Hoaglin, D.C., El Emam, K. and Rosenberg, J., Preliminary guidelines for empirical research in software engineering, *IEEE Transaction on Software Engineering,* 28(8): 721–734, 2002.

Land, L.P.W., Wong, B. and Jeffery, R., An extension of the behavioral theory of group performance in software development technical reviews, *Proceedings of the Tenth Asia-Pacific Software Engineering Conference Software Engineering Conference,* pp. 520–530, 2003.

Lewin, K., The research center for group dynamics at Massachusetts Institute of Technology, *Sociometry,* 8: 126–135, 1945.

Lindblom, C.E., Alternatives to validity. Some thoughts suggested by Campbell's guidelines, *Knowledge: Creation, Diffusion, Utilization,* 8: 509–520, 1987.

Lindsay, R.M. and Ehrenberg, A.S.C., The design of replicated studies, *The American Statistician,* 47: 217–228, 1993.

Lucas, J.W., Theory-testing, generalization, and the problem of external validity, *Sociological Theory,* 21: 236–253, 2003.

Lynham, S.A., The general method of theory-building research in applied disciplines, *Advances in Developing Human Resources,* 4(3): 221–241, 2002.

MacDonald, A., Russel, D. and Atchison, B. Model-driven development within a legacy system: an industry experience report, *Proceedings of the 2005 Australian Software Engineering Conference (ASWEC'2005). IEEE Computer Society,* pp. 14–22, April 2005.

March, S.T. and Smith, G.F., Design and natural science research on information technology, *Decision Support Systems,* 15(4): 251–266, 1995.

Markovsky, B., The structure of theories. In *Group Processes*, M. Foschi and E.J. Lawler, (eds.), Nelson-Hall Publishers, Chicago, pp. 3–24, 1994.

Merton, R.K., *Social Theory and Social Structure*, 3rd ed, The Free Press, New York, 1968.

Nagel, E., *The Structure of Science*, Hackett, Indianapolis, 1979.

Peirce, C.S., *Collected Papers*, Harvard University Press, Cambridge, MA, 1958.

Petit, R.G., Lessons learned applying UML in embedded software systems designs, *Proceedings of the Second IEEE Workshop on Software Technologies for Future Embedded and Ubiquitous Systems (WSTFEUS'04)*, Vienna, Austria, May 11–12, pp., 75–79, 2004.

Popper, K., *The Logic of Scientific Discovery*, Hutchison, London, 1959.

Ramanujan, S., Scamell, R.W. and Shah, J.R., An experimental investigation of the impact of individual, program, and organizational characteristics on software maintenance effort, *Journal of Systems and Software,* 54(2): 137–157, 2000.

Rosenberg, A., *Philosophy of Science: A Contemporary Introduction*, Routledge, London, 2001.

Ruse, M. (1995). Theory. *The Oxford Companion to Philosophy. T. Honderich*, Oxford University Press, New York, 870–871.

Salmon, W.C., Four decades of scientific explanation. In *Scientific Explanation*, P. Kitcher and W.C. Salmon, (eds.), *Minnesota Studies in the Philosophy of Science*, Vol. 13, Minnesota Press, Series, pp. 3–219, 1989.

Sandborg, D., Mathematical explanation and the theory of why-questions, *The British Journal for the Philosophy of Science,* 49(4): 603–624, 1998.

Sauer, C, Jeffery, D.R., Land, L. and Yetton, P., The effectiveness of software development technical reviews: a behaviorally Motivated program of research, *IEEE Transactions on Software Engineering,* 26(1): 1–14, 2000.

Shadish, W.R., Cook, T.D. and Campbell, D.T., *Experimental and Quasi-Experimental Designs for Generalized Causal Inference*, Houghton Mifflin, Boston, MA, 2002.

Simon, H.A., *The Sciences of the Artificial*, MIT Press, Cambridge, MA, 1996.

Sjøberg, D.I.K., Dybå, T. and Jørgensen, M., The future of empirical methods in software engineering research. In *Future of Software Engineering (FOSE '07)*, L. Briand and A. Wolf, (eds.), IEEE-CS Press, Minneapolis, US, pp. 358–378, 2007.

Sjøberg, D.I.K., Hannay, J.E., Hansen, O., Kampenes, V.B., Karahasanović, A., Liborg, N.-K. and Rekdal, A.C., A survey of controlled experiments in software engineering, *IEEE Transactions on Software Engineering*, 31(9): 733–753, 2005.

Strauss, A. and Corbin, J., *Basics of Qualitative Research: Techniques and Procedures for Developing Grounded Theory*, 2nd ed, Sage, Thousand Oaks, CA, 1998.

Sutton, R.I. and Staw, B.M., What theory is not, *Administrative Science Quarterly*, 40: 371–384, 1995.

Thagard, P., *Conceptual Revolutions*, Princeton University Press, Princeton, NJ, 1992.

Tichy, W.F., Should computer scientist experiment more? 16 excuses to avoid experimentation, *IEEE Computer*, 31(5): 32–40, 1998.

Van Dijk, T.A. and Kintsch, W., *Strategies of Discourse Comprehension*, Academic Press, New York, 1983.

Van Fraassen, B., *The Scientific Image*, Oxford University Press, New York, 1980.

Wagner, D.G., The growth of theories. In *Group Processes*, M. Foschi and E. J. Lawler, (eds.), Nelson-Hall Publishers, Chicago, pp. 25–42, 1994.

Weber, R., Editor's comments, *MIS Quarterly*, 27(3): 3–12, 2003.

Weick, K.E., Theory construction as disciplined imagination, *Academy of Management Review*, 14(4): 516–531, 1989.

Whetten, D.A., What constitutes a theoretical contribution, *Academy of Management Review*, 14(4): 490–495, 1989.

Yin, R.K., *Case Study Research: Design and Methods*, Sage Publications, Thousand Oaks, CA, 1984.

Yin, R.K., *Case Study Research: Design and Methods*, Applied Social Research Methods Series 5, 3rd ed, Sage Publications, Thousand Oaks, CA, 2003.

Chapter 13
Building Theories from Multiple Evidence Sources

Forrest Shull and Raimund L. Feldmann

Abstract As emphasized in other chapters of this book, useful results in empirical software engineering require a variety of data to be collected through different studies – focusing on a single context or single metric rarely tells a useful story. But, in each study, the requirements of the local context are liable to impose different constraints on study design, the metrics to be collected, and other factors. Thus, even when all the studies focus on the same phenomenon (say, software quality), such studies can validly collect a number of different measures that are not at all compatible (say, number of defects required to be fixed during development, number of problem reports received from the customer, total amount of effort that needed to be spent on rework). Can anything be done to build a useful body of knowledge from these disparate pieces?

This chapter addresses strategies that have been applied to date to draw conclusions from across such varied but valid data sets. Key approaches are compared and the data to which they are best suited are identified. Our analysis together with associated lessons learned provide decision support for readers interested in choosing and using such approaches to build up useful theories.

1. Introduction

Research in software engineering is often concerned with the development of new techniques, methods, or tools for software development. It has long been recognized that the weaknesses and benefits of such technologies can be identified by conducting empirical studies (Basili et al, 1986, 1999). Empirical information is necessary for researchers to refine the technologies, as well as for practitioners to understand when such technologies are likely to be useful. Empirical evidence can never *prove* that a technology will be useful under specific conditions, but such evidence helps build theories to that effect. The more evidence that can be accumulated, and the greater the extent to which the evidence is internally consistent, the more confidence can be had in the theories they support.

F. Shull et al. (eds.), *Guide to Advanced Empirical Software Engineering*.
© Springer 2008

The chapter by Sjøberg et al. (Sjøberg, 2007a) in this book discusses the difficulty of providing a precise definition of what a "theory" is. However, to avoid misconceptions, we adopt their convention of focusing on empirically-based theories, which are built on the basis of empirical research to offer explanations of why certain phenomena occur. We also adopt their criteria in saying that a good theory is constructed in such a way as to be testable; is supported by evidence, perhaps in the form of empirical studies; has explanatory power; contains the minimum number of concepts and prepositions; is independent of specific settings; and has relevance to the software industry. In accordance with Zelkowitz, we define empirical studies as a general form of research strategy that relies on analysis of the results of application in some context (Zelkowitz, 2001). Empirical studies include for example controlled experiments, case studies, and archival analyses.

Although a theory represents a proposed model of reality, these need not be formal models. An example of a theory that aims to support decision-making by practitioners might be, "When process conformance is good, software formal inspections will find and remove between 60% and 90% of the extant defects in an artifact, under typical conditions in many environments." Theories may also build implicit models by hypothesizing relationships between variables, such as "When applied by very small teams, the cost to apply software formal inspections may be prohibitive."

A single empirical study is a first step towards constructing theories related to the effectiveness of a technique, method, or tool. However, such single studies usually have a low power. The findings become more reliable (and we have greater confidence in the theories they support) if studies are replicated (i.e., are repeated or conducted in different settings). Similar findings in replications increase the confidence in the results. Multiple authors (e.g., Basili, 1999; Miller, 2000; Kitchenham et al, 2004) point out that it is necessary to accumulate the material of many studies to abstract robust and useful theories.

Based on our experiences, we define a "useful" theory as one which satisfies these criteria: (1) There must be traceability to the supporting data, such that a level of confidence is enabled. To have high confidence, there must be a rigorous way of showing which sources of evidence support a theory. (2) The theory must be abstract enough to be useful (i.e., it cannot hold only under certain unusual or unrealistic conditions, but it has to be relevant for some subset of software development projects).

Building theories is difficult, mainly because solid theories need to be supported by a significant body of evidence. But evidence is generated from many different environments, for many different reasons, and there are no universal standards for how to measure aspects of software development. For example, a researcher might want to theorize that a particular practice helps improve software quality. Supporting or extending this theory becomes difficult when some of the evidence on which it is based measures software quality in terms of customer satisfaction, some in terms of number of defects found after delivery, and some using the number of defects removed from work artifacts.

A number of techniques have been applied to accumulate bodies of knowledge and support theories based on them. The techniques range from informal, subjective, and unrigorous to formal, objective, and rigorous. In this chapter, we describe three such techniques and summarize the process for applying them. Since research techniques, just like development techniques, work well in some contexts and for some goals but not for all, we also assess all of the techniques along a standard set of dimensions to help understand the problems and conditions for which each is most appropriate.

2. Theory Building

After the more general introduction to the problem in the last section, we now take a closer look at the different tasks that need to be accomplished in order to build a useful body of knowledge. First, we will introduce a general process description of how theories can be built using available quantitative and qualitative evidence (Subsection 2.1). Based on these general process steps we will compare and contrast various existing approaches in the following sections. Second, we will identify and discuss a set of quality attributes for a body of knowledge (Subsection 2.2). This set of attributes will allow us to better classify the existing approaches.

2.1. A Process Model for Building Theories

Several approaches exist for how to build a body of knowledge out of discrete pieces of evidence. These approaches vary in specific details, such as the type of evidence considered for the evaluation, or in the way of handling different evidence pieces. However, all approaches need to integrate some essential process steps to be repeatable and systematic: (1) Define the topic, (2) identify search parameters, (3) find evidence, (4) analyze evidence, and (5) integrate evidence. Fig.1 displays how these steps are connected and emphasizes the iterative nature of the process.

For describing the process steps, and the basic activities associated with them, we will use the following schema:

Step number/name: Clearly identifies the process step.
Input: Lists products and preconditions needed to execute the process step.
Actions: Describes the basic activities performed in this process step.
Output: Identifies the products generated by the process and post conditions.
Comments: Provides a practical example of what needs to be done in this step or lists typical issues.

2.1.1. Define Topic

Before we can start collecting any evidence for a theory, the topic of the theory we want to describe needs to be defined. In this first step one has to clearly identify the object(s) that will be described by the theory. Ideally, this description not only

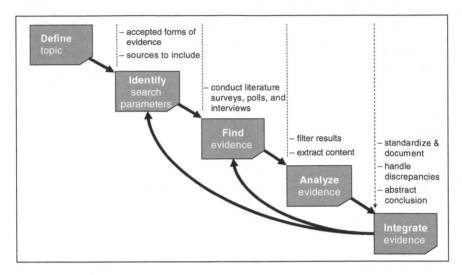

Fig. 1 Basic process steps for building a theory based on multiple pieces of evidence

identifies the topic(s) but also provides the basic definitions for key terms and concepts. Quality attributes, i.e., specific aspects of the object we are interested in, need to be included in this definition process, too. Examples for such quality attributes could be the effectiveness of the object regarding cost or time reduction.

This process step can be triggered for several reasons. Typical examples are the need for decision support on a given topic, or the interest of a researcher to identify missing studies in a certain field. As a result of this step we create a *Theory Topic Definition Document (TTDD)*, which will be the input and basic reference for the following process steps.

For formulating the goal in a more formal manner one might consider a specific template or other structured approaches. The Goal Question Metric (GQM) approach (Basili, 1994b; van Solingen and Berghout, 1999), for instance, provides a specific goal template for describing measurement goals. We have found the GQM goal template, as depicted in Fig.2 useful for helping to specify fairly straightforward theories, since it helps make explicit the object that is being theorized about as well as the properties of interest. Templates that are more comprehensive, for instance, have been proposed in Sjøberg (2007b).

Note that some researchers in the social sciences recommend mapping studies, prior to performing systematic review, in order to identify patterns in the research literature and identify areas suitable for systematic literature review or meta analysis or where more primary studies are needed (Petticrew and Roberts, 2006). This activity, however, may be most relevant under certain conditions or study topics.

Analyze the	[object]
for the purpose of	[purpose]
with respect to	[quality aspect]
from the perspective of	[view point]
in the context of	[context]

Fig. 2 GQM goal template according to Basili et al

Table 1 Overview of process step 1

Step number and name	❶ Define topic
Input	This process step can be started at any time; no specific input documents are required
Actions	Clearly describe the theory to be developed; provide basic definitions and include quality attributes
Output	Theory Topic Definition Document (TTDD)
Comments	Definitions may not be necessary if the relevant terms are commonly known

In conclusion, the first process step is summarized by using our schema in Table 1.

2.1.2. Identify Search Parameters

Using the concrete topic definition in the TTDD, the next process step in building a theory focuses on the search parameters for finding evidence. The evidence will be the basis for our body of knowledge. Hence, it is crucial to (a) clearly identify acceptable forms of evidence, and (b) describe how we will proceed to find the evidence.

By determining the forms of acceptable evidence it is indirectly determined how rigorous the overall process of building the body of knowledge will be. If, for instance, only the most significant and best documented empirical results will be considered, a highly rigorous process is most likely. The overall rigor becomes more relaxed if, for instance, qualitative evidence such as lessons learned is included.

Possible forms of evidence include: A rigorous empirical study with a comparison of the object under study to other existing practices, a controlled experiment in a research environment, an industrial case study, literature surveys, a qualitative statement of lessons learned, a poll, or even a single person's opinion captured in a white paper or interview. A good overview and classification of possible empirical evidence can be found in (Zelkowitz and Wallace, 1998).

Along with the types of accepted evidence goes the definition of accepted (i.e., trusted) sources for such evidence. Such sources can range from books and archival journals, where each piece of evidence is peer reviewed, to purely electronic sources on the Internet, which may include promotional material of technology vendors or companies.

Last but not least, we have to identify the possible search process we will use to find the evidence. This is in part connected to the list of accepted sources. For instance, evidence in journals can be found by searching specific internet catalogues of such journals (e.g., IEEE Computer Society Digital Library[1] or The ACM Digital Library[2]) or by a classical library search. A search for evidence on the Internet offers even more possibilities: Which search engines are going to be used? What keywords will be entered? How are the results filtered? In any case, it is necessary to document the intended (and later applied) search process and routines so it becomes obvious and repeatable for others.

As outcome products of our second process step, we generate a *List of Accepted Forms of Evidence (LAFE)*, a *List of Accepted (i.e., trusted) Sources for the Evidence (LASE)*, and a *Search Process Definition (SPD)*. All of these results can consist of separate documents, or can even be included in a single document. They even might be added to the TTDD. However, for our generic process we assume that each document will be handled separately.

We summarize the second process step by using our schema, in Table 2.

2.1.3. Find Evidence

While the first two process steps have been more concerned with the theoretical foundation of the theory building, this third process step marks the start of the practical work. The pieces of evidence for our body of knowledge are retrieved. Therefore, the search is executed as documented in the Search Process Definition (SPD).

Table 2 Overview of process step 2

Step number and name	❷ Identify search parameters
Input	Process ❶ needs to be terminated; complete Theory Topic Definition Document (TTDD)
Actions	Identify and list the accepted forms of (empirical) evidence. Provide an initial list of acceptable sources for the evidence. Describe the search process that will be applied
Output	List of Accepted Forms of Evidence (LAFE); List of Accepted Sources of Evidence (LASE); Search Process Definition (SPD)
Comments	Typically, this process step is executed in an iterative way. As soon as some of the produced documents exist, they may be evaluated and fine-tuned in the following process steps

[1] On-line at http://www.computer.org/portal/site/csdl/index.jsp

[2] On-line at http://portal.acm.org

Table 3 Overview of process step 3

Step number and name	❸ Find evidence
Input	Process step ❷ must have been started; initial versions of LAFE and LASE exist, and SPD has been created
Actions	Execute SPD; conduct literature surveys, polls, and/or interviews
Output	Collection of Retrieved Evidence for Theory (CRET)
Comments	For documentation purposes, the CET should include all of the retrieved evidence pieces that match the LAFE and LASE criteria. A filtering of these results will be conducted in the next process step ❹

This process step could include such activities as performing a literature survey, conducting specific polls, or holding interviews with practitioners and experts. All of the retrieved evidence should be documented in a *Collection of Retrieved Evidence for Theory (CRET)*. This step is summarized in Table 3.

2.1.4. Analyze Evidence

In this process step the potential evidence pieces in the CRET will be analyzed. Therefore, one first has to take a look at the CRET and define the process for the analysis. The process for analyzing the evidence has not necessarily been defined before (e.g., in step 2) because it may be dependant on the evidence itself (e.g., its quantity, quality, completeness, etc.). One also may have to further filter the CRET and prepare the single evidence pieces for the analysis. As part of the analysis activities the content of each evidence piece is extracted and prepared for the inclusion into the body of knowledge. This extraction is based on the defined quality attributes of the TTDD. Specific analysis methods will be discussed in the later sections of this chapter.

As results of this process step one creates a *Documentation of Chosen Analysis Process (DCAP)* and the *Analyzed Evidence for Theory (AET)*. See Table 4 for a summary of these actions and output.

2.1.5. Integrate Evidence

In this last step of the general process for building theories, summarized in Table 5, the actual body of knowledge is described and documented. This includes the clear identification and representation of all found and accepted pieces of evidence, the handling of possible discrepancies in these different evidence pieces, as well as an abstraction from the single evidence pieces. As a result of this final process step we create a *Structured Body of Knowledge (SBK)*.

To create the SBK several activities have to be performed. First of all the basis for the SBK needs to be documented. This may be simply done by referring to the AET or by integrating the AET evidence pieces into a specific data structure or

Table 4 Overview of process step 4

Step number and name	❹ Analyze evidence
Input	This process step can be started as soon as the first pieces of evidence are added to the CRET. TTDD is used as a basis
Actions	Define suitable process for analyzing the CRET
	Filter and prepare results from CRET according to process
	Extract content from evidence based on defined process
Output	Documentation of Chosen Analysis Process (DCAP)
	Analyzed Evidence for Theory (AET)
Comments	In the general process for building theories we include the DCAP in the analysis step. However, specific process may choose to perform this considerations already as part of the earlier process steps (e.g., step ❶ or ❷)

Table 5 Overview of process step 5

Step number and name	❺ Integrate evidence
Input	This process step can be started as soon as the DCAP is existent and the first pieces of evidence are available in the AET documentation
Actions	Standardize and make evidence available to users
	Identify and handle discrepancies in the evidence set
	Create an abstraction that integrates all evidence pieces into a transparent summary
Output	Structured Body of Knowledge (SBK)
Comments	If not enough evidence is available for this process step, it might be considered to redefine the search parameters (step ❷) or repeat the search step ❸

knowledge management system. Ideally, all evidence pieces have similar tendencies or the same findings regarding the quality attributes under study. In this case it is relatively easy to integrate all pieces of evidence into an abstraction. The abstraction is a transparent conclusion that summarizes the findings of all evidence pieces regarding the theory and the quality attributes under evaluation. This abstraction allows users to get a quick overview of the body of knowledge without having to take a look at all evidence pieces. Specific methods for accomplishing this combination and extraction of evidence will be discussed later in this chapter.

Regardless of which integration method is chosen, one important goal is that contradictory findings in the AET are clearly reflected in the final output. For instance, the results of the process so far may show that for seven out of nine pieces of evidence there are clear results that a technology reduces costs. But in the two other pieces of evidence it is reported that there has been no cost reduction or, even worse, that the cost has been increased. This inconsistency needs to be reflected somehow in the abstraction of the body of knowledge.

In analyzing these inconsistencies, it is important to note whether the evidence suggests that certain factors might be responsible for the different results.

For example, if the seven pieces of evidence, which support the idea that the technology reduces costs all come from large projects, and the contradictory evidence comes from small projects, then it is possible to hypothesize that project size influences the effectiveness of the technology. It is important to note that influencing factors may be attributes of the studies as well as attributes of the project; for example, analysts might notice that beneficial effects are seen only in the studies of one researcher and are missing in independent replications.

2.2. Quality Attributes for Classifying Theories

Before we take a detailed look at how different approaches instantiate the general process steps, we introduce some quality attributes that apply to theory building approaches. These quality attributes can be used to:

1. Characterize the specific aspects of a given theory building approach
2. Classify and compare the different theory building approaches so as to select the most suitable

Based on our experiences with decision support and technology transfer, we choose the following eight quality attributes as most relevant to robust and useful theories: (1) Applicability for qualitative data, (2) applicability for quantitative data, (3) scalability, (4) objectivity, (5) fairness, (6) ease of use, (7) openness, and (8) cost.

Since we are only intending to give tendencies on how these quality attributes are met by different approaches to theory building, we will rate each approach for each attribute as either: +, ±, or −. In this scheme a + indicates that the given approach can produce output that is rated well for this attribute, while a − definitely indicates that the approach is not well suited for users to whom this attribute is important. A ± is used in the case where no clear tendencies can be identified.

2.2.1. Applicability for Quantitative Data

This attribute indicates whether or not an approach makes use of quantitative data such as numeric measures of cost, quality, or schedule impact. Approaches that explicitly do not include such information will be indicated by a −, while others which explicitly include them will be indicated by a +.

2.2.2. Applicability for Qualitative Data

This attribute indicates whether or not an approach makes use of qualitative data such as lessons learned, whitepapers, or expert statements and interviews. Some approaches explicitly do not include such information (which will be indicated by a −) while others explicitly include them (indicated by a +).

2.2.3. Scalability

This attribute addresses the question of how easy or hard it is likely to be to find evidence that matches the constraints of the theory-building approach. That is, given the current state of the software engineering literature, does the approach scale up in that it can use a large set of publications as evidence, or is it limited to only a small subset? Obviously this will depend on the particular theory and the desired rigor of the analysis; however, this criterion attempts to give a (subjective) rating of, on balance, how many evidence sources in the software engineering domain will be found that are suitable inputs. A – indicates the approach is defined in such a way that suitable evidence sources will be difficult to find, while a + indicates the approach is designed to be more inclusive.

2.2.4. Objectivity

This attribute expresses how objective the approach is in handling the evidence. It describes the extent to which subjective influences of the person(s) executing the process are excluded. The more objective a process, the more deterministic its output becomes. Hence, this attribute indirectly captures the extent to which the process is repeatable. A + indicates the absence of subjective influences, while a – indicates the potential presence of such influences. A ± is used in the case where no determination can be made.

2.2.5. Fairness

This attribute describes the lack of bias in an approach. While objectivity describes whether repeatable conclusions will be drawn from a given set of evidence, fairness describes whether an approach will collect an appropriate set of evidence on which to base conclusions. Approaches with no bias will be marked with a + while a – indicates that the approach has the potential to include some bias.

2.2.6. Ease of Use

This attribute describes how easily the results can be accessed from a user's perspective. Are results clearly understandable by everyone, or does one need specific knowledge, for example about a domain, to interpret them? We rate outcomes that require no additional knowledge with a + while others which require highly specialized knowledge are rated with –.

2.2.7. Openness

This attribute describes how open the process steps are for the user. Can interested outside parties understand how the results were created? Are intermediate results available so that various process steps can be re-applied by outsiders and the results checked? Approaches which are explicitly open for users are rated with a + while a − indicates approaches that operate as more of a black-box (end users arc guaranteed only to see the inputs and outputs).

2.2.8. Cost

This is the last but definitely not the least important attribute in our list. "Cost" expresses the level of time and effort investment necessary to get results. Regardless of the benefits that can be achieved, some approaches may require substantial work to produce and document the results. In such cases we clearly flag them with a − while approaches with a + have exactly the opposite meaning, namely they are relatively cheap to apply.

3. Approaches to Theory-Building

Given the multiplicity of evidence types in the software engineering literature, it should not be surprising that multiple approaches have been applied to make sense of this information. It is important to note that the software engineering literature should be viewed as being stronger, not weaker, because it incorporates such a wide variety of types of evidence, ranging from a single expert's opinion, to aggregated opinions of multiple experts, to anecdotal case studies, to rigorously measured data from across dozens or hundreds of projects. However, this very disparity makes it hard to aggregate well-supported theories and marshal the supporting evidence in a way that is commonly accepted.

In this section, we introduce several approaches that have been proposed to rigorously and repeatably abstract well-formed theories from such data sets. Each is mapped to the general process described in the last section so as to facilitate comparison.

3.1. Systematic Literature Review

The approach to theory- and knowledge-building which has garnered the most attention recently is the systematic review. The systematic review can be defined as "a means of identifying, evaluating and interpreting all available research relevant to a particular research question, or topic area, or phenomenon of interest" (Kitchenham, 2004). It is in short a way to summarize across multiple studies on a given topic what conclusions can be drawn. Note the emphasis on completeness in the above definition ("…all available research…"), which is a major goal of the technique. By taking a highly procedural approach to defining the problem of study and searching the available literature, the technique aims to avoid the danger of selection bias, in which only a subset of studies are canvassed (which just might happen to be the subset that corresponds to a particular point of view). Systematic review was a key method proposed to support the goal of evidence-based software engineering, as articulated by Kitchenham et al. (2004).

The application of systematic review to software engineering was inspired by its success in the medical field, a domain in which researchers must also abstract actionable theories and conclusions from among many studies of the same phenomenon.

Procedure. The procedure for the systematic review is described in detail in a technical report compiled by Kitchenham (2004). The major activities, as mapped to our generic process description, are described below, and have been summarized from that source unless otherwise noted. Kitchenham does note that the process is likely to be highly iterative, with many transitions backwards and forwards among the following activities. An important part of this procedure is to document the planned activities for conducting the systematic review as a protocol, to facilitate the review of the plan and ensure that decisions are made so as to support a review that is as repeatable and rigorous as possible.

- *Define topic.* The guidelines state that the process should start from a well-defined question, in which the population, intervention, contrast, outcome, and context of interest have been made explicit. Kitchenham suggests starting in natural language but converting to a structured question as the ideas become refined.
- *Identify search parameters.* Next in the process, researchers must define a repeatable strategy for searching the literature. Doing so requires setting clear criteria for the following issues (among others):

  o Which sources will be searched
  o How sources will be filtered
  o How quality of sources will be assessed
  o What information will be extracted from sources
  o How missing information will be handled

- *Find evidence.* Assuming the search criteria and range of permissible sources have been defined in detail as above, finding evidence is then the process of exhaustively searching all sources for any paper that matches the criteria. Having the search specified in such detail helps ensure that the search process is repeatable, that is, that multiple users conducting a search according to the same criteria would find exactly the same sources.
- *Analyze evidence.* Analyzing the publications found in the search consists of first filtering out unsuitable publications and then extracting the information needed from those remaining.

  o During this round of filtering, only primary studies should be selected for inclusion in the systematic review. That is, researchers should analyze only reports of studies that directly examined the research question. Analysis or synthesis of studies performed by other researchers are not to be included in the study in combination with primary sources. (Such surveys should themselves be used as pointers to important primary sources or to compare against the final outcome of the systematic review.) An important question is whether certain types of studies or evidence should be excluded from consideration at this point. However, Kitchenham notes that due to the number of studies currently published in software engineering, researchers on most topics will not be able to be so selective: "In software engineering, we will usually accept all levels of evidence. The only threshold that might be viable would be to exclude level 5 evidence [expert opinion] when there are a reasonable number of primary studies at a greater level…" (Kitchenham, 2004). Still, the quality of each study included in the analysis must be assessed so that this can be considered when the results from each study are compared and contrasted during the integration phase.

o From each study that remains after the filtering is performed, the required data for the analysis must be extracted. The guidelines suggest that a template should be defined for each systematic review conducted and applied to each publication, so that complete information is extracted from each and organized consistently.

- *Integrate evidence.* Having defined in earlier phases concrete guidelines for what type of evidence will be included in the systematic review, the guidelines for how the evidence is to be integrated are not as specific. This is likely because the methods which are feasible for each systematic review will depend largely on how much and what type of evidence has been utilized, and on the specific research question under study. Kitchenham does note that conclusions in software engineering will need to be drawn from many different types of studies, but guidelines for combining different types of studies are not given. Although qualitative measures are allowed, it is recommended to convert each to a quantitative measure if at all possible. One way of reporting such results is via a forest plot, which is feasible if all studies measure the same treatment variable in the same units (or using different measures that can be converted to the same units).

Although not mentioned explicitly in our generic process, the systematic review guidelines do contain an addition activity for documenting the review. The justification for having this listed as a separate step is that the systematic review cannot be considered complete until it has been validated; the authors suggest that such validation is likely to happen via peer review. In the event that the report is published as a technical report or some other non-peer reviewed document, it should be made available via the web and a peer review organized for this purpose.

3.1.1. Lessons Learned in Application to Software Engineering

In the software engineering domain, this approach has been applied to a number of different analyses, which are increasing in number each year. After a relatively few applications published in 2004 and 2005, there has been a large increase in 2006 of the number of systematic reviews, especially in Master's theses and other student work. Some key examples in which systematic review was applied to test a research hypothesis include:

- Jørgensen (2004) conducted a systematic review of studies of estimating software development effort. He found, first, that estimation based on expert judgment was the most often-used approach. The systematic review found 15 different studies comparing expert estimates to estimates produced using more formal models. The results about which estimation approach produced more accurate estimates are inconclusive: five studies found expert judgment more effective; five found formal estimation models more effective; and five found no difference. However, Jørgensen was able to formulate a number of guidelines for improving expert estimation, which are each supported by at least some of the studies surveyed.
- Jørgensen and Moløkken-Østvold (2006) used a systematic review to test an assessment of the prevalence of software cost overruns done by the Standish Group. They investigated whether they could find evidence to support one of the often-cited claims of the 1994 "CHAOS" report, namely that "challenged" software engineering projects reported on average 189% cost overruns. This systematic review found three other surveys of software project costs. The comparison could not be definitive, since the Standish Group did not publish their source data or methodology. However, the researchers found that the conclusions of the Standish Group report were markedly different from the other studies surveyed, raising questions about the report's methodology and conclusions.
- Kitchenham et al. (2006) undertook a systematic review to investigate the conditions under which organizations could get accurate cost estimates from cross-company estimation models, specifically, the conditions under which those cross-company models were more accurate than within-company models. Seven papers were found that represented primary studies on this topic. The results were inconclusive: four found cross-company models were significantly worse than within-company models, while the remainder found that both types of models were equally effective.

Mendes (2005) applied systematic review for a slightly different goal: to assess the level of rigor of papers being published in the field of web engineering. In this case, it was not a single research hypothesis that was being explored; rather, Mendes was assessing the percentage of papers in the field that could be included in a systematic review of any hypothesis in this area, according to criteria for rigor that she set. 173 papers were reviewed and only 5% were deemed sufficiently rigorous, which emphasizes that this approach ensures rigor by being quite restrictive about the quality of papers accepted as input.

Some authors explicitly comment on the difficulty of applying the approach given the state of the software engineering literature. Jørgensen (2004), for example, mentions that few if any of the studies he identified met the criteria of reporting the statistical significance of their results, defining the population sampled, or using random sampling. For these reasons, it appears to be difficult to define the quality criteria too rigorously, in case the number of studies that can be included become too small to produce interesting results.

Because of the costly nature of applying this approach, some researchers have done some tailoring of the approach in application. For example, even though a best practice is to minimize bias by using two researchers to do the analysis, some researchers who are applying the method feel it is practical to use only one.

3.1.2. Assessment

Systematic review does cover a range of sources from different environments. To describe the conditions for which this analysis approach may best be suited, we examine it in reference to our quality criteria:

- *Applicability for quantitative data*: +
- The literature contains several examples of research questions addressed by systematic review of quantitative evidence sources.
- *Applicability for qualitative data*: −
- At the moment, this approach seems less well suited for evidence sources that contain qualitative data. Although methods for qualitative synthesis do exist (e.g., Noblitt and Hare, 1988), none of the applications of systematic review that we could find in the software engineering literature used qualitative data as a substantial source of information. Moreover, the guidelines in this field (Kitchenham, 2004) seem written with quantitative data in mind. It is likely that this will need to be explored further in future applications.
- *Scalability*: −
- An assessment of this attribute would depend on how a given application defines the quality and filtering criteria. However, we can say that applications to date have typically used fairly restrictive criteria. The lessons learned cited above do show that several authors have commented that a fairly small percentage of publications were suitable for inclusion in the systematic reviews that they ran.
- *Objectivity*: +
- The procedure is very well specified. Although key filtering criteria are allowed to be user-defined for each application, and so could theoretically be defined so as to impair the objectivity of the study, this would presumably be caught during the peer review of the study process and results.
- *Fairness*: +
- Fairness is typically high, since the search criteria are to be represented as search queries and repeated in several repositories. The researcher must take all documents matching the query; he or she is not allowed to pick and choose arbitrarily.
- *Ease of use*: +/−
- The procedure and results would be easily accessible to researchers, but the amount of detail in the report would not be user friendly for supporting decisions

by practitioners. This can be mitigated by applying additional effort aimed at creating multiple reports for different audiences, particularly by abstracting actionable guidelines for practitioners from the research (see for example Koyani et al., 2003).

- *Openness*: +
- The amount of detail that is required to be documented and included in the final report of results makes this a very open process. In fact, peer review of each step of the process is called for to ensure quality and rigor in the results.
- *Cost*: −
- Researchers have pointed out that systematic review is effort-intensive and hence high cost: "Systematic reviews require considerably more effort than traditional reviews" (Kitchenham, 2004). Part of this cost is due to the fact that this approach requires extensive and lengthy documentation. It is moreover not well suited for application by a single researcher, since a "best practice" is to use at least two researchers to minimize biases. Although we could find no comprehensive estimate of costs for performing systematic reviews, anecdotally we did hear from researchers who expressed some concern about their expensive nature in comparison to the benefits received. One researcher questioned the wisdom of adopting such techniques from the medical field, which has a research budget many times that of the budget for software engineering.

3.2. Meta-analysis

Meta-analysis is a method for combining data from different datasets collected during different studies, in order to statistically test a hypothesis. By using data from multiple datasets, the meta-analysis allows the investigation of whether the effect under study is robust across multiple contexts. By combining datasets across studies, meta-analysis provides for the statistical test a larger number of data which improves the chances of detecting smaller effect sizes than any test of a single dataset in isolation.

Meta-analysis should be seen as a special case of systematic review, rather than a distinct approach. It follows the same general process of systematically collecting, analyzing, and integrating evidence, but specifies certain techniques that are appropriate when the evidence is expressed in comparable, quantitative metrics.

Both meta-analysis and systematic review have a long history of use in other disciplines. Its applicability to software engineering has been studied relatively recently, as a way of getting greater benefit from the fairly few and expensive studies that are run on software engineering phenomena.

Procedure. The procedure for conducting meta-analysis in software engineering has been specified in previous publications. The information below has been summarized from Miller (Miller, 2000) unless otherwise noted. For purposes of comparison, we discuss the meta-analytic procedure for quantitative data using the same broad steps as we used for the more general systematic review approach. However, since this type of meta-analysis is concerned with a statistical test of quantitative data, many of the phases can be described in more detail, and require more constraints, than does the general systematic review process.[3] We map these activities to our generic knowledge-building process as follows:

- *Define topic.* The research topic investigated by a meta-analysis should be expressed in the form of a relationship between two variables. Although this is a matter of debate, the conservative approach is that the meta-analysis should be done between two variables only. Separate analyses should be run if there are more than two variables of interest.
- *Identify search parameters.* Although no specific guidelines are given on how to run the search, a number of important constraints govern which sources can be used in the meta-analysis:

    o Meta-analysis requires some knowledge about the individual data sets that it analyzes. Hence, only studies can be used which report the appropriate information regarding the results. If the raw data is not available, then the process requires from each source at least the mean, variance (or standard deviation), number of subjects, and details about the normality of the data. When non-significant results are reported an estimate of the statistical power of the experiment should be included.

    o Independence of the studies is important. Selecting studies among which some dependencies exist can weaken or invalidate the results.

    o Miller notes that "[c]urrently no work exists, which attempts to validate the use of meta-analysis for non-experimental results," and therefore recommends that researchers in software engineering not use evidential data from sources other than experiments in meta-analysis at this time. (The reasoning is that the randomization which takes place in experimental studies eliminates bias and confounding factors within the experimental results.) Thus it may be more appropriate, and is certainly safer, to analyze the results from different types of studies separately and then examine whether they tell a consistent story.

- *Find evidence.* This activity should take the form of an exhaustive literature search aimed at finding all empirical evaluations which describe relationships between the two variables of interest.
- *Analyze evidence.* As some authors have noted, there is a first pass that is necessary over the collected set of sources "to reconcile the primary experiments – i.e., define a common framework with which to compare different studies. This involves defining common terms, hypotheses, and metrics, and characterizing key differences" (Perry et al., 2000). In a second pass, the data must be examined more deeply for:

    o Errors in the individual data sets that could be corrected

---

[3] We recognize that procedures have been described for meta-analysis of qualitative data, e.g., Paterson et al., 2001, but as we are aware of no instances where they were applied in software engineering research we keep this section focused on quantitative applications.

○ Quality of the studies, in order to assign a weighting to each. In order to avoid bias, Miller notes that the recommended practice is to organize an independent panel of experts

- *Integrate evidence*. Having compiled and created a common framework for the individual data sets, integrating the evidence is done by means of running the proper calculation over the data values obtained. This will provide a quantitative, statistically valid answer to the question of whether there is a significant relationship between the two variables of interest. One important note for the analysis is that Miller recommends that meta-analysis not be employed to resolve differences among conflicting results. Meta-analysis was designed to combine results from similar experiments, not to deal with heterogeneous data sets.

3.2.1. Lessons Learned in Application to Software Engineering

In the software engineering domain, this approach has been applied in relatively few cases. Certainly one of the most relevant of these is the study by Miller (2000), in which meta-analysis was applied to abstract conclusions across defect detection experiments (i.e., experiments that ask the question: "Which (if any) defect detection technique is most effective at finding faults?"). This was an important test of meta-analysis in the software engineering domain, as defect detection techniques are among the most often-studied software engineering phenomena. Hence, if sufficient data could not be obtained on this topic, it would be difficult to understand how meta-analysis could be suitable for many other topics in software engineering.

However, the results from Miller's study were inconclusive. On a review of the literature, only five independent studies could be found which had investigated similar enough hypotheses and used similar enough measures to be compared. Upon analysis of the data the results of those studies were so divergent that meta-analysis was not deemed to be applicable. A possible reason for this is that the effectiveness of defect detection techniques is highly dependent upon the types of defects in the artifact being examined; the studies included in Miller's analysis did not describe the defect type information in sufficient detail that a mapping could be made to transform the results onto a common taxonomy. Thus, it could not be assessed whether those studies applied the techniques to defect profiles that were at all comparable.

A related use of this technique in software engineering was the attempt by Hayes to abstract results across five studies of inspection techniques, where four of the studies were either partial or full replications of the first (Hayes, 1999). In this case, the study designs were all very similar, which should have facilitated the ability to draw a common conclusion from this body of information. However, Hayes was forced to conclude that the effect sizes were significantly different across the studies and hence that a meta-analysis was not an appropriate method for reasoning about the underlying phenomenon. Hayes is able only to speculate about some causes for this – for example, that the studies were run in different cultural contexts and by subjects with different levels of experience – but it is worth noting that these resulting hypotheses may be of as much practical interest to the research community as a successful meta-analysis would have been.

A final application of meta-analysis in the software domain that is especially worthy of note was a study conducted by Galin and Avrahami (2005). These authors attempted to address the question of whether software quality assurance programs work by conducting a meta-analysis of studies examining the effects of the Capability Maturity Model (CMM) for software. The authors point out that CMM has been one of the most widely-deployed software process improvement methods for an extended number of years, and so would be among the most likely approaches for which sufficient data would exist. For the same reason, this analysis was also a good test of the suitability of meta-analysis for software engineering research. In this case, the results were more positive: 22 studies were found that examined the effects of the CMM on software process improvement and, of these, 19 contained sufficiently detailed quantitative information to be suitable for analysis. The analysis did find substantial productivity gains when organizations achieved the initial improvement levels of the CMM (although data was missing that addressed higher levels of achievement).

In the end, the lesson learned about applying meta-analysis to software engineering seems to be that: "...the heterogeneity of current empirical results is a major limitation in our ability to apply meta-analytic procedures" (Miller, 2000). Because of the large amounts of variation from so many different context variables, which exists in any set of software engineering experiments, we may be unable to generate statistically definitive answers for many phenomena other than those with the largest effect sizes (e.g., organizations going from an undisciplined development process to achieving initial levels of the CMM). This is true even in cases which seem to lend themselves to cross-study analysis, for example, topics for which there is a rich body of studies, some of which may even be replications of one another. For many other topics of interest which do not have such a rich set of studies, which tend to be the ones of most interest to researchers and practitioners, it is still an open question whether the studies undertaken so far are additive and can be combined via meta-analysis to contribute to an eventual body of knowledge.

3.2.2. Assessment

- *Applicability for quantitative data*: +
- When sufficient studies with quantitative results can be found, meta-analysis is the most rigorous way of combining those results.
- *Applicability for qualitative data*: –
- Meta-analysis commonly relies on statistical tests that are not suited for qualitative data. Methods for applying meta-analysis to qualitative analysis have been described but not yet applied in the field of software engineering.

- *Scalability*: +/−
- As with any technique, the number of suitable studies that could be found would depend on how the researcher defines the eligibility criteria. As an example, Miller's case study (Miller, 2000) starts with a relatively loose criteria (that all studies measure the same effect) but notes that it could be tightened, for example by stipulating that only a particular type of study design be used, or that small studies be either dropped from the analysis or given less weight. However, given the relative scarcity of software engineering data, the looser criteria is probably suitable for the field now. Although the study by Galin and Avrahami was able to use 19 out of 22 sources found, the more typical experience in software engineering studies at the moment seems to be that a sufficient number of studies is more difficult to find.
- *Objectivity*: +
- The objectivity of the approach should be seen as quite high: the procedure and statistical methods are very well specified. Different meta-analyses applied to the same datasets will always produce the same answer.
- *Fairness*: +/−
- Since no specific guidelines are given for how researchers should conduct the literature search to find evidence sources, the process will be as fair and unbiased as the researcher's search approach.
- *Ease of use*: −
- The outputs of this approach are aimed more at researchers than at practitioners. Training in statistical methods is necessary in order to apply the technique and interpret the results correctly.
- *Openness*: +/−
- There are no special requirements of the technique with respect to openness. It is to be expected that any serious meta-analysis would be subjected to peer review on its way to publication, and hence should theoretically allow reviewers to replicate the same analysis if desired.
- *Cost*: +/−
- There are no special constraints on cost. There are no special documentation requirements.

3.3. An Experience Portal-Centered Approach

Scientists at the Fraunhofer Center – Maryland developed an approach for accumulating and analyzing disparate evidence sources in 2002, to help the U.S. Department of Defense provide information for a central best practices clearinghouse about software acquisition and development. In contrast to the previous approaches discussed, there is no single comprehensive reference, although details of the approach have been published (Shull and Turner, 2005; Feldmann et al., 2006). The general method which was instantiated in the clearinghouse extends previous knowledge-building approaches used in the Experience Factory method (Basili et al, 1994a) and is known as EMPEROR (Experience Management Portal using Empirical Results as Organizational Resources).

An important way in which EMPEROR differs from the Experience Factory as well as from systematic reviews and meta-analysis is that it is designed to be executed via a community rather than a single research team. EMPEROR provides a mechanism for users in the field to submit their experiences with a given technology and for such experiences to be reflected in the summarized knowledge. Thus, it aims at abstracting conclusions at a different level than the previously mentioned methods.

This approach was primarily designed for decision support but is also useful for theory generation.

Procedure. The basic procedure for building knowledge through the EMPEROR approach was defined in several papers (Shull and Turner, 2005; Feldmann et al., 2006) and is summarized below. An important distinction from the previous approaches in this chapter is that EMPEROR imposes lower barriers to including information in the analysis, in order to be more inclusive of experiential information from participants. Less-than-rigorous information may therefore be entered as part of the knowledge base although it is labeled as such, and the summarized analysis is checked later to make sure that such information has not been overly relied on in forming conclusions.

- *Define topic.* As with other approaches, EMPEROR requires that the topic of knowledge gathering first be defined. Although this topic definition might be in the form of a hypothesis, it may also be simply a particular practice or technique about which the available evidence should be summarized. In general, topics investigated with this approach are of the form: What is the expected outcome of using a particular practice in a certain environment?
- *Identify search parameters.* Also similar to other approaches, EMPEROR contains a step in which the person applying the process must make explicit which types of evidence will be acceptable to the search and in which venues to look for that evidence. EMPEROR however is less restrictive and allows less rigorous types of evidence to be included (e.g., interviews, experience reports, white papers) both to get a more inclusive survey of the state of the practice and because for many questions sufficient amounts of highly rigorous studies are simply not to be found. This view of the software engineering literature is supported by many of the example applications of meta-analysis and systematic review discussed in previous sections.
- *Find evidence.* The search for the evidence is conducted given the constraints decided upon. When the published literature is found to be significantly lacking, researchers are advised to consider conducting interviews with representative practitioners in order to create additional workable knowledge. For each evidence source, a template is filled out; the information entered in such a template is expected to be largely textual. Where quantitative evidence is found it should be recorded taking special care to record the unit of measure along with the values. It is not expected that all evidence on the same topic will be recorded in the

same measures or in measures that can be translated one to the other. This phase of the procedure may go on for an extended period of time. Evidence may be allowed to accumulate opportunistically, with new templates being filled out as new evidence becomes available. The evidence found so far is made available for interested parties, e.g., at a website that can be updated as new evidence is found.

- *Analyze evidence.* As each evidence template is completed, it is assigned a measure of trustability based upon objective descriptions of how rigorously the practice under investigation was applied, the results were measured, and how results were reported. An example trustability scale (Feldmann et al., 2006) ranks each evidence source on a scale of 1 (signifying anecdotal evidence from a single source) to 20 (sustained and measured evidence that has undergone peer review).

- *Integrate evidence.* When sufficient evidence has been collected, a textual summary is constructed that describes the body of evidence that has been found. The summary is authored by a subject matter expert, that is, someone with sufficient knowledge of the topic area so as to be able to describe the important information from the knowledge accumulated. Before being published, the summary is reviewed by an objective, outside panel consisting of representatives from industry, government, and academia. This panel reviews the summary from the point of view of accuracy and objectivity (especially whether all of the conclusions can be traced back to a statement in the evidence templates) and representativeness (whether the evidence profiles that were used represent environments of interest and whether the evidence sources used do not represent a biased subset of users).

3.3.1. Lessons Learned in Application to Software Engineering

In the software engineering domain, this approach has been applied so far only in the context of the US Department of Defense's Best Practices Clearinghouse (Dangle et al., 2005). This single project contains analyses of several different practices, however, and hence several different example applications of the technique. These applications range from topics for which experiential data of all kinds is very easy to find (e.g., the costs and benefits of software inspections or spiral development) to topics for which the available data is much more scarce (e.g., the costs and benefits of a process variant known as performance-based earned value management).

As the project repository is currently in an initial phase, the approach will shortly undergo a more thorough evaluation as the project resources are opened up to the user community. Lessons learned will be analyzed and reported on in the near future. Among the most important aspects to be tested in this effort, however, is the question of whether an active community can be built around such a repository and whether it will work to contribute to and refine the evidence collection and hence the summarized information that can be built atop it.

3.3.2. Assessment

It is important to note again that the EMPEROR approach proceeds in a very different manner than the other ones discussed in this chapter. Analyses in this approach are always open to review by the user community, so as to elicit information that may have been missed in the initial review and to allow users to get the benefits of information before the entire review has been completed. Also, rather than take a restrictive approach and allow only the highest-quality evidence to be included in the analysis, EMPEROR will allow less-rigorous types of evidence (e.g., interviews, experiential anecdotes) as long as such evidence is always labeled with an appropriate caveat. Our discussions with our user advisory group has indicated that users are happy to get what guidance is available, as long as they know the appropriate level of confidence to place in it. Given the dearth of highly-rigorous studies that exists on many topics, there seems to be a need for workable interim solutions that can give some guidance.

- *Applicability for quantitative data*: +
- The process makes no special distinction between qualitative and quantitative data; it is equally well suited to both.
- *Applicability for qualitative data*: +
- Because the final summary of abstracted information is text-based, it is very well suited to incorporating qualitative data.
- *Scalability*: +
- The process has been designed to be as inclusive as possible. Any incoming evidence has only to pass a sanity check by a subject matter expert. However, each admitted evidence source is always tagged with an objective indicator of its quality.
- *Objectivity*: −
- The EMPEROR approach is more susceptible to subjectivity than the other approaches. However, it contains safeguards that do try to guard against such problems. For example, because the barriers to entry are low, evidence may be submitted that is anecdotal and subjective. However, this evidence would be tagged as of lower quality and should be marked as of less importance when the summary is created. As another example, the summary itself is a textual summary that needs to combine many disparate sources of evidence and many different measures of a practice's effectiveness. To guard against this, the process requires that the summary is always created by an expert in the topic under study and furthermore, that it be reviewed and accepted (or not) by an outside panel of experts representing different points of view.
- *Fairness*: −
- Similarly to objectivity, the approach is susceptible to bias but contains internal safeguards that attempt to mitigate this. For one example, there are no defined, repeatable search criteria for finding evidence sources. However, by stipulating that the in-process results are always visible to users, the approach allows users who do not see their own experiences represented in the repository to submit

new evidence that includes their own point of view, helping to correct any bias. As a second example, the textual summary may include bias if the included evidence sources exhibit bias. However, the objective outside panel of experts that reviews completed summaries is charged with assessing this. It may also be worth noting that, unlike the other two approaches discussed in this chapter, EMPEROR may suffer less from publication bias (i.e., the threat that negative results on a particular topic, or results that do not match the conventional wisdom, are less likely to be written up or accepted as part of the published literature). EMPEROR avoids this by allowing the submission of less rigorous unpublished experiential data (e.g., via interviews) that attempt to paint a more accurate picture of the state of the practice.

- *Ease of use*: +
  A unique point of the EMPEROR approach is that final vetting of summaries and results is done by representatives who look not only at the accuracy of results but also of the usefulness for the targeted users.
- *Openness*: +
- All in-process evidence and summary information are provided, with traceability links from one to another. Even the scoring models are made explicit, so that users looking to understand why an evidence source received a particular trustability rating can see the underlying scoring model. This openness has advantages that go beyond allowing peer review of the summaries that are produced. The open nature of the EMPEROR approach, as reflected by the requirement to publish in-process reviews, helps to identify areas where more evidence is most important to find. For example, practices for which there is a large degree of anecdotal information are ones which could benefit from a more rigorous study to either confirm or deny the conventional wisdom. The process can also work in the other direction: Practices for which there are a large number of rigorous academic studies but no experiential information from industrial contexts may be good candidates for early adopters in commercial environments to try out.
- *Cost*: +/−
- Another unique aspect is that the EMPEROR approach requires the publication of all materials and results to date, even though the process is ongoing. Thus, end users of the information need not wait until the entire process has been completed to get some benefit. Building up the evidence sets and the resulting summaries can be a costly process, but the entire cost is not required to be paid before any benefit is seen by users of the information.

4. Discussion and Conclusions

For a direct comparison of the approaches, we summarize the evaluations for each of the approaches along our eight quality attributes in Table 6.

The table helps to detect some interesting commonalities and differences among the techniques:

Table 6 Approaches and quality attributes

Quality attributes ⇒ ⇓ Approach	Applicability to quantitative data	Applicability to qualitative data	Scalability	Objectivity	Fairness	Ease of use	Openness	Cost
Systematic review	+	–	–	+	+	+/–	+	–
Meta-analysis	+	–	+/–	+	+/–	–	+/–	+/–
Portal-centered approach	+	+	+	–	–	+	+	+/–

- Basing theories on quantitative data seems to be the "standard" approach to building up theories from across multiple studies, as all of the approaches are designed to abstract theories from quantitative results. However, as has been noted in many of the previous sections, sufficient quantitative data cannot always be found for many topics of interest. For this reason, the additional quality attributes are especially helpful in making decisions about the applicability of approaches for different issues.
- If the majority of experiential information on a topic is expected to be in the form of qualitative data (or quantitative data collected using different incompatible measures), the portal-centered approach is an appropriate choice for combining the evidence sources to abstract a general theory. However, the price to be paid for this ability is a reduction in the rigor (objectivity and fairness) of the resulting conclusions. Although the portal-centered approach includes different levels of quality checking that attempt to remove subjectivity and bias, there is more risk in using this approach than there is for the other approaches, which remove unrigorous evidence by definition.
- Similarly, there is a tradeoff to be had between the inclusiveness of the technique (scalability) and the rigor of the results (fairness and objectivity). The portal-centered approach allows researchers to include less than rigorous evidence sources in the analysis, although the confidence in each is marked with a trustability score. However, again this introduces more risk than approaches which will only accept the most rigorous evidence sources as input. The final decision should of course be based on how much evidence is expected to be available to support interesting and relevant theories on the topic of interest – and the rigor of that decision should be understood and labeled.
- The ease of use attribute helps to highlight a major difference between the portal-centered approach and the other two approaches: The portal-centered approach focuses on providing decision support to practitioners (i.e., providing useful information at the expense of complete rigor), while systematic review

and meta-analysis are focused on providing highly rigorous results (while trading away ease of understandability to practitioners). A related issue is that the portal-centered approach intends to provide information that can support a given decision, not provide a definitive answer to a research question.

- All of the approaches are "open" in that they provide some transparency of the process to interested parties. Both, the systematic review and the portal-centered approach have this as an explicit goal for providing high-quality information.
- All of the approaches are costly; none are cheap to apply. Systematic review may have the most overhead in this regard, as has been commented by multiple researchers who attempted to apply the process guidelines with full rigor. The portal-centered approach is unique in defining useful in-process deliverables that can be published to provide value to users before the final analysis is completed.

As indicated by this comparison, there is no single approach that is capable of meeting all of the quality attributes. A major theme that comes through in the analysis is that full rigor is in tension with the ability to include all types of empirical information and provide easy-to-understand conclusions aimed at practitioners. A key challenge for the future may lie in managing these tradeoffs better, that is, in finding new approaches that combine aspects of the approaches discussed in this paper, to yield positive ratings along more of the quality attributes.

Ongoing research is attempting to address exactly this issue, for example by providing relatively easy-to-use approaches for converting qualitative data into the quantitative data that is usable by meta-analysis and systematic review (Port et al., 2006), or by providing easy-to-use approaches for combining different studies that retain more rigor (Mohagheghi and Conradi, 2006). As this work is fairly new and has not yet been applied in many contexts, it is an open question of how successful it will be in marrying rigor with a less costly, more practical approach. However, such exploration is necessary if we as a field are to aim for truly robust approaches to theory building that can best leverage the multiplicity of kinds and types of existing empirical evidence.

References

Basili, V.R., Selby, R., and Hutchens, D., (1986) Experimentation in software engineering. *IEEE Transactions on Software Engineering*, 12(7): 733–743.

Basili, V.R., Caldiera, G., and Rombach, H.D., (1994a) Experience factory. In *Encyclopedia of Software Engineering*, John, J. Marciniak, (ed.) Vol. 1, Wiley, New York, pp. 469–476.

Basili, V.R.,. Caldiera, G., and Rombach, H.D., (1994b) Goal question metric paradigm. In *Encyclopedia of Software Engineering*, John, J. Marciniak, (ed.) Vol. 1, Wiley, New York, pp. 528–532.

Basili, V.R., Shull, F., and Lanubile, F., (1999) Building knowledge through families of experiments. *IEEE Transactions on Software Engineering*, 25(4): 456–474.

Dangle, K., Dwinnell, L., Hickok, J., and Turner, R., (2005) Introducing the department of defense acquisition best practices clearinghouse. *CrossTalk*, 18(5): 4–5.

Feldmann, R., Shull F., and Shaw, M., (2006) Building decision support in an imperfect world. *Proceedings of International Symposium on Empirical Software Engineering (ISESE)*, Vol. II, Rio de Janeiro, Brazil, pp. 33–35.

Galin D. and Avrahami, M., (2005) Do SQA programs work – CMM work. A meta analysis. *Proceedings of IEEE International Conference on Software – Science, Technology and Engineering (SwSTE05)*, Herzelia, Israel, pp. 95–100.

Hayes, W., (1999) Research synthesis in software engineering: a case for meta-analysis. *Proceedings of the Sixth International Software Metrics Symposium (METRICS'99)*, Boca Raton, FL, p. 143.

Jørgensen, M., (2004) A review of studies on expert estimation of software development effort. *Journal of Systems and Software*, 70(1–2): 37–60.

Jørgensen, M., and Moløkken-Østvold, K. J., (2006) How large are software cost overruns? Critical comments on the Standish group's CHAOS reports. *Information and Software Technology*, 48(4): 297–301.

Kitchenham, B. (2004) *Procedures for Performing Systematic Reviews*, Joint Technical Report, Keele University TR/SE-0401 and NICTA 0400011T.1.

Kitchenham, B., Dybå, T., and Jørgensen, M., (2004) Evidence-based software engineering. *Proceedings of the International Conference on Software Engineering*, Edinburgh, UK, pp. 273–281.

Kitchenham, B., Mendes, E., and Travassos, G. H., (2006) Systematic review of cross- vs. within-company cost estimation studies. *Proceedings of the Evaluation & Assessment in Software Engineering (EASE)*, pp. 89–98.

Koyani, S.J., Bailey, R.W., and Nall, J.R., (2003) Research based web design and usability guidelines. National Cancer Institute. Available for download at http://usability.gov/pdfs/guidelines. html.

Mendes, E., (2005) A systematic review of web engineering research. *Proceedings of the ACM/IEEE International Symposium on Empirical Software Engineering*, Noosa Heads, Australia, pp. 408–418.

Miller, J., (2000) Applying meta-analytical procedures to software engineering experiments. *Journal of Systems and Software*, 54: 29–39.

Mohagheghi, P., and Conradi, R., (2006) Vote-counting for combining quantitative evidence from empirical studies – An example. *Proceedings of International Symposium on Empirical Software Engineering (ISESE)*, Vol. II, Rio de Janeiro, Brazil, pp.24–26.

Noblitt, G.W., and Hare, R.D, (1988) *Meta-Ethnography: Synthesizing Qualitative Studies (Qualitative Research Methods)*, Sage Publications Ltd., Thousand Oaks, CA..

Paterson, B., Thorne, S., Canam, C., and Jillings, C., (2001) *Meta-Study of Qualitative Health Research: A Practical Guide to Meta-Analysis and Meta-Synthesis*, Sage Publications Inc, Thousand Oaks, CA.

Perry, D., Porter, A., and Votta, L., (2000) Empirical studies of software engineering: a roadmap. *Proceedings of International Conference on Software Engineering*, Limerick, Ireland.

Petticrew, M. and Roberts, H., (2006) *Systematic Reviews in the Social Sciences. A Practical Guide*, Blackwell Publishing, Oxford.

Port, D., Kazman, R., Nakao, H., Hoshino, N., and Miyamoto, Y., (2006) Investigating a constructive scorecard model for creating meaningful quantitative data from qualitative inputs. *Proceedings of International Symposium on Empirical Software Engineering (ISESE)*, Vol. II, Rio de Janeiro, Brazil, pp. 27–29.

Shull, F. and Turner, R., (2005) An empirical approach to best practice identification and selection: the US department of defense acquisition best practices clearinghouse. *Proceedings of International Symposium on Empirical Software Engineering (ISESE)*, Noosa Heads, Australia, pp. 133–140.

Sjøberg, D.I.K, Dybå, T., Anda, B.C.D., and Hannay, J.E., (2007a) Building theories in software engineering. In *Advanced Topics in Empirical Software Engineering: A Handbook*, Shull, F., Singer, J., and Sjøberg, D.I.K (eds.), Springer, Berlin.

Sjøberg, D.I.K., (2007b) Documenting theories. In *Experimental Software Engineering Issues: Assessment and Future*, Basili, V.R., Rombach, D., Schneider, K., Kitchenham, B., Pfahl, D. and Selby, R, (eds.), Springer-Verlag, Berlin Heidelberg, pp. 111–114.

van Solingen, R. and Berghout, E., (1999) *The Goal/Question/Metric Method*, McGraw-Hill Education, New York.

Zelkowitz, M., (2001) Models for industrial validation of new technology. ISERN workshop at Strathclyde University. Available via http://isern.iese.de/network/ISERN/pub/meetings/Glasgow2001/Agenda.htm.

Zelkowitz, M. and Wallace, D., (1998) Experimental models for validating technology. *IEEE Computer*, 31(5), pp. 23–31.

Chapter 14
Replication's Role in Software Engineering

A. Brooks, M. Roper, M. Wood, J. Daly, and J. Miller

Abstract We provide motivation for researchers to replicate experiments in software engineering. The ideology of replication is discussed. We address the question: Is an experiment worth repeating? The current lack of replication studies is highlighted. We make clear that exact replication is unattainable and we draw on our first experience of performing an external replication. To categorise various kinds of replication, we propose a simple extension to Basili et al.'s framework for experimentation in software engineering. We present guidance as to the level of reported detail required to enable others perform a replication. Our conclusion is that there is only one route for empirical software engineering to follow: to make available laboratory packages of experimental materials to facilitate internal and external replications, especially the latter, which have greater confirming power.

1. Introduction

Experimental design is difficult and the experimental process can be error prone. As a consequence, all experimental results should be reproducible by an external agency. By other researchers successfully repeating an experiment, confidence is built in the procedure and the result. Without the confirming power of external replications, a result should be at best regarded as of limited importance and at worst with suspicion and mistrust.

We distinguish two main forms of replication: internal and external. Internal replication is undertaken by the original experimenters (or teams that contain members of the original experimental team): they repeat their own experiment. External replication is undertaken by independent researchers and is a critical verification step. We are not concerned here with replication as it applies to an individual experimental design.

The section that immediately follows provides motivation for researchers to replicate experiments in software engineering. There then follows sections on the theory of replication and replication in practice. As subsections of the latter, we discuss criteria for deciding whether an experiment is worth repeating, the frequency of replication studies, the unattainability of an exact replication, and

F. Shull et al. (eds.), *Guide to Advanced Empirical Software Engineering.*
© Springer 2008

our first experience of performing an external replication. In the section that then follows, to categorise various kinds of replication, we present a simple extension to Basili et al.'s (1986) framework for experimentation in software engineering. The penultimate section presents guidance as to the level of reported detail required to enable others perform a replication. In the final section, we conclude that there is only one route for empirical software engineering to follow: to make available laboratory packages of experimental materials to facilitate internal and external replications, especially the latter, which have greater confirming power.

2. Replication: The Motivation

No one doubts the need for software engineers to work from principles and guidelines in which the professional community has high confidence, all the more so if the application is safety critical. High levels of confidence are only attained when independent researchers successfully replicate an experiment. Without the confirming power of external replication, many principles and guidelines in software engineering should be treated with caution.

Much is to be gained, therefore, by critical examination of previous experiments, by identifying experiments that are worthy of replication, and by replicating these experiments externally.

Huxley (1965) has noted,

> And in science, as in common life, our confidence in a law is in exact proportion to the absence of variation in the result of our experimental verifications.

So the greater the number of experimental verifications the better, at least until such time as additional verifications carry no further power of confirmation. Moreover, given the human component and the rich variety of software and hardware technologies, it surely is beholden on the community to perform many, many, such verifications. Only under exceptional circumstances should one-shot studies involving subjects be relied upon. For example, when the following criteria are all met: (1) a large number of subjects were used, (2) the effect present is so large, the use of statistical tests to convince the reader that an effect exists are unnecessary, and (3) peer review has not found any criticism with the work. Even then of course the effect cannot be extrapolated to just any context. Thus, we strongly agree with Curtis (1980) when he says,

> ...results are far more impressive when they emerge from a program of research rather than from one-shot studies.

Much is said and written about quality control in software development (e.g. Card (1990)). It is ironic, to say the least, that the quality control mechanism of replication, especially external replication, is so little practiced amongst those doing the science behind the engineering. There is an additional irony: because of the current state of software development practice, N-version programming has been suggested as a fault recovery mechanism (see, for example Kelly et al. (1991)). We know so little about doing it right, we end up replicating system functionality across several programs.

Concerning a particular flawed study in psychology which was accepted as being valid for a long time, Broad and Wade (1986) wrote,

> Why did nobody helping to raise generations of undergraduates...replicate the study?

Such a question could equally as well be addressed to many educators of software engineering students regarding numerous studies whose results are communicated often quite uncritically to students. We should all be motivated to carry out replications or at least give support to those who do.

3. Replication: The Ideology

Subjecting theory to experimental test is a crucial scientific activity. Popper (1968), however, explains that researchers must be sure of their results before reporting them, stating,

> We do not take even our own observations quite seriously, or accept them as scientific observation, until we have repeated and tested them.

Coupled with this advice, modern scientific ideology now also demands that experimental results are replicable by an external agency. For example, as Lewis et al. (1991) rightly claim,

> The use of precise, repeatable experiments is the hallmark of a mature scientific or engineering discipline.

Furthermore, Goldstein and Goldstein (1978) take this one step further, stating,

> We now take for granted that any observation, any determination of a 'fact', even if made by a reputable and competent scientist, might be doubted. It may be necessary to repeat an observation to confirm or reject it. Science is thus limited to what we might call 'public' facts. Anybody must be able to check them; experimental observations must be repeatable.

Not only must the researcher make his work repeatable, however, some even regard it as being beholden on the scientific community to execute replications just to verify the experimental results, as we ourselves do. For example, Huxley (1965) has stated,

> In scientific inquiry it becomes a matter of duty to expose a supposed law to every possible kind of verification...

Broad and Wade (1986), in their description of the scientific ideology, consider replication to be the third check in verifying scientific claims, the first two being the peer review system that awards research grants and the journal refereeing that takes place prior to publication. They also describe the ideal of reporting experiments as follows,

> A scientist who claims a new discovery must do so in such a way that others can verify the claim. Thus in describing an experiment a researcher will list the type of equipment used and the procedure followed, much like a chef's recipe. The more important the new discovery, the sooner researchers will try to replicate it in their own laboratories.

Replication is also concerned with the way the original hypothesis is expressed. As Smith (1983) has stated,

> Replication does two things: first, it tests the linguistic formulation of the hypothesis; second, it tests the sufficiency of the explicit conditions for the occurrence of the phenomena.

For example, an original hypothesis may be linguistically expressed to almost encourage conclusions to be expressed with the wrong meaning. Henry and Humphrey (1990) state their hypothesis as follows: "the hypothesis of this study is that systems designed and implemented in an object-oriented manner are easier to maintain than those designed and implemented using structured techniques." In order to test this, their subjects were asked to make modifications to an object-oriented system and a functionally equivalent procedure-oriented system. After their data analysis, Henry and Humphrey concluded that the "experiment supports the hypothesis that subjects produce more maintainable code with an object-oriented language than with a procedure-oriented language," which turns around the meaning of the original hypothesis: the idea was not for subjects to produce code to be tested for maintainability, but rather to test the maintainability of two different systems by having subjects perform maintenance tasks on them.

Another important example is that criteria for subject participation in a software engineering experiment may be insufficiently specific and, as a result, the replication yields different results due to variability unaccounted for between the subjects.

4. Replication: In Practice

4.1. Determining Worthy Experiments

Even if an empirical study was found to be replicable in terms of the availability of experimental artifacts, there can be, and usually are, several other reasons why one should first be wary of devoting the resources necessary to performing a replication study. The background may not be properly researched and the empirical study may be addressing the wrong issue. Inappropriate methods may be used; for example, when people are involved, very strictly controlled laboratory experiments may be less useful than more qualitative or ethnographic forms of experimentation. Errors of commission or omission may be made or experimental variables may be incorrectly classified. For example, Scanlan (1989) criticises Shneiderman et al. (1977) for not making use of time as a measurable dependent variable (the subjects were all given as much time as they required) and claims as a result that "any significant difference may have been washed out." From his experimental result, however, Shneiderman et al. called into question the utility of detailed flowcharts, stating "we conjecture that detailed flowcharts are merely a redundant presentation of the information contained in the programming language statements." The experimental flaw identified by Scanlan can be classified as an error of omission, and one which, according to Scanlan, has seen "the decline of flowcharts as a way to represent algorithms." Scanlan then went on to design a new experiment to test the same hypothesis using time as a dependent measure and claimed "my experiment shows that significantly less time is required to comprehend algorithms represented as flowcharts."

Missing details may prevent the reader from forming their own view of the worth of the data, for example, error estimates may not be provided for some or all of the critical measures or raw data may be crudely summarised when it could have been presented in full. Statistical procedures may be misapplied. Alternative interpretations may not be presented: when people are involved it is more than likely that more than one interpretation can be placed on the data. We agree with Collins (1985) who regards an experiment to have been incompetently performed if some alternative explanation for the data has been overlooked. For example, in a comparative study of C and C++ development times involving only four subjects, Moreau and Dominick (1990) concluded that there was a significant difference in favour of C++. One of the four subjects, however, took very much longer on the third C++ task. The experimenters simply attributed this to a debugging difficulty, i.e. they appeared not to have checked that use of C++ itself was the real cause of the problem. Failure to discuss alternative interpretations of data can prevent a reviewer performing a meaningful meta-analysis of the research area. (Brooks and Vezza (1989) is an example of a paper providing the reader with alternative interpretations.)

Should the report of an experiment pass a detailed critical reading of its design, execution, analysis and interpretation, then it can be deemed worthy enough to replicate.

4.2. Frequency of Replication Studies

In schools, colleges, and universities, replication studies are performed daily. But such studies are usually scaled-down versions of an original experiment, are performed by students in the act of learning, and have no confirming power. As Collins (1985) notes,

> As more becomes known about an area however, the confirmatory power of similar-looking experiments becomes less. This is why the experiments performed every day in schools and universities as part of the scientific training of students have no confirming power; in no way are they tests of the results they are supposed to reveal.

Those employed in research rarely perform replication studies. Again, as Collins (1985) notes,

For the vast majority of science, replicability is an axiom rather than a matter of practice.

Broad and Wade (1986) also draw attention to the lack of replication work by stating,

How much erroneous…science might be turned up if replication were regularly practiced, if self-policing were a more than imaginary mechanism?

Broad and Wade (1986) reckon that the Simpson–Traction replication is,

…probably one of the very few occasions in the history of science in which the philosopher's ideal of replicability has been attained.

In 1961, Simpson had Traction watched while Traction unsuccessfully tried to repeat a biochemistry experiment concerned with protein synthesis.

Of course, since Broad and Wade's remark was made, there has been the saga of cold fusion. Many laboratories around the world tried to repeat the cold fusion experiment by Pons and Fleischmann – see Close (1990) or Amato (1993). Ordinarily, no scientist would have dreamt of trying to replicate a poorly reported experiment. The lure of cheap, relatively pollution free energy in abundance, was an exceptional motivation.

Historically the frequency of external replication work in software engineering research has been low. For example, no mention of external replication studies were made in Sharpe et al.'s (1991) investigation of the characteristics of empirical software maintenance studies between 1980 and 1989, nor in Roper's (1992) selected annotated bibliography of software testing.

More recently, even with the advent of a specialist journal such as the Empirical Software Engineering journal, the frequency of external replication work remains low, with fewer than 15 publications specifically addressing replication since the inception of the journal in 1996. A systematic survey of controlled experiments in software engineering between 1993 and 2002 by Sjoberg et al. (2005) found only twenty studies claiming to be replications of which only nine were external replications. Interestingly, six of these nine external replications are said to have failed to confirm the results of the original experiment.

This relative lack of output is likely because of the effort and resources needed to conduct an experiment, the lack of availability of laboratory packages of experimental materials, and last, but perhaps not least, the lack of glamour associated with replicating the work of others.

4.3. The Unattainability of Exact Replication

Care must be taken, however, to clarify what is meant by replication. The Universe is forever changing. Human observers and subjects are unique (Brooks (1980) and Curtis (1980) report on empirically discovered programming ability differences ranging from 4–1 to 25–1). There is no end to the number of measurements that can be made to describe the experimental setting. The art of experimental science is in making neither errors of commission or omission. Accuracy of observations can always be improved upon until such time as the Uncertainty Principle becomes important. Strictly speaking, it is more correct to talk of partial replication and the goal of performing as near exact replication as possible. Exact replication is unattainable.

According to Broad and Wade, exact replication is an impractical undertaking because the recipe of methods is incompletely reported, because to do so is very resource intensive, and because credit in science is won by performing original work. They do, however, draw attention to the important activity of improving upon experiments. They state,

> Scientists repeat the experiments of their rivals and colleagues, by and large, as ambitious cooks repeat recipes - for the purpose of improving them. All will be adaptations or improvements or extensions. It is in this recipe-improvement process, of course, that an experiment is corroborated.

With respect to poor statistical power levels caused by too few subjects, Baroudi and Orlikowski (1989) qualify this and note,

> Where a study fails to reject a null hypothesis due to low power, conclusions about the phenomenon are not possible. Replications of the study, with greater power, may resolve the indeterminacy.

Statistical power is the probability that a particular experiment will detect an effect between the control group (e.g. no use of inheritance) and the treatment group (e.g. use of inheritance). Calculations of statistical power probabilities depend on how many subjects take part, the size of any effect, and the p-value used in statistical tests (often 0.05). If the effect size is not large, and too few subjects are used, statistical power may be much less than 0.8 (a typical recommended level). The effect may go undetected. A replication with twice the number of subjects may boost the power level beyond 0.8 so that there is now a good chance of detecting the effect – at least eight out of ten experiments will detect the effect. In pioneering experimental work, it can be difficult knowing what effect size to expect, and it becomes the duty of the investigator to use as many subjects as is practically possible.

4.4. An Example: Our Replication of Korson's Experiment

Korson (1986) and Korson and Vaishnavi (1986) designed a series of four experiments each testing some aspect of maintenance. The experiment which was of greatest interest to us (Experiment 1) was designed to test if a modular program used to implement information hiding, which localizes changes required by a modification, is faster to modify than a non-modular but otherwise equivalent version of the same program. The non-modular (or monolithic) program was created by replacing every procedure and function call in the modular version with the body of that procedure or function. Programmers were asked to make functionally equivalent changes to an inventory, point of sale program – either the modular version (approximately 1,000 lines long) or the monolithic version (approximately 1,400 lines long). Both programs were written in Turbo Pascal. The changes required could be classified as perfective maintenance as defined by Lientz and Swanson (1980) i.e. changes made to enhance performance, cost effectiveness, efficiency, and maintainability of a program. Korson reckoned that the time taken to make the perfective maintenance changes would be significantly faster for the modular version. This is exactly what he found. On average, subjects working with a modular program took 19.3 min to make the required changes as opposed to the 85.9 min taken by subjects working with a monolithic version of the program. With a factor of 4 between the timings, and with the details provided in Korson's thesis, we were confident that we could successfully externally replicate Korson's first experiment.

Our external replication (Daly et al., 1994b), however, shocked us. On average, our subjects working with the modular program took 48 min to make the required changes as opposed to the 59.1 min taken with the monolithic version of the program. The factor between the timings was 1.3 rather than 4 and the difference was not found to be statistically significant.

To determine possible reasons for our failure to verify Korson's results, we resorted to an inductive analysis. A database of all our experimental findings was built and data-mining performed.

A suggested relationship was found between the total times taken for the experiment and a pretest that was part of subjects' initial orientation. All nine of the monolithic subjects appeared in the top twelve places when ranked by pretest timings. We had unwittingly assigned more able subjects to the monolithic program and less able subjects to the modular program. Subject assignment had simply been at random, whereas in retrospect it should have also been based on an ability measure such as that given by the pretest timings. The ability effect interpretation is the béte noir of performance studies with subjects and researchers must be vigilant regarding the lack of homogeneity of subjects across experimental conditions.

Our inductive analysis also revealed quite different approaches taken to program understanding by our subjects. Some subjects were observed tracing flows of execution to develop a deep understanding. We had evidence that the four slowest modular subjects all tried to understand the code more than was strictly necessary to satisfy the maintenance request. Others worked very pragmatically and focused simply on the editing actions that were required. We call this pragmatic maintenance. Our two fastest finishers with the monolithic program explained in a debriefing questionnaire that they had no real understanding of the code.

Our inductive analysis revealed at least two good reasons as to why we did not verify Korson's results and taught us many valuable lessons about conducting experimental research with human subjects. We were motivated to develop an experiment that would be easily replicable, and which would show once and for all that modular code is superior to monolithic code, but it was clear to us that it was more important to understand the nature of pragmatic maintenance. How do software maintainers in industry go about their work? Is pragmatic maintenance a good or bad thing?

5. A Simple Extension to Basili et al.'s Framework

As stated earlier, we are not concerned here with replication as it applies to an individual experimental design.

What we mean by internal replication is when researchers repeat their own experiments. For example, Korson (1986) and Korson and Vaishnavi (1986) claimed to have succeeded in providing internal replicability and stated,

> ...the study has demonstrated that a carefully designed empirical study using programmers can lead to replicable, unambiguous conclusions.

Internal replications involving an evolutionary series of experiments have some confirmatory power. In many areas of science, internal replications, carried out either by design, or as part of a program of research, or because the sensitivity of the results required improving, are relatively commonplace.

By external replication we mean published experiments carried out by researchers who are independent of those who originally carried out the empirical work. Greater confirmatory power inevitably comes with external replications.

Exact replication is unattainable, so it is important to consider and categorise the differences.

First, researchers must consider the experimental method. Should a similar or alternative method be used? A basic finding replicated over several different methods carries greater weight. As Brewer and Hunter (1989) have stated,

> The employment of multiple research methods adds to the strength of the evidence.

Does a keystroke analysis of a software engineering task yield the same conclusions as observing users' performance on the task? Are the conclusions the same as those obtained from a questionnaire survey of users who have performed the task?

As a first step, the existing method could be improved. For example, the replication might add a debriefing session with subjects after the formal experiment is over if no such debriefings too place during the original experiment. Such debriefings can provide many useful insights into the processes involved. This type of improvement does not compromise the integrity of the replication.

Second, researchers must consider the task. Should a similar or alternative task be used? A basic finding replicated over several different tasks carries greater weight. As Curtis (1980) has stated,

> When a basic finding...can be replicated over several different tasks...it becomes more convincing.

Does a complex refactoring task yield the same conclusions as a simple refactoring task?

Or should the task be improved by, for example, making it more realistic? For example, rather than refactor a small program of a few hundred lines, refactor widely used open source software of many tens of thousands of lines of code.

Third, researchers must consider the subjects. For example, should a similar or alternative group of subjects be used? A basic finding replicated over several different categories of subjects carries greater weight. Does working with undergraduates produce the same conclusions as working with postgraduates? Are the conclusions the same as those obtained working with professional software engineers?

Or should the group of subjects be improved by, for example, by using more subjects or more stringent criteria for participation?

A comprehensive framework for experimentation in software engineering was established by Basili et al. (1986). The four main phases of the framework are: definition, planning, operation, and interpretation.

In the definition phase, a study is characterized by six elements: motivation, object, purpose, perspective, domain, and scope. For example: A motivation might be to understand the benefits of inheritance. The object might be the maintenance process. The purpose might be to evaluate. The perspective might be that of the software maintainer. The domain might be the individual programmer working on a program. The scope might be several programmers working on several programs, which captures the notion of internal replication within an individual experimental design.

In the planning phase, a study is characterised by design, criteria, and measurement. For example: A 2×3 factorial design might be used if we have several observations from two types of programmers (inexperienced and experienced) across three types of programs (no existing inheritance, inheritance of depth three used, inheritance of depth five used). Criteria might be the cost of implementing a maintenance request. Measurement might be the time taken to fulfill the request, as well as programmers' views on the ease or difficulty of making the code changes.

In the operation phase, a study is characterised by three elements: preparation, execution, and analysis. For example: In preparation, a pilot study might be performed to check that implementing the maintenance request does not take an excessive amount of time. In execution, start and end times might be recorded and programmers' views taken in debriefing sessions. In analysis, a 2×3 analysis of variance might be applied and statistical results compared with programmers' views.

In the interpretation phase, a study is characterised by three elements: interpretation context, extrapolation, and impact. For example: The context might include the results of other published work on the maintenance of object-oriented programs. Extrapolation might suggest that the results from the laboratory study are generalizable to industry settings because professional programmers were employed in the study. Impact might involve applying the results in an industrial context. Basili et al. also point to another possible impact: that of replicating the experiment. They, however, do not explicitly distinguish between replication by the original experimenters (internal replication) and replication by independent researchers (external replication). We propose their framework should be extended to distinguish between internal and external replication and its various forms where method, task, and subjects can each be either similar, alternative, or improved. So, for example: Under impact in the interpretation phase, the original experimenters might declare their intention to (internally) replicate the experiment with an alternative group of subjects or they might declare that the experiment needs now to be externally replicated. Under motivation in the definition phase, independent researchers might declare a motivation to verify findings by externally replicating a study but with an improved method.

We believe it unnecessary at this stage to work with more detailed categorizations of replication. We note that Sjoberg et al. (2005) chose to categorise replications simply as close or differentiated. By close replications they mean that as far as possible the known conditions of the original experiment are retained. By differentiated replications they mean variations are present in key aspects of the experimental conditions such as the kind of subjects used.

Of course, if too many alternatives are used, or if the scale of any recipe-improving is too substantial, it becomes debatable whether the study counts as a replication. Initially, the power of confirmation will be high with external replication studies but there will come a point when a result is so well established that the replication ceases to have research value and the experiment should be moved from the research laboratory into the teaching laboratory.

Across the vector of (method, task, and subjects), we categorize our Korson (Daly et al., 1994b) replication as an example of (improved, similar, similar). The method is categorized as improved because we debriefed our subjects.

6. Reporting for Replications

Once an experiment has been performed, analyzed and the time comes for writing the findings, the researcher must provide as much detail surrounding the empirical work as possible in order to allow others to replicate. Jedlitschka and Pfahl (2005) have reviewed reporting guidelines for controlled experiments in software engineering, as is described elsewhere in this book, and present a proposal for a standard. As a minimum, their guidelines on the reporting of experimental design, analysis, and interpretation should be followed.

Unfortunately, numerous empirical studies in the software engineering literature are lacking in that the experimental methods are poorly reported so that it is impossible to perform an external replication study. For example, instructions and task materials given to subjects may not be given in full, or may otherwise be unobtainable. Various authors in the past have criticised poor reporting, for example Basili et al. (1986) and MacDonell (1991).

In our Korson replication (Daly et al., 1994a), we found problems with several details which prevented the fullest possible analysis and interpretation of both Korson's results and ours. Reporting inadequacies with the Korson experiment were:

1. The experimenter employed monitors to time his subjects, and sort out problems which might arise with hardware failure and the like. It was not reported, however, whether these monitors controlled when a subject was ready to move from one experimental phase to the next, or simply just noted each phase time. Such information would have prevented speculation about monitor variability across the two studies.
2. Subject selection criteria was subjective in that almost any computer science student who had completed a practical Pascal programming course could have met it. For example, one criterion was "an amount of programming experience." This should have been more objective by stating the minimum experience required, for example at least 2 years programming experience at college level. This may have reduced subject variability.
3. Expert times for testing the program were not published. There were three separate ways to test the program, one way taking much longer than the other two. A comparison of results is required in order to explain variability that might have arisen.
4. Pretest results were not published. This would have made important reading as all subjects performed the same task; this would have allowed a direct comparison with our subjects' times, and hence a direct comparison of the ability of our subjects to the original subjects. When timings such as these are collected they should always be published.
5. It was not made clear what was verbally communicated to the subjects prior to the experiment: was additional information given to them, were any points in the instructions highlighted, or was nothing said?

Of these reporting inadequacies, only the one regarding subjection selection is explicitly addressed by the guidelines proposed in Jedlitschka and Pfahl (2005). This illustrates the difficulties in conveying all necessary information required for external replication.

The original researcher, Korson, however, went much further than many researchers in reporting experimental details, and he must be commended for that. In his thesis he published his code for the experiments (both the pretest and the experimental code), and the instructions for both the pretest and experiment. He published individual subject timings rather than just averages, along with the statistical tests and their results. So, the original researcher has presented the major issues surrounding his experiment, but has unfortunately omitted details preventing the fullest possible interpretation of his work and the external replication.

We believe it is impractical to convey all the information necessary for external replication in a journal or conference paper. Experimental artifacts under consideration such as designs, code, instructions, questionnaires, and the raw data, would typically add too many pages as appendices. Such information is best conveyed over the internet as a downloadable laboratory package along with any underlying technical report or thesis. With a laboratory package in place, original researchers can more easily conduct internal replications, independent researchers more easily conduct external replications, and meta-analysts more easily combine raw data. Work by Basili et al. (1999) is exemplary in this regard, with the availability of laboratory packages (http://www.cs.umd.edu/projects/SoftEng/ESEG/downloads. html) stimulating a small family of internal and external replications and a consequent improved understanding of perspective-based reading. Without a laboratory package in some form, an experiment is unlikely ever to be verified through internal or external replication. Given the scale of effort and resources required to conduct an experiment, not to facilitate reuse of the experimental artifacts, by providing a laboratory package, seems folly.

We agree with Basili et al. (1999) that somewhere in the laboratory package, validity threats should be detailed so that these may be addressed in future replication attempts. There is no advantage in performing a close replication – similar, similar, similar – of an experiment where a serious validity threat is present. Making an improvement to address a serious threat will yield a better experiment and results.

We also recommend that any laboratory package should report even seemingly minor details, for example, verbal instructions made at the beginning of an experiment, to enable others perform an external replication. There may be times, however, when the only way reporting inadequacies are actually discovered is by replicating an experiment and analysing the results.

7. Conclusions

Basili et al. (1986) established a comprehensive experimental framework for software engineering in which replication is recognised in the scope of an individual experiment and as an impact on future work. We have proposed a simple extension to this framework to explicitly recognise internal and external replication and its various forms: similar, alternative, improved, across method, task, and subjects. This extension applies to the motivation and impact subsections of the framework.

Routinely we are told Tool X or Technique Y is a panacea to many of software engineering's problems, but where is the accompanying empirical evidence that can stand scrutiny, that has been verified by an independent research team? We conclude that there exists only one route for empirical software engineering to follow: to make available laboratory packages of experimental materials to facilitate internal and external replications, especially the latter, which have greater confirming power. The work of the replicator should be seen as glamorous not gruesome. By verifying results, so experiments can be subsequently crafted which software engineering students can repeat as laboratory exercises. If results are not verified, we need not be too despondent. As with our replication of Korson's experiment, it is very likely that the real issue requiring investigation comes to the fore. And those involved in conducting the replication will have improved their investigation skills enormously.

References

I Amato. Pons and fleischmann redux? *Science*, 260:895, 1993.
JJ Baroudi and WJ Orlikowski. The problem of statistical power in MIS research. *MIS Quarterly*, 13:87–106, 1989.
VR Basili, RW Selby, and DH Hutchens. Experimentation in software engineering. *IEEE Transactions in Software Engineering*, 12(7):733–743, 1986.
VR Basili, F Shull, and F Lanubile. Building knowledge through families of experiments. *IEEE Transactions on Software Engineering*, 25(4):456–473, 1999.
J Brewer and A Hunter. *Multimethod Research: A Synthesis of Styles*. SAGE Publications, Newbury Park, CA, 1989.
W Broad and N Wade. *Betrayers of the Truth*, page 17 and 81. Oxford University Press, New York, 1986.
RE Brooks. Studying programmer behavior experimentally: the problems of proper methodology. *Communications of the ACM*, 23(4):207–213, 1980.
A Brooks and P Vezza. Inductive analysis applied to the evaluation of a CAL tutorial. *Interacting with Computers, the Interdisciplinary Journal of Human-Computer Interaction*, 1(2):159–170, 1989.
DN Card. Software quality engineering. *Information and Software Technology*, 32(1):3–10, 1990.
F Close. *Too Hot to Handle The Story of the Race for Cold Fusion*. W H Allen Publishing, London, 1990.
HM Collins. *Changing Order Replication and Induction in Scientific Practice*, pages 19, 35, 43. SAGE Publications, London, 1985.
B Curtis. Measurement and experimentation in software engineering. *Proceedings of the IEEE*, 68(9):1144–1157, 1980.
J Daly, A Brooks, J Miller, M Roper, and M Wood. An external replication of korson's experiment. Research report EFoCS-4-94, Department of Computer Science, University of Strathclyde, Glasgow, 1994a.
J Daly, A Brooks, J Miller, M Roper, and M Wood. Verification of results in software maintenance through external replication. In *Proceedings of the IEEE International Conference on Software Maintenance*, pages 50–57. IEEE, Los Alamitos, CA, 1994b. ICSM'94.
M Goldstein and Inge F Goldstein. HOW WE KNOW *An Exploration of the Scientific Process*, page 207. Plenum Press, New York and London, 1978.
SM Henry and M Humphrey. A controlled experiment to evaluate maintainability of object-oriented software. In *Proceedings of the IEEE Conference on Software Maintenance*, pages 258–265, 1990.
TH Huxley. We are all scientists. In H Shapley, S Rapport, and H Wright, editors, *The New treasury of Science*, page 14. Collins, London and Glasgow, 1965.
A Jedlitschka and D Pfahl. Reporting Guidelines for Controlled Experiments in Software Engineering. Verification of results in software maintenance through external replication. In *International Symposium on Empirical Software Engineering*, pages 95–104. IEEE, Los Alamitos, CA, 2005. ISESE 2005.
JPJ Kelly, TI McVittie, and WI Yamamoto. Implementing design diversity to achieve fault tolerance. *IEEE Software*, 8(4):61–71, 1991.
TD Korson. *An Empirical Study of the Effects of Modularity on Program Modifiability*. PhD thesis, *College of Business Administration*, Georgia State University, 1986.
TD Korson and VK Vaishnavi. An empirical study of the effects of modularity on program modifiability. In E Soloway and Iyengar S S, editors, *Empirical Studies of Programmers: First Workshop*, pages 168–186. Ablex Publishing Corporation, Norwood, NJ, 1986. A Volume in the Ablex Human/Computer Interaction Series.
J Lewis, S Henry, D Kafura, and R Schulman. An empirical study of the object-oriented paradigm and software reuse. *OOPSLA*, 184–196, 1991.

B Lientz and E Swanson. *Software Maintenance Management.* Addison-Wesley, Reading, MA, 1st edition, 1980.

SG MacDonnell. Rigor in software complexity measurement experimentation. *Journal of Systems and Software*, 16:141–149, 1991.

DR Moreau and WD Dominick. A programming environment evaluation methodology for object-oriented systems: part ii – test case application. *Journal of Object-Oriented Programming*, 3(3):23–32, 1990.

KR Popper. *The Logic of Scientific Discovery.* Hutchinson, London, revised edition, 1968.

M Roper. Software testing: a selected annotated bibliography. *Software Testing, Verification and Reliability*, 2:113–132, 1992.

DA Scanlan. Structured flowcharts outperform pseudocode: an experimental comparison. *IEEE Software*, 6(5):28–36, September 1989.

S Sharpe, DA Haworth, and D Hale. Characteristics of empirical software maintenance studies: 1980–1989. *Journal of Software Maintenance: Research and Practice*, 3:1–15, 1991.

B Shneiderman, R Mayer, D McKay, and P Heller. Experimental investigations of the utility of detailed flowcharts in programming. *Communications of the ACM*, 20(6):373–381, 1977.

DIK Sjoberg, JE Hannay, O Hansen, VB Kampenes, A Karahasanovíc, N-K Liborg, and AC Rekdal. A survey of controlled experiments in software engineering. *IEEE Transactions on Software Engineering*, 31(9):733–752, 2005.

GP Smith. The problems of reduction and replication in the practice of the scientific method. *Annals of the New York Academy of Sciences*, 406:1–4, 1983.

University of Maryland Experimental Software Engineering Group. Lab packages. http://www.cs.umd.edu/projects/SoftEng/ESEG/downloads.html

Bibliography

Albrecht, A. J. & GaffneyJr., J. E. (1983), 'Software function, source lines of code, and development effort prediction: a software science validation', *IEEE Trans. Software Eng.* **9**(6), 639–648.

An, K. H., Gustafson, D. A. & Melton, A. C. (1987), A model for software maintenance, *in* 'Proceedings of the Conference in Software Maintenance', Austin, Texas, pp. 57–62.

Atkins, D., Ball, T., Graves, T. & Mockus, A. (1999), Using version control data to evaluate the effectiveness of software tools, *in* '1999 International Conference on Software Engineering', ACM Press, pp. 324–333.

Barnard, J. & Rubin, D. B. (1999), 'Small sample degrees of freedom with multiple imputation', *Biometrika* **86**(4).

Chidamber, S. R. & Kemerer, C. F. (1994), 'A metrics suite for object oriented design', *IEEE Trans. Software Eng.* **20**(6), 476–493.

Fleming, T. H. & Harrington, D. (1984), 'Nonparametric estimation of the survival distribution in censored data', *Comm. in Statistics* **13**, 2469–86.

Goldenson, D. R., Gopal, A. & Mukhopadhyay, T. (1999), Determinants of success in software measurement programs, *in* 'Sixth International Symoposium on Software Metrics', IEEE Computer Society, pp. 10–21.

Graves, T. L., Karr, A. F., Marron, J. S. & Siy, H. P. (2000), 'Predicting fault incidence using software change history', *IEEE Transactions on Software Engineering* **26**(7), 653–661.

Graves, T. L. & Mockus, A. (1998), Inferring change effort from configuration management databases, *in* 'Metrics 98: Fifth International Symposium on Software Metrics', Bethesda, Maryland, pp. 267–273.

Halstead, M. H. (1977), *Elements of Software Science*, Elsevier North-Holland.

Herbsleb, J. D. & Grinter, R. (1998), Conceptual simplicity meets organizational complexity: Case study of a corporate metrics program, *in* '20th International Conference on Software Engineering', IEEE Computer Society, pp. 271–280.

Herbsleb, J. D., Krishnan, M., Mockus, A., Siy, H. P. & Tucker, G. T. (2000), Lessons from ten years of software factory experience, Technical report, Bell Laboratories.

Jönsson, P. & Wohlin, C. (2004), An evaluation of k-nearest neighbour imputation using likert data, *in* 'Proc. of the 10th Int. Symp. on Software Metrics', pp. 108–118.

Kaplan, E. & Meyer, P. (1958), 'Non-paramentric estimation from incomplete observations', *J Am Stat Assoc* pp. 457–481.

Kim, J. & Curry, J. (1977), 'The treatment of missing data in multivariate analysis', *Social Methods and Research* **6**, 215–240.

Little, R. & Hyonggin, A. (2003), Robust likelihood-based analysis of multivariate data with missing values, Technical Report Working Paper 5, The University of Michigan Department of Biostatistics Working Paper Series. http://www.bepress.com/umichbiostat/paper5

Little, R. J. A. (1988), 'A test of missing completely at random for multivariate data with missing values', *Journal of the American Statistical Association* **83**(404), 1198–1202.

Little, R. J. A. & Rubin, D. B. (1987), *Statistical Analysis with Missing Data*, Willey Series in Probability and Mathematical Statistics, John Willey & Sons.

Little, R. J. A. & Rubin, D. B. (1989), 'The analysis of social science data with missing values', *Sociological Methods and Research* **18**(2), 292–326.

McCabe, T. (1976), 'A complexity measure', *IEEE Transactions on Software Engineering* **2**(4), 308–320.

Mockus, A. (2006), Empirical estimates of software availability of deployed systems, *in* '2006 International Symposium on Empirical Software Engineering', ACM Press, Rio de Janeiro, Brazil, pp. 222–231.

Mockus, A. (2007), Software support tools and experimental work, *in* V. Basili & et al, eds, 'Empirical Software Engineering Issues: LNCS 4336:', Springer, p. to appear.

Mockus, A. & Votta, L. G. (1997), Identifying reasons for software changes using historic databases, Technical Report BL0113590-980410-04, Bell Laboratories.

Myrtveit, I., Stensrud, E. & Olsson, U. (2001), 'Analyzing data sets with missing data: An empirical evaluation of imputation methods and likelihood-based methods', *IEEE Transactions on Software Engineering* **27**(11), 1999–1013.

Novo, A. (2002), 'Analysis of multivariate normal datasets with missing values'. Ported to R by Alvaro A. Novo. Original by J.L. Schafer.

R Development Core Team (2005), *R: A language and environment for statistical computing*, R Foundation for Statistical Computing, Vienna, Austria. ISBN 3-900051-07-0. http://www.R-project.org

Roth, P. L. (1994), 'Missing data: A conceptual review for applied psychologist', *Personel Psychology* **47**, 537–560.

Rubin, D. B. (1987), *Multiple Imputation for Nonresponse in Surveys*, John Willey & Sons.

Schafer, J. L. (1997), *Analysis of Incomplete Data*, Monograph on Statistics ans Applied Probability, Chapman & Hall.

Schafer, J. L. & Olsen, M. K. (1998), 'Multiple imputation for multivariate missing data problems', *Multivariate Behavioural Research* **33**(4), 545–571.

Schafer, J. S. (1999), 'Software for multiple imputation'. http://www.stat.psu.edu/~jls/misoftwa.html

Strike, K., Emam, K. E. & Madhavji, N. (2001), 'Software cost estimation with incomplete data', *IEEE Transactions on Software Engineering* **27**(10), 890–908.

Swanson, E. B. (1976), The dimensions of maintenance, *in* 'Proc. 2nd Conf. on Software Engineering', San Francisco, pp. 492–497.

Twala, B., Cartwright, M. & Shepperd, M. (2006), Ensemble of missing data techniques to improve software prediction accuracy, *in* 'ICSE'06', ACM, Shanghai, China, pp. 909–912.

Weisberg, S. (1985), *Applied Linear Regression, 2nd Edition*, John Wiley & Sons, USA.

Index